SLAVERY

AND THE

FOUNDERS

D0141137

SLAVERY
AND THE
FOUNDERS

RACE AND LIBERTY
IN THE AGE OF
JEFFERSON

SECOND EDITION

PAUL FINKELMAN

Library of Congress Cataloging-in-Publication Data

Finkelman, Paul, 1949–
    Slavery and the founders : race and liberty in the age of Jefferson / Paul Finkelman.—
2nd ed.
        p. cm.
    Includes bibliographical references and index.
    ISBN 0-7656-0438-8 (alk. paper) — ISBN 0-7656-0439-6 (pbk. : alk paper)
    1. Slavery—Law and legislation—United States—History. 2. Slavery—United
States—History. I. Title.

KF4545.S5 F565 2001
306.3´62´0973—dc21

                                                                00-053162

Printed in the United States of America

The paper used in this publication meets the minimum requirements of
American National Standard for Information Sciences
Permanence of Paper for Printed Library Materials,
ANSI Z 39.48-1984.

                                    ⊗

        BM (c)   10   9   8   7   6   5   4   3
        BM (p)   10   9   8   7

For Abby and Isaac

Contents

Preface

This book stems from my belief that slavery was a central issue of the American founding. My goal is to better understand how the first generation of leaders of the United States dealt with the profoundly important question of human bondage.

Slavery was legal in all of the thirteen colonies when the American Revolution began. When the Constitution was written, slaves could be found in all but two states, although three others were in the process of gradually abolishing the institution. This book explores the tension between the professed ideas of America, as stated in the Declaration of Independence, and the reality of early national America.

Jefferson's words from the Declaration ring true today. Americans continue to believe it is "self-evident" that we are all "created equal" and are "endowed" with the "unalienable Rights" of "Life, Liberty, and the Pursuit of Happiness." American political debate today, just as in the 1780s and 1790s, often focuses on how government may best help all Americans achieve these goals.

But despite Jefferson's fine words and our belief in this credo, it is clear that liberty was not available to most African-Americans at the time of the founding. In Chapters 6 and 7 of this book, I argue that Jefferson himself, who owned over 150 slaves when he wrote the Declaration, did not in fact believe that blacks were entitled to the same rights as other Americans. In other chapters I suggest that attempts to limit or undermine slavery in this period were weak and often ineffectual. I argue that the denial of the "blessings of liberty" to slaves profoundly affected the formation of the nation.

In the two decades before the Civil War, the Garrisonian abolitionists argued that the Constitution was proslavery. Garrison himself called it "a covenant with death" and an "agreement with hell." I am convinced that the Garrisonians were correct in their analysis of the Constitution as a slaveholders' compact. I do not, however, believe that the Garrisonians' response to that analysis was correct. They withdrew from politics to avoid the stain of working within an imperfect and morally corrupt system. Fortunately, not all antebellum northern opponents of slavery withdrew from politics. Some, like Salmon P. Chase, Charles Sumner, and Abraham Lincoln, were willing to participate in politics and challenge the nation to live up to its ideals. Through political success, constitutional change, and military victory, the United States was eventually able to implement the important ideals encapsulated in the Declaration of Independence.

But even those who jumped into politics to fight slavery understood (even if for tactical reasons they would not publicly admit it) that the Constitution was both imperfect and tainted. As I argue in Chapter 1, slavery permeated the debates of 1787 and, in the end, the slave owners got substantially what they wanted: a Constitution that protected slavery. Thus, from 1787 until the Missouri Compromise debates of 1819–1820, the national government and important national leaders pursued policies that protected slavery. This should not surprise us. With the exception of real estate, slaves were the most valuable form of privately held property in the United States at the end of the Revolution. A number of slave owners attended the Constitutional Convention. After the adoption of the Constitution, slave owners dominated the executive branch. Moreover, while the most important politician of the era—Thomas Jefferson, a slave owner—feared the negative effects that slavery had on his society, he feared emancipation and the presence of free blacks even more.

My exploration of these issues is neither enjoyable nor easy. The stain of racism and the legacy of slavery do not, after all, make pleasant reading. Nevertheless, we in the twenty-first century must confront and understand the actions of the Founders if we are to do better in our own times. Thus, this book reminds us of the extent to which early national America was a slaveholders' republic.

I wrote the first edition of this book over a number of years and began revision shortly after it appeared. I have published earlier versions of these chapters in a variety of places. For the first edition of this book I extensively revised and rewrote each chapter, taking into account new scholarship, my own new research, and the criticism of other scholars. Although some of my ideas have changed over time, I remain convinced of the importance of slavery to the founding. For this second edition I have rewritten Chapters 1, 6, and 7 and added a new Chapter 5, taking into account new scholarship and new information. This new information includes, of course, the results of DNA testing that prove that Jefferson did in fact father children with his slave Sally Hemings.

Grants from the National Endowment for the Humanities, the American Philosophical Society, and the Indiana Historical Society funded some of the research for this book. I thank the libraries and particularly the interlibrary loan staffs at the University of Tulsa College of Law, Lewis and Clark School of Law, Akron Law School, Brooklyn Law School, Virginia Tech, the University of Hawaii at Manoa, and Chicago-Kent College of Law, where I did much of the work on this book.

Many colleagues, friends, and students have read parts of this book; helped with the research, and provided important insights into the subjects discussed here. I owe special debts to David Brion Davis, John Hope Franklin, Stanley N. Katz, Rob Forbes, James Oakes, Peter Onuf, Peter Wallenstein, William M. Wiecek, Doron Ben-Atar, Barbara Oberg, Judith Schafer, Andrew Burstein, and Nancy Isenberg. William W. Freehling, Michael Les Benedict, and Earl Maltz continue, to a lesser or greater extent, to reject my analysis of the relationship between slavery and the founding. Over the years they have forced me to sharpen my own arguments, making this a better book. My friend and former editor at M.E. Sharpe, Michael Weber, pushed me hard (as a good editor should) to rework these chapters. They are better because of his criticism and persistence. Peter Coveney took over where Michael left off in bringing out the first and second edition of this book. Just as the second edition was about to come out, Peter left M.E. Sharpe for another position. With good humor and great skill Peter LaBella and Henrietta Toth took over the process of bringing out the edition. Laurie Lieb superbly copy-edited the second edition. My former student Natalie Duck read the entire first edition in manuscript, making invaluable suggestions along the way. In addition, I thank the following friends, colleagues, and students for their input on this book: Sara B. Bearss, Richard Beeman, Joan E. Cashin, Catherine Clinton, Robert J. Cottrol, Raymond T. Diamond, Woody Farrar, Stephen Gottlieb, Susan Huffman, Allison Lindsey, Robert McColley, Robert E. McGlone, James McPherson, Michael McReynolds, David Meek, Charles Miller, John Murrin, Kristin Onuf, Nell Painter, Jenni Parrish, Robert Post, Philip Presby, Renee Redman, Michael Riseman, Phil Schwarz, Larry Shumsky, Lucinda Stanton, Jean Tanaka, Dan Thorp, Melvin Urofsky, LeRoy Votto, and Peter Wood.

Finally, I owe a very special thanks to Rita Langford, my assistant at the University of Tulsa College of Law. Her hard work, good cheer, and wonderful computer skills were invaluable in producing this second edition.

I presented various versions of these chapters as works in progress at meetings of the American Historical Association, the Organization of American Historians, and the Society for Historians of the Early Republic; the Jeffersonian Legacies Conference at the University of Virginia; conferences on the Northwest Ordinance at Franklin College, Michigan State University, and Indiana University; and as lectures or symposia at Yale University's Gilder Lehrman Institute for the Study of Slavery and Abolition, Brooklyn Law School, Cornell Law School, Harvard Law School, Minnesota Historical Society, Princeton University, Southern Methodist University School of Law,

Tulane Law School, and Virginia Commonwealth University. I thank all the participants at those venues who gave me such helpful comments.

I thank the following publishers and journal editors for their many comments and suggestions and for their cooperation in reprinting portions of the following articles: "Slavery and the Constitutional Convention: Making a Covenant with Death," in Richard Beeman et al., eds., *Beyond Confederation: Origins of the Constitution and American National Identity* (Chapel Hill: University of North Carolina Press, 1987), 188–225; "The Kidnapping of John Davis and the Adoption of the Fugitive Slave Law of 1793," *Journal of Southern History* 56 (1990): 397–422; "Slavery and the Northwest Ordinance: A Study in Ambiguity," *Journal of the Early Republic* 6 (1986): 343–370; "Evading the Ordinance: The Persistence of Bondage in Indiana and Illinois," *Journal of the Early Republic* 9 (1989): 21–52; "The Problem of Slavery in the Age of Federalism," in Doron Ben-Atar and Barbara Olberg, eds. *Federalists Reconsidered* (Charlottesville: University Press of Virginia, 1998) 135–156; "Jefferson and Slavery: 'Treason Against the Hopes of the World,' " in Peter S. Onuf, ed., *Jeffersonian Legacies* (Charlottesville: University Press of Virginia, 1993), 181–221; "Thomas Jefferson and Antislavery: The Myth Goes On," *Virginia Magazine of History and Biography* 102 (1994): 193–228.

SLAVERY
AND THE
FOUNDERS

———— One ————

Making a Covenant with Death

Slavery and the Constitutional Convention

William Lloyd Garrison, the great nineteenth-century abolitionist, thought the Constitution was the result of a terrible bargain between freedom and slavery. The American states were, in Garrison's words, united by a "covenant with death" and "an agreement with Hell." Garrison and his followers refused to participate in American electoral politics, because to do so they would have had to support "the pro-slavery, war sanctioning Constitution of the United States." Instead, under the slogan "No Union with Slaveholders," the Garrisonians repeatedly argued for a dissolution of the Union.[1]

Part of their opposition to continuing the Union stemmed from their desire to avoid the corruption that came from participating in a government created by the proslavery Constitution. But their position was also at least theoretically pragmatic. The Garrisonians were convinced that the legal protection of slavery in the Constitution made political activity not only futile, but actually counterproductive. Traditional political activity created popular support for the constitutional order, which in turn strengthened the stranglehold slavery had on America. In 1845 Wendell Phillips pointed out that in the years since the adoption of the Constitution Americans had witnessed "the slaves trebling in numbers—slaveholders monopolizing the offices and dictating the policy of the Government—prostituting the strength and influence of the Nation to the support of slavery here and elsewhere—trampling on the rights of the free States, and making the courts of the country their tools." This experience proved "that it is impossible for free and slave States to unite on any terms, without all becoming partners in the guilt and responsible for the sin of slavery."[2]

The Garrisonians argued that by participating in politics they were strengthening slavery by supporting the Union and the Constitutional order. Furthermore, since the political system and the Constitution were stacked in favor of slavery, it was a pointless waste of their time and money to try to fight slavery through electoral politics. The Garrisonian critique of the Constitu-

3

tion logically led to the conclusion that the free states should secede from the union. Garrisonians thus rallied to the slogan of "No Union with Slaveholders."

It is easy to dismiss this argument more than a century and a half after it was first made. After all, we know that secession was a reactionary, proslavery movement that failed. But, in the 1830s and 1840s, the idea of a northern secession, as a way of destroying slavery, made some sense. The fugitive slave clause of the Constitution, for example, gave a master the right to hunt down a slave anywhere in the United States. Under the regime of the fugitive slave law, supported by a constitutional provision, slavery was a national institution.[3] But what would happen if the Garrisonians accomplished their goal, and the North left the Union to form a nation based on freedom instead of slavery? It would be like moving the Canadian border to the Mason-Dixon line. Suddenly, slavery would be threatened in Kentucky and Virginia because slaves could now escape to a free country just by crossing the Ohio River.

Garrison believed that such a change in political boundaries would prove fatal to slavery. As slaves crossed the Mason-Dixon Line or the Ohio and Mississippi Rivers into freedom, slavery would be weakened in the Upper South. Committed slave owners would move further south, which would further weaken slavery in the Upper South. Eventually Kentucky, Maryland, Delaware, and even Missouri might give up slavery and seek to join the free country. Pressure on Virginia would increase. Slavery, and hundreds of thousands of slaves, would be forced into the Deep South, where whites would become a desperate minority. Ultimately the institution would fall, perhaps after a series of rebellions in a region with a huge black majority, but just as likely simply from the weight of its own isolation.

Part of this theory was based on the notion that slavery was inherently unstable, needing force to be viable. The United States government provided that force, spending its resources to hunt fugitive slaves and, when necessary, suppress rebellions. Even when rebellions were put down by the local militia, those militias were armed by national government. The South also benefited from the strength of the northern economy. Southerners like James Henry Hammond of South Carolina thundered that "cotton is king" and declared "No, you dare not make war on cotton. No power on earth dares make war upon it."[4] But, as the Garrisonians saw it, without the North and the proslavery Constitution, the South was little more than a prosperous producer of commodities, devoid of industry and capital, lacking in population, arms, and manpower to hunt fugitive slaves and suppress rebellions. In the end, it was the proslavery bargain, and the North's contractual obligation under the Constitution to protect slavery, that made the system viable.

The Garrisonians did not necessarily see the Constitution as the result of a deliberate conspiracy of evil men; rather, they understood it to be the consequence of political give-and-take at the Convention of 1787. Indeed, before the publication of Madison's convention notes, the Garrisonians were not disunionist and, while unhappy with the Constitutional protections of slavery, were not yet ready to condemn the whole document. Some even argued that the Constitution favored liberty. However, the publication of *The Madison Papers*, which included Madison's notes on the Convention, convinced Garrison and his followers that the Constitution was in fact proslavery. Rev. Samuel J. May, for example, recalled that "the publication of the 'Madison Papers' . . . I confess, disconcerted me somewhat. I could not so easily maintain my ground in the discussions which afterwards agitated so seriously the Abolitionists themselves—some maintaining that the Constitution was, and was intended to be, proslavery."[5]

Thus, in *The Constitution, A Pro-Slavery Compact; or, Selections from the Madison Papers*, Wendell Phillips analyzed "that 'compromise,' which was made between slavery and freedom, in 1787; granting to the slaveholder distinct privileges and protection for his slave property, in return for certain commercial concessions upon his part toward the North." Using Madison's papers, Phillips argued that "the Nation at large were fully aware of this bargain at the time, and entered into it willingly and with open eyes."[6]

Phillips both exaggerated and understated the nature of the relationship between slavery and the Constitution. Some of those at the Convention "entered into" the bargain with great reservations, and many at the ratifying conventions may indeed have not seen the full extent of the "bargain." On the other hand, the bargain involved more than commerce and slavery: it concerned the very creation of the Union itself.

Other nineteenth-century antislavery leaders disagreed with the Garrisonians. Salmon P. Chase, the most successful antislavery politician, fought throughout the antebellum period to convince his colleagues, the judiciary, and northern voters that the Constitution was really antislavery. Despite his creative perseverance, Chase's efforts failed. The United States Supreme Court almost always protected slavery in the cases it heard. Likewise, almost all American presidents and their cabinet officers protected slavery in foreign and domestic politics. Perhaps most frustrating to the political abolitionists was the fact that some of their most brilliant allies in the crusade against slavery—the Garrisonians—agreed with their enemies on the meaning of the Constitution. Thus, one Ohio Liberty Party man ruefully noted after reading Wendell Phillips' pamphlet on the Constitution: "Garrison, Phillips, and Quincy; Calhoun, Rhett, and McDuffie; all harmoniously laboring to prevent such a construction of the Constitution as would abolish slavery."[7]

A careful reading of the Constitution reveals that the Garrisonians were correct: the national compact did favor slavery. A detailed examination of the Convention of 1787 explains how the Constitution evolved in this way. Both the text of the Constitution and the debates surrounding it help us understand that the "more perfect Union" created by this document was in fact fundamentally imperfect.

Slavery in the Constitutional Structure

The word "slavery" appears in only one place in the Constitution—in the Thirteenth Amendment, where the institution is abolished. Throughout the main body of the Constitution, slaves are referred to as "other persons," "such persons," or in the singular as a "person held to Service or Labour." Why is this the case?

Throughout the debates, the delegates talked about "blacks," "Negroes," and "slaves." But the final document avoided these terms. The change in language was clearly designed to make the Constitution more palatable to the North. In a debate over representation, William Paterson of New Jersey pointed out that under the Articles of Confederation Congress "had been ashamed to use the term 'Slaves' & had substituted a description." This shame over the word "slave" came up at the Convention during the debate over the African slave trade. The delegates from the Carolinas and Georgia vigorously demanded that the African trade remain open under the new Constitution. Gouverneur Morris of Pennsylvania, furious at this immoral compromise, suggested that the proposed clause read: the "Importation of slaves into N. Carolina, S— Carolina & Georgia" shall not be prohibited. Connecticut's Roger Sherman, who voted with the Deep South to allow the trade, objected, not only to the singling out of specific states, but also to the term "slave." He declared he "liked a description better than the terms proposed, which had been declined by the old Congs & were not pleasing to some people." George Clymer of Pennsylvania "concurred" with Sherman. In the North Carolina ratifying convention, James Iredell, who had been a delegate in Philadelphia, explained that "the word *slave* is not mentioned" because "the northern delegates, owing to their particular scruples on the subject of slavery, did not choose the word *slave* to be mentioned." Thus, southerners avoided the term because they did not want unnecessarily to antagonize their colleagues from the North. As long as they were assured of protection for their institution, the southerners at the Convention were willing to do without the word "slave."[8]

Despite the circumlocution, slavery was sanctioned throughout the Constitution. Five provisions dealt directly with slavery:[9]

Article I, Section 2, Paragraph 3. The three-fifths clause provided for counting three-fifths of all slaves for purposes of representation in Congress. This clause also provided that, if any "direct tax" was levied on the states, it could be imposed only proportionately, according to population, and that only three-fifths of all slaves would be counted in assessing what each state's contribution would be.

Article I, Section 9, Paragraph 1. Popularly known as the "slave trade clause," this provision prohibited Congress from banning the "Migration or Importation of such Persons as any of the States now existing shall think proper to admit" before the year 1808. Awkwardly phrased and designed to confuse readers, this clause prevented Congress from ending the African slave trade before 1808, but did not require Congress to ban the trade after that date. The clause was a significant exception to the general power granted to Congress to regulate all commerce.

Article I, Section 9, Paragraph 4. This clause declared that any "capitation" or other "direct tax" had to take into account the three-fifths clause. It ensured that, if a head tax were ever levied, slaves would be taxed at three-fifths the rate of whites. The "direct tax" portion of this clause was redundant, because that was provided for in the three-fifths clause.

Article V, Section 2, Paragraph 3. The fugitive slave clause prohibited the states from emancipating fugitive slaves and required that runaways be returned to their owners "on demand."

Article V. This article prohibited any amendment of the slave importation or capitation clauses before 1808.

Taken together, these five provisions gave the South a strong claim to "special treatment" for its peculiar institution. The three-fifths clause also gave the South extra political muscle—in the House of Representatives and in the electoral college—to support that claim.

Numerous other clauses of the Constitution supplemented the five clauses that directly protected slavery. Some provisions that indirectly guarded slavery, such as the prohibition on taxing exports, were included primarily to protect the interests of slaveholders. Others, such as the guarantee of federal support to "suppress Insurrections" and the creation of the electoral college, were written with slavery in mind, although delegates also supported them for reasons having nothing to do with slavery. The most prominent indirect protections of slavery were the following:

Article I, Section 8, Paragraph 15. The domestic insurrections clause empowered Congress to call "forth the Militia" to "suppress Insurrections," including slave rebellions.[10]

Article I, Section 9, Paragraph 5. This clause prohibited federal taxes on exports and thus prevented an indirect tax on slavery by taxing the staple products of slave labor, such as tobacco, rice, and eventually cotton.

Article I, Section 10, Paragraph 2. This clause prohibited the states from taxing exports or imports, thus preventing an indirect tax on the products of slave labor by a nonslaveholding state.[11]

Article II, Section 1, Paragraph 2. This clause provided for the indirect election of the president through an electoral college based on congressional representation. This provision incorporated the three-fifths clause into the electoral college and gave whites in slave states a disproportionate influence in the election of the president.

Article IV, Section 3, Paragraph 1. This clause allowed for the admission of new states. The delegates to the Convention anticipated the admission of new slave states to the Union.

Article IV, Section 4. The domestic violence provision guaranteed that the United States government would protect states from "domestic Violence," including slave rebellions.

Article V. By requiring a three-fourths majority of the states to ratify any amendment to the Constitution, this Article ensured that the slaveholding states would have a perpetual veto over any constitutional changes.[12]

Finally, some clauses did not inherently favor slavery, and were not necessarily considered to affect slavery when they were debated, but ultimately protected the institution when interpreted by the courts or implemented by Congress after the adoption of the Constitution. It would be wrong to argue that these illustrate the proslavery nature of the Constitutional Convention. However, these clauses do illustrate the way the Constitution set a proslavery tone, which enabled Congress and the courts to interpret seemingly neutral clauses in favor of slavery. Such clauses also directly challenge William W. Freehling's argument that the Framers were inherently antislavery and that "the impact of the Founding Fathers on slavery . . . must be seen in the long run not in terms of what changed in the late eighteenth century but in terms of how the Revolutionary experience changed the whole American antebellum history."[13] If we look at the "long run" impact of the Constitution on "American antebellum history," we find that the following clauses were used to protect slavery, not to harm it.

Article I, Section 8, Paragraph 4. The naturalization clause allowed Congress to prohibit the naturalization of nonwhites, even though it is likely that some of the new states, especially those that granted suffrage to blacks, would have also allowed foreign-born blacks to become citizens.

Article I, Section 8, Paragraph 17. The federal district clause allowed Congress to regulate institutions, including slavery, in what became the national capital. Under this clause, Congress allowed slavery in Washington, D.C. During the Convention, southerners expressed fear that the national capital would be in the North.

Article III, Section 2, Paragraph 1. The diversity jurisdiction clause limited the right to sue in federal courts to "Citizens of different States," rather than inhabitants. This clause allowed judges to deny slaves and free blacks access to federal courts.[14]

Article IV, Section 1. The full faith and credit clause required each state to grant legal recognition to the laws and judicial proceedings of other states, thus obligating free states to recognize laws creating and protecting slavery.

Article IV, Section 2, Paragraph 1. The privileges and immunities clause required that states grant equal privileges and immunities to "citizens" of other states; however, in *Dred Scott v. Sandford* (1857), the Supreme Court affirmed a long-standing position of the southern states that free blacks were not "citizens" under the Constitution and thus the slave states were free to deny privileges and immunities to them.[15]

Article IV, Section 3, Paragraph 2. This clause allowed Congress the power to regulate the territories. In 1820, Congress used this clause to limit slavery in the territories, but in *Dred Scott v. Sandford* the Supreme Court ruled that the clause authorized Congress to protect slavery in the territories, but not to ban the institution.[16]

Besides specific clauses of the Constitution, the structure of the entire document ensured against emancipation by the new federal government. Because the Constitution created a government of limited powers, Congress lacked the power to interfere in the domestic institutions of the states.[17] Thus, during the ratification debates only the most fearful southern antifederalists opposed the Constitution on the grounds that it threatened slavery. Most southerners, even those who opposed the Constitution for other reasons, agreed with General Charles Cotesworth Pinckney of South Carolina, who crowed to his state's house of representatives:

> We have a security that the general government can never emancipate them [slaves], for no such authority is granted and it is admitted, on all hands, that the general government has no powers but what are expressly granted by the Constitution, and that all rights not expressed were reserved by the several states.[18]

The Constitution was not "essentially open-ended with respect to slavery," as the late Don Fehrenbacher argued. Nor is it true, as Earl Maltz has argued, that "the Constitution took no position on the basic institution of slavery."[19] On the contrary, the Constitution provided enormous protections for the peculiar institution of the South at very little cost to that region. At the Virginia ratifying convention, Edmund Randolph denied that the Constitution posed any threat at all to slavery. He challenged opponents of the Constitution to show, "*Where* is the part that has a tendency to the *abolition of* slavery?" He answered his own question by asserting, "Were it right here to mention what passed in [the Philadelphia] convention. . . I might tell you *that the Southern States, even South Carolina herself, conceived this property to be secure*" and that "there was not a member of the Virginia delegation who had *the smallest suspicion of the abolition of slavery.*" South Carolinians, who had already ratified the Constitution, would have agreed with Randolph. In summing up the entire Constitution, General Charles Cotesworth Pinckney, who had been one of the ablest defenders of slavery at the Convention, proudly told the South Carolina House of Representatives: "In short, considering all circumstances, we have made the best terms for the security of this species of property it was in our power to make. We would have made better if we could; but on the whole, I do not think them bad."[20]

Slavery and Congressional Representation

General Pinckney had good reason to be proud of his role in Philadelphia. Throughout the Convention, Pinckney and other delegates from the Deep South tenaciously fought to protect the interests of slaveholders. In these struggles they were usually successful.

When they arrived at the Convention, the delegates probably did not think slavery would be a pressing issue. Rivalries between large and small states appeared to pose the greatest obstacle to a stronger Union. The nature of representation in Congress; the power of the national government to levy taxes, regulate commerce, and pay off the nation's debts; the role of the states under a new constitution; and the power of the executive were on the agenda. Yet, as the delegates debated these issues, the importance of slavery—and the sectional differences it caused—became clear.[21] Throughout the summer of 1787, slavery emerged to complicate almost every debate. Most important by far was the way slavery figured in the lengthy debate over representation.

On May 29, Governor Edmund Randolph of Virginia proposed the series of resolutions known as the Virginia Plan. Randolph introduced these resolutions in response to the "crisis" of the nation "and the necessity of preventing the fulfillment of the prophecies of the American downfall." This plan would create an entirely new form of government in the United States. The power of the central government would be vastly enhanced at the expense of the states. The new Congress would have greater powers to tax, to secure the nation "against foreign invasion," to settle disagreements between states, and to regulate commerce.[22]

Randolph's plan called for a radical restructuring of the American government by making population the basis for representation in the national Congress. Under the Articles of Confederation, each state had one vote in Congress. By changing the basis of representation to population, Randolph's plan immediately created tensions between the large and small states at the Convention. But the plan also raised the dilemma of whether slaves would be counted in allocating representation in the new Congress. This dilemma of how to count slaves, or whether to count them at all, would trouble the delegates throughout the Convention.

Virginia was the most populous state in the nation, and thus Randolph had a vested interest in basing Congressional representation on population. But how that population would be counted greatly affected the potential representation of Virginia and the rest of the South. Virginia's white population, as the 1790 census would reveal, was only slightly larger than Pennsylvania's. If representation were based solely on free persons, the North would overwhelm the South.[23] But if slaves were counted equally with free persons, the Virginia delegation would be the largest, and the South would have more members of Congress than the North. The Virginians of course realized that the northern states were unlikely to support counting slaves for purposes of representation. Thus, Randolph's plan hedged the issue, declaring "that the rights of suffrage in the National Legislature ought to be proportioned to the Quotas of contribution, or to the number of free inhabitants, as the one or the other rule may seem best in different cases."[24] Randolph's avoidance of the term "slaves" by referring to "quotas of contribution" indicates the sensitivity of the subject.

Squabbling over slavery began in earnest the next day, May 30. James Madison moved to delete the term "free inhabitants" from the Virginia Plan because he felt the phrase "might occasion debates which would divert" attention "from the general question whether the principle of representation should be changed" from states to population. Madison understood that an early debate on the role of slavery in the Union might destroy the Convention before it got started. But his proposal would have left representation based solely on "quotas of contribution," and this was also unacceptable to most of the northern delegates. Madison himself agreed "that some better rule ought to be found." Alexander Hamilton then proposed that representation be based solely on the number of "free inhabitants" in each state. This proposal was also too volatile and the delegates quickly tabled it. Other at-

tempts at compromise failed. Finally, the Delaware delegates put a temporary end to this divisive discussion by telling the Convention that they "were
restrained by their commission from assenting to any change on the rule of
suffrage," and if the body endorsed any change in representation, they would
be forced to leave the Convention. The Convention, having successfully
postponed this acrimonious debate, adjourned for the day.[25]

The Convention intermittently debated representation for the next two
weeks, but on June 11 slavery reemerged to complicate the debate, when the
Convention considered for the first time, and also approved provisionally,
the three-fifths clause. Over the next three months the Convention would, on
a number of occasions, redebate and reconsider the three-fifths clause before
finally adopting it.[26]

The evolution of the three-fifths clause during the Convention shows that
the clause was not essentially a compromise over taxation and representation,
as historians have traditionally claimed and as the structure of Article I, Section
2, Paragraph 3 implies.[27] Rather, it began as a compromise between those who
wanted to count slaves fully for purposes of representation and those who did
not want to count slaves at all. On this crucial question, the slave states won a
critical victory without making any important concessions.

On June 11, Roger Sherman of Connecticut proposed that representation
be based on the "numbers of free inhabitants" in each state. John Rutledge
and Pierce Butler of South Carolina objected, arguing for representation according to "quotas of contribution," which had become a euphemism for
counting slaves for representation.[28] James Wilson and Charles Pinckney,
the younger cousin of General Charles Cotesworth Pinckney, skillfully headed
off the Rutledge-Butler proposal.

Wilson proposed and Pinckney seconded a motion that ultimately became
the three-fifths clause. Here for the first time was an example of cooperation
between the North and the South over slavery. Significantly, Wilson was
known to oppose slavery and came from a state, Pennsylvania, which had
already adopted a gradual emancipation scheme. Nevertheless, harmony at
the Convention was more important to Wilson than the place of slavery in
the new nation. By teaming up, the nominally antislavery Pennsylvanian
and the rabidly proslavery Carolinian may have hoped to undercut the antislavery sentiments of other northern delegates while also satisfying the demands of the proslavery delegates like Butler and Rutledge.[29]

Most delegates seemed to accept this proposal. However, Elbridge Gerry
of Massachusetts was unwilling to compromise. With some irony he protested, "Blacks are property, and are used to the southward as horses and
cattle to the northward; and why should their representation be increased to
the southward on account of the number of slaves, than horses or oxen to the

north?" Gerry believed this would be an appropriate rule for taxation, but not for representation, because under it four southern voters would have more political power than ten northern voters. He also argued that this clause would degrade freemen in the North by equating them with slaves. He wondered "Are we to enter into a Compact with Slaves?"[30] No other northerner opposed counting slaves for representation at this time.

Thus, with little debate, the Convention initially accepted the three-fifths clause as a basis for representation. The clause, giving the South enormous political leverage in the nation, was accepted without any quid pro quo from the North. Application of the clause to taxation would not come until later in the Convention. Indeed, there was no reason in mid-June to believe it would ever be applied to taxation. A brief history of the three-fifths ratio, prior to 1787, bears this out.

The ratio of three slaves to five free persons was first proposed in the Congress in 1783 as part of an overall program for the national government to raise revenue from the states. The ratio was controversial. Southerners thought it overvalued slaves, and northerners thought it undervalued them. Delegates from Virginia and South Carolina, the states with the most slaves, wanted taxation based on land values. Congress initially rejected and then later resurrected the entire package, which called for taxation based on population. Congress then sent the package to the states as an amendment to the Articles of Confederation. However, this amendment failed to achieve the necessary unanimous support of all the states and so was not added to the Articles of Confederation.[31]

This history of the three-fifths clause shows there is little substance to the traditional view that the three-fifths clause "was a legacy from the Congress of 1783" or that "most northern delegates must have realized even before they arrived in Philadelphia that it would be the minimum price of southern acceptance of any new constitution." The only useful legacy of the Congress of 1783 was the numerical ratio itself, which Congress had applied only to taxation.[32] The application of the ratio to representation was an entirely new concept.

The meaning of the three-fifths clause to the delegates in Philadelphia was clear in the report of the Committee of the Whole on June 13, which stated that representation would be "in proportion to the whole number of white and other free citizens and inhabitants, of every age, sex and condition, including those bound to servitude for a term of years and three fifths of all other persons not comprehended in the foregoing description, except Indians, not paying taxes in each State." The phrasing of the term "white and other free citizens and inhabitants" clearly implied that the "other persons" were neither white nor free.[33] By mid-June a majority in the Convention had accepted the principle that representation in the national Congress would be based on population and that three-fifths of the slave population would be added to the free population in determining representation. However, a minority of the delegates, led by those from New Jersey, were still unhappy with this plan.

On June 15 William Paterson introduced what is commonly known as the New Jersey Plan. The plan rejected congressional representation based on population and, instead, retained the system of representation then in force under the Articles of Confederation: that the states would have an equal number of delegates in the Congress. For the next fifteen days, the Convention debated, without any reference to slavery, whether representation in Congress would be based on population. In most of the votes on this issue, the South (except Delaware) supported population based on representation. These votes were predicated on the assumption that the three-fifths clause, which had already been accepted, would be part of the basis of representation. The southern delegates also expected their region to grow faster than the North, and thus representation based on population would help them in the long run. But, even if whites did not move south, slaves could still be imported. Southerners, confident that a growing slave population would augment their representation in Congress, consistently supported population as the basis of that representation.[34]

By June 30 the Convention was at a standstill. The states in favor of population-based representation had enough votes to adopt their scheme. But if they were unable to persuade the delegates from the smaller states to acquiesce on this point, the Convention itself would fail. In the middle of this debate, Madison offered a new mode of analysis for the delegates. He argued

> that the States were divided into different interests not by their difference of size, but by other circumstances; the most material of which resulted partly from climate, but principally from their having or not having slaves. These two causes concurred in forming the great division of interests in the U. States. It did not lie between the large and small States: it lay between the Northern and Southern, and if any defensive power were necessary, it ought to be mutually given to these two interests.

So Madison proposed two branches of Congress, one in which slaves would be counted equally with free people to determine how many representatives each state would have, and one in which slaves would not be counted at all. Under this arrangement, "the Southern Scale would have the advantage in one House, and the Northern in the other." Madison made this proposal despite his reluctance to "urge any diversity of interests" among the delegates.[35]

The Convention ignored Madison's proposal. He may have offered it simply to divert attention from the heated debate between the large and small states. If this was indeed his goal, he was not immediately successful. The small states, led by Delaware, continued to express fear that they would be swallowed up by larger states if representation in the Congress were based solely on population.[36]

Subsequent debates, however, reveal the validity of Madison's analysis that sectionalism—caused by slavery—created a major division within the Convention and the nation. Indeed, slavery continued to complicate the Convention debates long after the conflict between large and small states had evaporated. On July 2, Charles Pinckney argued that there was "a solid distinction as to interest between the southern and northern states." He noted that the Carolinas and Georgia "in their Rice and Indigo had a peculiar interest which might be sacrificed" if they did not have sufficient power in any new Congress.[37] Immediately after this speech the Convention accepted a proposal by General Charles Cotesworth Pinckney to send the entire question of representation to a committee of one delegate from each state. The Convention then adjourned until July 5.

On July 5 the committee proposed what historians have since called the Great Compromise. Under this plan, representation in the lower house of the legislature would be based on population, and in the upper house the states would have an equal vote. The three-fifths clause was a part of this proposal.[38]

On July 6 the Convention once again approved the concept of representation based on population for the lower house of the Congress. The Convention then chose a five-man committee to redraft the clause. In the absence of a census, this committee would also have to recommend to the Convention the number of representatives that each state would get in the first congress. Before the Convention adjourned for the day, Charles Pinckney again raised sectional issues connected to slavery, arguing that "blacks ought to stand on an equality with whites," but he "w[oul]d. . . . agree to the ratio settled by Congs."[39]

Pinckney's argument here was doubly significant. First, in a debate that had nothing to do with slavery per se, Pinckney raised the issue, as if to warn the Convention not to forget the special needs of the South. Second, Pinckney made it clear that he (and presumably other southerners) thought that the three-fifths rule for counting slaves was a great concession.

On July 9, the committee of five reported its recommendations. Gouverneur Morris, who was on the committee, admitted that the allocations in the report were "little more than a guess." A number of delegates were dissatisfied with these guesses, because in allocating representation for the first congress the committee had taken into account "the number of blacks and whites." This action led William Paterson to register a protest—only the second so far in the Convention—against the three-fifths clause. This was the beginning of a four-day debate over slavery and representation. Paterson declared that he regarded

> negroes slaves in no light but as property. They are no free agents, have no personal liberty, no faculty of acquiring property, but on the contrary are themselves property, and like other property entirely at the will of the Master.

Paterson pointedly asked, "Has a man in Virga. a number of votes in proportion to the number of his slaves?" He noted that slaves were not counted in allocating representation in southern state legislatures, and asked, "Why should they be represented in the Genl. Gov't.[?]" Finally, Paterson argued that counting slaves for purposes of representation encouraged the slave trade.[40]

In response, Madison once again proposed that representation in one house of the legislature be based on total population and the other on just the free population. Pierce Butler again argued for wealth as a basis for representation. This proposal, of course, meant that slaves would be counted equally with whites. Rufus King of Massachusetts gave unexpected support to Butler, warning that the South would not unite with the rest of the country "unless some respect were paid to their superior wealth." Furthermore, King reminded his northern colleagues that, if they expected "preferential distinctions in Commerce," they should be willing to give up something. At least at this point in the Convention, King was willing to accept the three-fifths ratio for representation.[41] Here was the beginning of a major compromise between the Deep South and the commercially oriented states of the North. But the moment, King and other northerners were offering the three-fifths clause to the South, without asking southerners for any concession in return.

This debate resulted in the appointment of yet another committee to come up with a new proposal for representation in the first congress. This committee reported its deliberations the next day, July 10, and the Convention debated them. Like the previous committee, this one had to calculate representation in the first congress without the benefit of a census. This allocation, which was later written into the Constitution, gave the North thirty-five seats in the first congress while giving the South thirty.[42] Not surprisingly, some delegates objected to the apportionment for their states. More important, though, was the sectional animosity that these allocations stimulated.

Almost immediately, John Rutledge and Charles Cotesworth Pinckney of South Carolina moved to reduce New Hampshire's representatives from three to two. Although on the previous day Rufus King had supported Pierce Butler's demand for more southern representation, he now defended the committee's apportionment, warning that the New England states would not accept any reduction in their representation. King also endorsed Madison's analysis of sectionalism, arguing that "a difference of interests did not lie where it had hitherto been discussed, between the great and small States; but between the Southern and Eastern." King nevertheless continued to seek compromise and explicitly recognized the need "for the security of the Southern" interests. For this reason he acquiesced to the three-fifths rule and was even willing to consider "a still greater security" for the South, although he admitted he did not know what that might be. But he also asserted that "no principle would justify giving" the South "a majority" in Congress.[43]

Charles Cotesworth Pinckney responded that the South did not require "a majority of representatives, but [he] wished them to have something like an equality." Otherwise, Congress would pass commercial regulations favorable to the North, and the southern states would "be nothing more than overseers for the Northern States." Hugh Williamson of North Carolina agreed, arguing that under the present system the North would get a majority in Congress that it would never relinquish, and thus "the Southern Interest must be extremely endangered."[44]

Gouverneur Morris of Pennsylvania, who was emerging as the Convention's most vocal opponent of concessions to slavery, became the first delegate to challenge the assumption that the South was richer than the North and therefore deserved greater representation in Congress. He also argued that, in time of emergency, northerners would have to "spill their blood."[45] Madison's notes do not contain the full text of Morris's statement, but its implications are clear. Northerners would have to "spill their blood" because there were more free people in the North than in the South and because slavery made the South an unreliable ally in wartime.

After various unsuccessful attempts to reduce representation for some northern states or increase representation for some southern states, the Convention adopted an apportionment scheme for representation in the first congress by a vote of nine to two. The negative votes did not come from the smallest states, but from the most southern.[46] The delegates from South Carolina and Georgia made their point: they must have protection for slavery or they would oppose the Constitution.

The next day, July 11, the Convention debated the provision for a census to determine future representation in Congress. Hugh Williamson of North Carolina amended the provision under consideration to explicitly include the three-fifths clause for counting slaves. Still dissatisfied with the three-fifths clause, Butler and Charles Cotesworth Pinckney of South Carolina "insisted that blacks be included in the rule of Representation, equally with the Whites," and moved to delete the three-fifths clause. Butler argued that "the labour of a slave in South Carolina was as productive and valuable as that of a freeman in Massachusetts," and since the national government "was instituted principally for the protection of property," slaves should be counted fully for representation.[47] The Convention quickly rejected the Butler-Pinckney proposal.

The defeat of the Butler-Pinckney resolution did not end the debate over slavery and representation. A motion to require Congress to take a census of all "free inhabitants" passed on a slim six-to-four vote, with four slave states voting no. The Convention then began debating the motion to count three-fifths of all slaves. King and Gorham of Massachusetts expressed reservations, and Sherman of Connecticut urged conciliation.

James Wilson of Pennsylvania, who had initially proposed the three-fifths clause, supported it on pragmatic grounds. Admitting he "did not well see on what principle the admission of blacks in the proportion of three fifths could be explained," he asked, if slaves were citizens, "why are they not admitted on an equality with White Citizens?" But, if slaves were "admitted as property," it was reasonable to ask, "Then why is not other property admitted into the computation?" Wilson argued, however, that these logical inconsistencies "must be overruled by the necessity of compromise." Gouverneur Morris, also representing Pennsylvania, was not so willing to sacrifice principle. Having been "reduced to the dilemma of doing injustice to the Southern States or to human nature," Morris chose the former, asserting that he "could never agree to give such encouragement to the slave trade" by allowing the slave states "a representation for their negroes." The three-fifths clause then failed, by a vote of four to six. However, this defeat was not solely the result of Morris's arguments in favor of principle: two slave states that were still holding out for fully counting slaves for representation opposed the measure, while three northern states hoped not to count slaves at all.[48]

The next day, July 12, the three-fifths clause was back on the floor, directly tied to taxation for the first time. The debate on slavery was the most divisive yet. Six southerners, representing Virginia, North Carolina, and South Carolina, addressed the issue. Their collective demand was clear: either give the South substantial representation for its slave population or the South would oppose the Constitution. Randolph, who had so far avoided the debates over slavery, "lamented that such a species of property existed," but nevertheless "urged strenuously that express security ought to be provided for including slaves in the ratio of Representation." Meanwhile, the South Carolinians, as might be expected, demanded full representation for slaves, declaring themselves willing, even eager, to be taxed fully for their slaves in return for full representation for their slaves.[49] William R. Davie of North Carolina, who had been virtually silent throughout the Convention, declared "it was high time now to speak out." Davie warned that North Carolina would "never confederate" unless slaves were counted, at the very least, under a three-fifths ratio. Davie threatened that if some representation for slaves was not adopted, "the business [of the convention] was at an end."[50]

Only Gouverneur Morris was prepared to call Davie's bluff, warning that Pennsylvania would "never agree to a representation of Negroes." But he also agreed that it was "vain for the Eastern states to insist on what the Southern States will never agree to." As much as Morris wished "to form a compact for the good of America," he seemed ready to risk failure on the issue of slave representation.[51] No other northerner joined Morris on this issue. However, Oliver Ellsworth and William Samuel Johnson of Connecticut strongly supported southern interests, foreshadowing an emerging compromise between New England and the South over slavery and commerce. After a heated debate, the Convention finally adopted the three-fifths clause by a vote of six to two, with two states divided.[52]

After more than a month and a half of anguished argument, the Convention had finally resolved the issue of representation for what would become the House of Representatives. Throughout, slavery had constantly confused the issue and thwarted compromise. Sectional interests caused by slavery had emerged as a major threat to the Union. At this juncture in the Convention, the smaller states still feared the larger ones; however, the northern and southern states had also come to openly distrust each other. In the last debate over representation, General Charles Cotesworth Pinckney declared he was "alarmed" over statements about slavery by northerners.[53] His alarm would soon spread to other southern delegates.

No sooner had the Convention laid to rest the issue of representation than it reemerged as part of the debate over taxation. On July 13, Elbridge Gerry proposed that, until an actual census could be taken, taxation would be based on the initial representation in the House. This seemingly reasonable proposal set the stage for a partial reopening of the debate over representation.

Reviving an earlier proposal, Hugh Williamson of North Carolina tried to cut New Hampshire's representation in the House of Representatives from three to two. Williamson argued that because New Hampshire had not yet sent any delegates to the Convention, it was unfair to force the state to pay taxes on the basis of three representatives. This explanation fooled no one, and Williamson's maneuver failed. Next, Read of Delaware expressed the fear that Gerry's motion was a plot by the larger states to tax the smaller ones. This led Madison to reiterate his belief that "the difference of interest in the United States lay not between the large and small, but the Northern and Southern States." Madison supported Gerry's motion "because it tended to moderate the views both of the opponents and advocates for rating very high, the negroes." After three votes, Gerry's motion passed. The Convention had deepened its commitment to the three-fifths clause, both for representation and for taxation.[54]

With the sense of the Convention on this issue apparently clear, Randolph moved to bring language previously used in the working document into conformity with the three-fifths clause. Earlier in the Convention, the body had declared that representation would be based on "wealth." Randolph now proposed substituting the wording of the three-fifths clause for the word "wealth."[55] This led to yet one more debate over the three-fifths clause. This debate revealed the deep animosities that had developed between some northern and southern delegates.

Gouverneur Morris mocked the attempt to replace the word "wealth" with the three-fifths clause. If slaves were "property," then "the word wealth was right, and striking it out would produce the very inconsistency which it was meant to get rid of." Morris then launched into a full-scale attack on southern demands. In the process he suggested that a peaceful end to the Convention, and the Union itself, might be in order. Morris asserted that, until this point in the Convention, he had believed that the distinction between northern and southern states was "heretical." Somewhat disingenuously, he declared that he "still thought the [sectional] distinction groundless." But he saw that it was "persisted in; and that the Southern Gentlemen will not be satisfied unless they see the way open to their gaining a majority in the public Councils." The North naturally demanded "some defence" against this. Morris thus concluded:

> Either this distinction is fictitious or real: if fictitious let it be dismissed and let us proceed with due confidence. If it be real, instead of attempting to blend incompatible things, let us at once take a friendly leave of each other. There can be no end of demands for security if every particular interest is to be entitled to it.

Morris argued that the North had as much to fear from the South as the South had to fear from the North.[56]

South Carolina's Pierce Butler responded with equal candor: "The security the Southn. States want is that their negroes may not be taken from them which some gentlemen within or without doors, have a very good mind to do."[57] For the rest of the Convention, Butler and his southern colleagues would remain vigilant in protecting this interest.

By Saturday the fourteenth, sectional tempers had cooled. The Convention now reconsidered the makeup of the Senate. The small states again reiterated their fears that the large states would overwhelm them in a legislature based entirely on population. Delegates from New Jersey and Connecticut made it clear that they would not support the emerging Constitution unless there was state equality in at least one branch of the legislature. Charles Pinckney once again proposed that representation in both houses of the legislature be based on population. In supporting this motion, Madison yet again argued that "the real difference of interests lay, not between the large and small but between the Northern and Southern States. The institution of slavery and its consequences formed the line of discrimination." Madison seemed particularly worried that state equality would give the North a perpetual majority in one branch of the legislature.[58]

Over Madison's protests, the equality of the states in the Senate remained part of the Constitution. On the final vote on this issue, three of the four negative votes came from the South.[59] This vote indicates that Madison's sense of sectional division was at least as important as the division between large and small states.

On July 16, when debate over the powers of Congress resumed, Butler and Rutledge opposed giving Congress the power to legislate where the states were "incompetent." The southerners feared this "vague" and, therefore, dangerous power, and thus four slave states supported a futile attempt to recommit this clause. This debate illustrates that sectional fears, more than rivalries between large and small states, had emerged as the major problem for the Convention. Butler and Rutledge, after all, were fearful of what a Congress dominated by the North might do. Any vagueness in language might be used to harm slavery.[60]

The irony of the shifting sentiments of the Carolinians became clearer a day later, when Gunning Bedford offered compromise language for this clause. Bedford, of Delaware, had up to this time vociferously represented the needs, and fears, of the small states. During the debates over representation, he had emphatically told his fellow delegates, "I do not gentlemen, trust you." Bedford was probably as jealous of state power, and as fearful of national power, as any man at the Convention. Yet on this issue he was not fearful and was willing to compromise, because even he saw nothing dangerous in the proposed clause, especially if it contained his compromise language. Bedford's amendment did not mollify the delegates from South Carolina and Georgia. These Deep South delegates remained opposed to allowing the national government to legislate for the "general interest of the Union,"[61] suspecting that such power might somehow, some day, threaten the particular interest of slavery.

Slavery and the Executive Branch

The Convention was deeply divided over how the nation's chief executive should be chosen. Slavery complicated the debates on this question and affected their outcome. On July 17, the Convention considered, and rejected by wide margins, election by the Congress, direct election by the people, and election by the state legislatures. Significantly, the most vocal opposition to election by the people came from three southerners: Charles Pinckney, George Mason, and Hugh Williamson. While Pinckney and Mason argued against the competence of the "people," Williamson was more open about the reasons for southern opposition. He noted that Virginia—and by extension the rest of the South—would not be able to elect her leaders president because "her slaves will have no suffrage."[62]

For James Madison the debate over the presidency was particularly difficult. Because he believed that "concepts of right and justice were paramount expressions of majority rule,"[63] Madison instinctively favored election of the president by the people. He told the Convention that "the people at large" were "the fittest" to choose the president. But "one difficulty . . . of a serious nature" made election by the people impossible. Madison noted that the "right of suffrage was much more diffusive in the Northern than the Southern States; and the latter could have no influence in the election on the score of the Negroes." In order to guarantee that the nonvoting slaves could nevertheless influence the presidential election, Madison favored the creation of the electoral college.[64] Under this system, each state was given a number of electors equal to its total congressional and senatorial representation. This meant that the three-fifths clause would help determine the outcome of presidential elections.[65] Thus, the fundamentally antidemocratic electoral college developed, at least in part, to protect the interests of slavery.

Commerce and Slavery: The Dirty Compromise

By late July, the Convention had hammered out the basic outline of the Constitution. On July 23, the Convention agreed to send the draft of the Constitution to a Committee of Detail. At this juncture, General Charles Cotesworth Pinckney "reminded the Convention that if the Committee should fail to insert some security to the Southern States against an emancipation of slaves, and taxes on exports, he should be bound by duty to his State to vote against their Report."[66] This protest must have surprised the Convention. In the previous nine days slavery had not been directly debated; and where it had come up at all, such as in the discussion of the election of the president, the South had had its way. Now, just as the work of many weeks was about to go to a committee for what many hoped was a final redrafting, Pinckney raised new demands for the protection for slavery.

Pinckney's outburst provoked no immediate reaction. The Convention remained in session for three more days, redebating how the executive should be chosen and numerous minor details. Finally, on July 26, the Convention adjourned until August 6, to allow the Committee of Detail to put the Convention's work into some coherent form. This five-man committee included two southerners, Rutledge and Randolph, while a third member, Oliver Ellsworth of Connecticut, came from a state that had consistently supported southern interests in the Convention.

The report of the Committee of Detail contained a number of provisions aimed at the protection of slavery. The new Congress could not interfere with the African slave trade and would need a two-thirds majority to pass navigation acts. The new government would be obligated to provide military support to suppress rebellions and insurrections in the states. Although Clause IV provided for representation based on "the number of inhabitants, according to the provisions herein after made," no such provisions were in fact in this draft. Thus, the committee report implied that the slaves would be counted equally with all other "inhabitants" when determining representation in Congress. The three-fifths clause was in the Committee report, but applied only to "direct" taxes and "capitation" taxes, not to representation. The committee report also prohibited taxation of both exports and imported slaves. With the exception of a clause allowing Congress to regulate commerce by a simple majority, the draft Constitution seemed to give the South everything it wanted.[67] The Committee of Detail appeared to have taken to heart Pinckney's demand for "some security to the Southern States."

On August 7, the Convention began to debate the committee report. On the next day, yet another debate over the three-fifths clause took place. Hugh Williamson moved to clarify the status of this clause by replacing the phrase "the provisions herein after made" with a direct reference to the three-fifths provision. After the Convention adopted Williamson's motion, Rufus King protested that counting slaves for representation "was a most grating circumstance," especially because the draft of the Constitution also prohibited Congress from banning the slave trade or even taxing the produce of slave labor. He thought that some provision ought to be made for ending the slave trade, but at minimum he argued that "either slaves should not be represented, or exports should be taxable."[68]

Roger Sherman, who would prove to be the Deep South's most vocal northern ally, agreed with King that the slave trade was "iniquitous" but believed that this issue should not be raised in connection with the question of representation, which had "been settled after much difficulty and deliberation." Madison, Ellsworth, and Sherman then tried to discuss other topics. But Gouverneur Morris would not let the slavery issue drop. He moved to insert the word "free" in front of the word "inhabitants" in the clause directing how representation would be determined. Believing that "much . . . would

depend on this point," Morris said that he could "never . . . concur in upholding domestic slavery," which was "the curse of heaven on the States where it
prevailed." Morris compared the "rich and noble cultivation" of the middle
states with "the misery and poverty which overspread the barren wastes of
Virginia, Maryland and the other slave states" and concluded that counting
slaves for representation

> when fairly explained comes to this: that the inhabitant of Georgia and
> South Carolina who goes to the Coast of Africa, and in defiance of the
> most sacred laws of humanity tears away his fellow creatures from their
> dearest connections and damns them to the most cruel bondages, shall have
> more votes in a Government instituted for protection of the rights of man-
> kind, than the Citizen of Pennsylvania or New Jersey who views with a
> laudable horror, so nefarious a practice.[69]

According to Morris, the draft Constitution compelled the North "to march
their militia for the defense of the Southern States; for their defense against
those very slaves of whom they complain." Furthermore, the government lacked
the power to levy a tax on imported slaves or on the goods they produced. Worst
of all, counting slaves for representation encouraged the South to import more
of them. Morris scoffed at the idea that there could ever be a direct tax, such as
the three-fifths clause allowed, because it was "idle to suppose that the General
Government can stretch its hand directly into the pockets of the people scattered
over so vast a Country." Thus the South would get extra representation in Congress for its slaves and have to pay nothing in return. Morris declared he "would
sooner submit himself to a tax for paying for all the Negroes in the United States
than saddle posterity with such a Constitution."[70]

For the first time in the Convention, two northerners—King and Morris—
had denounced slavery in the same debate. A third, Jonathan Dayton of New
Jersey, joined them by seconding Morris's motion. Curiously, no one responded in kind to these attacks. Roger Sherman calmly answered his northern neighbors, declaring he saw no "insuperable objections" to "the admission
of the Negroes into the ratio of representation." He argued, "It was the freemen of the Southn. States who were in fact to be represented according to
the taxes paid by them, and the Negroes are only included in the Estimate of
the taxes." This response reflected claims made by delegates from South
Carolina since the beginning of the Convention that wealth as well as population had to be represented in the Congress. James Wilson added that the
objections by Morris and King were premature. Charles Pinckney merely
indicated that he would reply "if the occasion were a proper one." The Convention then overwhelmingly rejected Morris's amendment.[71]

For the South, this debate, along with the vote that followed it, was a major victory. The debate exposed many of the weaknesses of slavery; some delegates had made powerful moral and practical arguments against the institution. Yet all the northern states except New Jersey voted with the South.

In the following week, the Convention managed to avoid rancorous debates over slavery, even though sectional distrust sometimes appeared.[72] This period of calm ended on August 16, when the Convention began reviewing the powers of Congress. During a routine discussion of the taxing power, George Mason raised the issue of the power of Congress to tax exports. A part of the draft Constitution that had not yet been debated specifically prohibited Congress from taxing exports. Mason wanted to debate the issue out of order. He did not want to give Congress the right to levy any tax without simultaneously adopting a corresponding prohibition on export taxes. Mason "was unwilling to trust to its being done in a future article" and "professed his jealousy for the productions of the Southern or as he called them, the staple States." Sherman and Rutledge quickly reassured Mason that such a provision could be dealt with later. Mason could not, however, have been totally reassured when Gouverneur Morris declared that a prohibition on taxing exports was "radically objectionable." A number of other delegates then debated this issue. With the exception of Madison, all the southerners opposed taxing exports; all the northerners, except those from Connecticut and Massachusetts, favored the idea.[73] The Convention then postponed the question of taxing exports.

This short debate gave hints of a developing bargain between New Englanders and delegates from the Deep South. In reassuring Mason, South Carolina's John Rutledge noted that he would vote for the commerce clause as it stood, but only "on condition that the subsequent part relating to negroes should also be agreed to."[74] Rutledge clearly equated an export tax with an attack on slavery. Delegates from Connecticut and Massachusetts indicated some support for Rutledge's position. The "dirty compromise" of the Convention was taking shape. The South Carolina delegation would support the commerce clause if New England would support a prohibition on export taxes and a protection for the slave trade. This understanding solidified during the next two weeks.

On August 21, the New England states joined five slave states on three crucial votes. On the first vote, all three New England states voted to defeat an amendment to the draft Constitution that would have allowed Congress, by a simple majority vote, to tax exports. During the debate over this motion, Connecticut's Ellsworth argued against taxing exports because such taxes would unfairly hurt the South, which produced major export crops such as "Tobo. rice and indigo." Ellsworth believed "a tax on these alone would be partial and unjust." Next, in a key five-to-six vote, Connecticut joined the five slave states to defeat a proposal, made by James Madison, to allow taxes on exports by a two-thirds vote of Congress. On the final vote, to absolutely ban all export taxes, Massachusetts joined Connecticut, and the measure to prohibit export taxes, favored by the South passed, seven to four. During the debate, the Virginia delegation was divided, three to two, with James Madison and George Washington unsuccessfully favoring Congressional power to tax exports.[75]

The Convention then debated a motion by Luther Martin to allow an import tax on slaves. Martin represented Maryland, a slave state, but one with a surplus of slaves, a fact that helps explain his opposition to the African trade. Rutledge opposed Martin's motion with a two-pronged attack. He first told the Convention that the "true question at present is whether the Southern States shall or shall not be parties to the Union." The implied threat of secession was clear. He then told the northern delegates that, if they would "consult their interest," they would "not oppose the increase of slaves which will increase the commodities of which they will become the carriers." Ellsworth of Connecticut agreed, refusing to debate the "morality or wisdom of slavery" and simply asserting that "what enriches a part enriches the whole." The alliance for profit between the Deep South and New England was now fully developed. Charles Pinckney then reaffirmed that South Carolina would "never receive the plan if it prohibits the slave trade."[76] Shrewdly, Pinckney equated a tax on imported slaves with a prohibition on the trade itself. On this note, the Convention retired for the day.

Roger Sherman opened debate the next day by adopting a familiar pose. He declared his personal disapproval of slavery but refused to condemn it in other parts of the nation. He then argued against a prohibition of the slave trade, asserting that "the public good did not require" an end to the trade. Noting that the states already had the right to import slaves, Sherman saw no point in taking a right away from the states unnecessarily because "it was expedient to have as few objections as possible" to the new Constitution. Here Sherman assumed it was necessary to defuse southern opposition to the Constitution, which might result from a ban on the slave trade, but he did not think it necessary to placate those who might oppose the Constitution if it allowed the slave trade to continue. Sherman was prepared to appease those who supported the slave trade, but he apparently was unconcerned about the strong opposition to the slave trade in his own region. Next, Sherman observed that "the abolition of slavery seemed to be going on in the U.S." If left alone, the "good sense of the several States" would soon put an end to all slavery in the country. In making this argument, Sherman either confused the abolition of the slave trade with the abolition of slavery itself, or he foolishly believed that because New England and Pennsylvania had begun to abolish slavery, the rest of the nation would soon follow. Finally, revealing his priorities, Sherman urged the Convention to hurry and finish its business.[77] After almost three months of meetings, this argument doubtless resounded well with some delegates.

George Mason of Virginia responded to Sherman with a fierce attack on the "infernal traffic" in slaves, which he blamed on "the avarice of British Merchants." Reflecting the sectional hostilities at the Convention, as well as trying to lay blame on anyone but Virginians for the problem of slavery, Mason then "lamented" that his "Eastern brethren had from a lust of gain embarked in this nefarious traffic." Mason leveled some of the strongest criticism of slavery yet heard at the Convention, declaring it an "evil" system that produced "the most pernicious effect on manners." He declared that "every master of slaves is born a petty tyrant" and warned that slavery would "bring the judgment of heaven on a Country" and ultimately produce "national calamities." Despite this apparent attack on the whole institution, Mason ended his speech by demanding only that the national government "have power to prevent the increase of slavery" by prohibiting the African trade. As Peter Wallenstein has argued, "Whatever his occasional rhetoric, George Mason was—if one must choose—proslavery, not antislavery. He acted in behalf of Virginia slaveholders, not Virginia slaves," when he opposed a continuation of the African trade.[78]

Others at the Convention understood this quite well. Mason failed to say that Virginia, like Maryland, had a surplus of slaves and did not need the African slave trade any longer. But James McHenry candidly wrote in his private notes: "That the population or increase of slaves in Virginia exceeded their calls for their services," and thus a prohibition of the slave trade "would be a monopoly" in Virginia's "favor." Under such conditions "Virginia etc would make their own terms for such [slaves] as they might sell."[79] The "etc" no doubt included McHenry's own state of Maryland.

Ellsworth of Connecticut, adopting the same pose as Sherman, answered Mason. Because "he had never owned a slave," Ellsworth declared he "could not judge of the effects of slavery on character." However, if slavery were as wrong as Mason had suggested, merely ending the trade was insufficient. Ellsworth, of course, knew that the Virginians opposed allowing the national government to abolish slavery. Since there were many slaves in Virginia and Maryland and fewer in the Deep South, any prohibition on the trade would be "unjust towards S. Carolina and Georgia." Ellsworth thus urged the Convention not to "intermeddle" in the affairs of other states.[80] The Convention had now witnessed the unusual phenomenon of a New Englander defending the slave trade against the attacks of a Virginian.

The Carolinians were of course quite capable of defending their own institution. Charles Pinckney, citing ancient Rome and Greece, declared that slavery was "justified by the example of all the world." He warned that any prohibition of the slave trade would "produce serious objections to the Constitution which he wished to see adopted."[81] His cousin, General Pinckney, also declared his support for the Constitution, but noted that his "personal influence . . . would be of no avail towards obtaining the assent" of his home state. He believed Virginia's opposition to the trade was more pecuniary than moral. Virginia would "gain by stopping the importations" because "her slaves will rise in value, and she has more than she wants." Prohibiting the trade would force South Carolina and Georgia "to confederate" on "unequal terms." While Virginia might gain, the nation as a whole would not. More slaves would produce more goods, and that result would help not only the South but also states involved in "the carrying trade." Seeing the slave trade solely as an economic issue, Pinckney thought it "reasonable" that imported slaves be taxed. But a prohibition of the slave trade would be "an exclusion of S. Carola from the Union." As he had made clear at the beginning of his speech, "S. Carolina and Georgia cannot do without slaves." Rutledge and Butler added similar sentiments, as did Abraham Baldwin of Georgia and Williamson of North Carolina.[82]

New England twangs now supported the Southern drawls. Gerry of Massachusetts offered some conciliatory remarks, and Sherman, ever the ally of the South, declared that "it was better to let the S. States import slaves than to part with them, if they made that a sine qua non." However, in what may have been an attempt to give his remarks an antislavery tone, he argued that taxing imported slaves was morally wrong, because that "implied they were property."[83] This position undoubtedly pleased Sherman's southern allies, who did not want to pay taxes on any slaves they imported. Sherman's speech also underscored the profound support that the Carolinians and Georgians found among some New Englanders.

The reasons for cooperation between New England and the Deep South on this issue were now clear. All the New England states had banned the slave trade and prohibited their ships from transporting slaves from Africa. But New Englanders involved in the "carrying trade" would profit from transporting rice and other products produced by slave labor. And the South Carolinians seemed willing to support the New Englanders' demands for Congressional power to regulate all commerce. In return, New Englanders would support the right of the Carolinas and Georgia to import the slaves they could not "do without."

On the other side of the issue, only John Langdon of New Hampshire and John Dickinson of Delaware vigorously opposed allowing the slave trade to continue. Dickinson argued that the trade was "inadmissible on every principle of honor and safety." Furthermore, he was prepared to call the Carolinians' bluff on the question of Union, doubting that the Deep South would reject the Constitution if the trade were prohibited. James Wilson was also skeptical of southern threats, but he did not offer any strong rebuttal. Nor did Rufus King, who only pointed out that prohibiting a tax on imported Africans was an "inequality that could not fail to strike the commercial sagacity of the Northern and middle States."[84]

The most surprising contribution to this debate came from Gouverneur Morris of Pennsylvania, who had previously been the most consistent opponent of slavery at the Convention. He suggested that the subject of commercial regulation acts and the slave trade be sent to committee. "These things may form a bargain among the Northern and Southern States," he shrewdly noted. The Convention quickly accepted his suggestion.[85]

On August 26, the Convention began to debate the committee's compromise proposal. The committee proposed that Congress be barred from prohibiting the African slave trade until 1800, but that in the meantime a reasonable tax could be levied on imported slaves. General Charles C. Pinckney immediately proposed that the date be changed to 1808, which would be twenty years after the Constitution was ratified. Gorham of Massachusetts seconded this motion. Madison complained that this provision was "dishonorable to the National character" and to the Constitution and that the "twenty years will produce all the mischief that can be apprehended from the liberty to import slaves." Nevertheless, the delegates accepted Pinckney's change by a seven-to-four vote, three New England states, Maryland, and the three Deep South states supporting it.[86]

Gouverneur Morris, still resisting a continuation of the slave trade, then proposed that the clause specifically declare that the "importation of slaves" be limited to the Carolinas and Georgia. Morris wanted it known "that this part of the Constitution was a compliance with those States." Having made this motion only to embarrass supporters of the trade, Morris withdrew it. By a seven-to-four vote, the Convention then adopted the slave trade provision. The three New England states once again joined Maryland and the Deep South to allow the slave trade to continue for twenty years.[87] This vote formed a key component of the "dirty compromise."

On August 28, the Convention debated what would become the privileges and immunities clause of the Constitution. Charles Cotesworth Pinckney "seemed to wish some provision should be included in favor of property in slaves," but he did not press the point, and the Convention accepted the clause with only South Carolina voting no. Pinckney's concern was apparently over the right of masters to travel from state to state with their slaves.

In fact, those states that had already passed gradual emancipation statues, like Pennsylvania, had made provisions for slave transit. Perhaps for this reason, other southern delegates did not share Pinckney's concern. This seems to have been the only time during the Convention when southerners perceived a threat to slavery but were unable to muster the votes, or perhaps their own energies, to head it off.[88]

The Convention immediately turned to the fugitives from justice clause. Butler and Charles Pinckney attempted to amend this provision "to require fugitive slaves and servants to be delivered up like criminals." Roger Sherman sarcastically countered that he "saw no more propriety in the public seizing and surrendering a slave or servant, than a horse." James Wilson objected that this would cost the free states money. Significantly, this opposition came from two delegates who usually sided with the South. Butler wisely "withdrew his proposition in order that some particular provision might be made apart from this article."[89]

The next day, the debates over commerce, the slave trade, and fugitive slaves were all joined to complete the "dirty compromise." In a discussion of the commerce clause, Charles Pinckney, the younger and more impetuous of the two cousins, moved that a two-thirds majority be required for all commercial regulations. He argued that "the power of regulating commerce was a pure concession on the part of the S. States" and that therefore the two-thirds requirement was reasonable.[90]

General Charles Cotesworth Pinckney agreed that "it was the true interest of the S. States to have no regulation of commerce." But, in one of the most revealing statements of the Convention, he explained his support for a clause requiring only a simple majority for passage of commercial legislation. Pinckney said he took this position because of "their [the eastern states'] liberal conduct towards the views of South Carolina." The "views of South Carolina" concerned the slave trade. In the margins of his notes, Madison made this clear. Madison wrote that Pinckney

> meant the permission to import slaves. An understanding on the two subjects of navigation and slavery, had taken place between those parts of the Union, which explains the vote on the Motion depending, as well as the language of General Pinckney and others.

Other delegates confirmed this analysis. Luther Martin later reported that "the eastern States, notwithstanding their aversion to slavery, were very willing to indulge the southern States, at least with a temporary liberty to prosecute the slave trade, provided the southern States would in their turn gratify them, by laying no restriction on navigation acts; and after a very little time, the committee by a great majority agreed on a report, by which the general government was to be prohibited from preventing the importation of slaves for a limited time, and the restrictive clause relative to navigation acts was to be omitted."[91]

Subsequent debate confirmed that New Englanders and South Carolinians had indeed struck a bargain. Butler, for example, declared that the interests of the southern and eastern states were "as different as the interests of Russia and Turkey." Nevertheless, he was "desirous of conciliating the affections of the East" and so opposed the two-thirds requirement. The Virginians, who had opposed the slave trade provisions, now supported the demand for a two-thirds requirement for commercial legislation. But they were in the minority. South Carolina joined all the northern states to defeat the motion to require a two-thirds vote to regulate commerce. The Convention then adopted the clause, allowing a simply majority to regulate commerce.[92]

Immediately after this vote, Butler reintroduced the fugitive slave clause. Without debate or recorded vote, it too passed.[93] The last bargain over slavery had been made. The northerners who had opposed the fugitive slave provision only a day before were now silent.

The debates of late August reveal how willing the northern delegates—especially the New Englanders—were to support slavery and the demands of the Deep South. Some years ago, William W. Freehling argued that the slave trade clause was adopted to "lure Georgia and South Carolina into the Union."[94] The Convention debates, however, suggest that the Deep South did not need to be lured into the Union; the delegates from the Carolinas and Georgia were already deeply committed to the Constitution by the time the slave trade debate occurred. Moreover, the South had already won major concessions on the three-fifths clause and the prohibition on taxing exports. These were permanent features of the Constitution, unlike the slave trade provision, which would lapse in twenty years. Although some southerners talked of not joining the Union unless the slave trade were allowed, it seems unlikely they would have risked going it alone over a temporary right of importation.[95]

This prospect is even more unlikely because at the time of the Convention none of these states was actively importing slaves from Africa. This fact cuts against Professor Earl Maltz's contention that giving Congress the "authority to ban the importation of new slaves" would "have done serious damage to the economies of a number of southern states."[96] From 1787 until 1803 South Carolina did not import any slaves from Africa. From 1803 to 1808 South Carolina imported about 80,000 new slaves. These importations created enormous human tragedies for the individual victims of the trade—and they doubtless provided huge profits to individual importers and purchasers—but these importations did not dramatically affect the economy of South Carolina or the Deep South.

The arguments of Freehling and Maltz rest on the assumption that the states of the Deep South would have rejected the Constitution over the right to import slaves in the future when they in fact were not currently importing them. Furthermore, even without constitutional protection for the slave trade, importations from Africa would have been legal until the Congress actually took the time, and mustered the votes, to prohibit them. At no time did the Convention consider a clause flatly prohibiting the trade; the entire debate was over whether the Constitution would explicitly protect the trade. Earl Maltz writes that "under the Articles of Confederation, no federal action against the slave trade was possible; if this is the appropriate starting point then even a delayed grant of authority over the importation of slaves must be considered anti-slavery and nationalistic."[97] However, this analysis ignores the fact that the slave trade clause is a specific exception to the general rule giving Congress complete power to regulate all commerce *but* slave importation. In essence, the Convention granted Congress the general power to regulate *all* international commerce except the African slave trade. It is not surprising that the South Carolina delegation considered this a great victory for their special interest in slave importations.[98]

However one views the African trade, it is hard to see how anyone could assert that the fugitive slave clause was also a "lure." Added at the last possible moment, without any serious debate or discussion, this clause was a boon to the South without any quid pro quo for the North. On this vote the northern delegates either did not understand the importance of the issue or were too tired to fight it.

The August debates also reveal that the northern delegates could have had no illusions about the nature of the covenant they were forming with the South. The northern delegates could not have forgotten General Charles Cotesworth Pinckney's earlier assertion that "S. Carolina and Georgia cannot do without slaves." While the "Fathers liked to call [slavery] temporary," the evidence of the Convention shows they should have known better.[99] Throughout the Convention, the delegates from the slave states made no attempt to hide their belief that slavery would be a permanent part of their culture and society. No one who attended the Philadelphia Convention could have believed that slavery was "temporary" in the South.

Toward Sectional Harmony

With the adoption of the commerce clause and the fugitive slave clause, the issues of immediate concern to slave owners seemed to be settled. However, on August 30, a conflict over slavery briefly emerged during a discussion of the domestic violence clause of what became Article IV of the Constitution. John Dickinson of Delaware attempted to delete the limitation that permitted the national government to intervene to prevent violence only "on the application" of a state legislature. This change would have allowed the national government, and not the states, to determine when intervention was necessary. The Convention quickly defeated this motion, with the five slave states voting no, apparently because they did not want the national government to interfere in their domestic affairs. However, on a vote to change the wording of the clause from "domestic violence" to "insurrections," the four slave states south of Virginia voted yes, but the motion lost five to six.[100] Fear of slave insurrections no doubt motivated the South to wish for explicit protection on this matter.

The Convention now turned to the numerous proposals that had been tabled throughout the summer. North-South cooperation remained high. Motions introduced by a delegate from one section were often seconded by one from the other. Although some patterns of sectional voting can be found in these debates, they are rare and may be more coincidental than significant.[101] Some delegates, particularly Mason of Virginia, raised sectional fears. But by this time Mason was so clearly opposed to the Constitution that he was apparently willing to make any argument to derail the work of the Convention.[102]

Even on that divisive issue—the slave trade—the sectional compromise held. On September 10, the last day of debate before the Constitution went to a final Committee of Style, John Rutledge of South Carolina noted his opposition to the amendment procedure because "the articles relating to slaves might be altered by the states not interested in that property and prejudiced against it." At Rutledge's insistence, the Convention added a clause forbidding any amendment of the slave trade provision and the capitation tax provision before 1808.[103] As they had throughout the Convention, the delegates from the Deep South left almost nothing to chance in their zeal to protect slavery.

Emerging from the Committee of Style on September 14, the penultimate version of the Constitution produced further debate on issues relating to slavery and sectionalism. On September 15, an attempt to increase the representation of North Carolina in the first congress failed, on a strictly sectional vote. Similarly, the Convention rejected an attempt to change the clause on export taxes to make it yet more favorable to the South. Here, however, Maryland and South Carolina joined the North in defeating the measure.[104] The Convention's last substantive action on slavery-related matters concerned the fugitive slave clause. The Committee of Detail had reported the clause with the language "No person legally held to service or labour in one state escaping into another shall . . . be discharged from such service or labour. . . ."

The Convention substituted the term "under the laws thereof" after the word "state" for the term "legally." The delegates made this change "in compliance with the wish of some who thought the term [legally] equivocal, and favoring the idea that slavery was legal in a moral view."[105] This was a minor victory for those who were squeamish about slavery, but it had no practical effect.

The Proslavery Compact

This final compromise over the wording of the fugitive slave clause was an entirely appropriate way to end discussion of slavery at the Convention. Throughout the Convention, the delegates had fought over the place of slavery in the Constitution. Northerners opposed representation for slavery because it would give the South a political advantage; Virginians opposed the slave trade, at least in part, because it would undermine the value of their excess slaves. A few delegates had expressed moral qualms over slavery, but most of the criticism had been political and economic. The initial reaction to the fugitive slave clause typified this. When Pierce Butler and Charles Pinckney first proposed it, James Wilson complained, "This would oblige the Executive of the State to do it, at public expense."[106] The costs Wilson worried about were more financial than moral.

The word "slavery" was never mentioned in the Constitution, yet its presence was felt everywhere. The new wording of the fugitive slave clause was characteristic. Fugitive slaves were called "persons owing service or Labour," and the word "legally" was omitted so as not to offend northern sensibilities. Northern delegates could return home asserting that the Constitution did not recognize the legality of slavery. In the most technical linguistic sense, they were perhaps right. Southerners, on the other hand, could tell their neighbors, as General Charles Cotesworth Pinckney told his, "We have obtained a right to recover our slaves in whatever part of America they may take refuge, which is a right we had not before."[107]

Indeed, the slave states had obtained significant concessions at the Convention. Through the three-fifths clause they gained extra representation in Congress. Through the electoral college their votes for president were far more potent than the votes of northerners. The prohibition on export taxes favored the products of slave labor. The slave trade clause guaranteed their right to import new slaves for at least twenty years. The domestic violence clause guaranteed them federal aid if they should need it to suppress a slave rebellion. The limited nature of federal power and the cumbersome amendment process guaranteed that, as long as they remained in the Union, their system of labor and race relations would remain free from national interference. On every issue at the Convention, slave owners had won major concessions from the rest of the nation, and with the exception of the commerce clause they had given up very little to win these concessions. The northern delegates had been eager for a stronger Union with a national court system and a unified commercial system. Although some had expressed concern over the justice or safety of slavery, in the end they were able to justify their compromises and ignore their qualms.

At the close of the Convention, two delegates, Elbridge Gerry of Massachusetts and George Mason of Virginia, explained why they could not sign the document they had helped create. Both had a plethora of objections that included slavery-related issues. But their objections were not grounded in moral or philosophical opposition to slavery; rather, like the arguments of those delegates who ultimately supported the compromises over slavery, the objections of Gerry and Mason were practical and political. Gerry objected to the three-fifths clause because it gave the South too much political power at the expense of New England. Mason opposed allowing the slave trade to continue because "such importations render the United States weaker, more vulnerable, and less capable of defense."[108]

During the ratification struggles, others would take more principled stands against the compromises over slavery. A New Yorker complained that the Constitution condoned "drenching the bowels of Africa in gore, for the sake of enslaving its free-born innocent inhabitants." In New Hampshire, "A Friend of the Rights of People" asked, "Can we then hold up our hands for a Constitution that licenses this bloody practice? Can we who have fought so hard for Liberty give our consent to have it taken away from others? May the powers above forbid." The anonymous "Friend" was particularly troubled because even after twenty years the Constitution did not require that "this cruel and barbarous practice . . . shall cease." A Virginian thought the slave trade provision was an "excellent clause" for "an Algerian constitution: but not so well calculated (I hope) for the latitude of America."[109]

It was more than just the slave trade that northern antifederalists feared. Three opponents of the Constitution in Massachusetts noted that the Constitution bound the states together as a "whole" so "the states" were "under obligation . . . reciprocally to aid each other in defense and support of every thing to which they are entitled thereby, right or wrong." Thus, they might be called to suppress a slave revolt or in some other way defend the institution. They could not predict how slavery might entangle them in the future, but they did know that "this lust for slavery, [was] portentous of much evil in America, for the cry of innocent blood, . . . hath undoubtedly reached to the Heavens, to which that cry is always directed, and will draw down upon them vengeance adequate to the enormity of the crime."[110]

The events of 1861–1865 would prove the three Massachusetts antifederalists of 1788 correct. Only after a civil war of unparalleled bloodshed and three constitutional amendments could the Union be made more perfect by finally expunging slavery from the Constitution.

——— Two ———

Slavery and
the Northwest Ordinance, 1787

A Study in Ambiguity

For many antebellum northerners, the Northwest Ordinance's prohibition of slavery was almost a sacred text. Article VI of the Ordinance stated:

> There shall be neither slavery nor involuntary servitude in the said territory, otherwise than in the punishment of crimes, whereof the party shall have been duly convicted: provided always, that any person escaping into the same, from whom labour or service is lawfully claimed in any one of the original states, such fugitive may be lawfully reclaimed, and conveyed to the person claiming his or her labour or service as aforesaid.[1]

In the early 1830s, a young Salmon P. Chase, who would become Chief Justice of the United States Supreme Court in 1864, described the provision as a "remarkable instrument . . . the last gift of the congress of the old confederation to the country . . . a fit consummation of their glorious labors." Writing in the 1850s, when sectional tensions over slavery in the territories were at their height, Edward Coles, the antislavery former governor of Illinois, declared that the Ordinance of 1787 was "marvellous" and showed "the profound wisdom of those who framed such an efficacious measure for our country." Coles contrasted the debate over slavery in Kansas and Nebraska in 1854 to the earlier period, when "the Territories subject to it [the Ordinance] were quiet, happy, and prosperous." Coles believed that if American politicians had followed the pattern set by the Ordinance of 1787, the turmoil of the 1850s might have been avoided. Men like Chase and Coles praised the Ordinance for creating the free states along the Ohio River. Many antebellum northerners had no doubt that without the Ordinance the Midwest would have become a bastion of slavery.[2]

In spite of the praise that Article VI received in the nineteenth century, modern scholars have, for the most part, ignored it. Although Ulrich B. Phillips described it as "the first and last antislavery achievement by the central government" in this period, a careful examination of the provisions and its implementation suggests that it is unclear exactly what the article was intended to accomplish. At the time of its passage the Ordinance did not threaten slavery in the South. It may even have strengthened slavery there. Nor did the Ordinance immediately or directly affect slavery in the territory north of the Ohio River. Slavery continued in the region for decades. Thus in the nineteenth-century usage of the term, the Ordinance was not abolitionist and was only barely "antislavery."[3]

Certainly it is unlikely that all those who voted for the Ordinance saw the provision as antislavery. The congressmen from the Deep South who voted for it were not consciously undermining slavery. On the contrary, some of the slaveholders who voted for the legislation may have believed that Article VI actually fortified slavery. The fact that the Ordinance was specifically limited to the territory north of the Ohio River seemed to imply that the territories south of the river were open to slavery. This assumption was reinforced by the fact that in 1784 Congress had defeated a proposal to prohibit slavery in *all* the western territories after the year 1800.[4] Furthermore, the Ordinance's fugitive slave clause offered protection to the slave owners whose property might escape into the territory. Since the Articles of Confederation contained no such protection and the Constitutional Convention had not yet added a similar clause to the proposed new compact, this was an important victory for slavery.[5]

While the Ordinance gave support to slavery in the South, it did not destroy slavery north of the Ohio. Article VI was not an emancipation proclamation for the Northwest. No slaves were freed immediately because of the Ordinance. Neither it nor the state constitutions of the free states in the Northwest led to an immediate end to slavery throughout the area.

In the long run, of course, Article VI became a powerful force in the development of the ideology of free soil. As historian David Brion Davis points out, "It provided the core of the Republican party's ideology, an ideology that seemed convincing to millions of northerners who had no sympathy for the abolitionist cause." Thus, in the 1850s, northern Republicans, who had no interest in interfering with slavery in the South, nevertheless adopted the notion implicit in the Ordinance that slavery should not be allowed in the western territories. The Ordinance also set the stage for the emergence of five free states in the region. By discouraging slave owners from moving into the region, the Ordinance helped create a white majority in the Northwest that was hostile to slavery. This proved especially crucial in Illinois, where in 1823–1824 opponents of slavery led by Governor Edward Coles soundly defeated an attempt to amend the Illinois Constitution of 1818 to allow slavery. Yet, even after the defeat of the proslavery forces, some Illinois blacks remained in bondage for nearly thirty years. Slavery lingered so long in the Northwest at least in part because the Ordinance itself was ambiguous, internally inconsistent, and written by men who were uncertain of their own objectives.[6]

Article VI of the Northwest Ordinance

An examination of the transition from slavery to liberty in the Northwest illustrates the ambivalence of the founding generation over slavery, the naïveté of the early opponents of the peculiar institution, the tenacity of slave owners in maintaining control over their "servants," even when they lived in theoretically "free" jurisdictions, and the support for slavery expansion that existed in the early national period.[7] Finally, this examination illustrates the difficulty of ending an entrenched institution merely by constitutional dictates and without the support of legislative enactments or executive enforcement.

The failure of the Ordinance and state constitutions to end slavery immediately has a fourfold explanation. First, Congress drafted and adopted Article VI without debate. Such debate might have clarified its intent and meaning. After approving Article VI, the Confederation Congress did not change the rest of the Ordinance to provide internal consistency in the document. Thus, specific dictates of the Ordinance protected some slavery in the region, even while Article VI seemed to proclaim an end to slavery. For example, throughout the Ordinance there are references to "free" inhabitants of the territory, indicating that "unfree" inhabitants might also be allowed to live there.

Second, slavery had a certain staying power—a power of inertia—which made eradication of the institution difficult. Slavery existed in the Northwest before Congress enacted the Ordinance, and the mere passage of a law by a distant and virtually powerless Congress could hardly effect immediate change. Nor would a state constitution necessarily end slavery immediately. Notions of private property fundamental to the ideology of the American Revolution further strengthened existing slavery in the territory. Was it fair, asked men raised on Lockean concepts of "life, liberty, and property," to deprive one man of his property to give another his liberty? Chief Justice William Tilghman of Pennsylvania, for example, concluded in an 1815 case that property was as important as liberty. In rejecting a slave's claim to freedom, he wrote: "I know that freedom is to be favoured, but we have no right to favour it at the expense of property." Tilghman articulated an attitude prevalent throughout much of the nation. Thus, perhaps it is not surprising that the Illinois Constitution of 1818 protected slavery and involuntary servitude and that until 1845 the Illinois Supreme Court was unwilling to free all the slaves (or their descendants) in that state.[8]

Third, the abolition of slavery in the Northwest Territory created serious conflict-of-laws questions. The three most important antebellum states in the area—Ohio, Indiana, and Illinois—shared long borders with slave states. The two great river highways of the American interior, the Ohio and the Mississippi, demarcated these borders. Numerous masters traveling with their slaves on these waterways found it necessary or convenient to land on the free side of these rivers. In later years the National Road would begin in the slave state of Maryland, but pass through two northwestern states and terminate in a third. If these states did not allow transit with slaves, then comity among the states and harmony within the union would be disrupted. On the other hand, to allow such transit would require the states to violate their own constitutional prohibitions of slavery. This was so because even slaves temporarily in a free state were, nevertheless, slaves. Freedom was essentially indivisible. It was impossible to bring slaves into a free jurisdiction without bringing some or all of the attributes of a system of slavery with them. If the slave followed the master into a free territory or state, so would the whip, the chain, and the other coercions of the institution.[9]

Finally, there was a lack of will on the part of many local officials actually to enforce either the spirit or the precise letter of the Ordinance. Important national leaders, such as Thomas Jefferson, were willing to allow the institution to survive in the Northwest on the theory that the diffusion of slaves throughout the nation would benefit both the slaves and the white population. Many slaveholding settlers in the territory also supported this theory in hopes it would undermine the antislavery thrust of the Ordinance.

The Adoption of the Slavery Prohibition

The Northwest Ordinance, which Congress adopted in 1787, consists of fourteen paragraphs and six articles that set out the method for governing the territory north and west of the Ohio River, which today encompasses the states of Ohio, Indiana, Illinois, Michigan, Wisconsin, and part of Minnesota. The adoption of the Ordinance was one of the most significant acts of the national congress under the Articles of Confederation.

The Ordinance directly addressed slavery in its last article:

> There shall be neither slavery nor involuntary servitude in the said territory, otherwise than in the punishment of crimes, whereof the party shall have been duly convicted: provided always, that any person escaping into

the same, from whom labour or service is lawfully claimed in any one of the original states, such fugitive may be lawfully reclaimed, and conveyed to the person claiming his or her labour or service as aforesaid.[10]

On its face this language appears to be straightforward and conclusive. The words "there shall be neither slavery nor involuntary servitude" seem to mean that all slavery is prohibited in the territory and that the status of "slave" cannot be recognized by the laws of the territory. Yet the fugitive slave provision of the same article partially compromised this apparently conclusive language. The article gives no hint as to how a fugitive slave was to be treated in the territory. Could a master beat his fugitive with impunity? Might a master rape his female fugitive slave? What would be the status of a child born in the territory to a fugitive? These questions, and similar ones, suggest that slavery presented problems that might not be easily overcome by a single article in the Ordinance.

The apparent simplicity of Article VI is further undermined by other provisions of the Ordinance and by the circumstances of the drafting of Article VI itself. The Ordinance initially consisted of fourteen paragraphs that outlined how the territory was to be governed, and five "articles" that would "forever remain unalterable, unless by common consent."[11] Between May 1786 and May 1787, Congress intermittently discussed this proposed document with no mention of slavery. In April and May 1787, the proposal received two favorable readings in Congress. A third reading, set for May 10, was postponed, and by May 12 Congress lacked a quorum. When Congress resumed deliberations in July, it appointed a new committee to finish work on the Ordinance. On July 11, when the committee brought it to the full house, the Ordinance did not contain the slavery prohibition. On the twelfth, the Ordinance was given a second reading and scheduled for a final vote the next day. Again, there was no mention of slavery in the Ordinance or on the floor of Congress. On July 13, Nathan Dane, a delegate from Massachusetts, proposed the addition of Article VI. Congress apparently accepted this amendment without debate or protest. The Ordinance, with the slavery prohibition now added to it, passed by a unanimous vote of all the states present.[12]

Historians have long puzzled over this chain of events. Although Nathan Dane drafted Article VI in committee, some have doubted that he really deserved credit for the famous provision.[13] While this point remains unresolved, it is not as compelling as the question why the southern majority then in Congress so readily accepted the clause. When Congress passed the Ordinance, one state present, Massachusetts, had ended slavery. New Hampshire had also ended slavery, while Rhode Island, Connecticut, and Pennsylvania had passed gradual emancipation statutes. But delegates from those states did not vote on the matter. The five southern states present—Delaware, Virginia, South Carolina, North Carolina, and Georgia—would retain slavery until the Civil War. The two remaining states, New York and New Jersey, would be the last northern states to take steps to end slavery, not doing so until 1799 and 1804, respectively. Staughton Lynd and Peter Onuf offer two plausible interpretations for this vote: southerners expected the Northwest to be sympathetic to southern issues even if it had no slaves, and the Northwest Ordinance tacitly implied that the Southwest would remain open to slavery.[14]

A third explanation for southern support comes from Congressman William Grayson, a Virginian on the congressional committee that had drafted the Ordinance. Grayson wrote to James Monroe that the slavery prohibition "was agreed to by the Southern members for the purpose of preventing Tobacco and Indigo from being made" in the Northwest. The Ordinance would thus prevent the Northwest from competing with the emerging Southwest. This explanation also supports the notion that the Ordinance implied that the territory south of the Ohio would remain open to slavery. The fugitive slave clause in Article VI doubtless helped gain the votes of southerners and may have in fact been the necessary element in obtaining their support for the ban on slavery.[15]

There is a fourth possible reason for southern support of the Ordinance with the slavery provision: the need to pass an ordinance that would satisfy Manasseh Cutler, the lobbyist for the New England investors who formed the Ohio Land Company. The final impetus for passage of the Ordinance, for both southern and northern congressmen, was the possibility of selling some five million acres of land to Cutler and his associates. In two letters written immediately after passage of the Ordinance, Richard Henry Lee asserted that it was passed as "preparatory to the sale of that Country [Ohio]." Lee noted that as soon as the Ordinance was passed, Congress turned "to consider of [*sic*] a proposition made for the purchase of 5 or 6 millions of Acres, in order to lessen the domestic debt." Evidence of this sort led the nineteenth-century historian William F. Poole to conclude that the "chief motive of the Southern members in voting unanimously for the Ordinance was doubtless to relieve the financial embarrassment of the government, and to bring the public lands into the market at the highest price." Poole further argued that the slavery prohibition was placed in the Ordinance at the insistence of Manasseh Cutler, because Congress felt it must frame "an instrument which would be satisfactory to the party proposing to purchase these lands." Perhaps informed by the realities of Gilded Age politics, Poole saw the lobbyist for the land company as the most important actor on the scene.[16]

Cutler came to New York on July 6 to lobby for the right to purchase land for the Ohio Company. On the tenth he presented the committee with some suggestions for amendments to the Ordinance and then immediately left New York for Philadelphia. On the thirteenth, Congress adopted the Ordinance with the slavery prohibition.[17] It is unknown if Cutler would have agreed to purchase Ohio lands if the Ordinance had not contained the prohibition of slavery. It is impossible to know if his proposed amendments even included the prohibition of slavery, because Cutler's diary entry on this subject gives absolutely no indication of what the amendments were. However, his known antipathy to slavery suggests that he was instrumental in persuading the committee, and the Congress, to accept the clause. On the other hand, he apparently was willing to accept the version of the Ordinance he read on July 10, which did not include the slavery prohibition, because he left New York immediately after giving his suggested amendments to the committee. Had he been overwhelmingly concerned with the fate of his suggestions, Cutler probably would have stayed in New York for the vote on the thirteenth.[18]

Poole's assertion that Cutler was responsible for the slavery prohibition is, then, subject to the Scotch verdict—not proved. Poole seems more correct in his conclusion that the "Ordinance of 1787 and the Ohio purchase were parts of one and the same transaction. The purchase *would* not have been made without the Ordinance, and the Ordinance *could* not have been enacted except as an essential condition of the purchase." As noted above, the Ordinance, in some form, had been under consideration since at least 1785. It is likely that a version of the Ordinance would have passed, sooner or later, simply because at some point pressure to settle the West would have forced Congress to act. But the evidence does suggest that Cutler's lobbying and the interest of the Massachusetts land speculators in purchasing land in Ohio did spur Congress to act.[19]

In the final analysis it may not matter who proposed Article VI, whether Cutler's lobbying made it possible, or why Congress enacted the Ordinance when it did. What is important is that the history of the Ordinance shows (1) that there was virtually no debate over the slavery provision; (2) that it was added at the last possible moment, without careful consideration; (3) that the rest of the Ordinance was not redrafted to make it consistent with Article VI; and (4) that although the plain meaning of the language of Article VI is that slavery could not exist in the territory (except for fugitives), it is unlikely that the southern majority that passed the Ordinance understood the article to mean this.

Whatever the reasons were, the prohibition of slavery was added to the Ordinance at the eleventh hour. This was, of course, not the first time that a prohibition on slavery in the territories had been considered. In 1784 Jefferson had proposed the prohibition of slavery in *all* the national territories, but it would not go into effect until 1800. It is difficult to imagine how Jefferson's proposal would have worked, had it been accepted; by 1800 some of the territories probably would have had large slave populations and politically powerful masters who would have worked to undermine the Ordinance of 1784 had it included Jefferson's prohibition. With no enforcement clause, it is almost impossible to imagine a territorial or state legislature voluntarily ending slavery after the institution had been allowed to grow until 1800. There is no indication that anyone at the time considered or discussed how the proposal might have been implemented. As historian William Cohen has observed, under Jefferson's proposal "bondage would have been legal in the area for sixteen years; and it seems likely that, if the institution of slavery had been allowed to get a foothold in the territory, the prohibition would have been repealed." One of Jefferson's most important biographers, Merrill Peterson, concludes that the proposal would have been "ineffectual." Whatever enforcement problems Jefferson's clause might have caused became moot when Congress defeated the proposal with strong and vocal opposition from the southern states.[20] In 1785 Rufus King proposed a similar provision, but Congress rejected it without debate. Nor did Congress debate the slavery prohibition in 1787. Nathan Dane, King's successor in Congress, also wanted slavery prohibited, but he initially excluded such a provision from the Ordinance because he thought the attempt would be futile. When the last-minute amendment was accepted with apparently no discussion and little comment, Dane could offer no explanation. He wrote Rufus King that he "had no idea the States would agree to the sixth article, prohibiting slavery, as only Massachusetts of the Eastern States, was present," and thus he "omitted it" from the draft; "but finding the House favorably disposed on the subject, after we had completed the other parts, I moved the article, which was agreed to without opposition." No one in Congress seemed to think this clause was extraordinary. Dane's comments on it in his letter to King were immediately followed by a discussion of what seemed to matter most to Dane, King, and Cutler: the purchase of land in Ohio. Besides Dane, William Grayson is the only other member of the committee to comment on the slavery prohibition in any existing letter. The lack of debate on the article or comment on it by members of Congress, especially the many southerners present, suggests that the clause was not considered particularly important.[21]

Conflicting Clauses Within the Ordinance

The lack of debate on the clause, and the fact that it was tacked on to the document at the last moment, explains why the rest of the Ordinance conflicts with the famed Article VI. Throughout the Ordinance there are indirect references to slavery. Paragraph 2 provides that "the French and Canadian inhabitants, and other settlers of the Kaska[s]kies, St. Vincent's, and the neighbouring villages, who have heretofore professed themselves citizens of Virginia [may retain] their laws and customs now in force among them, relative to the descent and conveyance of property." The main purpose of this clause was to allow the French settlers to follow French inheritance practices, rather than Anglo-American ones. Much of the property to be inherited, however, consisted of slaves, and it is reasonable to believe that this "property" could still be conveyed through sales and passed on through wills. Much litigation in Missouri and Illinois would eventually focus on the status of the slaves owned by these early settlers of the Northwest.[22]

Article II of the Ordinance provided protection for all private property and required compensation for private property taken for the public good. Did Article VI provide an exception to Article II where slave property was concerned? Article II also provided that the territorial government could never pass legislation that would "interfere with, or affect private contracts or engagements, *bona fide*, and without fraud previously formed." It would not be far-fetched to argue, as many slave owners would, that slave property purchased or acquired before 1787 could not be taken—or freed—without compensation to the master, and that contracts for the purchase, sale, or rent of slaves, made before 1787, were still enforceable in the territory.[23] Article IV of the Ordinance provided for free navigation of the "waters leading into the Mississippi and St. Lawrence, and the carrying places between the same" for all Americans.[24] It is doubtful if the congressmen from the southern states who voted for the Ordinance understood it to mean that they could not take their slaves with them when traveling on the important inland water routes of the United States.

Finally, despite the slavery prohibition in Article VI, in other places the Ordinance refers to "free male inhabitants" (Paragraph 9) and "free inhabitants" (Article II). Until the Congress added Article VI at the very last moment, there was no doubt that slavery would be perfectly legal in the area. But, after the addition of Article VI, Congress did not rewrite the rest of the Ordinance, and thus the document contained logical and linguistic contradictions. If there were "free inhabitants" then there must also have been "unfree" inhabitants. This language suggests that the congressmen who initially wrote the Ordinance expected slaves to be there and that after adding Article VI they made no effort to insure that the rest of the language conformed with the new article.[25] Had they done so, the sweeping language of Article VI might have been debated and clarified. Without such clarification and redrafting, the entire Ordinance remained at odds with Article VI. These inconsistencies would enable slave owners in the area to argue that their property rights had not been affected by Article VI.

A Mandate Without an Enforcement Provision

Despite the intentions of Dane and others to guarantee that the Northwest would be "free soil," Article VI of the Ordinance was ill suited to the task of ending slavery in the Northwest Territory. Unlike the Civil War Amendments ending slavery and making blacks citizens, with the right to vote, Article VI of the Ordinance contained no enforcement clause empowering Congress to pass legislation ending slavery in the territory. The article did not indicate what organ of government—the territorial governor, the territorial judiciary, the territorial legislature (which would not be formed until the territory's voting population reached 5,000), or the national Congress—would take action to end slavery. Since an end to slavery would require an innovative change in public policy and social institutions, some governmental intervention was necessary.

In its failure to provide a mechanism for enforcement, Article VI must be compared and contrasted to other parts of the Ordinance. Article II of the Ordinance, for example, protected such civil liberties as access to the writ of habeas corpus, jury trial, and bail while prohibiting "cruel or unusual punishments," excessive fines, and the taking of property without legal authority or just compensation. These protections could be enforced by the people of the territory through their elected representatives, through petitions to Congress, or by appeals to courts when they were created. With the exception of initiating legal action, slaves in the territory had no way to vindicate their rights. Initiating legal action was made more difficult by the low level of literacy among slaves, their lack of mobility, their lack of money to hire counsel, and laws that prohibited them from testifying against whites. A comparison between Articles II and VI suggests that granting constitutional rights to people is effective only if those people have the power, resources, and liberty to protect their rights.

Similarly, Article III declared that "schools and the means of education shall forever be encouraged." But it neither required that schools be built nor provided an enforcement mechanism. In this way Article III and Article VI are similar. But the substance of the Articles was so different that in one an enforcement mechanism was unnecessary while in the other it was vital.

Article III did not require an enforcement clause. The requirement that schools be built was unnecessary because for more than a century local communities had been building schools. Americans knew what schools were and knew how to build them. But few Americans had any experience with dismantling an entrenched social system, such as slavery, that provided wealth for those who had political power at the expense of those who lacked all power. The education clause could be implemented by those who would benefit from the clause. But those people who would most directly benefit from Article VI—slaves—could not legally participate in the political process and thus could not insure the implementation of the article. Finally, both the creation of public schools and the abolition of slavery would have financial costs. While the Ordinance of 1787 provided no funds for either object, the Land Ordinance of 1785 had provided that one section in each township would be reserved "for the maintenance of public schools, within the said township."[26] Thus, the national government had committed financial resources to the education provisions of Article III but not to the prohibition of slavery in Article VI.

Article III also admonished the settlers to treat the Native Americans fairly, requiring that

> the utmost good faith shall always be observed towards the Indians, their lands and property shall never be taken from them without their consent; and in their property, rights and liberty, they never shall be invaded or disturbed, unless in just and lawful wars authorized by Congress; but laws founded in justice and humanity shall from time to time be made, for preventing wrongs being done to them, and for preserving peace and friendship with them.

Unlike slaves, the Indians were in a position to defend their property rights, either in court or on the battlefield. Indeed, as Peter Onuf has noted, "emigration to the Northwest [was] . . . sluggish . . . because it took so long to pacify the Indian frontier." The settlers knew that peaceful relations with the Indians might be maintained if this provision of Article III were carried out. Thus, this part of the Ordinance could be enforced. Just to make sure, however, Article III also explicitly reserved for Congress the right to declare war and explicitly directed that "laws founded in justice and humanity" would "be made" to protect Native rights. The policy towards Indians was clear: either the settlers would observe "good faith" towards the Indians or the Congress would intervene.[27] No such threat of intervention existed for Article VI. Nor were the settlers in the territory even admonished to treat the slaves with "good faith."

The slavery prohibition compared unfavorably to the civil liberties aspects of Article II and both the education and the Indian provisions of Article III. Those who would benefit most from Article VI lacked the political power to implement it, the legal rights or support to enforce it in court, or the military might to fight for it on the battlefield. Neither the Congress nor the territorial government was directed to pass any enforcement legislation. Moreover, those in the territory who had the power to implement the slavery prohibition were the men least likely to do so.

The Ordinance illustrates the danger of hastily drafted legislation. This statement is not meant to blame Dane and the others who were responsible for Article VI. On the contrary, they deserve great credit for acting quickly when the moment was right to pass an antislavery provision in a pending bill. The great tragedy of the American founding may be that this is the *only* time legislators acted in this way. When dealing with great social issues—with such monumental questions as human freedom—it may be better to pass what legislation you can, when you can, than to wait until something better can be accomplished at a later date.

Nevertheless, the Ordinance is worth reading and studying as an example of *how not to* draft a statute. It serves to remind legislators, lawyers, and jurists that hastily drafted and poorly planned amendments to legislation, added at the last minute, may not accomplish what their authors wish. Besides not giving any indication how the slavery prohibition was to be enforced, the framers of the Ordinance did not resolve the internal contradictions created by Article VI. Thus, its meaning was left to whoever held power in the territory. Had there been a full-fledged debate over Article VI, a clearer sense of its meaning might have emerged. Someone might have asked if the Ordinance was meant to free the slaves then living in the territory. The legislators might also have clarified the status of the children of slaves in the region.

It is possible, as David Brion Davis has argued, that a more serious debate over Article VI would have "destroyed . . . any chance of agreement on an antislavery provision."[28] However, a more elaborate debate might have led to a law modeled on the gradual emancipation statutes that had been passed in Pennsylvania, Connecticut, and Rhode Island. Such a law would probably not have threatened southerners; indeed, they may have had such a law in mind when they voted for Article VI. Such a law would have specified the status of the existing slaves, their children, and any slaves brought into the territory, either as transients, sojourners, or residents. However, when Congress debated the Ordinance, there were no delegates present from Pennsylvania, Rhode Island, or Connecticut. In fact, all of the delegates who voted for the Ordinance came from states where emancipation had never been a political issue. Thus, the exact meaning of Article VI, and how it was to be implemented, was not debated and remained in doubt.[29]

In another context, the Ordinance can be seen as an example of the tension between liberty and property inherent in revolutionary America. The "self-evident" truths of the Declaration of Independence—"that all men are created equal" and are endowed with the rights to "Life, Liberty and the pursuit of Happiness"—were, of course, written by a man who owned approximately 175 slaves. There were numerous slave owners in the Continental Congress and at the Constitutional Convention. Many of those who struggled against "enslavement" by King George III apparently had few scruples about enslaving others.

Resistance to Article VI

Over the years, "the Ordinance has become a symbol of the Revolution's liberalism" towards race, at least in part because it was the only important act by the national government under the Articles of Confederation that indicated disapproval for the peculiar institution.[30] During the Revolution, Dr. Samuel Johnson, the English literary figure, chided the rebellious colonists by asking, "How is it that we hear the *loudest yelps* for liberty among the drivers of negroes?"[31] Unfortunately, there were no comfortable answers to the question. The American revolutionaries were trapped in an ideology of private property that made it difficult for them collectively to give up their own pursuit of happiness for the liberty of others. In the Ordinance, the ideals of liberty came into conflict with the selfish happiness of the ruling race. Thus, the Congress could easily declare there would be no slavery in the Northwest; it was quite another matter to actually eliminate the institution in the territory.

Whatever it was supposed to accomplish, Article VI had little immediate impact on the legal status of slaves in the area that would become the states of Indiana and Illinois, where the bulk of the slaves in the territory lived.[32] France had owned this area until 1763, when Britain took possession after the Seven Years War. The Treaty of Paris ending that war guaranteed the property rights of the original French settlers. During the Revolution, patriot soldiers led by George Rogers Clark, whose home state of Virginia claimed the area under its charter of 1609, seized the Northwest. Other states also claimed the territory under their charters. Although Virginia never intended to govern the area indefinitely, for a number of political reasons Virginia continued to assert authority over the area until ceding it to the national government in 1784. The Virginia law transferring possession of the area to the United States government also protected the property rights of the residents of the territory. When the territory came into the hands of the United States, slave owners were living there and the national government was obligated to protect their property.[33]

Although Article VI of the Ordinance contained no enforcement mechanism and would in fact remain unenforced for many years, it nevertheless troubled the slave owners living in the territory. The Franco-American slave owners, coming out of a civil law tradition, may have believed that the Ordinance was self-enforcing or would be enforced by the national government. Thus, shortly after the passage of the Ordinance, various settlers in the area that later became Indiana and Illinois appointed Barthelemi Tardiveau as their agent to lobby Congress on matters involving land titles and other issues of concern to the Northwest. In July 1788, Tardiveau petitioned Congress "By order & in behalf of the french [*sic*] inhabitants of the Illinois [Country]." The petition asked Congress to secure certain land titles, reimburse the settlers for goods impressed by American soldiers, and to protect the rights of the French settlers in other ways. The last part of the petition noted:

> There is in an Ordinance of Congress, an Ex post facto law[34] . . . which declares that Slavery Shall not take place in the Western territory. Many of the inhabitants of these districts have Slaves, and Some have no other property but Slaves. If they wish to preserve their property, they must transport themselves to the Spanish Side of the Mississipi [*sic*]; but if they do, they Shall lose the lands granted them by Congress. One law tells them: leave the country, or ye Shall forfeit your negroes: the other Saith; Stay in the country, or your lands shall be taken from ye.[35]

The French settlers hoped Congress would resolve their dilemma by allowing them to keep their slaves in the territory and thus hold on to their lands as well. When Congress ignored this request, Tardiveau presented a second petition asking Congress either to modify the slavery prohibition of the Ordinance or to "abrogate that part of their Resolve which binds them [the white residents] to a three years residence in the country in order to be entitled to the property of the lands granted them." Once again Tardiveau inaccurately asserted that the slavery prohibition of the Ordinance "operates as an Ex post facto law."[36]

The settlers of the Illinois Country believed that the Ordinance violated their property rights. The emancipation of slaves could not technically be considered an ex post facto law,[37] but the assertion that the Ordinance was such a law underscored the popular hostility to it. Ex post facto laws symbolized tyranny and oppression; they were also simply bad policy. It was against such arbitrary lawmaking that Americans fought the Revolution. The new national Constitution—which had only just been ratified—prohibited such laws in the United States. The message from Tardiveau and the other French settlers was clear: by ending slavery, Congress was destroying the property rights of the slaveowners and violating its revolutionary commitment to fair government and the protection of private property. The French settlers were also asserting that the law violated the new Constitution.

For many of those living in the Illinois Country, the new United States was simply another "government." Since 1763 the area had been ruled by France, Great Britain, and Virginia. Certainly the settlers could not have felt great loyalty—or even much attachment at all—to the United States. The Revolution had not been *their* revolution. Thus, when the Congress failed to respond positively to their petitions, many of the French settlers voted with their feet. In July 1789, Major John Hamtramck reported that "the King [of Spain] has permitted to the inhabitants living on the American side to settle themselves" in the Spanish territory west of the Mississippi. A few weeks later he noted that "a number of people had gone & were about going from the Illinois to the Spanish Side, in consequence of a resolve of Congress respecting negroes, who . . . were to be free."[38]

Tardiveau could not blame the slaveholding settlers for leaving. He explained to Governor Arthur St. Clair that "the wretched inhabitants of Illinois, who had seen themselves for ten years neglected by that [national] power from which alone they could expect protection, now found that the very first act of attention paid to them pronounced their utter ruin." With the passage of the Ordinance, "many aggravating circumstances rumored that the very moment" the territorial governor arrived "all their slaves would be set free." Thus, a "panic seized upon their minds" and the wealthiest settlers sought "from the Spanish Government that security which they conceived was refused to them" by the United States.[39]

Congressional Interpretation: The Failure to Implement the Ordinance

Those slave owners who remained in the Northwest Territory quickly discovered that the words of the Ordinance were much like the words of the Declaration of Independence. They sounded idealistic but had little force. Although Congress refused to modify the Ordinance along the lines suggested by Tardiveau's petitions, neither did Congress take any steps to implement the Ordinance. Indeed, Tardiveau explained to Governor St. Clair that he had failed to pressure Congress for a definitive answer to his memorial because "it was needless" and he had already "troubled that body with a number of petitions." Tardiveau assured St. Clair that certain unnamed "gentlemen" in Congress "remarked that the intention of the obnoxious resolution had been solely to prevent the future importation of slaves into the Federal country; that it was not meant to affect the rights of the ancient inhabitants." Tardiveau wanted St. Clair to convey this information to the settlers in the territory. In addition to informing St. Clair of this interpretation of the Ordinance, in the summer of 1789 Tardiveau wrote friends in Illinois that "the resolve of Congress respecting the Slavery of this Country was not intended to extend to the negroes of the old French inhabitants." Major Hamtramck "immediately published" this information in an effort to stem the tide of emigration from the Northwest.[40]

Tardiveau was not entirely correct in his assessment of congressional intent. Congress had in fact made no dispositive interpretation of Article VI of the Ordinance. Rather, Congress had referred Tardiveau's petitions to a committee made up of Abraham Clark of New Jersey, Hugh Williamson of North Carolina, and James Madison of Virginia. This committee of slave state congressmen offered a resolution that declared that the

> Ordinance for the government of the Western territory, shall not be construed to deprive the Inhabitants of Kaskaskies Illinois[,] Post St. Vincents and the other Villages formerly settled by the French and Canadians, of their Right and property in Negro or other Slaves which they were possessed of at the time of passing the said Ordinance, or in any manner to Manumit or Set free any such negroes or other persons under Servitude within any part of sd. Western territory; any thing in the said Ordinance to the contrary notwithstanding.[41]

The committee report seemed to distort the plain meaning of the Ordinance. The committee urged the Congress to "construe" it to mean that slaves living in the territory were not in fact emancipated and that the French inhabitants (and by this time a good number of Anglo-American inhabitants as well) would not be deprived of their property. Slave owners throughout the nation assumed that their property right in slaves included a right to the children of their female slaves. Thus, the committee report implied some sort of perpetual slavery for the descendants of those slaves living in the territory in 1787, in spite of the Ordinance. The committee asked Congress to accept this construction, "any thing in the said Ordinance to the contrary notwithstanding." This statement implies that the committee knew that its proposed interpretation of the language violated the plain meaning of the clause.

The committee's resolution never reached the floor of Congress for debate or a vote. Therefore, it could not really be said to explain congressional intent. At best, it indicated what some men in Congress believed to be the best application of the Ordinance. As the new Constitution of the United States went into effect, the meaning of the Ordinance, passed under the old Articles of Confederation, remained unclear.

On another level, however, this committee report suggests how truly *uncommitted* the Founders were to ending slavery in the Northwest territory. James Madison's presence on this committee is particularly revealing. On the eve of the adoption of the Constitution, the "father" of that document was unwilling to interpret the Ordinance in an antislavery light, despite language in it which not only supported such an interpretation, but seemed to mandate it.

In his prizewinning biography of the fourth president, Drew McCoy argues that "on the level of principle," Madison's "antislavery credentials can be fairly described as impeccable" and that "his categorical opposition to slavery generated an unyielding commitment to abolishing it in the United States." But McCoy also notes that for Madison "the question was never if, but rather when and how." Madison's position on slavery in the 1788 Congress must cause us to reconsider his position on the spread of slavery. McCoy argues that Madison opposed the spread of slavery in 1787 because, as long as the slave trade remained open, new slave territories would lead to more slaves being imported into the country. After 1808, when the slave trade ended, however, Madison favored allowing slavery in new territories and states because the spread of slavery would not lead to more slaves, but only to diffusing them across the country, thus lessening the power of slavery. McCoy uses this argument to explain why in 1820 Madison opposed the slavery restrictions in the Missouri Compromise.[42] The problem with this analysis, however, is that in 1788 Madison also supported the continuation of slavery in the Northwest.

Madison's position on the Ordinance would have led to the perpetual enslavement of a number of people and their descendants. Such an outcome would of course have done nothing to diminish the power of slavery in the society, nor would it have discouraged the slave trade. Had Madison and the committee declared that masters could not keep their slaves in the Northwest, either the slaves there would have become free or the masters would have moved them south—perhaps to Kentucky or Tennessee—thus diminishing the demand for slavery there and presumably diminishing the need for more slaves from Africa. Either way, enforcement of the Ordinance would have helped decrease the number of slaves in the United States.

Despite this logic, Madison was unwilling to take any concrete steps to abolish slavery in one corner of the country where it was relatively weak. If Madison—whose "antislavery credentials can be fairly described as impeccable"—could not take a stronger position on liberating the slaves in the Northwest, then it is perhaps understandable that others of the founding generation failed to confront the problem of slavery where the institution was more entrenched and the number of slaves was greater. Thus, the committee supported the interests of the slave owners in the Northwest.

Like the congressional committee, territorial Governor Arthur St. Clair had no interest in interfering with the master-slave relations of those he governed. Despite the language of the Ordinance, St. Clair saw no reason to take action to end slavery. In 1790 he reported to President Washington that settlers were still moving west of the Mississippi to protect their slave property. To help stop this depopulation, St. Clair told the president:

> I have thought proper to explain the Article respecting Slaves as a prohibi-
> tion to any future introduction of them, but not to extend to the liberation
> of those the People were already possessed of, and accquired [*sic*] under
> the Sanction of the Laws they were subject, at the same time I have given
> them to understand that Steps would probably be taken for the gradual
> Abolition of Slavery, with which they seem perfectly satisfied.[43]

This interpretation assumed that the Ordinance was only a directive to the
territorial authorities and that without further legislation slavery might continue. St. Clair was concerned about satisfying the desires of his white,
slaveholding constituency and not with any rights slaves might have under
the Ordinance. There is no extant record that anyone in the new national
government challenged St. Clair's interpretation, perhaps because Washington and his cabinet agreed with it.

A year later, however, St. Clair revealed to Secretary of State Thomas
Jefferson that neither he nor his constituents were happy with his earlier
interpretation of the Ordinance. His initial understanding would prevent the
return of those slaveholders who had fled to the Spanish territory because
they thought the Ordinance would emancipate their slaves. St. Clair felt that
those slave owners who had left the territory should be allowed to return
with their slaves. The governor was certain "that the [Spanish] Country itself
is much less desirable than on the American side—could they be allowed to
bring them [their slaves] back with them, all those" who had moved to the
western side of the Mississippi "would return to a man."[44]

Two years later, the territorial governor no longer wished to be held to
either of the interpretations he offered Washington and Jefferson. St. Clair
wrote that the Ordinance was "no more than the Declaration of a Principle
which was to Govern the Legislature in all Acts respecting that matter, and
the Courts of Justice in their Decisions upon Cases arising after the Date of
the Ordinance." He had implied this in his 1790 letter to Washington. Now
he spelled it out. But St. Clair went further in reinterpreting the Ordinance.
He asserted that "the Sense of Congress is very well to be known on this
Subject by what they have actually done. . . . making it unlawful to import
into any of the States any Negroes after a certain specified Time, and which
is yet to come—so that if any person after the Arrival of that period should
import a Cargoe of Negroes there is no Doubt that they would all be free
while those that were in the Country before remain in Slavery according to
the former Laws."[45]

In his official duties, St. Clair never had an opportunity to implement this
interpretation of the Ordinance. He did, however, use his office to discourage profreedom interpretations of it. In 1794, territorial Judge George Turner

issued a writ of habeas corpus for slaves owned by another territorial official, Henry Vanderburgh. Turner asserted that all slaves were "free by the Constitution of the Territory" but, before the case could come to trial, a group of men, allegedly employed by Vanderburgh, kidnapped the blacks and reenslaved them. Turner sought indictments for kidnapping against Vanderburgh and his associates, but St. Clair interceded to protect the kidnappers. St. Clair also informed Turner that the Ordinance was prospective only and could not be used to emancipate slaves living in the territory before 1787.[46]

Turner later tried to liberate other slaves through the use of habeas corpus. Slave owners complained to St. Clair about Turner, and residents of the Illinois Country successfully petitioned Congress to remove him from office. In 1796, United States Attorney General Charles Lee reported to the House of Representatives that Turner should be prosecuted in a territorial court for abusing his office and, if convicted, he might then be impeached and removed from office. In 1797, a congressional committee concurred with Lee's advice, and under this threat Judge Turner resigned his office and left the territory.[47]

At the end of Washington's administration, the status of slaves in the Northwest remained substantially what it had been before the Ordinance. The territorial governor had publicly and privately asserted that the Ordinance applied only to those slaves brought into the Northwest *after* 1787. But slaveholders in the territory, who were often the most politically powerful men in the region, were not even content with this interpretation. Some had brought slaves into the territory since 1787. Others hoped to bring more slaves into the territory. By 1797—a decade after Congress passed the Ordinance—no slaves appear to have gained their freedom as a result of Article VI of the Ordinance. But the language of the Ordinance posed a potential threat to slavery north of the Ohio River, especially for those who owned slaves brought to the territory after July 1787. In the early years of the nineteenth century slave owners would unsuccessfully petition Congress to modify the Ordinance to protect their slaves.[48] In the meantime, the territorial governments in Indiana and Illinois would adopt laws to protect slavery and involuntary servitude in their jurisdictions. Not until the second decade of the nineteenth century would slavery begin to disappear in those places. And not until the adoption of the second Illinois constitution in 1848, more than sixty years after Congress passed the Ordinance, would all slavery end in the region.[49]

The Ordinance As an Antislavery Document

The sixty-year lag from the adoption of the Ordinance to the final abolition of slavery in the Northwest reflects the ambiguous nature of the Ordinance.

As suggested at the beginning of this chapter, many nineteenth-century northerners venerated the Northwest Ordinance, in part because of Article VI. Much of this veneration was politically motivated. Those who opposed slavery sought to wrap themselves in the memory of the Founders. Article VI enabled them to do this. Thus, when some settlers in Illinois tried to make it into a slave state, the words of the Ordinance and the memory of those who were involved in its passage became important weapons for Edward Coles and his antislavery supporters.

Similarly, in the Webster-Hayne debate, Daniel Webster not only used the Ordinance to his advantage but tried to claim that a Massachusetts man, Nathan Dane, deserved the credit for its passage. Thomas Hart Benton, who also opposed South Carolina's extremism, invoked the Ordinance as well, but claimed the glory for his political hero, the southerner Thomas Jefferson.[50]

The use of the Ordinance in the debates over slavery suggests its impact on the nation's political culture. As David Brion Davis reminds us, we should not "ignore the extraordinary power of antislavery ideology" embodied in the Ordinance.[51] Indeed, it is clear that the Ordinance took on an ideological life of its own, especially after 1840.

But its impact on slavery in the Northwest, especially in what became Indiana and Illinois, is more ambiguous. Slavery continued in Indiana until after statehood, which the Hoosiers achieved in 1816. Not until 1820, in *State v. Lasselle*, did the Indiana Supreme Court declare that slavery violated the new state constitution. Even then, a few Hoosier masters held slaves until the 1830s.[52]

In Illinois the record is even more dismal. Here slavery remained vigorous throughout the territorial period. Illinois would most likely have adopted a full-fledged system of slavery in 1818 if the territorial leaders had not been certain that Congress would not have granted statehood under a constitution which allowed slavery.[53] Congressional opposition to slavery in Illinois was directly connected to the reverence that some northerners in Congress had for the Ordinance. Here the ideological power of the Ordinance affected politics at the national level. But at the local level it was the threat of rejection of a proslavery constitution by Congress, rather than the ideological or legal force of the Ordinance itself, that preserved Illinois as a nominally free state. Nevertheless, slaveholders in Illinois were powerful enough to protect the institution in the state's Constitution of 1818 and in subsequent legislation.[54]

No slaves living in the state explicitly gained their freedom under the first Illinois constitution, and the Illinois Supreme Court did not follow Indiana's lead in interpreting either the Ordinance or the state constitution to have ended slavery. On the contrary, the court continued to support slavery and servitude in the state until the 1840s. Not until the Constitution of 1848 did Illinois finally abolish slavery.[55]

Had the Ordinance been drafted more clearly, it might have provided a better guide for the legislators of the Northwest.[56] A requirement of gradual emancipation, such as Pennsylvania adopted in 1780, or one of absolute abolition, such as Vermont adopted in its first constitution, might have clarified the intent of the framers of the Ordinance and given guidance to the settlers of the territory. Such clarification could have headed off the struggle to legalize slavery completely in Illinois in 1823–1824. It might also have led to freedom for the 2,000 to 3,000 blacks who remained enslaved in the Northwest between 1787 and 1848.[57] In at least one small corner of revolutionary America, the legacy of freedom written into Article VI would then have been a reality to those who were denied their natural rights under existing laws.

Three

Evading the Ordinance

The Persistence of Bondage in Indiana and Illinois

The Ordinance of 1787 is probably most famous for its Article VI, which prohibited slavery and involuntary servitude in the Northwest Territory. Eventually, all of the states carved out of the area would enter the union as free states. Yet the Northwest Ordinance did not end slavery in what would become Indiana and Illinois. Nor did the Illinois Constitution of 1818 lead to an immediate end to slavery in that state. Indeed, not until 1845 would the Illinois Supreme Court be willing to free the slaves (or their descendants) born in the Northwest after adoption of the Ordinance of 1787. Not until 1848—over six decades after the adoption of the Ordinance—did that state's second constitution finally abolish all human bondage in the Prairie State.

The persistence of slavery in Indiana and Illinois was due to a number of factors. The ambiguous intentions of its framers, combined with internal contradictions within the Ordinance itself, allowed for an evasion of the apparent abolitionist implications of Article VI.[1] The many slaveholding settlers living in the territory before the adoption of the Ordinance tenaciously fought to retain the institution. Many of the nonslaveholding settlers also favored the institution. Territorial officials, especially Governors Arthur St. Clair, William Henry Harrison, and Ninian Edwards, opposed any immediate emancipation of slaves within the region and were hostile to the prohibition of slavery itself. Both Harrison and Edwards were themselves slave owners.

From the 1790s until Illinois achieved statehood in 1818, these territorial officials implemented policies and adopted laws that protected existing slavery and encouraged the introduction of new bondsmen and bondswomen into the territory. These policymakers were remarkably innovative. They did not actually introduce de jure slavery throughout the region. Such an action would have been in direct violation of the Ordinance. Rather, they creatively developed de facto slavery through a system of long-term indentures, rental contracts, enforcement statutes, and the recognition of the status of slaves who had been brought to the territory before 1787. The proslavery position of the territorial officials pleased those white settlers in Indiana and Illinois who owned slaves and feared that Article VI of the Ordinance would deprive them of their human property. The policies also enabled those who did not yet own slaves to acquire their equivalent: blacks held to service under long-term indentures.

A careful examination of slavery in Indiana and Illinois reveals the difficulty of banning a popular institution or commodity. The record in the Northwest illustrates the ability of nineteenth-century Americans to develop law as they needed it, even in the face of apparent constitutional restrictions. In this respect, the early history of laws creating bondage in the Northwest Territory may be seen as an example of the development of law as an instrument for economic growth and the release of creative energy, which many legal scholars have argued is the paradigm of antebellum American legal development.[2] Ironically, in Indiana and Illinois the early settlers did not use the law to release their own creative energies, but rather to release themselves from an apparent constitutional prohibition of slavery. The settlers used their creative energies to reshape the law so that they could have others work for them.

Early Opposition to the Slavery Prohibition

The slaveholders of the Northwest did not want to rely solely on their ability to create new laws that evaded the Ordinance. From 1787 through 1807, the slaveholding residents and settlers of the Northwest petitioned Congress to modify or repeal Article VI. These proslavery petitions combined a variety of economic, political, and racist arguments. The petitioners did not stridently argue, as South Carolinians had at the federal Constitutional Convention, that slavery was an unmixed blessing to the owners. Unlike the Carolinians, they did not claim that they wanted to keep slavery forever.[3]

Most of the petitioners accepted the idea that slavery was a violation of republican principles. The settlers' acknowledgment of republican principles in fact led to one of their strongest arguments in favor of retaining slavery: they argued that by allowing slavery for a limited time in the Northwest, Congress would actually be helping generations of unborn slaves to live in freedom. The petitioners asked for the right to bring slaves into the territory while at the same time indicating their willingness to adopt a gradual emancipation scheme to end the system eventually. For example, one group of petitioners prefaced their proslavery requests by admitting that they were "opposed to an unconditional state of Slavery" and that they in fact "venerate[d] the philanthropy which caused the prohibition of it [slavery] and of involuntary Servitude in the Ordinance." Indeed, they argued that by allowing temporary slavery, Congress would be setting the stage for future emancipation.[4]

The concept of gradual emancipation led to another important prudential argument in favor of relaxing the Ordinance. This argument was based on the racist belief that a high concentration of blacks in any single region threatened the security of the entire nation. By allowing slaves into the Northwest, the settlers argued, they were diffusing the problem presented by blacks—slave or free—in white American society. In 1805, the Indiana territorial legislature sounded almost philanthropic in proposing that if migrants from "the Southern and Western States where slaves are most numerous" were allowed to move to Indiana with their property, "in less than a century the colour would be so disseminated as to be scarcely discoverable."[5]

The proposals for the gradual emancipation of slaves brought into the Northwest were combined with various economic, social, and legal arguments, all aimed at convincing Congress to modify the Ordinance. Congress never acted favorably on these petitions, but neither did Congress or the executive branch take steps to implement Article VI of the Ordinance during the territorial period. As a result, the indenture system went forward without congressional or executive interference. By the time Congress divided the Northwest Territory in preparation for Ohio statehood in 1800, black servitude was well entrenched in the newly created Indiana Territory, which included the Illinois Country. After this subdivision, the Indiana territorial government took important steps to preserve and protect bondage in the region. Later, officials in Illinois would take similar steps. Thus, when Illinois entered the union as a "free" state in 1818, slavery was a fact of life for numerous residents.

Shortly after the adoption of the Northwest Ordinance, settlers in what later became Indiana and Illinois appointed Barthelemi Tardiveau as their agent to lobby Congress for confirmations of land titles and other matters. In July 1788, Tardiveau asked Congress to modify the Ordinance to allow masters to retain slaves they already held in the territory. Tardiveau explained to territorial Governor Arthur St. Clair that without a change in the Ordinance the inhabitants of the Illinois Country would move to the western side of the Mississippi River, which was then owned by Spain. The Spanish government allowed slavery. Although a Congressional committee that included James Madison of Virginia and Hugh Williamson of North Carolina urged favorable action on Tardiveau's petition, the whole Congress never acted on the report. Thus, while the nation debated its new Constitution, the slavery prohibition in the Ordinance remained both unaltered and unimplemented.[6]

Slavery and the Territorial Governors

By the time the new national government came to power in 1789, no one had taken any steps to free the slaves living in the Northwest. Indeed, Governor

St. Clair had made it clear that he did not believe that the Ordinance was meant to accomplish this. In 1790, St. Clair told President George Washington that he had "thought proper to explain the Article respecting Slaves as a prohibition to any future introduction of them, but not to extend to the liberation of those [slaves] the People were already possessed of, and accquired [*sic*] under the Sanction of the Laws." St. Clair indicated to the settlers that there might be a gradual emancipation sometime in the future, but he did not indicate when this might take place.[7]

By 1793 St. Clair had retreated from this position. He argued that Article VI was "no more than the Declaration of a Principle which was to Govern the Legislature in all Acts respecting that matter." He believed that the Ordinance was only meant to free any new slaves brought into the territory, but could have no effect on any slaves living there before 1787.[8]

Petitions from the Indiana Territory

The likelihood that for the foreseeable future—or even forever—they could keep their slaves may have satisfied some masters already in the territory, but it was little comfort to the new settlers entering the region, to those already there who did not yet own slaves, or to those who owned some slaves but wanted more. Thus, in 1796, four community leaders from St. Clair and Randolph counties in the Illinois Country became the first residents of the Northwest to formally petition Congress to allow slavery in the region. These slave owners—John Edgar, William Morrison, William St. Clair, and John Dumoulin—asked Congress to repeal Article VI of the Ordinance, to allow unlimited slavery in the region. If Congress would not do this, the petitioners requested that Congress at least modify the Ordinance "so as to give permission to introduce slaves into the said Territory from any of the original States . . . [and] that a law may be made permitting the introduction of such slaves as servants for life, and that it may be enacted for what period the children of such servants shall serve the master of their parents."[9] While petitioning for themselves, it was clear that these men reflected the sentiments of a good number of their white neighbors and fellow settlers.

The petitioners began with a three-pronged pragmatic argument: that slavery would benefit the economy of the territory, that it would keep slave owners from moving to the Spanish side of the Mississippi, and that the diffusion of slaves throughout the West would benefit the slaves themselves as well as the nation's white population. The men believed that a statutory change allowing slavery would stimulate settlement of the territory and increase the value of land in Illinois. This would be personally advantageous to the four petitioners, because they were large landowners and speculators.

But it would also enrich their neighbors. In the wilds of the Illinois Country, anything that would stimulate settlement and growth would benefit those settlers who had already moved to the territory and acquired land. The four community leaders did not, however, frame their petition in such crass terms. Rather, they argued that the high price of labor impeded cultivation of the rich farmland of Illinois and suggested that without slaves the territory could never be developed. These arguments were similar to those made by South Carolinians at the Constitutional Convention nine years earlier in support of the continuation of the African slave trade. Unlike the South Carolinians, the Illinois Country petitioners did not want to import slaves from Africa. Rather, they wanted the right to bring slaves that were already in the nation into the Northwest. But, like the Carolinians, the Illinois petitioners argued that slavery was essential to their economic development.[10]

The petitioners also predicted that the settlers who lacked slaves, and thus the labor to cultivate Illinois, would move west "to the Spanish dominions, where slavery is permitted, and consequently, the price of labor much lower." The petition implied that the growth and economic development of the territory would be at risk unless slaves could be brought to Illinois. Ironically, in the 1840s and 1850s, Free Soilers and Republicans would use the same argument to oppose the spread of slavery into new territories. The backbone of the Republican critique of slavery in the territories was that cheap slave labor drove out more expensive, but inherently better (so the Free Soilers argued) free labor.[11] The Illinois settlers, however, believed that the cheaper slave labor was not only inherently better, but absolutely necessary for the economic development of the region. This argument also paralleled the arguments made by politicians from the Deep South who opposed federal restrictions on the African slave trade.

These petitioners also argued that allowing slaves in Illinois would not increase the total number of slaves in the nation, but only diffuse them over a larger geographic area. They asserted that their petition would "not be objected to as unreasonable, even by the greatest opposers to slavery, seeing they do not pray for the introduction of any foreign slaves into the Territory."[12] This argument showed that the petitioners did not understand the distinction between opposition to the African slave trade, which was common among slaveholders in Virginia and other parts of the Upper South, and the outright opposition to human bondage, which was gaining strength throughout the northern states, where slavery was gradually being brought to an end.

The petitioners did understand the concept of diffusion, which was popular with some southerners, including Thomas Jefferson. Proponents of diffusion were concerned about the concentration of large numbers of blacks in relatively few states. The diffusion argument, made in this petition, implied that allowing slaves in the Illinois Country would be beneficial both to the slaves brought there and to those left at home. The more spread-out slavery was, the diffusion argument went, the better slaves would be treated, in part because whites would be less fearful of them. Equally important, the diffusion principle implied that the nation as a whole would be better off if slavery were spread out, rather than concentrated in a single region.[13] A critical part of the diffusion argument was the petitioners' assertion that the children of slaves brought to Illinois would be servants for life, rather than slaves, and thus their children might be free after an unspecified period of indenture. This implied some kind of gradual—albeit *very* gradual—emancipation.

The petitioners supported these practical arguments by various claims based on history and law. The petitioners argued that Article VI violated the promises given to the residents of the area by George Rogers Clark and by the Virginia government when the British acknowledged Virginia's sovereignty over the area at the end of the Revolution. They also argued, incorrectly, that Article VI was an ex post facto law because it took property away from people who already had title to that property. This misunderstanding of what constituted an *ex post facto,* law led to the conclusion that Article VI violated the fundamental principles of republican government. The petitioners pointed out that the Ordinance was "made *ex parte* by the original States only." These four residents of the territory asserted that "if the people then in the Territory had been called upon to make such compact, they never would have consented to enter into one that would deprive them of their most valuable property." Finally, the petitioners asserted that the Ordinance violated the fundamental principles of private property. Citing William Blackstone's *Commentaries on the Law of England*, the petitioners determined that "it may then be clearly deduced . . . that any person purchasing, or otherwise acquiring a slave in any of the States, is entitled to his perpetual service in this Territory as a servant."[14] To protect this right, the petitioners sought a repeal, modification, or clarification of the Ordinance.

The Illinois Country slave owners raised important questions about the nature of republican government in the new nation. They had not been represented in 1787, when the Congress appeared to have voted to free their slaves. Indeed, had the residents of the territory been represented in 1787, it is conceivable that Congress would have clarified Article VI of the Ordinance, or not passed it at all, in deference to those slave owners already living in the Northwest.

In raising the issues of representation, property rights, and republicanism, the petitioners were somewhat disingenuous, because they did not actually complain about any emancipation of their existing slaves that the Ordinance might mandate. Apparently relying on the interpretation of Governor St. Clair, they did not seem to believe that the Ordinance threatened their claims to slaves they had owned in the territory before the adoption of the Ordinance. Instead, they asked Congress to modify or change the Ordinance to allow the introduction of new slaves in the region. This raised a different and more profound question of republican theory. Was it fair, this petition implied, for Congress to bind the people of the territory to a compact that the majority of the residents opposed, especially when no one living in the territory had had any opportunity to vote or express any opinions about the compact? The petitioners did not articulate, but they certainly implied, that a theory of popular sovereignty was appropriate for the existing residents. In other words, they thought that the settlers, and not some geographically distant and politically remote Congress, should decide what the status of slavery should be in the Illinois Country.[15]

When this petition reached Congress, a committee chaired by Joshua Coit of Connecticut noted that the petitioners were "only four in number" and had produced "no power by which they claim to petition, even in behalf of the inhabitants" of the area. On these grounds, and not on the substantive issues raised by the petitioners, Coit's committee successfully urged rejection of the petition.[16]

In 1799, "several officers of the late Virginia line" bypassed Congress and petitioned the territorial legislature "for toleration to bring their slaves into this Territory, on the military lands" they had been granted.[17] Unlike the petitioners of 1796, these Revolutionary War veterans did not seek to profit by encouraging others to bring their slaves into the territory. They simply wanted to settle the lands they had received in payment for their wartime service. They may have wondered what had been the purpose of fighting in the war if, after the victory, they could not enjoy the land they were entitled to *and* enjoy the property (in slaves) they already owned. Their petition, however, was futile, since the legislature rejected it as "incompatible" with the "Ordinance of Congress."[18]

Petitions from the Illinois Territory

On July 4, 1800, legislation went into effect dividing the Northwest Territory into two parts: the Ohio Territory and the Indiana Territory.[19] Virtually all of the slaves and slave owners in the region lived in the new Indiana Territory. Less than three months after the establishment of this new territory, the proslavery citizens began organizing to protect and expand their interest in slavery.

On October 1, 1800, over 265 residents of St. Clair and Randolph counties asked the United States Senate to reconsider the question of slavery in the territory. These petitioners were more realistic than those of 1796. They petitioned in great enough numbers so that the Senate could not summarily dismiss their claims. More significantly, they did not ask for a complete repeal of Article VI, as the four petitioners in 1796 had done. Rather, they asked for a modification of Article VI that would include a gradual emancipation scheme.[20]

The petitioners began by shrewdly declaring that they were "opposed to an unconditional state of Slavery, and venerate the philanthropy which caused the prohibition of it and of involuntary Servitude in the Ordinance." In fact, they claimed that their proposal for a modification of the Ordinance was designed to "ameliorate the Condition of the unfortunate people concerned as to establish a gradual abolition of Slavery." The petitioners sought permission to bring unlimited numbers of new slaves into the territory. These people would be kept in lifetime servitude. The children of these slaves, however, would be emancipated at birth. The male children would serve as indentured servants until age thirty-one and the female until age twenty-eight. The petitioners argued that this was a humanitarian project and that under it "in the course of a very few years [it] will, in all human probability, rescue from the vilest state of Bondage a number, and without doubt a considerable number, of Souls yet unborn." Rather than contributing to the growth of slavery in the nation, the petitioners bragged that their scheme would "tend considerably to diminish the number by emancipating those who . . . would otherwise be born Slaves." The Senate, singularly unimpressed by the "philanthropy" of the Illinois Country petitioners, permanently tabled the petition.[21]

Two years later, in 1802, a convention of settlers met at Vincennes and once again asked Congress to relax the provisions of Article VI. These petitioners wanted the right to import slaves for ten years. The "president" of this convention was territorial Governor William Henry Harrison. These petitioners stressed that many liberty-loving Americans were moving to the Spanish territory west of the Mississippi because the Ordinance forced them "to seek an Asylum in that country where they can be permitted to enjoy their property." With unintended irony, the petitioners appealed to the American ideals of liberty, freedom, and property—to America as an asylum from Spanish "tyranny"—as a reason for instituting slavery in the Indiana Territory.[22]

Between 1803 and 1806, various congressional committees considered the Vincennes petition. In 1803, a committee chaired by John Randolph of Virginia but dominated by northerners reported that it was unnecessary to change the Ordinance. The committee noted that the rapid development of Ohio proved "that the labor of slaves is not necessary to promote the growth and settlement" of the Northwest. The committee felt that slave labor was "demonstrably the dearest of any" and could "only be employed to advantage in the cultivation of products more valuable than any known to that quarter of the United States." This was, of course, arguable, because crops that grew on the southern side of the Ohio River, in Kentucky and Virginia, could certainly have been cultivated on the northern bank. Slaves could also have been profitably used in mining, on riverboats, and in other nonagrarian pursuits. Indeed, the Illinois Constitution of 1818 would specifically allow for the use of slaves in the state's salt mines.[23]

The Randolph committee opposed an introduction of slavery in the region for more than just economic and humanitarian reasons. The committee also rejected the petition on national security grounds. Ever since Lord Dunmore's proclamation in 1775—offering freedom to Virginia slaves who would fight against their masters during the Revolution—Americans had been aware of the danger that slaves might pose during wartime. In 1800, the British and the Spanish both posed military threats to the Northwest. Slaves would weaken the region; they were a potential enemy living within the homes of the American settlers. The congressional committee thought the Ordinance gave "strength and security to that extensive frontier"[24] precisely because it prohibited slavery in the region.

In 1804, a second committee, consisting entirely of southerners, reconsidered the Vincennes petition and, not surprisingly, endorsed the introduction of slavery into the Northwest. This committee urged Congress to allow slave importations for ten years provided that the children of slaves born in the territory would be free, the males at age twenty-five and the females at age twenty-one. Such a scheme would have allowed a vigorous system of slavery and servitude to flourish for at least fifty years. Congress never acted on this committee report.[25]

In addition to allowing bondage to flourish in the Northwest, this scheme would also have encouraged greater importations of slaves from Africa, because allowing people to bring slaves to the Northwest would have decreased the supply of slaves in the South and thus led to greater demands for imported slaves to be sold to the emerging cotton kingdom. Indeed, if diffusion made any sense at all, it was only in conjunction with an absolute ban on the African slave trade. As long as South Carolina could import new slaves into the country, allowing the movement of slaves into the Northwest just decreased the supply of slaves in the South, leading to greater pressures to import more slaves from Africa and ultimately to more total slaves in the nation.

In 1806, yet a third committee considered the Vincennes petition along with a new petition, adopted in 1805 by the recently organized Indiana territorial legislature, and a new memorial from residents of St. Clair and Randolph counties. These two new documents indicate that the residents of the territory had not yet given up on a congressional alteration of the Ordinance. All three documents asked Congress to sanction slavery in the region.

The petition from the territorial legislature was a remarkably frank appraisal of slavery. The Indiana legislators conceded that slavery was "evil" and "repugnant" to "principles of republican form of Government." Nevertheless, they wished to adopt slavery to strengthen the local economy. Like their predecessors, the Indiana legislators also endorsed the diffusion principle as a way of limiting this "evil." The petition noted that the presence of so many slaves "south of the Potomac render[s] the future peace and tranquility of those states highly problematical."[26] The Hoosiers were willing to accept the institution and thus patriotically help the nation redistribute slaves throughout the country.

The 1806 congressional committee, dominated by southerners and westerners,[27] urged Congress to allow the "removal of persons, already slaves, from one part of the country to another." The committee believed that this would fulfill the wishes of the settlers, "accelerate the population [growth] of that Territory," and benefit the slaves. Explicitly endorsing the concept of diffusion, the committee asserted that slaves brought to Indiana would be better off because "the more they are separated and diffused, the more care and attention are bestowed on them by their masters." In addition, the congressmen believed that the "dangers . . . from too large a black population existing in any one section of country, would certainly be very much diminished, if not entirely removed." Thus, on economic, political, humanitarian, and racist grounds, as well as for reasons of public safety, the committee urged a ten-year suspension of Article VI. Once again, Congress took no action.[28]

The residents of the territory remained undaunted by their failures and continued to petition Congress for a modification of the Ordinance. The failure of Congress to act on these petitions was not necessarily an indication of congressional sentiment. Congress often took no action on committee reports because the press of business did not allow debates and votes on minor matters. The status of slavery in the Indiana Territory was certainly of little import to Congress when compared to the Jeffersonian revolution taking place in Washington, the purchase of Louisiana from France, and the growing international tensions caused by the Napoleonic wars.

Residents of the territory may also have been encouraged by the committee reports of 1804 and 1806, both of which supported the goals of the petitioners. In 1806 and 1807, Congress received a number of new petitions favoring slavery.[29] The latter year was, however, the last time that territorial residents petitioned for a change in the Ordinance.

There are a number of explanations for the drop-off in petitions after 1807.

In spite of a series of favorable committee reports, including a House report in February 1807 urging a suspension of Article VI for ten years, the residents of the territory may have concluded that petitions were futile. The proslavery forces in the West may also have feared that future petitions might backfire. In November 1807, a Senate committee concluded that any suspension of Article VI would be inexpedient. This, the first negative reaction in four years, may have indicated to the supporters of slavery that they might end up losing if they pushed Congress for a vote on their petitions and memorials. Future negative reactions in Congress were also likely because, for the first time since the adoption of the Ordinance, Congress, in 1807, received a number of serious antislavery petitions from Indiana and Illinois.[30] Those who wished to see a modification or repeal of Article VI may have understood that the antislavery opposition, although still in the minority, might pose a serious threat to any congressional action. Indeed, even a small amount of opposition to slavery in the territory might lead to a reaffirmation of Article VI, if the Congress were pushed to act on the subject.

The most important reason for a cessation of petitions may have been the realization that congressional action was unnecessary for the goals of proslavery settlers in the Indiana Territory. By 1807, the would-be slave owners in the Northwest had discovered a new method of living under the Ordinance and owning slaves.

Proslavery Legislation in the Indiana Territory

In 1802, territorial Governor Harrison had presided at the Vincennes Convention, which had petitioned Congress for an alteration or suspension of Article VI. He had also been a prime mover in organizing the petition campaign that set the stage for the convention. As a Virginian and a slave owner himself, Harrison was more than just sympathetic to those who favored slavery: he was one of them.[31] Harrison's failure to persuade Congress to allow slavery in the territory was only a temporary setback. As territorial governor, he was able to use his power to circumvent the Ordinance.

Before 1805, the Indiana Territory was under what Congress called the "first stage" of territorial government. In this stage there was no self-government in the territory. Instead, a governor and three judges, all appointed by the president, governed the territory. Territory laws were not passed by a legislature; rather, the governor and judges simply adopted laws from the existing statutes of other states. Such laws were subject to the review of Congress, which could override them. But the affairs of the Indiana Territory were not a burning issue for Congress. Harrison "and his allies knew that Congress would not interfere [with laws establishing bondage] as long as lip service was paid to the Ordinance and slaves were called 'servants.'"[32] Starting in 1803, Harrison and the territorial judges implemented this strategy by adopting laws that allowed slavery to grow in Indiana. After 1805, when the second stage of territorial government went into effect, the new territorial legislature reenacted these laws, or passed new ones, to protect bondage in the region.

The territorial laws did not establish de jure slavery. That would have directly violated the Northwest Ordinance and perhaps led to congressional intervention. Nevertheless, the territory adopted laws that sanctioned and supported bondage and involuntary servitude. Thus "A Law concerning Servants," adopted in 1803,[33] in conjunction with similar acts adopted in 1805 and 1806, became the basis of all regulation of slavery and involuntary servitude in the Indiana Territory. In 1809, when it became a separate territory, Illinois adopted similar laws, which remained in force until well after statehood, which was achieved in 1818.

The law of 1803 was based on a Virginia statute for the regulation of slaves and indentured servants. In many ways the law resembled the harsh colonial codes used to virtually enslave indentured servants in the seventeenth century. The 1803 law also bore a striking resemblance to contemporary slave codes. The first section declared that "All negroes and mulattoes . . . who shall come into this territory under contract to serve another . . . shall be compelled to perform such contract specifically during the term thereof." Other sections provided punishments—usually in the form of whipping— for servants who would not perform their duties. The law also allowed masters to add time to the agreed-upon contract to make up for lost labor due to laziness, running away, or other infractions. As with slaves, "the benefit of the said contract" for the indentured black could be sold or assigned to a new master, as well as bequeathed to a master's heirs. The law prohibited third parties from doing business with servants, entertaining them, or harboring them.[34]

While not a slave code, the statute did establish bondage in the Indiana Territory. The statute avoided a prima facie conflict with Article VI of the Ordinance through a legal fiction. The statute assumed that all blacks who came into the territory were indentured servants who had *voluntarily* contracted with their masters before entering Indiana. Thus, Indiana was merely giving "full faith and credit" to the contracts made in other states. Furthermore, these indentures were for a specific term of years and, unlike slavery, did not guarantee perpetual servitude. The 1803 law (and subsequent acts) placed certain obligations on the master and gave the servant some protections and legal rights. Masters were obligated to feed, clothe, and house their servants. At the end of an indenture, the master was required to give the ex-servant a blanket and some clothes. A servant had to "freely consent" in the "presence of a justice of the peace" before the sale of a contract to a new master would be valid. Finally, the law empowered the courts to hear complaints from mistreated servants.[35]

In fact, however, the differences between this law and a slave code were largely illusory. Most of these "servants" were slaves brought to Indiana by their masters in the guise of servants. As slaves, they had no legal power to enter into a contract with anyone, including their masters. Thus, any contracts for indenture made in a slave state were void under the laws of the state in which they were made. Even if the contracts between the master and the servant were somehow legal, the coercive power of the master in a slave state made any notion of "freedom of contract" ludicrous. The terms of service in these contracts were often for periods far longer than the life expectancy of either the master or the servant. Few servants would know that they had recourse to the courts under the law and fewer still would have access to attorneys. And those blacks who understood their rights nevertheless might have been reluctant to risk the wrath of an angry master by bringing suit against him. A master brought to court might not mend his ways, but instead take revenge on his servant. Similarly, few servants would dare tell a justice of the peace that they did not consent to being sold to another master. That would just leave them in the hands of their original master, who would no doubt be angry at the servant for ruining a business deal. The servants did not have even the theoretical right to protest if they were rented, given away, bequeathed to a new master, or sold to pay a master's debts.

Servants faced with intolerable masters had two alternatives. They could run away, though the 1803 law, of course, provided punishments for those who did so. Or they could complain to civil authorities. Here, however, the 1803 law offered them little protection. It required a certain standard of treatment by masters—food, clothing, housing, and so forth—but the statute provided no punishment for a master who violated his obligations to his servants.

Whatever rights servants theoretically had were limited in one more significant way. Two days before Indiana adopted the 1803 law regulating servants, Harrison and the judges adopted another law prohibiting blacks from testifying against whites. Thus, even if a servant did take an abusive master to court, this new law barred the servant from testifying before that court.[36]

In 1804, Indiana became a territory of the "second grade," which meant that an elected territorial legislature would participate with Governor Harrison in adopting laws for the area. Harrison believed that a majority of the residents in the territory wanted some type of slavery in the region, but that this majority might not exist in a few years. Thus, he pushed the first legislature to adopt a code for regulating slaves brought into the territory.

The first legislature was well suited to this task. Five of its seven members were from the slave states of Virginia and Maryland. A sixth was a slaveholder from the Illinois Country. The seventh, Benjamin Parke, would eventually become a congressman and federal judge from Indiana. Although born in New Jersey, Parke had practiced law in the slave state of Kentucky before moving to Indiana and was as proslavery as the native southerners in the legislature. Less than three weeks after it was organized, the new territorial legislature passed "An Act concerning the introduction of Negroes and Mulattoes into this Territory."[37] Under this law, owners of slaves could hold them in the territory for up to sixty days. During the first thirty days, the master and slave were permitted to contract for a term of servitude, and this agreement would be recorded by the county court clerk. Masters could return to the slave state from which they had come any slaves who refused to acquiesce to such an agreement. Children of indentured blacks would serve their masters, the males until age thirty and the females until age twenty-eight.

Under this law slaves were powerless to refuse an indenture. Such a refusal simply meant that the slave would be returned to a slave state. This made sense, because the purpose of the law was not to protect the rights of the slave, but rather to allow the master to keep his slaves in a theoretically free territory. Some masters indentured their slaves for as many as forty, fifty, or even ninety years under this law. The law did not prohibit the removal of indentured blacks from the state. Thus, the freeborn children of servants could easily be taken to a slave state and sold. Similarly, pregnant servants could be taken back to the South, where their newborn children could be claimed as slaves. Combined with the police provisions of the 1803 law, this act created involuntary servitude, if not outright slavery, in Indiana and Illinois. As one historian has noted, this law was "clearly a brazen attempt to evade the prohibition against involuntary servitude in the Northwest Ordinance."[38]

In 1806, the territory adopted a new law aptly titled "An Act concerning Slaves and Servants." This was nothing less than a full slave code for Indiana. Under this law, servants and slaves found without passes could be whipped on the orders of a justice of the peace. Similarly, the law provided whippings for slaves and servants charged with trespass, riot, unlawful assembly, or giving "seditious speeches." Persons harboring servants or slaves or aiding runaways could be severely punished. The text of the statute consistently referred to "slave or servant." Such wording, combined with the statute's provisions, gave legal recognition to slavery in the territory and provided the mechanisms to control the institution. Acts passed in 1807 and 1808 further protected bondage in the territory, while other laws recognized the institution and indirectly supported it.[39]

The legislation adopted between 1803 and 1808 created a presumption that all blacks in the territory were slaves or long-term servants. This is particularly striking, because, however one interpreted the Ordinance of 1787, at a minimum it was written to create a jurisdiction where freedom would be the general rule and goal of the society. But this was neither the goal nor the likely result of the territorial legislation. By 1809 the situation was not simply that some slaves, and the vestiges of a slave system, could be found in Indiana and Illinois. Rather, the legislature was protecting and nurturing bondage and de facto slavery.

The End of Slavery in Indiana

In February 1809, Congress created the Illinois Territory. The political separation of Indiana and Illinois allowed the two areas to treat slavery according to the wishes of the settlers in each place. A substantial amount of support for bondage had always come from Randolph and St. Clair counties, which were now part of Illinois. Thus, with the division of the territory, the supporters of slavery in Indiana lost many allies. In addition, by this time opposition to slavery had become quite strong in Indiana, as more settlers from the North and Northeast moved into the region. These new settlers in Indiana realized, as Peter Onuf has noted, "that the effective authority of Article VI depended on the will of the people" to implement it. Thus, in 1810, the newly constituted Indiana legislature repealed some of the territory's proslavery legislation and prohibited the introduction of any new slaves or indentured servants.[40]

When Indiana entered the union in 1816, opponents of slavery permanently dismantled the institution with two clauses. Article XI of the new constitution read as follows:

> There shall be neither slavery nor involuntary servitude in this state, otherwise than for the punishment of crimes, whereof the party shall have been duly convicted. Nor shall any indenture of any negro or mulatto hereafter made, and executed out of the bounds of this state be of any validity within the state.[41]

This clause not only prohibited the introduction of new slaves, but also ended the practice of bringing slaves into Indiana under the subterfuge of an indenture. Indiana's constitution makers also took care to ensure that future lawmakers would respect their distaste for the peculiar institution. In a unique clause, the constitution declared:

> But, as the holding any part of the human Creation in slavery, or involuntary servitude, can only originate in usurpation and tyranny, no alteration of this constitution shall ever take place so as to introduce slavery or invol-

untary servitude in this State, otherwise than for the punishment of crimes, whereof the party shall have been duly convicted.[42]

With the adoption of this constitution in 1816, many slave owners left Indiana. Some slave owners who remained perhaps assumed that the state constitution would be as ineffective in actually freeing slaves as the Northwest Ordinance had been. Those who gambled with their human property in this way lost. In 1820, the Indiana Supreme Court ruled that the 1816 constitution immediately freed all slaves in the state. Implementation of the state constitution turned out to be far more effective than implementation of the Ordinance. By 1830 slavery had virtually ceased in Indiana, as the census found only three slaves in the state.[43] But it had taken over forty years for Article VI of the Ordinance to take effect.

Proslavery Activity in the Illinois Territory

In 1809, Congress carved out of the Indiana Territory the area that eventually became the state of Illinois and organized it as the Illinois Territory. Illinois adopted the earlier Indiana laws and added to them. By the time Illinois achieved statehood, more than a thousand slaves and indentured blacks lived there.[44] After statehood, Illinois continued to sanction black servitude through legislation and court decisions.

The residents of the Illinois Country had been, from 1787 on, among the most active and vocal opponents of Article VI. The earliest petitions in favor of slavery in the territory came from this region. As early as 1801, residents along the Mississippi sought to separate from the rest of the territory, and "from 1804 until 1809, separation and slavery were constantly sought by the people of the Illinois Country."[45]

In 1809, the new Illinois Territory adopted the statutes that had supported slavery and servitude in the Indiana Territory. In 1813, the Illinois leaders dealt with an issue that had been ignored by previous territorial governments but that most slave states considered important: the problem of free blacks. Like the slave states of the South, in 1813 Illinois prohibited the immigration of free blacks into the territory. The act provided for the whipping and expulsion of any free blacks entering Illinois and required county officials to register or expel any who were already there. This law placed Illinois in a unique position. Other northwestern jurisdictions discouraged the immigration of free blacks. Ohio, for example, had an onerous statute requiring immigrant blacks to prove their freedom and find sureties for their good behavior.[46] But in 1813 Illinois was the only free territory or state to absolutely prohibit the immigration of free blacks. In this way the territory was more like a slave, than a free, jurisdiction.

A year later the new territorial legislature made certain that the opposition to free blacks did not discourage the further introduction of slaves. In 1814, "An Act concerning negroes and Mullattoes [*sic*]" allowed the hiring within the territory of southern slaves for periods of up to a year.[47] Illinois settlers who could not afford to purchase an indentured black would now have access to slaves.

The 1814 law was designed to stimulate settlement and economic development in Illinois. The legislators noted that "the erection of mills and other valuable improvements are greatly retarded in this Territory, from the want of Laborers." The lawmakers especially lamented that the production of salt could not be "successfully carried on by white laborers." Thus the law allowed one-year hirings of slaves in the territory and specifically declared that such hirings would "not operate in any way whatever to injure the right of property in the master, in and to the services of such slave or slaves." This law, like earlier ones, required that the slaves hired out in Illinois had to agree to such a hiring and that they were to be "examined privately, separate and apart from his or her owner by a Justice of the peace" or other court official.[48] Nevertheless, as with the similar laws adopted by the Indiana territorial government, there is no reason to believe that any slaves would have dared to complain about being forced to labor in the mines, mills, and salt works of Illinois, even if they feared or hated such jobs.

It is not at all clear, however, that slaves sent to Illinois in fact worked in those industries. Although the preamble to the statute talked of the need for laborers in such manufacturing and building, there was nothing in the statute that required this. As one observer noted, "To roll a barrel of salt once a year or to put salt into a saltcellar was sufficient excuse for any man to hire a slave and raise a field of corn." Many settlers did just that, and slaves were hired throughout Illinois, even where it was impossible to make salt or erect mills.[49]

Besides allowing masters to bring slaves into Illinois, in 1814 the territorial legislature also severely regulated the activities of blacks in Illinois. Three years later, however, a temporary antislavery majority in the legislature passed a bill abolishing the indenture system in the state. Governor Ninian Edwards, himself a slave owner, vetoed the bill and then immediately prorogued the legislature.[50]

In August 1818, delegates to the Illinois Constitutional Convention met at Kaskaskia. By this time there were about 1,200 blacks in the state, most of whom were slaves or indentured servants. A majority of the delegates at Kaskaskia probably favored making Illinois a slave state. The statehood movement itself was viewed as "a proslavery plot" by those opposed to human bondage. One opponent of slavery warned readers of the *Kaskaskia Western Intelligencer* that the people should resist "the fascinating bate [*sic*] of '*state government*' " until those opposed to slavery were in the majority.[51]

Supporters of statehood and rapid growth often favored slavery for practical economic reasons. Proponents of human bondage argued that slavery would "promote the speedy settlement and improvement of the country"[52] both because southerners would be likely to move into the region and because slave labor would allow for a rapid clearing of the forests and the development of the salt and lead industries in Illinois. Indeed, by this time it was quite clear that slave owners were able to clear and settle large areas of land far more rapidly than farmers dependent solely on free labor. The rapid settlement of the Southwest "demonstrated . . . that whatever moral opinions might have been abroad, the advantage of slave labor for clearing a wilderness was simply too attractive to forgo."[53] By this time, westward movement had emerged as part of the "ideology" of America's slave owners. Many statehood enthusiasts no doubt believed that opening Illinois to slavery would attract a stream of southern masters and their bondsmen.[54]

For many slave owners living in southern Illinois, these economic arguments were superfluous. They already held people in bondage and hoped to have more. For them slavery was not a method of achieving statehood; rather, statehood was a method of turning Illinois into a full-fledged slave society.

Slavery in the State of Illinois

That the 1818 constitution ultimately prohibited slavery was probably not due to any humanitarian ideals of the majority of the convention delegates. Rather, it reflected the political wisdom of the day that the northern majority in Congress would not let Illinois into the Union as a slave state. Indeed, when the convention wrote a constitution that prohibited slavery while at the same time allowing indentured servitude and a limited use of slave labor in the state, there was some question whether Congress would admit Illinois into the Union. Ultimately Congress accepted Illinois with its 1818 constitution, but only over the protests of Congressman James Talmadge of New York. Talmadge's opposition to the limited toleration of slavery under the Illinois Constitution turned out to be a prelude to his more vigorous and more nearly successful opposition to the admission of Missouri as a slave state a year later.[55]

For someone concerned with the spread of slavery, the Illinois Constitution was truly a troubling document. Article VI of the constitution began with the statement—by 1818 almost pro forma in northern state constitutions—that "Neither slavery nor involuntary servitude shall hereafter be introduced into this state otherwise than for the punishment of crimes whereof the party shall have been duly convicted."[56] Yet even in this apparently forthright assault on slavery there was a catch. Unlike the slavery prohibition in the Indiana Constitution, this clause was restricted to slavery that might *here- after* be introduced and thus implied that existing slavery was permissible. At this time there were still hundreds of slaves in Illinois. These slaves either had been living in Illinois in 1787 or were the children of such longtime inhabitants. These slaves did not become free under the new constitution.

The rest of the constitution's provision on slavery was also problematic. The remainder of the first clause prohibited the indenturing of males over age twenty-one and females over age eighteen, "unless such person shall enter into such indenture while in a state of perfect freedom, and on condition of a bona fide consideration received or to be received for their service. Nor shall any indenture of any negro or mulatto hereafter made and executed out of this state, or if made in this state, where the term of service exceeds one year, be of the least validity except those given in cases of apprenticeship."[57]

This clause gave Illinois residents a number of options for bringing blacks into the state and holding them as involuntary servants. First, the clause did not apply to minors, who might be indentured for periods extending beyond their childhood. Second, it is unclear how an "apprenticeship" of a black, especially a minor, might differ from an indenture. Thus, under the guise of apprenticing blacks, servitude for more than one year might have been possible. Nor does this clause indicate what "bona fide consideration" might mean. It is likely that Illinois jurists would have accepted promises to house, feed, and clothe servants as "bona fide consideration." Finally, this clause, like similar ones in the territorial statutes, raises the issue of freedom of contract in transactions involving slaves. The term "state of perfect freedom" might have been easily manipulated in the proslavery regions of southern Illinois.

The remaining two sections of Article VI also undercut the prohibition on slavery. Section 2 declared: "No person bound to labour in any other state shall be hired to labour in this state, except within the tract reserved for the salt works near Shawnee-town; nor even at that place for a longer period than one year at any one time; nor shall it be allowed thereafter the year [1825]. Any violation of this article shall effect the emancipation of such person from his obligation to service."[58] Practically, this provision meant that slaves could be hired in Illinois until 1825 without any legal interference. Yearly contracts could be extended annually for seven years. Although slaves were supposed to be hired only to work in salt manufacturing, it would have taken little imagination to foresee that slaves brought to work in salt manufacturing could then be hired out for other manufacturing or agricultural jobs.

Section 3 of the constitution confirmed the status of any involuntary servants already in Illinois:

Each and every person who has been bound to service by contract or indenture in virtue of the laws of Illinois Territory heretofore existing, and in conformity to the provisions of the same, without fraud or collusion, shall be held to a specific performance of their contracts or indentures; and such negroes and mulattos as have been registered in conformity with the aforesaid laws, shall serve out the time appointed by said laws; Provided, however that the children hereafter born of such persons, negros, or mulattos, shall become free, the males at age twenty one years, the females at the age of eighteen years. Each and every child born of indentured parents shall be entered with the clerk of the county in which they reside by their owners within six months after the birth of said child.[59]

This section of the constitution confirmed and supported any indentures—even those for the expected lifetime of the servant—made under the territorial laws. Moreover, it ensured that the children of such indentured servants would be held in service for a number of years. The provision did not, however, ensure that any children of indentured servants would gain their freedom. Unlike the gradual emancipation statutes of the eastern states,[60] this clause did not provide any specific protections for the children of lifetime servants. There were no penalties for masters who removed such children from the state and sold them into lifetime servitude.

The section on indentures also contained a major loophole in its timing. The constitution was written in August 1818 but did not go into effect until December. In the interim, masters were free to import and indenture as many servants as they wished. Many did so, as "a rush to indenture Negroes and a brisk trading of slaves with the French occurred in White and Gallatin counties during those months."[61]

Ultimately, the most important part of the constitution and its relationship to slavery may have been not what the document said about slavery, but what it did not say. Nowhere in the constitution was there a declaration that the hundreds of slaves living in Illinois at the time of statehood were to be free. Nor did the document indicate the status of the children who might be born to slaves living in Illinois at the time of statehood. Under this constitution, the holding of slaves, if not the complete institution of slavery, might continue for years. Slave owners could continue owning any slaves they held in Illinois before 1818.[62] This had been the interpretation of the far less equivocal language of the Northwest Ordinance given by a string of territorial governors. Such an interpretation could have been extended to the children of slaves as well, because part of the slave owner's property right was in the future increase of his slaves. Thus, despite the Northwest Ordinance and the assumption that Illinois would enter the union as a free state, slavery was protected in the state and would not be ended immediately.

The case for a proslavery interpretation of the Constitution of 1818 is strongly supported by the actions of the state legislature immediately after Congress admitted Illinois into the Union. In 1819, the legislature passed an elaborate statute entitled "An Act respecting Free Negroes, Mulattoes, Servants, and Slaves."[63] While not explicitly declaring that slavery was still legal in Illinois, the statute recognized the existence of slaves in the state and implied that there was nothing improper about this. Indeed, this statute underscored the presumption that the 1818 constitution was not meant to free all slaves in Illinois.

The 1819 law required the registration of all slaves in Illinois, severely restricted the movement of slaves, and provided whipping as punishment for slaves and servants violating the act's many provisions. The law strictly regulated free blacks while giving owners of slaves and servants the authority to buy and sell such persons, punish them, force them to work, and strictly control them. If masters failed to control their slaves, the statute allowed individual citizens or law enforcement authorities to act.

The law resembled the slave codes of the South in many ways. The most important part of this law, however, was not the way it regulated persons held in bondage but rather the legal presumptions it created and the future it seemed to imply. Unlike laws of every other free state, this statute created a presumption of slavery or servitude for all blacks in the state. In addition, the law, along with the constitution, provided no hope that slavery in Illinois would end soon. The constitution makers and lawmakers in Illinois apparently had no interest in taking steps to end slavery. On the contrary, both the 1818 constitutional convention and the 1819 legislature wanted to protect the rights of slave owners and to perpetuate slavery and bondage wherever possible. This they did with remarkable skill. Not until 1845 would the Illinois Supreme Court conclude that slaves born in Illinois after 1787 were free.[64] Not until 1848 would a new state constitution end all slavery in the state.

The Illinois Constitution of 1818 and the statute of 1819 make greater sense when they are examined in light of the events of 1822–1823. In 1822, Governor Edward Coles, himself a former slave owner from Virginia, "asked legislators to revise the state's black code and take steps to liberate the French slaves" living in the state.[65] This set the stage for a proslavery counterattack. Those who favored slavery declared that only through a constitutional convention could such an alteration in the state's laws and constitution take place. It quickly became clear that those who favored a constitutional convention did so not to end slavery, but to engraft it to the state permanently. Through the heroic efforts of Coles, the fortuitous collapse of a proslavery newspaper, and a gradual shift in the nature of the Illinois population, the movement for a new convention was soundly defeated.[66] This defeat of the referendum calling for a new constitutional convention sealed the fate of the proslavery forces in Illinois, although slaveholding would linger for more than two decades.

Debate over the convention referendum centered in part on the meaning of the Northwest Ordinance. Those who favored slavery argued that as a sovereign state Illinois was free to ignore the Ordinance and create whatever institutions the state wished to have. This was surely the correct constitutional interpretation. There seems little intellectual or constitutional support for the notion that Congress could bind a state to enforce a territorial regulation. Indeed, in 1850 the Supreme Court would unanimously hold that, once a territory became a state, the Northwest Ordinance was no longer in effect.[67]

Some of those who opposed slavery argued that the Ordinance prohibited Illinois from ever adopting slavery. This argument, however, did not even persuade all those who wanted Illinois to be permanently free. As one opponent of slavery told his followers, "Rely upon yourselves. The Congress of 1787, with parental solicitude, have confided to you the sacred boon of liberty. It is your duty to protect and preserve it."[68] This they did, and in the process made the Ordinance into what historian Peter Onuf has aptly described as a "higher law,"[69] albeit one which the people had to implement.

Had the 1823 vote on the referendum gone the other way, the constitution of 1818 and the law of 1819 would be of greater significance. The constitution and the statute allowed the slave owners a grace period, at least until 1825, to maintain their system of bondage. In that period they could bring rented slaves in from other states. They could also keep the slaves and indentured servants already in the state. The 1818 constitution put the question of slavery on hold—to be decided by the people of Illinois after statehood. The virtue of this, from the perspective of the slaveholders, was that it allowed the people to decide this issue without the interference of Congress or the Northwest Ordinance.

It is, of course, impossible to prove that those who wrote the constitution in 1818 planned later to amend it to create a full-blown system of slavery in Illinois. The documentary records simply do not exist. However, the text of the constitution, combined with the law of 1819, certainly suggests that this was the direction many people in Illinois, including a phalanx of powerful politicians, wanted to take their state. The referendum in 1823 shows that more than 40 percent of the state's voters were willing to make Illinois into a slave state.

The Final Defeat of Slavery in Illinois

The constitution of 1818 allowed Illinois masters the use of their slave property for the indefinite future. It reaffirmed the proslavery policies of the territorial governors and legislators. Moreover, it set the stage for converting Illinois into a full-fledged slave state. Had the slave owners been more prescient, they might have forced a vote on the issue in 1819, when they clearly controlled the legislature and probably dominated the electorate. Instead, they waited too long. By the time they acted, Illinois had an antislavery governor and a growing number of settlers who came from the free states of the north rather than the slave states of the South. The result was a free state that would ultimately become the "Land of Lincoln."

To some extent, the final outcome was a result of the Ordinance. It surely gave easterners an expectation that the territories in the Northwest would enter the union as free states. That expectation was enough to discourage the establishment of a full-blown slave state in 1818. The Ordinance may have also discouraged some slave owners from moving into Indiana and Illinois. But, as the territorial laws and the Illinois constitution both indicate, the Ordinance did not prevent a majority of the early settlers from favoring bondage. Other factors, especially the southwestern cotton boom, led slave owners to move south, rather than north.

In the end, the result in Indiana and Illinois was neither preordained by geography nor dictated by the Northwest Ordinance. Rather, it was the result of the people of the state making a conscious decision to reject slavery. Even this result was an incomplete victory for freedom, as men and women remained in bondage for more than two decades after the 1823 referendum. This illustrates how close Illinois came to being a slave state. The story of bondage in Indiana and Illinois also·shows how the issue of slavery and freedom was dangerously present in the early national period.

———— Four ————

Implementing the
Proslavery Constitution

The Adoption of the Fugitive Slave Law
of 1793

For most Americans, the return of a fugitive slave conjures up the image of fleeing blacks chased by men on horses with bloodhounds leading the way. Many fugitives were doubtless taken in "hot pursuit." But, from the 1790s until the Civil War, the most famous fugitive slave cases usually involved blacks who had lived in the North for months or even years. The return of a fugitive slave could lead to great human tragedies. The seizure of a fugitive slave who had lived for years in a community disrupted the life not only of that individual, but of spouse, children, neighbors, employers—indeed the entire community. Also, the seizure of fugitive slaves could and did lead to the enslavement of free blacks. The case of John Davis, which led to the enactment of the first fugitive slave law, illustrates these problems.

In 1791 Governor Thomas Mifflin of Pennsylvania requested the extradition of three Virginians who were accused of kidnapping a black named John, or John Davis, and taking him from Pennsylvania to Virginia, where he was enslaved. Governor Beverley Randolph of Virginia ultimately refused to extradite the three men, claiming that Davis was really a fugitive slave who had escaped into Pennsylvania. Mifflin then turned to President George Washington, who asked Congress to pass legislation on both interstate extradition and fugitive slave rendition. The result was the adoption, in February 1793, of a four-part statute dealing with both questions, which is commonly known as the Fugitive Slave Law of 1793. How Congress came to adopt that law tells us much about the way the founding generation dealt with slavery. Ironically, Governor Mifflin's attempt to protect free blacks from kidnapping resulted in legislation that provided slave owners with a vehicle for recovering runaway slaves and possibly enhancing opportunities for kidnapping.

The Fugitive Slave Clause of the Constitution

In 1788, while summing up the entire Constitution, General Charles Cotesworth Pinckney crowed to the South Carolina House of Representatives: "In short, considering all circumstances, we have made the best terms for the security of this species of property it was in our power to make. We would have made better if we could; but on the whole, I do not think them bad."[1] The Constitution was proslavery, and most southerners knew it. Nevertheless, the document left many unanswered questions about the nature of the new national government and its relationship to slavery.

During the first decade under the Constitution, Congress dealt with issues of the slave trade, the problem of slavery in the territories, and the admission of new slave states. Most important, in 1793 Congress passed the first Fugitive Slave Law, which aided southerners hunting after their runaway human chattel. This law was a major boon to the South with no reciprocal gain for the North. In addition to the substance of the law, the adoption of the law was an important constitutional change.

The fugitive slave clause of the Constitution provided: "No person held to Service or Labour in one State, under the Laws thereof, escaping into another, shall, in Consequence of any Law or Regulation therein, be discharged from such Service or Labour, but shall be delivered up on Claim of the Party to whom such Service or Labour may be due."[2] Arguably, this clause did not give Congress the power to pass any statute to enforce the provision, but merely admonished the states to act in a certain way. By interpreting the clause in the way it did, Congress made the Constitution even more proslavery than it perhaps was.

Late in the Constitutional Convention of 1787 Pierce Butler and Charles Pinckney, both of South Carolina, proposed that a fugitive slave clause be added to the provision requiring the interstate extradition of fugitives from justice. James Wilson of Pennsylvania objected to the juxtaposition because "this would oblige the Executive of the State to do it, at the public expence." Butler discreetly "withdrew his proposition in order that some particular provision might be made apart from this article." A day later, the Convention, without debate or formal vote, adopted the fugitive slave provision.[3] Eventually the two clauses emerged as succeeding paragraphs in Article IV, Section 2 of the Constitution.

The paucity of debate over the fugitive slave clause is remarkable because by the end of August 1787, when the Convention adopted the clause, slavery had emerged as one of the major stumbling blocks to a stronger union. While it was morally offensive to a number of northern delegates, some southerners defended slavery with an analysis that anticipated the "positive good" arguments of the antebellum period. Nevertheless, unlike the debates over the slave trade, the three-fifths clause, the taxation of exports, and the regulation of commerce, the proposal for a fugitive slave clause generated no serious opposition. The delegates to the Constitutional Convention may have been simply too exhausted for further strenuous debate. It is more likely, however, that the northern delegates failed to appreciate the legal problems and moral dilemmas that the rendition of fugitive slaves would pose. In 1787 even those northern states that were in the process of gradual abolition, such as Pennsylvania, recognized the need to return runaway slaves to their owners.[4]

Both the fugitives from justice clause and the fugitive slave clause dealt with a similar problem—the return to one state of persons found in another. Both clauses contained an implicit expectation of interstate cooperation. The criminal extradition clause appeared to guarantee a pro forma process between governors. The fugitive slave clause suggested a similar process between a slave owner and local authorities. The slim records of the Philadelphia Convention indicate that most of the Framers assumed, incorrectly as it turned out, that state and local authorities would cooperate in the extradition of fugitives from justice and the rendition of fugitive slaves.

The subsequent history of the two clauses shows that the Framers miscalculated. The Virginia-Pennsylvania controversy of 1788–1791 quickly put the nation on notice that the interstate cooperation necessary for a smooth implementation of these clauses had failed to materialize. This controversy, over the kidnapping of John Davis, is particularly important because it led to the adoption of the 1793 act dealing with both fugitives from justice and fugitive slaves.[5]

The Davis case had important implications for the rendition of fugitive slaves because the three fugitives from justice that Pennsylvania sought were charged with kidnapping a free black. The problem of kidnapping free blacks quickly emerged as a mirror image of the problem of fugitive slaves. Just as southern states demanded the right to retrieve runaway slaves, northern states demanded the right to protect their free black residents from being kidnapped and sold into servitude in the South. The rights of personal liberty and the claims of personal property caused sectional strife from 1787 until the Civil War.[6]

The history of the adoption of the 1793 law illustrates the importance of slavery to national politics in the early national period.[7] Southerners were quick to perceive a threat to slavery and to organize to protect that institution. Northerners were unwilling to endorse slavery, and the institution disturbed many of them. But in congressional battles from 1791 to 1793, northerners were less willing, or less able, to protect free blacks and fugitives seeking refuge in the emerging free states. The northern lawmakers also failed to protect their white constituents who aided fugitive slaves for humanitarian reasons, hired fugitive slaves purely for business reasons, or protected runaways on the assumption that they were actually free people.

Finally, northerners in Congress apparently failed to appreciate the dangers that slave hunting posed to both free blacks and antislavery whites. In 1793 northern congressmen and senators who opposed slavery nevertheless voted in favor of an extradition law that provided for the return of fugitive slaves, no doubt on the assumption that good faith enforcement of the law would lead to a more harmonious union. This assumption, of course, proved to be quite wrong. The immediate catalyst for the 1793 law—the conflict between Pennsylvania and Virginia—should have put northern legislators on notice that cooperation and interstate harmony were unlikely when southerners felt their slave property was even slightly endangered.

The John Davis Case

The conflict between Pennsylvania and Virginia emerged from Pennsylvania's program to end all slavery in that commonwealth and the confusion caused by uncertainty over the location of state boundaries in the wake of the Revolution. Immediately at issue was the status of John Davis and the three Virginians accused of kidnapping him. The conflict was complicated by Virginia officials' proslavery views, which were already quite evident in the early 1790s.[8] This conflict eventually led to the passage of the 1793 federal law regulating both the extradition of fugitives from justice and the rendition of fugitive slaves.

John Davis gained his freedom under Pennsylvania's Gradual Emancipation Act of 1780. That law declared that all children born of slaves in Pennsylvania after March 1, 1780, were free at birth, subject to a period of indenture.[9] The law allowed masters to retain any slaves they owned in Pennsylvania on March 1, 1780, provided they registered each slave with a court clerk before November 1, 1780. The registration fee was two dollars per slave, and any slave not registered by that date immediately became free.[10]

The 1780 law put all slave owners in Pennsylvania on notice that they needed to register their slaves. It also left some slave owners in a quandary. Throughout the 1770s, the exact location of the Pennsylvania-Virginia border remained uncertain. Inhabitants of what ultimately became Pennsylvania's Westmoreland and Washington counties lived in an area claimed by Pennsylvania under its charter but dominated by Virginia. Some people in the area no doubt actually believed they lived in Virginia. Others certainly expected that in the end they would come under Virginia's jurisdiction. As late as 1783, Virginians living in the area "cherished the hope that a final determination would return them to Virginia." Still others believed that western

Pennsylvania would be turned into a separate state, especially after Congress's resolutions of September and October 1780 indicated the national legislature's "intention to form new states in its prospective national domain. . . ."[11] The combination of the political and jurisdictional confusion and the "cherished" hopes of some settlers made many slave owners in the area unwilling to register their slaves under Pennsylvania law. Registration not only cost money but also implied an acceptance of Pennsylvania's jurisdiction over them, when in fact they still either maintained their allegiance to Virginia or wanted to create their own state.[12]

Slave owners who did not register their slaves risked losing them if in fact it turned out that they lived in Pennsylvania. Nevertheless, many slave owners in western Pennsylvania did not register their slaves under the 1780 law, even though on August 31, 1779, commissioners from the two states finally agreed on the exact location of the border and on September 23, 1780, the Pennsylvania legislature adopted a resolution accepting the work of the commissioners. This agreement, however, was not finally ratified by both state legislatures until April 1, 1784.[13]

In 1782, two years before final action on this agreement, Pennsylvania provided some relief for slave owners in the two western counties. The 1782 law allowed slave owners in the disputed territory until January 1, 1783, to register their slaves, provided they proved that they had owned those slaves, in Pennsylvania, on September 23, 1780.[14] This statute showed Pennsylvania's desire to woo the loyalty of the western settlers. It may also have been a response to Virginia's demand that Pennsylvania respect "the private property and rights of all persons, acquired under, founded on, or recognized by the laws of either" state. In any event, whatever its impetus, most slave owners in the area probably welcomed Pennsylvania's 1782 law and registered their slaves under it.[15]

One owner who did not take advantage of this law was a master named Davis, who had moved from Maryland to what he thought was Virginia or what he hoped would become Virginia, but what in fact turned out to be Pennsylvania. In 1782 Davis failed to register his slave John. In 1788 Davis took John to Virginia, where he rented John to a man named Miller. A group of John's former neighbors, allegedly members of the Pennsylvania Abolition Society,[16] found John in Virginia and brought him back to Pennsylvania. Miller, fearful that Davis would hold him liable for the value of the slave, hired three Virginians, Francis McGuire, Baldwin Parsons, and Absolom Wells, to recover John. In May 1788 they went to Pennsylvania, found John, and forcibly brought him back to Virginia. Davis subsequently sold John to a planter who lived along the Potomac River in eastern Virginia. In November 1788 the court of oyer and terminer in Washington County, Pennsylvania,

indicted the three Virginians for kidnapping. This precipitated the first interstate conflict over the extradition of fugitives from justice.[17]

The Pennsylvania–Virginia Conflict

Early in 1790 members of the Washington County branch of the Pennsylvania Abolition Society (PAS) asked the parent society in Philadelphia for help
in recovering John. The Philadelphia society had little advice, except to suggest that John abscond from his new owner and return to Pennsylvania. The
Washington County group found this suggestion dangerous, because if the
escape was unsuccessful it would lead to "an aggravated repetition of his
past sufferings," and after a failed escape John's new owner "might have
hurried him beyond our reach forever." Instead, the Washington County society hired a Virginia attorney named White, a nephew of Congressman
Alexander White, to recover John. This tactic proved unsuccessful, and John
remained a slave in Virginia.[18]

By this time the three kidnappers, McGuire, Parsons, and Wells, had been
under indictment for over two years but remained at large in Virginia. In
December 1790 the Washington County society again sought the aid of their
more prestigious brethren in Philadelphia, this time to help secure the extradition of the three kidnappers. In May 1791 the Philadelphia society petitioned Governor Thomas Mifflin of Pennsylvania, telling him that "a crime
of deeper die" could not be found in the Pennsylvania "criminal code . . .
than that of taking off a freeman and carrying off with intent to sell him, and
actually selling him as a slave."[19]

In June, Governor Mifflin sent Virginia's governor, Beverley Randolph,
copies of the indictments and a cordial note, requesting the extradition of the
three Virginians, "agreeably to the provisions contained in the second section of the fourth article of the constitution of the United States." Mifflin also
asked Randolph to "extend your interference on this occasion as far as it
may be expedient to restore the negro to his freedom." In this last matter
Mifflin relied on Randolph's "regard for justice and humanity."[20]

Instead of responding directly to Mifflin's request, Governor Randolph
turned the matter over to James Innes, Virginia's attorney general. Innes
objected to the extradition procedure for a variety of technical and procedural reasons. He argued that because the indictments accused the three
men of kidnapping "*violently*, and not *feloniously*," the alleged crimes could
not be considered felonies but were merely "*other crimes*" under the extradition clause of the Constitution. Innes further argued that the kidnapping of a
free black, under Virginia law, amounted only "to a trespass . . . as between
the parties" and merely "to a breach of the Peace" between the state and the

defendants. Having explained how Virginia law treated the kidnapping of free blacks, he then asserted, incorrectly, that the laws of Pennsylvania on this subject were the same as those of Virginia. This led Innes to the bizarre conclusion that in cases involving minor crimes extradition was only possible when there was "an exclusive Jurisdiction in the State making the demand." Innes advised Governor Randolph that if the three kidnappers were tried in Pennsylvania and found guilty of the crime of trespass or breach of the peace "and their personal presence should be necessary for their punishment, it will be then time enough to make a demand of them."[21]

Innes's position was that the alleged kidnappers had committed only a minor offense over which either Virginia or Pennsylvania had jurisdiction. Therefore, Virginia need not extradite the men unless they were actually convicted of the offense. But while arguing for Virginia's jurisdiction over the alleged kidnappers, Innes did not suggest that the state of Virginia was under any obligation to arrest them and bring them to trial. He did, however, make it clear that if Virginia actually prosecuted them, the charge would not be kidnapping or any other felony. Rather, they would be tried for the minor crime of "trespass."

The weakness of these arguments and conclusions must have been apparent, even to Innes. Thus he offered a second set of arguments. Innes conceded that all constitutional "requisites [had] been satisfied" and that Pennsylvania had "an exclusive Jurisdiction over" the crimes. Still he opposed extradition. Innes argued that "every free man in Virginia is entitled to the unmolested enjoyment of his liberty, unless" deprived of it by federal law, the Constitution, or Virginia law. Since the kidnappers had not run afoul of any of these, Innes believed that Virginia authorities had no legal right to arrest the men. Since they could not be arrested in Virginia, they obviously could not be returned to Pennsylvania.[22]

The Controversy and the National Government

In July, Governor Randolph sent Mifflin his formal refusal to order the arrest and extradition of the three fugitives from justice along with a copy of Innes's report. Mifflin responded by sending copies of the indictments and his correspondence with Randolph, including the Innes opinion, to President George Washington. Mifflin argued that Innes's analysis of the criminal extradition clause of the Constitution was "inaccurate." He told Washington that the three Virginians were charged with serious offenses, which upon conviction could lead to heavy fines and up to twelve months' confinement at hard labor. This was hardly a mere "trespass," as Innes had asserted. Mifflin asked Washington to consider the entire problem and to seek "the interposition of the Federal Legislature" so as to "obviate all doubt and embarrassment upon a constitutional question so delicate and important." Washington forwarded the communications to Secretary of State Thomas Jefferson, who in turn gave them to United States Attorney General Edmund Randolph.[23]

After reviewing all the papers sent by Governor Mifflin, Attorney General Randolph concluded that fault for the conflict lay with both governors. The attorney general thought that Mifflin's extradition requisition was defective in two ways. First, Mifflin had failed to provide an authenticated copy of the laws that the three kidnappers had allegedly violated. Second, Mifflin had neglected to provide some basis for the conclusion that the three men had actually fled from Pennsylvania into Virginia. Randolph noted that one of the three men, Absolom Wells, was in fact under arrest and in custody in Pennsylvania.[24]

On the other side of the question, Attorney General Randolph had little sympathy for Innes's arguments. Randolph thought it "notorious, that the crime is cognizable in Pennsylvania only." Virginia had no jurisdiction over the issue. The Constitution directed that an offender be tried "in the State where crimes shall have been committed," which in this case was Pennsylvania. Nor did Randolph have any patience for the suggestion that the state of Virginia lacked the authority to arrest the offenders. Indeed, to preserve interstate peace and harmony, Randolph considered it the duty of the governor to act. The only alternative was for one state to invade another, searching for criminals.[25]

Attorney General Randolph concluded his analysis by noting "that it would have been more precise in the Governor of Pennsylvania" to send his counterpart "an authenticated copy of the law declaring the offence" and "that it was essential that he should transmit sufficient evidence" of the alleged criminals "having fled from . . . justice" in Pennsylvania and into Virginia. Without that evidence, the governor of Virginia was correct in not delivering the fugitives from justice. But "with it" Virginia's governor "ought not to refuse."[26]

Randolph then gave Washington some political advice. Randolph noted that Governor Mifflin was "anxious that this matter should be laid before Congress." Randolph did not think this was advisable "at this stage of the business." He noted that "a single letter has gone from the Governor of Pennsylvania to the Governor of Virginia." Furthermore, although the Virginia governor had refused to comply with the request, this "proceeded from a deficiency of proof." The attorney general urged Washington to give the Pennsylvania governor time to supply full proof. Only if the governor of Virginia still denied the request should the president intervene. To do so at this point "would establish a precedent" for federal intervention "in every embryo dispute between States."[27]

Partially following Randolph's advice, Washington sent copies of the attorney general's analysis to both governors. The governors continued to correspond, and Governor Mifflin indicated his willingness to follow Attorney General Randolph's suggestion for a more complete extradition request and, as he reported to the Pennsylvania legislature, he "took measures for a scrupulous adherence to the forms which were expected."[28]

Despite Mifflin's implementation of Attorney General Randolph's suggestions and his conciliatory stance with Governor Randolph, aid from the Virginia executive was not forthcoming. Virginia's governor soon came under pressure from citizens in the western part of the state to refuse to extradite McGuire and Parsons. These petitions accused members of the Pennsylvania Abolition Society of stealing slaves in Virginia and of seizing the slaves of Virginians traveling west. The state legislators from McGuire's county told Governor Randolph that John was in fact a slave who had been "seduced" into Pennsylvania and that when McGuire, Parsons, and Wells heard about this they were "roused by a just indignation against such nefarious practices" and "went out and brought the negro back."[29]

In January 1792 Governor Mifflin reported to the Pennsylvania legislature that Virginia still refused to return the fugitives from justice. Instead, the Virginia governor complained that Pennsylvanians were "seducing and harboring the slaves of the Virginians." Mifflin promised to investigate this allegation while continuing the correspondence in the hope—a futile hope, as it turned out—that the kidnappers might be returned for trial.[30]

The Controversy Goes to Congress

While the governors of Pennsylvania and Virginia sparred inconclusively, President Washington decided to act. On October 27, 1791, Washington sent Congress Attorney General Randolph's report and copies of his correspondence with Governor Mifflin.

The House Bill of 1791

On October 31 the House appointed a three-man committee—Theodore Sedgwick and Shearjashub Bourne, both of Massachusetts, and Alexander White of Virginia—"to prepare and bring in a bill or bills, providing the means" for the extradition of fugitives from justice. The committee was also charged with the responsibility of "providing the mode by which" fugitive slaves might be returned to their owners. Thus, from the onset, extradition and rendition were tied together. On November 15 Sedgwick reported "a bill respecting fugitives from justice and from the service of masters."[31]

Extradition and rendition seem to have been linked for two reasons. Most immediately, the controversy between Virginia and Pennsylvania involved both issues. Virginia asserted that John Davis was a runaway slave and thus his return was a vindication of the fugitive slave clause; Pennsylvania, on the other hand, claimed that he had become free under the Pennsylvania Gradual Abolition Act and had then been kidnapped and that those who took him to Virginia should be extradited to face prosecution. From the beginning, Congress was forced to face both issues in tandem. A second reason for the linkage of the two issues no doubt stems from their juxtaposition in the Constitution. The Philadelphia Convention had seen them as related problems, and so did Congress. Both dealt with a similar procedural question and with the important constitutional issue of interstate comity. Not surprisingly, Congress dealt with both issues simultaneously.

The proposed House bill treated fugitives from justice and fugitive slaves in much the same way. In the case of a fugitive from justice, the governor in one state communicated his request for an extradition to the governor of another state. When seeking a fugitive slave, the claimant was required to apply for an arrest warrant to the governor of the state where the fugitive was found. In both cases, the governor of the state where the alleged fugitive was hiding would issue warrants "to all sheriffs, their deputies, and other officers" empowered to "execute warrants in criminal prosecutions" in the state, "commanding" them to arrest the fugitive. The fugitive would then be delivered to officers of the state making the claim or, in the case of slaves, to the claimant. The House bill contained no requirement for a hearing or other proceeding before a judge or magistrate. In the case of a fugitive from justice, the state authorities making the claim returned the alleged criminal to the state where he was wanted, and he would be tried. In the case of a slave, the claimant simply took the alleged fugitive back to the slave state he supposedly came from. Any officer failing to act on either type of warrant or anyone interfering with the rendition process was subject to fines, which were to be "recovered by indictment" in federal courts.[32]

Significantly, the House bill treated the rendition of both fugitives from justice and fugitives slaves as quasi-criminal matters. Thus the bill obligated northern states to pay their officers to hunt fugitive slaves. This is ironic because at the Constitutional Convention one reason for not tying rendition to extradition in the same clause was northern opposition to the costs imposed on the free states.[33]

Under the House bill, both rendition procedures were summary and did not allow the person seized as a fugitive to make any defense before extradition. This procedure raised due process questions for fugitives from justice and similar, but much weightier, questions for blacks claimed as runaway slaves.

The drafters of the House bill no doubt assumed that requests for fugitives from justice would be based on probable cause, arrest warrants, or actual indictments. The bill required that the request be "by an instrument in writing, authenticated by the signature of the Governor or other first executive officer and by the seal of such state."[34] Furthermore, the House members must have assumed that, once returned, a fugitive from justice (other than an escaped convict) would face a trial where he would be presumed innocent until the state proved otherwise.

This procedure contrasts sharply with the provisions in the House bill for returning fugitive slaves. The bill required that fugitive slaves be seized at the request of the claimant, based on "the depositions of two or more credible persons, that the person so claimed doth owe, under the laws of the state from which he fled, service or labor to the person claiming" the slave. The proposed bill did not say who could witness the depositions or if they had to be taken under oath.[35] This was a far cry from the standards of evidence necessary to obtain an arrest warrant or a grand jury indictment, which presumably a governor would want before he committed his signature to an extradition request for a fugitive from justice. Courts and grand juries issued warrants and indictments only after probable cause had been presented to judges or members of grand juries, all of whom were uninterested third parties. Under the proposed House bill, alleged fugitive slaves could be seized on the basis of depositions from private claimants with obvious pecuniary interests in the outcome. Even more important, the lawmakers had no reason to expect that alleged fugitive slaves would receive any hearing or trial once they were returned to a slave state. These procedures invited abuse by kidnappers.

The House bill also threatened the integrity of the states in the new republic. The bill placed the entire authority for fugitive slave rendition in the hands of governors and sheriffs, and yet if these officers failed to act on a deposition or interfered with rendition, they faced harsh monetary penalties enforced in the federal courts. Slave owners seeking fugitives were to turn first to state officials for aid. But if they failed to act, slave owners had recourse to the national government. Most state and local officials would probably have cooperated with the law,[36] but under pressure from the early abolition societies, it is possible that some would have either ignored the law or resisted it, thus setting the stage for state-federal conflicts at a time when the national government was weak. The bill, as drafted, may also have been unconstitutional because it required state officials to act. It is not clear if the Congress had the power to require actions by state officials. In 1842, in *Prigg v. Pennsylvania*, the United States Supreme Court would in fact rule that Congress could not compel state officials to enforce a federal law.[37]

Whether constitutional or not, the bill never came to a final vote. On November 15, 1791, the committee introduced the bill on the floor of the House, where it went through two readings and was scheduled for a third. Despite this energetic start, for reasons that are uncertain the House ceased consideration of the issue. It may be, as William R. Leslie argued, "that Congress thought it more fitting for the upper chamber to draft bills pertaining to interstate relations since the upper chamber represented states as states." Thus the House may have ceased action on the bill in deference to the Senate.[38] But it is also likely that, once congressmen studied the bill, they found it severely flawed since it threatened the powers of the states in the new nation, the liberty of free northern blacks, and the pocketbooks of northerners who interfered with the rendition of a fugitive. Many fugitive slaves had lived so long in the North that their white neighbors might have defended them on the assumption that they were free. Under this proposed law, such action could have resulted in a costly fine.

Fugitives and the Senate

The following March, the Senate appointed George Cabot of Massachusetts, Roger Sherman of Connecticut, and Ralph Izard of South Carolina "to consider the expediency of . . . a bill respecting fugitives from justice and from the service of masters." This committee had not reported back to the Senate by the time the session ended in May 1792.[39]

At the beginning of the next session of Congress, the Senate appointed a new three-man committee, chaired by Cabot, to consider criminal extradition and fugitive slave rendition. During much of the next two months, the Senate considered a number of proposals on this issue that, for the sake of clarity, will be designated Senate Bill 1, Senate Bill 2, Senate Bill 3, and the Final Senate Bill. On December 20, 1792, the Cabot committee reported a bill that Congress debated until December 28, when it recommitted the bill. This was Senate Bill 1. On January 3, 1793, the Cabot committee, which had been expanded to five members, reported a series of amendments that completely rewrote Senate Bill 1. This amended bill will be designated Senate Bill 2. On January 14 the Senate amended Senate Bill 2 with a series of deletions and additions that resulted in Senate Bill 3.[40] On January 18 the Senate passed a combination of Senate Bills 2 and 3 along with amendments made between January 15 and January 17. This will be designated as the Final Senate Bill. The House made only minor changes, which the Senate accepted. President Washington signed the bill on February 12, 1793.

An analysis of the legislative odyssey from Senate Bill 1 to the Final Senate Bill shows the alternatives the Senate considered. The fugitive slave provision of the various bills created great conflict in the Senate. The record suggests that the southerners in the Senate generally had the upper hand. With the exception of one clause introduced in Senate Bill 2 and deleted in the Final Senate Bill, all of the bills favored slave owners at the expense of northern whites, free blacks, and fugitive slaves. The law that emerged from these debates ultimately offered little protection for the North and at the same time satisfied most of the slave owners in Congress. From the beginning of the session, southerners dominated the committee responsible for drafting the bill. While northerners ultimately succeeded in eliminating some of the most proslavery features of Senate Bill 1 and Senate Bill 2, the Final Bill nevertheless was a southern victory.

Senate Bill 1

This victory began on November 22, 1792, with the appointment of a committee consisting of George Cabot of Massachusetts and two slave owners, George Read of Delaware and Samuel Johnston of North Carolina. While Cabot chaired the committee, Johnston seems to have been its dominant force. On December 20 Johnston presented Senate Bill 1, and on December 21 the Senate began a second reading of the bill, which consisted of three sections. The first two dealt with fugitives from justice, the last with fugitive slaves. Senate Bill 1 was awkwardly drafted and poorly written. More important, it threatened the emerging balance between the states and the national government.

In many ways, Senate Bill 1 posed a direct threat to the power of the states. The bill authorized governors to call on all citizens of a state to help capture a fugitive from justice and provided fines and jail terms for citizens who refused to aid in the capture of fugitives. Senate Bill 1 would also have required state officials to aid in the rendition of fugitive slaves.

The threat Senate Bill 1 posed to the states was minor in comparison to its threat to free blacks, fugitive slaves, and their white supporters. In many ways, this bill was more threatening and less fair than the House bill of the previous year. Senate Bill 1 permitted the return of a fugitive slave based on the deposition of one "credible person." As with the House Bill of 1791, there was no requirement that this deposition be sworn before any court or public official. Moreover, a single deposition, even if sworn, established such a low evidentiary threshold that Senate Bill 1, had Congress adopted it, would have set the stage for the kidnapping of free blacks.

Senate Bill 1 required state and local law enforcement officials to arrest fugitive slaves and turn them over to claimants on the basis of this single deposition. Law enforcement officers who refused to cooperate were subject to fines, and citizens who harbored fugitive slaves or obstructed their return could also be fined. Senate Bill 1 called for a specific sum of money to be determined by Congress to be forfeited to the claimant "for every day the person owing such labour or service shall be harboured or concealed." Beyond that, the claimant retained the right to sue those who helped his slaves. Under Senate Bill 1, such suits could be brought in either the state or the federal courts.[41] Depending on how much the daily penalty turned out to be and how courts interpreted the terms "harboured" and "concealed," the law might have meant bankruptcy for northerners who simply hired runaway slaves.

Opposition to Senate Bill 1 grew until December 28, when the Senate defeated a motion to postpone all consideration of the question until the next session of Congress. Instead, the Senate returned Senate Bill 1 to an expanded committee that included Roger Sherman of Connecticut and Virginia's John Taylor who was known as John Taylor of Caroline. Southerners, voting as a block, made sure that the committee continued to be dominated by slave owners.[42]

Senate Bill 2

On January 3 this newly constituted committee presented a series of amendments that effectively created a new bill: Senate Bill 2. The Senate gave this bill a first reading and then ordered it to "be printed for the use of the Senate." Senate Bill 2 also contained three sections, but only one focused on fugitives from justice; the other two dealt with fugitive slaves.[43]

Senate Bill 2 reflected a compromise between slave owners seeking to protect their property and northerners seeking to protect the rights of blacks. The bill protected free blacks in three ways. First, Senate Bill 2 required that anyone seized as a fugitive slave be brought before a judge or magistrate before being removed from the state, thereby preventing some kidnappings by requiring a judicial proceeding before removal. Second, Senate Bill 2 made two changes in the evidentiary requirement necessary to remove a fugitive slave. Under the House Bill of 1791 and under Senate Bill 1, either one or two depositions were sufficient to require that a magistrate order the seizure of an alleged fugitive slave. Senate Bill 2 required "proof to the satisfaction" of the judge or magistrate hearing the case. This proof had to be sworn, either in the form of "oral testimony or affidavit taken before and certified by a magistrate."

Finally, Senate Bill 2 provided that no judge could grant a certificate of removal if the alleged fugitive was "a native of, or hath resided in the state or territory wherein he or she shall be so arrested for a term of __ years immediately previous to such arrest, and shall moreover show probable cause that he or she is entitled to Freedom." Instead, the claimant and the alleged fugitive were to "be left to contest their rights under the laws of the state where such arrest shall be made." This language established a type of "statute of limitations" on fugitive slave rendition for whatever number of years had been inserted in the blank in the phrase "term of __ years." This provision created a presumption of freedom for blacks who were born in free states or who had lived in them for many years. This presumption could not be rebutted by deposition, affidavit, or even oral testimony. It could be overturned only through a trial in the state where the alleged fugitive was found. This procedure would have protected some free blacks from being kidnapped and would have also prevented the rendition of some fugitives. In parts of New England and Pennsylvania, it would have been impossible to win custody of a black under the "laws of the state where" the fugitive was found. Some judges and many jurors would have sided with alleged fugitives. Equally important, this provision helped preserve the power of the states by giving them exclusive jurisdiction over the status of blacks who had lived within their territory for a sufficient length of time.[44]

Slave owners, however, also stood to gain some new benefits from Senate Bill 2. Owners or their agents were empowered to seize fugitive slaves on their own, without first going before a magistrate to obtain a warrant or waiting for a local law enforcement official to act. This right of self-help was also in the final version of the law. Senate Bill 2 required slave owners to bring the captured fugitive before a magistrate in order to obtain a certificate of removal. However, the revised bill allowed claimants to prove ownership using "oral testimony." Thus a master could seize a slave while in "hot pursuit" without first obtaining depositions or affidavits. The test for removal was "proof to the satisfaction of the judge or magistrate." This open-ended requirement could have worked to the benefit of slave owners in many cases. Also useful to slave owners was a provision that allowed the seizure and arrest of a fugitive slave in absence of the claimant. Under Senate Bill 2 local law enforcement officials could be required to arrest a fugitive slave and then to notify the owner of the capture. As with Senate Bill 1, Senate Bill 2, allowed monetary damages against law enforcement officials for noncooperation and provided for fines or imprisonment for private citizens who interfered with the rendition of fugitive slaves.[45]

The Senate debated Senate Bill 2 on and off from January 3 until January 13. During this debate, the Senate fixed the amount of the fine for helping fugitive slaves at $500. However, the Senate made little progress toward final passage of the bill. Instead, senators raised objections to some parts of the bill and offered various amendments to improve it. South Carolina's Senator Pierce Butler—the man who had first proposed the fugitive slave clause at the Constitutional Convention—unsuccessfully proposed amendments that would have aided masters seeking runaways.[46]

Senate Bill 3

On January 14 various senators proposed another series of amendments. Senate Bill 3 consists of these amendments combined with what remained from Senate Bill 2. The Senate debated Bill 3 for the next three days. On January 14 and 16 the Senate journal reported that there had been "progress," while on January 15 the journal only noted that there had been "debate." During the three days of debate, the Senate accepted a number of these newest amendments.[47]

In the debates over Bill 3, the Senate expanded the definition of what constituted a breach of the law. Senate Bill 2 had limited the penalty—which was set at $500—to those who might "knowingly and wilfully obstruct" the return of a fugitive slave. Sometime between January 14 and January 17, the Senate added new language, penalizing anyone who would "obstruct or hinder" a "claimant his Agent or attorney" in "seizing and arresting" an alleged fugitive.[48] This was clearly a last-minute victory for slave owners. The word "hinder" implied that the penalty might be recovered from someone who did little more than delay a rendition in order to find evidence that helped the alleged fugitive. The use of the word suggests that the Senate wanted to create a rendition process that would be quick and streamlined.

This change, which benefited slave owners, was at least partially offset by the removal of clauses from the proposed bill requiring local law enforcement officials to seize fugitive slaves at the direction of masters or their agents, or, in the absence of an owner or agent, to arrest and incarcerate them until their owner arrived. These clauses would have turned northerners into slave catchers, which was intolerable to a society that was gradually dismantling slavery altogether. Without these provisions, a slave owner would have to capture a runaway slave on his own and then bring the slave before a judge or magistrate for a certificate of removal. Removing northern law enforcement officials from the rendition process was seen as a victory for opponents of slavery.

Northerners were no doubt happy to see their role in enforcement removed from the bill, but this change was also a blessing to slave owners, who then were not dependent on northerners for aid in the rendition process. Slave owners acting on their own could now seize alleged fugitive slaves and take them back to the South. In 1842 the U.S. Supreme Court approved this sort of fugitive slave rendition as long as it was done without a breach of the peace.[49] Thus, after 1842 unscrupulous slave catchers could more easily remove free blacks because the slave catchers did not have to rely on the cooperation of northern judges and police officials. There is no indication that this concerned members of the House and Senate. This is ironic, since the bill before Congress originated because of such a problem.

The Final Bill

The final debates on Senate Bill 3 led to two other changes beneficial to the South. The Senate deleted a provision mandating that civil suits for damages against those who interfered with the return of fugitive slaves be brought "in any court of the United States." At this time very few federal courts existed, and this provision limited the ability of slave owners to sue people who harbored or rescued their slaves.[50] The removal of this provision allowed slave owners to choose the most convenient forum—federal or state—for suing those who aided their runaway slaves. The most important victory for slave owners in the final shaping of the law concerned alleged fugitives who had lived for a long time or who had been born in the state where they were captured. The proposed bill would have guaranteed such blacks a right to a hearing in the state where they were living at the time of their capture. The deletion of this clause meant that no alleged fugitive could interpose a claim that he or she was born free or had been emancipated and then obtain a trial to prove that right to freedom in the place where he or she lived. In order to remove a black from a free state—even one born in that state—the claimant had only to meet the minimal evidentiary requirements of the law.

There was an eleventh-hour attempt to roll back one proslavery change in the bill. On January 17 a senator whose name was not mentioned in the record, proposed that the $500 penalty for those who aided fugitive slaves be deleted "for the purpose of inserting a less sum." The Senate defeated this proposal and in an unrecorded vote passed the entire measure and sent it on to the House.[51]

The House received the Senate bill on Friday, January 18. On January 21 the House gave the bill two readings and ordered that one hundred copies of it be printed. The House scheduled a third reading for January 30, but the bill did not come up until February 4, when, in a committee of the whole, the House made a minor change in the wording of the first section, which dealt with fugitives from justice. Andrew Moore of Virginia then proposed a substantial increase in fines for people who helped fugitive slaves. According to the *Pennsylvania Journal*, "this motion occasioned some debate" in the House, which then rejected the amendment. The next day the House passed the bill by a vote of forty-eight to seven. Five of the negative votes came from northerners. The two southern opponents, John Francis Mercer of Maryland and Josiah Parker of Virginia, had been active Anti-Federalists during the ratification struggle, and they probably opposed the nationalizing tendencies of the bill. Six northerners, some of whom opposed slavery in subsequent congressional debates, failed to vote on the bill.[52] However, a few northerners who actively opposed slavery, such as Elias Boudinot and Jonathan Dayton of New Jersey, voted in favor of the bill, probably because they thought it was an adequate compromise between the two sections.[53] Later that day the Senate concurred in the House version. The next day, February 8, Congress sent the bill to President Washington, who signed it into law on February 12.[54]

Because the records of Congress for this period are scant, it is impossible to reconstruct fully the debates. It is clear, however, that the fugitive slave law did not sail smoothly through Congress. The debates in the Senate were particularly bitter. The deletion of virtually all of Senate Bill 1 and many of the provisions of Senate Bills 2 and 3 indicates the divisions within the Senate. The report in the *Journal of the Senate* that "progress" was made on January 14 and 16 suggests that progress had been slow up to that point.

The last-minute effort in the Senate to lower the penalty for those who aided fugitive slaves also suggests the sectional aspects of the debate. Some northern senators were obviously unhappy with a law that might financially destroy their ethically motivated constituents: in 1793, $500 was a substantial sum of money. This northern opposition indicates that even in the 1790s opposition to slavery had some force. The defeat of this amendment, combined with other changes in the law favorable to the South, similarly suggests that the southern senators were far more unified in debate than their northern counterparts. The southerners, although outnumbered in the Senate, were able to mold the 1793 act to protect their interests. This was similar to what southern politicians had successfully accomplished at the Constitutional Convention in 1787 and also in the first Congress.

The attempt by Congressman Moore to increase the penalties for those who helped fugitive slaves escape suggests that some southerners doubted the bill would be effective in preventing northerners from aiding fugitive slaves. But the failure of his motion should not be seen as a defeat of southern interests. More likely, it indicated that most members of the House, including those from the South, did not want to prolong debate over a bill that, in one form or another, had been under consideration for over a year. A full debate of Moore's amendment might have undermined the whole bill. Most southerners in the House must have realized that a $500 penalty was high enough, especially since the bill preserved a suit at common law for any other costs or losses associated with someone interfering with the rendition process. This included a suit for the full value of any slaves actually lost.

The Fugitive Slave Law of 1793

The law that Washington signed contained four separate sections. The first two dealt with the extradition of fugitives from justice and the last two with the rendition of fugitive slaves. This order of the sections mirrored the form of Article IV, Section 2, of the Constitution.

Sections one and two set out the responsibilities of the governors in criminal extradition cases. A governor seeking a fugitive from justice was required to send to his counterpart a copy of an indictment, "or an affidavit made before a magistrate," charging the alleged fugitive with a crime. These had to be certified by the governor of the state "from whence the person so charged fled." The governor receiving this information was to then arrest the fugitive and notify "the executive authority making such demand" or his appointed agent. If no agent claimed the fugitive within six months, the fugitive was to be released. Anyone rescuing a fugitive from custody would be subject to a fine of up to $500 and up to a year in prison.[55]

The criminal extradition provision of the law declared that "it shall be the duty of the executive authority" to act on an extradition requisition. The law did not, however, indicate what might happen if a governor failed to act. Following the language of the Constitution, the statute simply set out the mode of procedure for the governors to follow. In 1861 the Supreme Court would hold that this procedure, while required by the Constitution, could not be imposed on a governor. If a state governor refused to act, there was nothing the Supreme Court or any other branch of the federal government could do to compel his cooperation.[56]

Sections three and four of the law, dealing with the rendition of fugitive slaves, failed to vest responsibility for the enforcement of the law in any one person or official. Nor was the requirement of proof precise. Section three outlined a three-stage process for rendition. First, a slave owner, or the owner's agent, seized a runaway slave. The alleged slave was then brought before any federal judge, state judge, "or before any magistrate of a county, city or town corporate" where the fugitive was seized. The claimant then had to offer "proof to the satisfaction of such judge or magistrate" that the person claimed was a fugitive slave owned by the claimant. This proof could be oral or through an "affidavit taken before, and certified by, a magistrate" of the state from which the alleged slave had fled. Upon satisfactory proof, the official hearing the case issued a certificate of removal to the claimant. Under section four of the act, any person interfering with this process could be sued for a $500 penalty by the owner of the alleged slave. In addition, the owner could initiate a separate suit for any "injuries" caused by this interference. Injuries, in this context, might include both loss of the slave, physical damages to the claimant or the slave, or the costs of the rendition.

Was the 1793 Law Constitutional?

On the day that George Washington signed the 1793 law, the Pennsylvania Abolition Society (PAS) warned its members of the pending legislation. Society members worried about the use of affidavits sworn before southern judges. They did not trust southerners who sought to capture runaway slaves or to kidnap free blacks. They also feared that northern magistrates would allow renditions based on suspect affidavits. The society's committee of correspondence reported that there was "reason to fear" that the new law would "be productive of mischievous consequences to the poor Negro Slaves appearing to be calculated with very unfavorable intentions towards them." The society complained that the bill was "artfully framed" with "the word Slave avoided," which meant that only the most vigilant opponents of bondage would be aware of the danger. Society members feared that the new law would "strengthen the hands of weak magistrates" who would be used by masters to recover fugitive slaves.[57]

Curiously, however, neither members of the Pennsylvania Abolition Society, nor anyone else questioned the constitutionality of the 1793 law. In the 1790s Americans were not yet in the habit, as they are today, of raising all issues of public policy and politics to the level of a constitutional controversy. Forty years later, some northern judges, as well as many abolitionists, would argue that the 1793 law was unconstitutional.[58] But in the 1790s, no one was making such an argument.

This is perhaps because in the 1790s the political activists most likely to raise a constitutional question about federal legislation were the followers of Thomas Jefferson, who were skeptical of national power and centralized authority. However, the Jeffersonians were also the most proslavery element in American politics. Jefferson and his southern followers no doubt saw the 1793 law as a beneficial act to help them to recover their own runaways. Jefferson's northern followers were more hostile to black rights than the Federalists and thus likely to support any law that would aid in the removal of blacks from their midst.

Most opponents of slavery were firmly in the camp of the Federalists. In Pennsylvania, for example, the majority of the Quaker abolitionists were affiliated with the Federalists. In Philadelphia it was "almost an oddity" to find a Jeffersonian involved with the Pennsylvania Abolition Society. "Among several hundred members of the Democratic-Republican Society of Philadelphia," an organization that supported Thomas Jefferson, "only two belonged to the PAS." By the 1790s, the Jeffersonian newspapers, including William Duane's *Aurora*, were among the few in the city that continued to run advertisements for slave sales. Such advertisements suggest that people interested in buying and selling slaves were most likely to be Jeffersonians and the fact that Federalist editors may have been uninterested in such business. Similarly, in New York, Federalists like John Jay, Gouverneur Morris, and Alexander Hamilton were active in the New York Abolition Society.[59]

The new fugitive slave law was supported by the Federalist administration of President Washington and was consistent with Federalist notions of strengthening the national government. Thus, it would have been unlikely that Federalists—even those openly opposed to slavery like Jay, Morris, Joseph Bloomfield, or Elias Boudinot—would have opposed the new law on constitutional grounds.

Had someone challenged the constitutionality of the law, three lines of attack would been obvious. First, everyone admitted that the Constitution created a government of limited power. As General Charles Cotesworth Pinckney of South Carolina had argued in support of the Constitution:

> We have a security that the general government can never emancipate them [slaves], for no such authority is granted and it is admitted, on all hands, that the general government has no powers but what are expressly granted by the Constitution, and that all rights not expressed were reserved by the several states.[60]

While Pinckney made this argument to illustrate how secure slavery was, the same argument might have been made against a fugitive slave law. Since the Constitution did not specifically empower Congress to pass such a law, Congress lacked the power to do so.

A second argument against the constitutionality of the 1793 law could have emerged from a structural analysis of the Constitution. The Framers left no record of how they expected the fugitive slave clause to operate. Textually and structurally, it seems that they anticipated some sort of state action to enforce it because the clause is in Article IV, which deals with interstate relations. The clause immediately follows the criminal extradition clause, which directly imposes this obligation on the governors of the states. In addition, by using the phrase "shall be delivered up," the fugitive slave clause implies some official action. The implication is that a state judge or county sheriff would seize and "deliver up" the fugitive.

Indeed, the entire structure of the Constitution supports the idea that the Framers contemplated that the states would implement the clause, *without* congressional action. Although limiting what the states might do, this clause is not in Article I, Section 10, where most other limitations on state power are found. Nor is it elsewhere in Article I, where Congress is granted legislative powers. Thus, structurally, the clause is more like an admonition to the states than a grant of power to Congress.

Of course, Article I is not the only place where the Constitution explicitly grants legislative powers to Congress. Articles II and III contain grants of power. Article IV also contains specific enumerations of congressional legislative power. However, these specific grants of power in Article IV strengthen the case against congressional power over fugitive slave rendition.

Article IV consists of four separate sections. Three of these sections explicitly authorize the federal government to act. Only Section 2, which contains the fugitive slave clause, lacks such a grant of power.

Article IV, Section 1, the full faith and credit clause, states that "Congress may by general Laws prescribe the Manner in which such Acts, Records and Proceedings shall be proved, and the Effect thereof." Section 3 of Article IV concerns the admission of new states and the regulation of federal territories. Both of these paragraphs contain explicit grants of power to Congress. Section 4, the guarantee clause, preserves "a Republican Form of Government" in the states. This clause does not allocate power to Congress, but rather empowers the United States government to act "on the Application of the Legislature, or of the Executive (when the Legislature cannot be convened) against domestic Violence."

Unlike the other three sections of Article IV, Section 2 contains neither a general grant of power to the United States government nor any specific grant of power to the legislative or executive branches. This fact implies that the Framers intended Section 2 to be implemented directly by the states. The Framers may have contemplated a right of appeal to the federal courts if the states failed to respect this clause, but it seems unlikely that the Framers thought Congress itself should directly implement the provisions of this section.

Section 2, Paragraph 1 is a general statement: "The Citizens of each State shall be entitled to all Privileges and Immunities of Citizens of the several States." The clause directs the states to treat citizens of other states more or less as they treat their own citizens. The clause does not mention the national government, and it has always been understood as setting a standard for the states to follow, rather than as a provision subject to congressional enforcement. During the early national period, the national government largely ignored this provision.

Article IV, Section 2, Paragraph 2, the fugitives from justice clause, provides that a fleeing criminal "shall on Demand of the executive Authority of the State from which he fled, be delivered up, to be removed" to the state claiming jurisdiction over him. The text of this clause implies governor-to-governor communication and action. Criminal extradition has always worked in that way. Nothing in the text of this clause indicates or even implies that Congress may legislate on the subject. Even if Congress has some power to regulate or to standardize the extradition process, the text of the clause clearly places the power to implement it solely in the hands of the state governors.

Given the foregoing analysis of the structure of the Constitution and of Article IV, it is reasonable to conclude that the Framers did not intend federal enforcement of the fugitive slave clause. Structurally at least, fugitive slave rendition, like privileges and immunities and criminal extradition, seemed to be a matter of comity.

State law at the time of the adoption of the Constitution supports this assertion. In 1787, Pennsylvania, Connecticut, and Rhode Island were ending slavery through gradual emancipation statutes. Nevertheless, these northern states recognized that slaves from other states might enter their jurisdictions seeking freedom. Thus, Pennsylvania provided for the return of fugitive slaves. Rhode Island and Connecticut followed Pennsylvania's lead. So did New York and New Jersey, which had not taken any steps to end slavery by 1787. Even Massachusetts, which had fully abolished slavery by 1787, provided for the return of fugitive slaves.[61]

The existence of these statutes supports the argument that the fugitive slave clause was merely an admonition to the states to return fugitive slaves. Under this analysis, the only role of the federal government would be judicial review of any state law that purported to authorize the emancipation of fugitive slaves.

The third argument against the constitutionality of the 1793 law could have come from an analysis of the Bill of Rights, which the nation had adopted only two years earlier. Those amendments contained a variety of provisions to guarantee fair trials and due process of law. While a hearing over the rendition of a fugitive slave was not a criminal trial, it certainly came close to being one. It would not have been far-fetched to argue that the lack of a jury trial to prove the claim of the master—and the status of the alleged slave—made the law unconstitutional.

However valid these constitutional arguments might have been, no one seems to have made them in 1793. The lack of such arguments does not prove the constitutionality of the 1793 law, especially in the abstract. Rather, the failure to make such arguments illustrates the extent to which the founding generation accepted what historian William M. Wiecek has called the "federal consensus" on slavery—that the national government could not interfere with slavery in the states and that support for slavery was part of the national compact necessary to keep the union together.[62] This analysis helps to explain the debates that led to the fugitive slave law and the failure of opponents of the law to raise constitutional objections to it.

The Law of 1793 and Federal Consensus

The members of the Pennsylvania Abolition Society must have recognized the irony of this new situation. They had initially written to Governor Mifflin to secure the extradition of whites accused of kidnapping a free black. Their letter set in motion a chain of events that led to a weak criminal extradition law and a relatively strong fugitive slave law. Under the new law, the governor of Virginia could have resisted the demands for the three kidnappers. But under the same law, many fugitive slaves were unable to protect their newly found freedom.

Even blacks like John Davis, who had a bona fide claim to freedom, could not protect their liberty under the new law. Ironically, the well-intentioned letter of the abolition society and the equally well-intentioned letter of Governor Mifflin to President Washington led to this dangerous result. The Pennsylvania abolitionists probably had not expected Mifflin to turn to Washington for help. Nor could the Pennsylvania abolitionists have foreseen that Washington would turn the matter over to Congress. Had they realized that their letter would lead to federal legislation, they might not have written it. After all, they knew from the experience of 1790 that the northern majority in Congress was weak on slavery issues. The adoption of the 1793 law only underscores this.

In 1790 northern congressmen had failed to support antislavery petitions presented by the Pennsylvania Abolition Society. The northerners perhaps had taken this position as part of a quid pro quo for southern support for various economic programs, such as the Bank of the United States and the federal assumption of state revolutionary war debts.[63] In 1792 and 1793 northern congressmen and senators did not seek an economic quid pro quo from the South, as they had in 1790. Assumption of the state debt was already in place, as was the Bank of the United States. Thus the northerners, who dominated both houses of Congress, might have taken a stronger stand on extradition and fugitive slave rendition. That they did not do so suggests that the "federal consensus" was already in place.

In addition to the "federal consensus," three other factors explain the adoption of the 1793 law. First, a majority of northerners were not overly concerned about slavery even though they opposed the institution. Second, the southerners were able, even in the early 1790s, to create a united front to defend their most valuable institution. Finally, those few northerners who did oppose slavery appear to have misunderstood the stakes of the fugitive slave question. They voted for a bill northerners later grew to hate.

Ironically, southerners also came to despise the law of 1793. However harsh it was, southerners continuously demanded even stronger measures. The federal courts were too few to aid them, and after 1842 many northern state courts refused to take jurisdiction in fugitive slave cases.[64]

In the end then, the 1793 law worked poorly. It did not even resolve the issues immediately surrounding its passage: the three Virginians who were wanted as fugitives from justice were never tried in Pennsylvania on kidnapping charges and John Davis remained a slave, his freedom lost forever. In 1850 southerners obtained new and harsher amendments to the 1793 law. These amendments, in a number of ways, resembled the bill drafted by the House in 1791. The 1850 amendments came too late, however, to restore sectional harmony; they only undermined it further.

—————— Five ——————

The Problem of Slavery in the Age of Federalism

Historians of the founding often have difficulty dealing with slavery. It is an uncomfortable subject. William M. Wiecek brilliantly compares discussions of slavery at the Constitutional Convention to the "Witch at the Christening" in a fairy tale—the uninvited, evil guest who comes along to curse the newborn child, in this case the new American nation. Scholars of the early national period—the age of federalism or, if one prefers, the age of Jefferson—want to talk about the creation of political institutions, the adoption of the Bill of Rights, the rise of a great nation.[1] Thus, Stanley Elkins and Eric McKitrick write that, after the Revolution, Americans

> possessed—or imagined they did—the one essential element, hitherto lacking, for releasing the creative energies of an already favored people. This was individual liberty. An all-but-miraculous force, liberty would give wings to every conceivable endeavor.[2]

While personal liberty and constitutional government—both embodied in the Constitution of 1787 and the Bill of Rights of 1791—were surely the great accomplishments of the Revolution, slavery is nevertheless a striking reminder of the incompleteness of that Revolution. Many scholars who focus on the early national period ignore slavery or explain it away.[3] For example, in their 900-page magnum opus *The Age of Federalism*, Elkins and McKitrick barely acknowledge the existence of slavery and never discuss it.[4] It is as though slavery was epiphenomenal—an institution existing outside of the political, economic, constitutional, diplomatic, and social structures of the society.

This is peculiar for two reasons. First, because, as we have seen throughout this book, the United States began as a slaveholding nation. In 1776 slavery was legal in all of the newly independent states, although its importance as an economic and social institution varied tremendously. By 1787 two states—Massachusetts and New Hampshire—had abolished the institution, and three others—Pennsylvania, Connecticut, and Rhode Island—had adopted gradual emancipation statutes, guaranteeing its eventual end. New York and New Jersey joined this "first emancipation" before the end of Jefferson's first presidential term. By the end of the early national period, new states, slave and free, had entered the Union, and the nation had clearly become, in a phrase Abraham Lincoln would coin a half century later, "half slave and half free."[5] The emergence of the free North during the age of federalism was in itself a tremendous accomplishment. Rarely has a master class so peacefully voted itself out of existence.

The second oddity about the virtual absence of slavery from *The Age of Federalism* is the important notion that the early national period was an "Age of Passion."[6] Nothing stirred passions greater than the revulsion some Americans felt toward human enslavement and the emerging defense of that institution by other Americans. As we saw in Chapter 1, slavery was one of the key issues debated at the Constitutional Convention, which surely must be seen as the birthplace of the age of federalism.[7] Some of the most passionate opposition to the Constitution came from northerners opposed to slavery. Similarly, during the age of federalism southerners began to passionately defend slavery and argue for the necessity of a permanent system of racially based bondage in the new nation. The age of federalism spawned a firming of resolve on the part of southerners and the emergence of a proslavery ideology to defend slavery.

Defining the Age of Federalism

Coming to terms with the importance of slavery in the age of federalism requires setting some parameters for both the age and the term itself. Elkins and McKitrick have a weirdly constricted notion of the age of federalism, ending with Jefferson's inauguration. Like John Adams climbing into a stagecoach to start his long trek back to Boston at four o'clock on the morning of Jefferson's inauguration, the age of federalism, as Elkins and McKitrick imagine it, disappeared into the night air sometime between sundown on March 3, 1801, and sunrise on March 4.[8] Implicitly, they define the "age" to coincide with the time the Federalist Party controlled the presidency.

This is a curious notion. At the national level, the Federalist Party had the potential of regaining national power at least until 1812.[9] While the Federalist Party never did regain the presidency, it continued to be a factor in national and state politics for at least twenty years—approximately twice as long as it had been in power. In New York, for example, Federalists sometimes held power after 1801 and "remained a substantial electoral threat to their opponents until 1820."[10] In other parts of the North, especially New England, the party remained in power even longer. Josiah Quincy was the Federalist speaker of the Massachusetts House of Representatives in 1822 and mayor of Boston from 1823 to 1829.

During the Missouri debates of 1819–1821, the Federalists, for the last time, acted as a recognizable national political force, marshaling most northerners in Congress to support at least some restriction on slavery in the western territories acquired by Jefferson. While the Missouri debates were the last gasp of organized Federalist political activity, federalism lived on. "Federalist" politicians were successful without their party. John Quincy Adams, for example, was a "federalist" in his policies and ideas, despite his rejection of the party before the War of 1812.[11]

Finally, it is worth remembering that, especially after Chief Justice John Marshall's decision in *Marbury v. Madison*,[12] the Supreme Court constituted a third, if not quite equal, branch of the national government. That branch remained ideologically and jurisprudentially federalist until the 1830s.

Indeed, one might argue that the final coup de grâce to federalism came, not at the hands of Thomas Jefferson, but rather at the hands of Andrew Jackson. Major rejections of federalism in the age of Jackson include the bank veto, an end to federally supported internal improvements, a sea change on the Supreme Court, the Indian removal, the belligerent western expansion culminating in a war of aggression against Mexico, and the disfranchisement of blacks in Pennsylvania, North Carolina, and Tennessee, where they had previously voted. Such an argument does not mean that federalism dominated politics after 1801, for clearly it did not. Rather, policies and ideas, such as Marshall's vision of the commerce clause, Hamilton's concept of a national bank, and Washington's notion of reasonably fair treatment for Native Americans, remained viable well after the Federalist Party had lost most of its power and in fact ceased to exist. However, Jacksonian democracy finished off these ideas and policies.

Slavery and Politics in the Age of Federalism

Throughout the age of federalism, as we have seen earlier in this book, slavery was a significant factor in politics. We conventionally date the emergence of slavery as the dominant issue in American political life with the Missouri Compromise controversy, which also marks the time when the Federalist Party fizzled out of existence. But this chronology misses the mark in two ways.

First, it underestimates the way slavery shaped politics from the late 1780s to the Missouri debates. The sectionalism so apparent during the Constitutional Convention did not lie dormant until 1819. On the contrary, as historian James Roger Sharp has noted, during the early national period "sectionalism, as it had been since the Revolution and as it would be throughout the antebellum period, was the main catalyst inciting political conflict."[13] Slavery, of course, was at the center of that sectionalism.

Second, by ignoring the role of slavery in the critical first decades, historians have missed the important ways federalism affected the debate over slavery both before and after the crisis of 1819–1820. Although their party was no more, after 1821 a number of prominent Federalists and former Federalists took strong stands against slavery and the emerging "slave power." These include Josiah Quincy and John Quincy Adams of Massachusetts, Joseph C. Hornblower of New Jersey, Samuel Fessenden of Maine, and William Jay of New York.[14] In addition to prominent political leaders, many antislavery activists were the cultural (and often the biological) descendants of the Federalists. Abolitionists Wendell Phillips, Edmund Quincy, Theodore Sedgwick Jr., and the poet James Russell Lowell were the sons of federalist politicians. William Lloyd Garrison's father supported the Federalists, although he held no offices. Garrison began his career as an apprentice to "Ephriam W. Allen, owner and editor of the staunchly Federalist *Newberryport Herald*," who greatly influenced the impressionable young man. More than Allen, the young Garrison found a "model, perhaps a father image, in Timothy Pickering," the very embodiment of New England federalism, who had a strong distaste for slavery and the South.[15] Indeed, Garrison's later secessionist demands—"No Union with Slaveholders"—may have originated with federalists flirtation with secession in 1804[16] or, more likely, with the secessionist arguments of Federalists at the Hartford Convention. In both movements, the three-fifths compromise and the overall power of slavery in the federal government loomed large.

These second- and third-generation Federalists resurrected ideas about slavery that Federalists of their parents' generation had used. For example, Federalists understood that the three-fifths clause gave the South—especially Virginia—undue power in the national government. Had slaves not been counted for purposes of representation and the electoral college, John Adams, not Thomas Jefferson, would have been elected president in 1800. Not surprisingly, opposition to the three-fifths clause was a major component of demands of the Hartford Convention, where extreme Federalists had justified calls for secession at least in part over this issue. Abolitionists later made similar points.[17] In the 1840s, Wendell Phillips, the scion of a Massachusetts federalist family, analyzed and denounced the proslavery compromises in 1787, which, among other things, gave the South extra political muscle through the three-fifths clause.[18]

Thus it was that Federalists and federalist ideas persisted past the demise of the Adams administration and the dissolution of the party itself. Federalists helped lay the groundwork for what would become the abolitionist and antislavery critique of American politics. Moreover, the Federalists advocated some measure of racial equality, in contrast to the Jeffersonians, who fostered the emerging, racially based, proslavery argument and a concomitant attack on the rights of free blacks.

In approaching problems affected by slavery, or affecting slavery, from the Constitutional Convention to the Missouri Compromise, Federalists often implemented policies quite different from those of the Republicans. When lacking power to accomplish their policies, Federalists continued to oppose the proslavery racism of the Jeffersonians. As Linda Kerber has demonstrated, Federalists "in dissent" were antislavery.[19]

The Northwest Ordinance

While the Constitutional Convention was in session in Philadelphia, Congress, operating under the Articles of Confederation, adopted the Northwest Ordinance, with its famous, although not immediately successful, ban on slavery in the western territories north of the Ohio River. Between 1787 and 1861, this was the only national law limiting slavery adopted without a great sectional debate in Congress.[20]

Congress was able to pass the slavery prohibition in the Ordinance without a heated and emotional debate because most of the delegates did not know that slavery already existed in the Old Northwest and most southerners did not think slavery was viable there. Moreover, the Ordinance implicitly sanctioned the development of slavery in the Southwest.[21]

It is, of course, anachronistic to ascribe the Northwest Ordinance to "federalists," since there were none at the time of its passage. However, the two men most responsible for the prohibition of slavery in the Ordinance, Manasseh Cutler and Nathan Dane, soon became federalist politicians of "the old school."[22] Furthermore, the slavery prohibition in the Ordinance may be seen as a "proto-federalist measure" in that it embodied three themes the Federalists later embraced: the notion that the central government should have the power to set economic policy for the nation, the idea that commerce (in this case land sales) was important to the nation, and an opposition to slavery. When the Federalists did take power, under the new Constitution, they reenacted the Ordinance.

The Constitution and Its Adoption

While the Confederation Congress was adopting the Ordinance with relatively little debate, the Constitutional Convention vigorously debated the place of slavery in the new republic. As we saw in Chapter 1, Madison argued that the great difference between the states was not size, but was "principally from their having or not having slaves." A number of delegates who would later become Federalists, like Rufus King, Alexander Hamilton, and Gouverneur Morris, expressed similar sentiments. Frustrated by the constant southern demands for special considerations for slavery, Morris wondered if the Union was worth strengthening or maintaining.

> Either this distinction is fictitious or real: if fictitious let it be dismissed and let us proceed with due confidence. If it be real, instead of attempting to blend incompatible things, let us at once take a friendly leave of each other. There can be no end of demands for security if every particular interest is to be entitled to it.[23]

What little opposition to slavery can be found in the Convention generally came from future Federalists, like King, Hamilton, Morris, and William Paterson. In the end, the place of slavery within the constitutional structure led to numerous and often heated debates. Morris argued that counting slaves for representation

> when fairly explained comes to this: that the inhabitant of Georgia and South Carolina who goes to the Coast of Africa, and in defiance of the most sacred laws of humanity tears away his fellow creatures from their dearest connections and damns them to the most cruel bondages, shall have more votes in a Government instituted for protection of the rights of mankind, than the Citizen of Pennsylvania or New Jersey who views with a laudable horror, so nefarious a practice.[24]

The document that emerged accommodated the needs and demands of slavery at almost every turn. Slavery affected the makeup of Congress, the method of choosing the president, interstate relations, and the regulation of commerce. As we saw in Chapter 1 of this book, the document that launched the "Age of Federalism" was subsequently called a "covenant with death" and an "agreement in Hell" by the Garrisonian abolitionists, who condemned its many proslavery compromises.

The proslavery implications of the Constitution were apparent to many northern Anti-Federalists, who opposed the Constitution in part because of the three-fifths clause, the prohibition until at least 1808 against ending the slave trade, and the guarantee that the national government would suppress slave rebellions. "A Countryman from Dutchess County" thought that Americans might become "a happy and respectable people" if under the Constitution the states were forced into "relinquishing every idea of drenching the bowels of Africa in gore, for the sake of enslaving its free-born innocent inhabitants." Similarly, "A Friend of the Rights of People" asked, "Can we then hold up our hands for a Constitution that licences this bloody practice? Can we who have fought so hard for Liberty give our consent to have it taken away from others? May the powers above forbid."[25]

This critique of the Constitution forced northern supporters of the document—the original "federalists"—to offer less than candid answers on how the document dealt with slavery. James Wilson, who surely knew better, tried to convince the Pennsylvania ratifying convention that the slave trade clause would allow Congress to end all slavery in the United States: after "the lapse of a few years, . . . Congress will have power to exterminate Slavery within our borders."[26] This, of course, was decidedly not the case.

Wilson, Hamilton, Jay, King, and other supporters of the Constitution overlooked, talked around, or ignored the proslavery implications of the Constitution. This was politically smart. Having made compromises over slavery, they now wanted to get the document ratified.

Once ratified, however, Federalists were more likely than Democratic-Republicans to oppose slavery in state and national politics. After ratification, some Federalists would devote a good deal of their energy to undoing or modifying the very compromises over slavery they helped make.

Slavery in Politics: The 1790s

Hardly had the new government begun when slavery threatened to disrupt Congress and interstate harmony. "[S]ome of the sharpest remarks heard by the first Congress" followed a proposal that the national government tax slaves imported from Africa. South Carolinians and Georgians vociferously defended slavery and the African slave trade with arguments that presaged the "positive good" defense of slavery that became common a generation later. James Jackson, who would later become a stalwart Jeffersonian, attacked the idea of allowing free blacks in the United States, declaring "he was opposed to the 'liberty of negroes' under any circumstances."[27] A year later, Congress erupted in an even more vigorous debate over a petition from Benjamin Franklin urging action to curb slavery and the slave trade. The most virulent opposition to this proposal came from Thomas Tudor Tucker, who would later become the Treasurer of the United States under Jefferson. Aedenus Burke, who had been an Anti-Federalist in 1787–1788 and later emerged as a Jeffersonian, threatened an end to the new union if Congress considered any limitation on the African trade.[28]

Although slavery had the potential to disrupt politics and national harmony, sectional cooperation also worked on some slavery-related issues. This is quite clear from the earlier discussion in this volume over the passage of the 1793 criminal extradition statute, which also included the first fugitive slave law.[29]

In this period, party affiliation was uncertain, and the connection between party affiliation and slavery was tenuous. A careful analysis of all roll call votes on slavery in Congress would probably reveal a pattern showing that Federalists or future Federalists were more inclined to oppose slavery than Republicans or future Republicans. More significant than the party affiliation is the understanding that, in this early period, slavery was already a divisive issue with a potential to undermine sectional harmony. In other words, slavery was a significant political issue in the very early part of the age of federalism, even if it was not yet the nation's central political issue, as it would be a generation later.

Slavery and the Growth of the Nation

Slavery was also part of the story of the growth of the nation in the age of federalism. Delegates to the Constitutional Convention assumed (incorrectly, as it turned out) that the South would grow faster than the North. In 1791 Vermont entered the Union with a constitution that flatly prohibited slavery. Ohio followed in 1803 and Indiana in 1816. Illinois was less emphatic in its opposition to slavery, allowing some forms of bondage to continue in what was clearly not yet "the Land of Lincoln." In 1799, as already noted, New York passed its gradual emancipation statute, putting that state on the road to freedom. New Jersey followed suit in 1804. By 1819 the North had clearly emerged as a region free of slavery. Meanwhile, five new states—Kentucky (1793), Tennessee (1798), Louisiana (1812), Mississippi (1817), and Alabama (1819)—strengthened the South. By the time Congress debated the admission of Missouri, sectionalism was obvious to anyone who cared to notice it.

The debate over Missouri is often seen as the opening salvo in the sectional war. In that debate, northern Federalists—or politicians who had once been Federalists—took the high ground in attacking slavery. Jeffersonian Republicans, who had so successfully vanquished the Federalists in the preceding two decades, fought hard to allow slavery to spread into the territory that their hero had acquired from France and called an "Empire for Liberty." This position was consistent with the Republican emphasis on westward expansion. Federalists viewed trade and commerce as the way to make the nation grow; Republicans wanted more land and westward settlement, including the spread of slavery.[30]

In his mountaintop mansion outside of Charlottesville, the leader of the Republicans brooded over this debate. The Federalists seemed to have come alive once again, threatening to curtail both the settlement of the West and the institution of slavery. Congressman John Holmes, who had drifted into the Republican Party when his own Federalist Party began to collapse, asked the Sage of Monticello to endorse a restriction on slavery. Jefferson responded that the Missouri crisis had "like a fire bell in the night, awakened and filled" him "with terror." Jefferson feared that the crisis would destroy the nation he had helped build. Rebuffing Holmes, Jefferson wrote, "I regret, that I am now to die in the belief, that the useless sacrifice of themselves by the generation of 1776, to acquire self-government and happiness to their country, is to be thrown away by the unwise and unworthy passions of their sons." Jefferson bemoaned that his countrymen, misled by Federalists like Rufus King, Daniel Webster, and Justice Joseph Story,[31] were willing to risk the stability of the nation over slavery and blacks. Jefferson despaired that his fellow white citizens could "perpetrate this act of suicide on themselves, and of treason against the hopes of the world,"[32] over, of all things, the place in society of a people Jefferson believed were inferior.

Slavery and Foreign Policy in the Age of Federalism

Slavery was also an important aspect of foreign policy. After the Revolution, America negotiated to regain custody of slaves who ran to British lines or joined the British army. American diplomats also sought to gain access to the port of New Orleans, which at the time was owned by Spain. Access to this Mississippi port would have most directly served the interests of slave owners moving into Kentucky, Tennessee, and what later became Mississippi and Alabama.

Federalist foreign policy was ambivalent or hostile to slavery. The Federalists never pushed hard for the actual return of slaves who had escaped with the British army at the end of the Revolution. Hamilton argued that the British should "make indemnification for, not restoration of, Negroes carried away." Washington "discouraged his fellow Virginians from their efforts to regain slaves freed by the British."[33] In contrast, Jefferson wanted the British to return the former slaves who had gained their freedom by entering British lines. In 1794 the newly organized Republicans secured House (but not Senate) passage of a resolution calling for a boycott of British trade until, among other things, the British returned slaves who had escaped with them at the end of the war.[34]

While John Jay believed that the Treaty of Paris required the actual restoration of the slaves taken from America, in his negotiations with England that led to the treaty which bore his name, Jay, "in a strongly humanitarian way," was willing to accept monetary compensation. Jeffersonians in South Carolina asserted that the failure to gain full "compensation for the value of the Negroes" who gained their freedom by leaving with the British army was an "insurmountable objection" to Jay's Treaty. When debating the treaty, the Senate Republicans initially attempted to force the issue of compensation for slaves. This may have simply been a ploy to defeat the treaty by splitting off southern Federalists who otherwise supported the treaty. The move failed by a vote of fifteen to twelve. After the Senate had ratified the treaty by the necessary two-thirds majority, the Republicans "in a last gasp of protest" once again "moved to renew discussion on compensation for the Negroes."[35]

The contrast between Jay and Jefferson on this issue illustrates the difference between Federalists and Republicans on much that had to do with slavery. Jay refused to press for the return of slaves because there was obviously something horrible in the new American nation demanding that people who had escaped to find liberty should be returned to bondage. Furthermore, Jay "believed that satisfaction for the Negroes had been obtained, 'though not in express words,' when he gained the northwestern ports and won privileges for his country's vessels in the British West Indies."[36] For the Federalists, trade was clearly a higher priority than the right to own slaves or to regain custody of slaves who had escaped with the British army.

For the Jeffersonians, on the other hand, regaining their slaves, or at least obtaining direct compensation for them, was a matter of principle. It became an inordinately high priority for them. Even after ratification of the treaty, the Jeffersonian press "recurrently reminded" Americans "that England continued to violate the treaty of 1783 by withholding compensation for kidnapped negro slaves." Jeffersonian newspapers attacked Jay's Treaty in part because "the carrying of Negro slaves" was "not even mentioned." Ironically, while concerned about the recovery of their own slaves, the Jeffersonians also used the rhetoric of the enslavement of whites to attack the Federalists. Thus, in the aftermath of the XYZ affair, Jeffersonians complained that a British victory over the French, which federalist policy might lead to, would "insure slavery to man for centuries to come."[37] Presumably, if the Jeffersonians had their way, the people of France would be free, while in the United States Jefferson and his followers would have been free to continue to enslave their own blacks for "centuries to come."

Explaining the Federalists

Most opponents of slavery in the early national period were motivated by religion, revolutionary sentiments, or both.[38] There was no such thing as an "antislavery" party until the emergence of the Liberty Party in 1840. The first political parties were surely uninterested in discussing the issue at all since it was, as we have seen, so divisive at the Constitutional Convention and had the potential to rip apart the fragile bonds of Union in the early years. Nevertheless, slavery was a constant and pervasive issue in American politics from the Revolution until the Missouri debates.[39]

Slavery was, of course, central to the development of sectional interests and conflicts in this period. By 1804, with the passage of New Jersey's gradual emancipation statute, the North had emerged as a free section, the South as a slave section. Where tobacco, rice, and cotton grew, slavery flourished. It also did well where wheat, corn, and hogs were common and less well where commerce, fishing, dairy farming, and manufacturing were taking hold. Federalists, as we know, were more powerful in the North, especially in New England and parts of New York.

But, beyond the economic and geographic aspects of slavery, there was also a political or ideological dimension to the Federalists' opposition to slavery. Northern Federalists were more hostile to slavery than their Republican neighbors. Southern Republicans were more rabid in defense of slavery than their Federalist neighbors. The few southerners who genuinely opposed slavery, like George Washington, were Federalists. Why were Federalists somehow different from the Democratic-Republicans when it came to thinking and legislating about slavery and race?

Federalists and Opposition to Slavery

While the political parties did not take a position against slavery, many politicians did. Republicans were severely constrained in their opposition to slavery because their party was dominated by the slaveholding elite of Virginia. After 1800 any criticism of slavery was an implicit criticism of Jefferson and his cohorts. Those northern Republicans opposed to slavery were "by and large, embarrassed by their partisan connections with Southern slaveholders."[40]

Federalists, on the other hand, were in a strong position to attack slavery. Not only was the party more solidly based in the North, but *their* slaveholding president, George Washington, voluntarily freed his slaves in his will.[41] Furthermore, except for South Carolina, southern "Federalism was not associated with plantation agriculture, and few of its leaders exhibited the siege mentality that affected" many Republicans in the South.[42] Thus, some Federalists opposed slavery through private actions; others did so through state and local politics or through participation in manumission societies; still others tried to shape national policies to challenge the institution. While there are some important exceptions to this, generally speaking, Federalists were more likely to oppose slavery than Republicans. Similarly, on the related question of the rights of free blacks, Federalists tended to be less racist and more accommodating than their Republican opponents. Indeed, after the Revolution, "what remained of the antislavery cause in the North therefore passed into the Federalist Party."[43]

The most obvious example of this can be seen in the three "federalist" presidents of the nation's early years, George Washington, John Adams, and John Quincy Adams.[44] Two of these—John Adams and John Quincy Adams—were the only presidents elected before 1836 who had never owned slaves. Moreover, both Adamses, but especially John Quincy, were the only northern presidents before Lincoln who actually opposed slavery. The other northern presidents were either former slave owners, like William Henry Harrison, with a long track record of supporting slavery, or doughfaces—northern men with southern principles—like Franklin Pierce and James Buchanan, who spent their entire political careers supporting slavery.[45]

George Washington, the first federalist president, was the only southern president to manumit his slaves, and although a slave owner, he was never committed to slavery. At the Constitutional Convention, he was a strong nationalist, ready to sacrifice slavery to strengthen the Union.[46] His opposition to the institution stands out, especially when he is compared to Jefferson. "As President, Washington was sensitive to the scandal of a national leader holding slaves, and he hired white servants to do the publicly visible work at his residence." By contrast, Jefferson brought his choice slaves with him to the new presidential mansion in the new capital, Washington.[47]

Many leading northern Federalists, like Alexander Hamilton, John Jay, Gouverneur Morris, Jared Ingersoll, Joseph Bloomfield, Joseph Hopkinson, Elias Boudinot, and Josiah Quincy, joined abolition societies or worked against slavery in some other way. These men, and their children, continued to oppose slavery in the early nineteenth century and beyond. "Most of the great American philanthropists in 1819 were Federalists, and these had opposed slavery all their lives, regardless of whether they had a political ax to grind."[48]

Starting with the election of 1800, northern Federalists constantly reminded voters of the connection between Jeffersonianism and slavery. Sometimes the connection was personal. In 1800 there were allegations of "Mr. Jefferson's Congo Harem." After 1802 there was the story of Sally Hemings, "The African Venus."[49]

Most scholars and commentators have been so caught up in this debate over Jefferson's personal morality and the excitement of illicit—and interracial and exploitative[50]—sex in the bedroom of an American president that they have failed to explore adequately why the Federalists would have raised such an issue and why it should have mattered. The allegations about Jefferson and Hemings go to the heart of the emerging federalist critique of slavery—upon which abolitionists would later expand. The Federalists pointed out—with the Master of Monticello as their prime evidence—that slavery was a fundamentally immoral institution, which led to the exploitation of blacks, laziness and personal sinfulness among whites, and the natural corruption of American politics. It was the essence of hypocrisy to be a slave owner and call oneself a democrat. Federalists zeroed in on the "domestic monarch [who] writes and spouts incessantly about . . . the *danger of power*" but abused others with his power.[51] From the view of the Federalists, this was Jefferson in his home and in the office of president. Josiah Quincy "mocked Jefferson's first inaugural: 'Intimacy . . . with all women—matrimonial alliance with none.'"[52] Even if the Federalists could not prove that Jefferson was the father of the children of Sally Hemings, he nevertheless provided a convenient proxy for all southern white men who *did* father children with their slaves, in violation of Federalist notions of morality and religion. It is likely that the New England Federalists, many of whom still accepted Puritan concepts of morality and community, found Jefferson's marital circumstances—as a healthy and young widower who insisted on remaining single—somewhat suspect.

Federalists—especially in New England—pointed out that slavery produced a lazy, dissolute society filled with pompous, domineering planters. Josiah Quincy suggested that "Democracy" was really "an Indian word, signifying *'a great tobacco planter, who had herds of black slaves.'*" "They starve their Negroes," Roger Griswold complained, while Thomas Boylston Adams argued, "There is a spirit of domination engrafted on the character of the southern people" that made them the "most imperious" and arrogant "inhabitants of this continent."[53] Federalist merchants and businessmen, embodying a Calvinist work ethic, were righteously, and perhaps rightly, contemptuous of the southern planters who dominated the Democratic-Republican Party, babbled on and on about the "rights of men," and continued to own hundreds of slaves. Federalists honestly employed men at an honest wage; Democrats dishonestly owned men and paid them no wage.

Free Blacks and Federalists

During the age of federalism, blacks could vote in a number of states, including New York, Pennsylvania, and Massachusetts. Where they voted, they generally supported the Federalists. Before 1811, Massachusetts had universal suffrage only for state offices, but in that year changed its suffrage laws by opening "the vote for town officers to all adult males except paupers." This led to increased voter participation in 1812. In Salem, blacks who had previously not voted did so, resulting in Federalists taking over what had previously been a Republican-controlled town meeting.[54] Given an opportunity to cast a ballot against the party of slaveholding Virginians and Jefferson's embargo,[55] the blacks in Salem naturally gravitated to the Federalists.

In Pennsylvania, the majority of the Quaker abolitionists were Federalists. In Philadelphia, it was "almost an oddity" to find a Jeffersonian in the Pennsylvania Abolition Society. Indeed only two of the hundreds of members of the Democratic-Republican Society of Philadelphia were also members of the PAS.[56] By the 1790s, only a few Jeffersonian newspapers, including William Duane's *Aurora*, ran advertisements for slave sales. Such advertisements suggest that people buying and selling slaves were most likely to be Jeffersonians as well as the possibility that Federalist editors may have refused to accept advertisements for the sale of human beings.

By 1800, as Gary Nash and Jean Soderlund have concluded, "the antislavery impulse" in Philadelphia was in the hands of Quakers and "those who subscribed to a failing Federalist political persuasion." The Republicans, meanwhile, began to war against black rights. In 1813 a Republican paper declared that free blacks were "useless," while that same year a Republican politician proposed legislation to prohibit free blacks from entering the state and to sell into servitude any black convicted of a crime.[57] In the 1830s the Democrats had enough power in Pennsylvania to successfully disfranchise all black voters in that state. Jacksonian democracy, the child of Jeffersonian democracy, in fact spelled doom for black voting in Pennsylvania, Tennessee, and North Carolina.

In most cities, the Jeffersonians appealed to the white working class. In the seventeenth century, blacks and whites had worked side by side: "the two despised groups initially saw each other as sharing the same predicament."[58] But, by the 1790s, this was largely a forgotten past. In northern cities, white workers, particularly Irish immigrants, were already pitted against blacks. In Philadelphia, the Republicans appealed to the Irish while at the same time "becoming overtly hostile to the city's growing black population."[59]

New York provides a good case study. Many important and wealthy New Yorkers owned slaves. It would not have been out of character for an aristocrat like John Jay or a parvenu like Alexander Hamilton to accept slavery and even own slaves themselves, as Jay did. But Jay also helped organize the New York Manumission Society, while other leading New York Federalists, like Hamilton, Gouverneur Morris, James Duane, and Philip Schuyler, were early and active opponents of slavery in the state. Finally, in 1799 New York became the penultimate state to adopt a gradual abolition law, followed by New Jersey in 1804. New York's 1799 gradual emancipation statute was "enacted by a Federalist legislature and signed by" Jay, "a Federalist governor," although there was some support from Republicans as well.[60] Jay's antislavery legacy was later carried on by his son, Judge William Jay, and his grandson and namesake, John Jay, Jr. In the antebellum period, both of the younger Jays were active abolitionists who viewed their opposition to slavery as a continuation of Chief Justice Jay's federalist ideology.

In comparison to Jay and Hamilton, there is no evidence that any leading Jeffersonians in New York, with the exception of Chancellor Robert R. Livingston, cared much about slavery or the plight of free blacks.[61] Governor George Clinton, who served as vice president under Jefferson and Madison, never raised a finger to end slavery during his six successive terms as governor of New York. His nephew, Governor DeWitt Clinton, sought the repeal of a portion of the gradual emancipation law that encouraged masters to free their slaves. By 1820 Clinton's faction in New York at least openly opposed the extension of slavery in the West. However, Martin Van Buren, who would soon come to control the Democrats in New York, supported the interests of slavery at the end of the federalist period and beyond. The Silver Fox of Kinderhook refused even to take a public stand on the Missouri Compromise, while his followers, the Bucktails, "were generally lukewarm" in support of any antislavery measures and "opposed" to any restrictions on slavery in Missouri or the West. According to Rufus King, the Federalist Senator from New York, Van Buren's ally, Senator Daniel Tomkins, "fled the field . . . of battle" on the day of the vote in Congress over restricting slavery in Missouri and the West. In the mid-1820s, Van Buren tried to resurrect the old Jeffersonian alliance of "the planters of the South and the plain Republicans of the North."[62] In the 1830s, Van Buren would become the first doughface Democrat, supporting slavery in his one term as U.S. president.

Before 1821 blacks in New York could vote under the same rules as whites. Not surprisingly, given the views of the Clintons and other Jeffersonians on race and slavery, New York's blacks generally supported Federalists. The traditional explanation for this is that free blacks had been owned by kindly Federalist masters: the "slaves, who had been well treated, stood by the 'families' after freedom almost faithfully as before." Thus, free blacks voted Federalist.[63]

This explanation may have some truth to it, but more likely, free blacks in New York and elsewhere supported the Federalists for three concrete reasons. First, blacks agreed with Federalist policies on race and slavery. Federalists supported emancipation in the North, they favored trade with Haiti and eventual diplomatic recognition of that black revolutionary nation, and they hated the African slave trade.[64] Federalists filled the ranks of the emancipation societies from Delaware to New England. Second, Federalist economic policy, especially expanded overseas trade, dovetailed with the heavy concentration of free blacks in the maritime industry. Third, blacks clearly saw no alternative in the Republicans. Jefferson's was the party of slavery. The party leaders were Virginia masters. In the North, the party supported slavery and opposed black rights. "Anti-Negro prejudice eventually became a test of party regularity for the New York Republican party."[65] Jefferson and his party wanted to destroy the "black Republic" in Haiti. Thus, for quite logical reasons, having nothing to do with the kindness of their former owners, blacks in New York and elsewhere gravitated to the Federalist Party, which accepted them; similarly, blacks moved away from the Republican Party, which in fact wanted nothing to do with them. In the 1790s, for example, the Philadelphia Democratic-Republican society rejected a black who wished to join.[66]

In the election of 1808, Republicans in New York attacked Federalists with a campaign song that included the verse, "Federalists with blacks unite." Black voters, meanwhile, endorsed the Federalists and attacked Jefferson's embargo, which probably hurt free blacks in the North harder than any other single group because so many of the men in that community were either sailors or involved in shipbuilding, repairs, and sail making.[67] Before the War of 1812, the "Federalists defended black voting rights and foiled several attempts" by the Jeffersonians "to institute racial restrictions." When Republicans gained control of the New York legislature in 1811, they attempted to restrict black voters by requiring them to show proof of their status as freemen. Federalists who controlled the Council of Revision defeated this "humiliating" and "wanton insult . . . on account of their complexion."[68] Not surprisingly, free blacks in New York continued to vote for Federalists, who, throughout the North, stood for emancipation and black rights.

In 1821, when the New York Constitutional Convention debated revising the requirements for suffrage in the state, Republicans pushed for the removal of property requirements for white male voters and the full disfranchisement of blacks. This was the essence of Jeffersonian "democracy." Federalists supported the right of black men to vote. Noting that blacks with property could already vote, Chancellor James Kent, one of the last of the New York Federalist leaders, argued that the goal of the convention was not "to *disfranchise* any portion of the community or to take away their rights." Peter Augustus Jay, Judge Jonas Platt, and other Federalists joined Kent in arguing against racial discrimination in the franchise. Leading the charge against black suffrage were the Republicans who had supported Jefferson and would soon follow Andrew Jackson. Here ideology and political strategy went hand in hand: blacks in New York generally supported the Federalists, so disfranchising them made good sense to the Republicans.[69] Significantly, however, Republicans never tried to disfranchise any other identifiable group that supported the Federalists. In other words, black disfranchisement may have been good politics for the Republicans, but their motivation was mostly racism and bigotry.

Haiti as a Test Case for Federalist and Republican Attitudes Toward Race

The most profound example of the difference between Federalist and Jeffersonian policies over slavery can be found in American relations with St. Domingue, or Haiti, as it is now called. In the 1790s, a series of slave revolts destroyed the system of human bondage on the island. Some Americans, particularly John Adams and his Federalist administration, viewed this revolution with great sympathy, seeing Toussaint L'Ouverture as the Haitian Washington, leading his people out of colonial domination. Adams encouraged the new regime and quickly developed a strong economic relationship with Haiti. While not according Haiti full diplomatic recognition, the Adams administration seemed to be moving in that direction.

But not all Americans welcomed the tumultuous prospect of black slaves on St. Domingue overthrowing their French and creole masters. While not directly affecting the United States, the image of slaves emulating the American revolutionaries sent shivers of fear through the South. Southern Republicans, dreading that their own slaves might follow the lead of Toussaint L'Ouverture, naturally opposed the Haitian revolution.

Reflecting on the possibility that the Haitian Revolution would spread to America, Thomas Jefferson wrote to a friend, "If something is not done & soon done, we shall be the murderers of our own children."[70] Other Republicans opposed the new Haitian regime because of their close ties to France. Even a scholar sympathetic to the Republicans concedes that "although there were scores of resolutions adopted by the popular societies hailing and supporting the French Revolution, not one was passed supporting another revolution occurring at the same time—the black revolution of slaves in the French West Indies."[71]

Federalists were more friendly to Haitian liberty. The revolt against French rule dovetailed with their Francophobia. But antislavery ideology was also important in shaping Federalist policy. Thus, despite their Anglophilia, the Federalists "lent little aid or comfort to the British while His Majesty's forces mounted a savage four-year-long assault on the island, though American interests in trade lay manifestly more with monarchical Britain than with incendiary St. Domingue."[72] By 1799 the United States was actively trading with Haiti and, more importantly, providing arms and supplies to Toussaint. The Federalists rejected the concerns of the British, who looked upon this support of Toussaint with "horror."[73] An act of February 1799, passed by the Federalist-dominated Congress, authorized President Adams to lift the embargo on Haiti. Secretary of State Timothy Pickering immediately sent a diplomatic envoy, Edward Stevens, to the island for face-to-face negotiations with L'Ouverture. Stevens traveled "in a ship loaded with provisions for Toussaint, escorted by an American warship."[74] Quickly Stevens negotiated an agreement that allowed British and American merchants access to the Haitian markets.

A variety of circumstances—including the quasi war with France and the interests of New England merchants—led Federalists to support the revolution of Toussaint L'Ouverture. As early as June 1798, Pickering indicated that America would look kindly on an independent black republic in Haiti with L'Ouverture at the top. It is impossible to imagine Secretary of State Jefferson taking such a position. Indeed, at the very time his nation was aiding L'Ouverture, Jefferson was fretting about the possibility that the example of Haiti would spread to the United States, and worrying about becoming "the murderers of our own children."[75]

By 1800 Haiti was in the throes of a civil war, not between the master class and the slaves, but between an army of mulattoes—*gens de couleur*—led by General André Rigaud, and L'Ouverture's army of ex-slaves. In the final battle of this war, an American frigate "stood off the port, cutting out Rigaud's supply vessels, and in the final assault used her artillery to bombard Rigaud's harbor forts and compel their evacuation." Some months later another American ship captured Rigaud at sea.[76]

Under the Federalist regime of Adams and Pickering, the United States urged the Haitians to declare their independence; under Jefferson and Secretary of State James Madison, the nation offered France help to suppress the slave rebellion. Republican policies reflected the fears of their leaders and of the slaveholding elite of the South.

The results of these differences are clear. When Federalists controlled the national government, trade with Haiti ballooned. "Before Jefferson became president, the value of the American exchange with St. Domingue was perhaps seven times the value of the French commerce on the Island." This ended with the end of Federalist rule, as Jefferson and his colleagues in the House and Senate imposed an embargo on the black republic. As historian Rayford Logan observed, "In 1799 a strong Federalist majority had been in favor of reopening trade with Haiti. In 1806 an overwhelming Democratic majority closed that trade."[77] When Jefferson became president, he recalled Edward Stevens and replaced him with Tobias Lear, a cipher of limited abilities. When Lear arrived in Haiti, he carried no letter or other official greeting from the new president. Toussaint L'Ouverture "complained bitterly" about this, but Lear lamely replied that because he was merely a commercial agent it was not "customary" to present such a letter or other commission from the president. L'Ouverture knew better. He declared to Lear that "his colour was the cause of his being neglected."[78] More precisely, it was the color prejudices of the president and his party. Thus, in St. Domingue it was the Federalists who held far more closely to the faith of the founders and the Jeffersonian Republicans who tried far more tenaciously to tether and traduce the will of the people. It was the Federalists who were keen to aid the oppressed in their effort at independence and the Republicans who resisted that effort. It was the Federalists who fostered freedom and the Republicans who attempted the restoration of a colonial regime and, indeed, the reimposition of slavery itself.[79]

The debate over the Haitian embargo illustrates the distinction between Federalists and Republicans on questions of race and slavery. This embargo preceded Jefferson's general embargo on all foreign trade and lasted longer than the general embargo.

Once in power, the Jeffersonians tried mightily to destroy the black republic. In 1805 and 1806, Congress debated an absolute embargo on trade with the island. During this period, Republicans raved about the need to undermine Haiti. Secretary of the Treasury Albert Gallatin believed that any American trade with Haiti was "illicit" and "contrary to the law of nations." Senator James Jackson of Georgia argued that the black government "must be destroyed." Virginia Congressman John Wayles Eppes, Jefferson's son-in-law, denied that Haiti was free and declared that he would "pledge the Treasury of the United States that the Negro government should be destroyed."[80] By this time, even the French had written off the island. The United States could gain nothing from the embargo, except to harm its own economic interests. Nevertheless, Jefferson insisted on the embargo.[81]

Senator Samuel White, a Federalist from the slave state of Delaware, spoke out against the embargo bill, which he called a "disgrace." White discussed at great length the fact that the Haitian slaves were free under French law and that they were "de facto the governors of the country, and in every respect act as an independent people." The Senate voted twenty-one to eight in favor of the embargo against Haiti. All the opposition came from Federalists.[82] In the House, Congressman Eppes was so anxious to embargo Haiti that he "violently opposed" a motion to delay consideration of the bill by even a day. On the final vote, almost all of the opponents of the measure were Federalists. Some Southern Federalists, like Joseph Lewis of Virginia, who dared not vote against the measure because they might be labeled as supporters of the Haitian Revolution, managed to be absent and thus avoid the roll call.[83]

In this debate, the Republicans could not countenance the possibility of free black people having their own country and trading with the United States. The Federalists, while certainly not racial egalitarians, were willing to accept the reality of Haiti, recognize the nation, and trade with the black republic. As Michael Zuckerman has observed about Haiti, "In the realm of race, the Federalists clung to the ideological inheritance of the Revolution far more than the Jeffersonians."[84]

Geography, Economics, and Moral Culture

Clearly, Federalists and Jeffersonian Republicans had a different approach to slavery. With a few exceptions, Federalists were more likely to oppose slavery than Democratic-Republicans; the Republicans were more likely to support slavery than Federalists. In the North, Federalists were more likely to support gradual abolition programs and Republicans were more likely to oppose them, although sometimes such laws seem to have had substantial support from both groups. On black rights the division is more clear. Federalists were far more likely to support the rights of free blacks, and Republicans were clearly more likely to oppose them. Not surprisingly, in New York, Pennsylvania, and New England, where blacks voted, they voted for Federalists.

The division between federalists and Republican on race and slavery is most obvious in the North. While most southern Federalists supported slavery and opposed black rights, this was not always the case. Southern Federalists were more likely than their Jeffersonian neighbors to free their own slaves and to favor programs that limited slavery "by opposing the slave trade, encouraging voluntary manumission, and reducing discrimination against both slaves and free Negroes."[85] In Virginia, Federalists like Josiah Parker, John Marshall, George Washington, and Bushrod Washington showed ambivalence or hostility to slavery. The Virginia Federalist congressman Charles Fenton Mercer was "an honest opponent of slavery."[86] Similarly, as a young man, Roger B. Taney was a Federalist attorney-politician who defended alleged abolitionists in Maryland and freed his own slaves. Only after he became a Jacksonian Democrat did he adopt the racism and proslavery positions for which he is most famous.[87] Between 1802 and 1805, the Federalists in the South Carolina legislature opposed both the African slave trade and the interstate slave trade, while the Republican majority voted to reopen the African trade.[88]

Federalists in Virginia, South Carolina, and North Carolina voted to liberalize laws allowing for private manumission, while the Jeffersonians opposed these laws. Similarly, between 1803 and 1814, a majority of Federalists in the North Carolina and Virginia legislatures voted for various laws to ameliorate the condition of free blacks. For example, in 1805 Federalists voted three to one against a bill to compel emancipated slaves to leave the state, while Republicans voted two to one in favor of the bill.[89]

North Carolina, where blacks voted until 1835, also provides some evidence of Federalist support for free blacks. While "it is difficult to ascertain the extent to which free Negroes were a factor in politics during the national period," evidence suggests that those who voted sided with the Federalists. John Chavis, one of the few politically active blacks in North Carolina, complained about the possibility of the reelection of Andrew Jackson, noting that the nation really needed "a Hamilton, a Jay, or an old Adams bottomed upon G. Washington." In 1835, North Carolina disfranchised all blacks. The supporters of this disfranchisement included not only the new Jacksonian Democrats, but longtime Jeffersonians, like Nathaniel Macon. Old-line Federalists like William Gaston fought this racist assault on black rights. As justices on the North Carolina Supreme Court, Gaston and the Federalist Archibald Henderson often wrote decisions favorable to slaves and free blacks. John Culpepper, an active Federalist and Baptist minister, signed a published resolution urging that a black minister be allowed to preach. Similarly, the Federalist William Boylan signed a petition to the legislature urging that a free black family be allowed to remain in the state.[90] Some of these are minor issues, to be sure. And men like Gaston and Henderson were not closet abolitionists, but, like Federalists in the North, they were more respectful of black rights, less openly racist, and generally more humane toward free blacks than their Jeffersonian and Jacksonian counterparts.

On the big controversies—like extending of slavery into the West or allowing Missouri to enter the Union as a slave state—the issues were clearly drawn. Northern Federalists led the charge against slavery; Republicans from the North and the South defended against that charge.

Why was there such a split in the two parties? Why were the Republicans so proslavery? Why were the Federalists less proslavery and even antislavery? Four answers seems to emerge.

Proslavery Republicans

In the 1790s the Republicans emerged as the party of Virginia and Thomas Jefferson. While undoubtedly uncomfortable with slavery and fearful of the dangers that he thought slaves posed to white society, "Jefferson had only a theoretical interest in promoting the cause of abolition." From the time he returned from France in 1789 until his death in 1826, Jefferson never took a public position in opposition to slavery, while often supporting the institution. His positions on race were extreme, even by the standards of his own age. As Winthrop Jordan has noted, Jefferson's attitude about race "constituted, for all its qualifications, the most intense, extensive, and extreme formulation of anti-Negro 'thought' offered by any American in the thirty years after the Revolution."[91] While Madison and Monroe may have been less negrophobic, they certainly never gave any support to opponents of slavery or supporters of black rights. It should not surprise us, then, that a party led by such men would have been proslavery and antiblack. To support the Democratic-Republicans meant to support slave owners at the top of the ticket. In northern cities, the Republicans appealed to working-class whites and recent immigrants, who quickly came to believe that free blacks threatened their economic status. One of the "wages" that white urban workers earned, as early as the 1790s, was their privilege of being white.[92] The Jeffersonian Republicans openly played the race card early on in American history. Their party, which became known as the Democratic Party after 1828, would continue to play it, in the Jacksonian era, the antebellum period, during the Civil War, and well into the twentieth century. Ironically, the second Republican Party, which emerged in 1854 and sent Lincoln to the White House, was distinctly antislavery, and many of its members were racial egalitarians.

Elitism and Racial Acceptance

Thus, blacks rejected the Jeffersonian Republicans. The dishonorable attempt of New York Republicans to disfranchise blacks illustrates why African-Americans supported the Federalists. The proslavery, negrophobic policies of the Democratic-Republicans left them no choice.

But why were the northern (and some southern) Federalists both receptive to free blacks and hostile to slavery? Why didn't Federalists also play the race card? Or, to put it another way, why were they less concerned about paying themselves and their constituents in the wages of whiteness?

Part of the answer has to do with the elitist views of many Federalists. Their social position and aristocratic nature allowed Federalists to grant blacks political rights without thinking of them as equals. Federalists did not see or want "equality" among all Americans; thus, they had less need to relegate one group of people—blacks—to a permanent underclass status in order to uplift themselves.

In the South, the master class had long understood the necessity of keeping blacks and whites separated. As historian Edmund Morgan has so eloquently argued, in the American South freedom was dependent on American slavery.[93] Slavery made all whites equal by creating what South Carolina senator James Henry Hammond would call in 1858 the "mudsill" for American society, on top of which all whites could compete as equals. The Republicans easily carried this idea to the North, where it was used to organize whites. Jeffersonian democracy led to racism, elevating all whites to equality on the backs of slaves and free blacks. Federalists did not need the "wages of whiteness" to feel secure in their social place; Democratic-Republicans, north and south, needed to suppress blacks to feel better about themselves. Indeed, southern Federalists, secure in their elite status, were apparently neither frightened nor threatened by free blacks in their midst. Southern Republicans, on other hand, were often deeply paranoid on this issue.[94]

Economic Interests

Economic ideology went hand in hand with Federalist notions of racial accommodation and hostility to slavery. As supporters of property, Federalists were able to reward property-owning free blacks with the franchise as easily as they would have denied the franchise to propertyless whites. Similarly, as men of commerce, they were more interested in economic efficiency than race. Selling goods to the British West Indies was far more important than compensation for slaves who escaped to freedom with the British army; selling goods to Haiti was far more important than worrying about the color of their trading partners. Yankee traders went to China, India, and Polynesia. Haiti was just one more port to the New York, Philadelphia, or New England ship captain, who was likely to hire black crewmen, to have his ship repaired by a black worker, or even to have purchased his sails from a black sailmaker.[95]

Both Federalists and Republicans had notions of manifest destiny in this early period. They both wanted to make America a great nation. But for Federalists, this greatness would come through free trade and economic expansion across the oceans, in ships manned by integrated crews sailing to ports where the people were of many colors. Republicans, and later the Jacksonians, wanted to move west, eliminating the nonwhites in their way and bringing their black slaves with them.

Religion, Culture, and Morality

Finally, concepts of morality and justice help explain Federalist policy. As elitists, many Federalists had a strong sense of noblesse oblige. Washington, the greatest Federalist of all, was the embodiment of moral rectitude. This ideology led him to believe that slavery was morally wrong, and he acted on this belief in many ways. As commander-in-chief of the army, he ultimately accepted black soldiers and came to see them as men in uniform, no better or worse than white soldiers. Although a slave owner, he refused to buy and sell slaves, "as you would do cattle at a market," even though he owned more slaves than he needed or could profitably employ.[96] As a planter, he ultimately put his lands and crops in the hands of his own slaves and slave overseers, thus preparing them for freedom. And, finally, in his will he manumitted his slaves. The contrast with Jefferson is striking. As a slave owner, Jefferson sold scores of bondspeople—at least eighty in one ten-year period ending in the early 1790s—all the while protesting that he had "scruples about selling negroes but for delinquency or on their own request."[97]

In the North and parts of the Upper South, Federalists joined manumission societies and other philanthropic endeavors that made them sympathetic to the least fortunate in American society. "The New Englanders' version of republicanism was bound up with the Northerners' piety and morality and their belief that the United States was a national organic community striving to build a 'Christian Sparta.'"[98] Such ideas were also common among some New Yorkers, Pennsylvanians, and other northerners. Such ideas naturally led them to oppose—even hate—slavery.

Slavery was the opposite of all that the Federalists stood for. It was also immoral, in fundamental ways that bothered the inheritors of the traditions of the Calvinists, Huguenots, and Quakers. To explain why some northerners continued these traditions, and others did not, is beyond the scope of this book. But, clearly, the difference was there for the early national period, just as it would be for the antebellum period. We need not explain why Lincoln found slavery morally wrong and Stephen A. Douglas did not, to understand that the difference was real. Similarly, while we await a fuller explanation of what motivated Washington or John Jay to act as they did and Jefferson or Martin Van Buren to act as they did, it is nevertheless important to understand that their approaches to slavery and race were quite different. Thus, in the age of Jefferson, the Federalists were the people most committed to liberty and racial fairness, if not necessarily equality and fraternity.

——— Six ———

"Treason Against the Hopes of the World"

Thomas Jefferson and Slavery

His words ring true and strong more than two centuries after he wrote them. It is "self-evident" that all persons "are created equal, that they are endowed by their Creator with certain unalienable Rights, that among these are Life, Liberty, and the pursuit of Happiness." The message is clear; it is a fundamental credo of American culture.

The author of these words has been called "the greatest champion of liberty this country has ever had." Even historians who have concentrated on his faults argue that Jefferson, along with Lincoln, "is the central figure in the history of American democracy."[1] Yet this "apostle of liberty" could never reconcile the ideals of freedom expressed in the Declaration of Independence and his other writings with the reality of his ownership of men and women and his leadership of a slaveholding society.[2]

An understanding of Jefferson's relationship to slavery requires analysis of his statements and beliefs and an account of his actions as a public leader and a private individual. Scrutinizing the contradictions between Jefferson's professed ideals and his actions does not impose twenty-first-century values on an eighteenth-century man. Because Jefferson was the author of the Declaration of Independence and a leader of the American enlightenment, the test of his position on slavery is not whether he was better than the worst of his generation, but whether he was the leader of the best; not whether he responded as a southerner and a planter, but whether he was able to transcend his economic interests and his sectional background in order to implement the ideals he articulated. Jefferson fails the test.

When Jefferson wrote the Declaration of Independence, he owned over 175 slaves. While many of his contemporaries freed their slaves during and after the Revolution, Jefferson did not. In the fifty years from 1776 until his death in 1826, a period of extraordinary public service, he did little to end slavery or to dissociate himself from his role as the master of Monticello. To the contrary, as he accumulated more slaves he worked assiduously to increase the productivity and the property values of his labor force. Nor did he encourage his countrymen to liberate their slaves, even when they sought his blessing.[3] Even at his death, Jefferson failed to fulfill the promise of his rhetoric. In his will he emancipated only five bondsmen, condemning nearly 200 others to the auction block.

On the fiftieth anniversary of the Declaration, Jefferson expired, a monument to the giant chasm between his words and his deeds on the question of race and liberty. His slaves, and those of his countrymen, may have been "endowed by their Creator" with a right to "liberty," but Jefferson had done nothing to secure that right for them.

Jefferson's ideas about slavery and his relationship to the institution were complex and contradictory. A proponent of legal reform and humane criminal codes, he advocated harsh, almost barbaric, criminal punishments for slaves or free blacks; known for expansive views of citizenship, he nevertheless proposed legislation to make emancipated blacks "outlaws" in the land of their birth; opposed to "attainders for corruption of the blood," he proposed expelling from Virginia the children of white women and black men solely because they had "corrupt"—mixed—blood.[4]

The public Jefferson avoided the problem of slavery, forgoing opportunities to undermine the institution and its growing stranglehold on national politics. Throughout his life, Jefferson tried to dodge discussions of slavery. When he did speak of the institution, as in his *Notes on the State of Virginia*, it was at the prompting of others, or to serve his polemical purposes (most notably in denouncing British tyranny), or when his business dealings required it.[5] When unable to evade the issue, Jefferson sought to avoid confrontation and friction. When corresponding with other slave owners, he sounded just like one of them—which he was;[6] to opponents of slavery, Jefferson sounded like an abolitionist who would do anything to end slavery if only the circumstances were right. Dumas Malone has noted Jefferson's "extreme distaste for personal controversy" and admits that this habit of avoiding conflict "was a defect of his politeness and amiability which caused him to seem deceptive."[7] Nowhere is this deceptiveness more apparent than when he talked about slavery. Joseph J. Ellis argues that "what his critics took to be hypocrisy" about slavery "was not really that at all. In some cases it was the desire to please different constituencies, to avoid conflict with colleagues. In other cases it was an orchestration of his internal voice, to avoid conflict within himself."[8] Conscious or not, planned and calculated or a function of his unconscious need to please everyone and to avoid conflict, hypocritical or merely self-deluding, the result was the same: throughout his life Jefferson was Janus-faced about slavery, talking about liberty to those who believed in liberty and giving advice and succor to his fellow slave owners. In the end, through his deeds as both private slave owner and public leader, time and again, Jefferson sided with slavery and against freedom.

Jefferson opposed the circulation of his *Notes on Virginia* in part because his comments on slavery might "produce an irritation."[9] We might well join David Brion Davis in asking "how he expected to encourage the cause of emancipation without producing irritation?" This is exactly the problem. Ultimately, Jefferson was more concerned with avoiding "irritation" than promoting emancipation. He was, in William Freehling's words, a "Conditional Terminator," never able to argue for an end to slavery without conditions that were always impossible to meet.[10] For Jefferson, any cost of ending slavery, however low, was too high.

Perhaps because he regularly faced slaves in the daily management of his lands and farms, as well as his mountaintop mansion, Jefferson simply could not allow himself to reflect on their lack of liberty. Jefferson remained strikingly unconcerned about slaves as individuals. He barely noticed those slaves who served him at home and in his fields and all too often became ready forms of capital to pay his debts. He seems to have suffered no qualms when he separated families, selling children from parents and husbands from wives, in order to pay bills resulting from his poor management or his insatiable appetite for Bordeaux, furniture, and other fine things. This lack of concern was possible because, as historian Andrew Burstein notes, Jefferson "separated himself emotionally" from his slaves.[11]

Of course, at some abstract level Jefferson knew slavery was wrong. It could not have been otherwise for an eighteenth-century natural law theorist. Many of his closest European and American friends and colleagues were leaders of the new abolition societies. Jefferson was part of a cosmopolitan "republic of letters" that was overwhelmingly hostile to slavery.[12] But, for the most part, he suppressed his doubts while doing virtually nothing to challenge the institution. On this issue, Jefferson's genius failed him. As Davis observes, "Jefferson had only a theoretical interest in promoting the cause of abolition."[13]

Jefferson could not live without slaves. They built his house, cooked his meals, and tilled his fields. In contrast to George Washington, Jefferson failed to carefully manage his lands and finances and lived far beyond his means. Washington refused to traffic in slaves. James Madison chose to sell land when in debt and agreed to sell a few slaves to close friends only when his reduced landholding made it impossible for him to keep so many slaves. Jefferson professed to have "scruples about selling negroes but for delinquency or on their own request." But, chronically in debt, he overcame his "scruples," selling scores of slaves in order to make ends meet. In just one

"sold at least 85 slaves"
-- Jefferson

ten-year period between 1784 to 1794, Jefferson sold at least eighty-five slaves.[14] Without his slaves, Jefferson could not maintain his extravagant lifestyle, which to judge from his lifelong behavior, was far more important than the natural rights of his slaves.

Jefferson, Race, and Republicanism

Even if he had put his financial house in order and been able to extricate himself from his role as master and slave owner, a general emancipation posed other problems for Jefferson. Who would replace the slaves in the fields and in other menial positions? A permanent lower class of free people would threaten his notion of a republican society.

Contemporaries of Jefferson, as well as historians, have commented on the relationship between slavery and republicanism in the South. During Jefferson's presidency, Sir Augustus John Foster, an English diplomat, observed that Virginia planters could "profess an unbounded love of liberty and of democracy in consequence of the mass of the people, who in other countries might become mobs, being there nearly altogether composed of their own Negro slaves." Historian Edmund Morgan agrees: "Aristocrats could more safely preach equality in a slave society than in a free one. Slaves did not become leveling mobs."[15] The liberty and political equality of the white masses rested on the slavery of the black masses.

Even if all whites could somehow remain politically and legally equal without slavery, race presented an insurmountable barrier to emancipation. Jefferson could not accept blacks as his equals. He believed blacks were swayed by emotion, lacked intellectual abilities, and were not equipped to participate in a free republican society. As John Hope Franklin insightfully notes, "it would seem hardly likely that anyone with such pronounced views on the inferiority of blacks, who, at the same time, believed blacks and whites could not live together as free persons could entertain a deeply serious belief that slaves should be emancipated." Jefferson was not alone in excluding blacks from the vision of equality. William M. Wiecek persuasively argues that for Virginians and other southerners, Jefferson's "self-evident truths contain[ed] an implicit racial exception" and "the lines, properly read in the light of American social conditions of 1776, contain[ed] the word 'white' before the word 'men.'" But, in revolutionary America, as Jack Pole notes, "strikingly similar expressions" of equality "did not always mean the same things."[16] Many northerners considered blacks—even slaves—entitled to their self-evident rights. In Massachusetts, the Supreme Judicial Court interpreted the state's 1780 constitution, with language almost identical to that which Jefferson used in the Declaration, to have ended slavery in that commonwealth. Every revolutionary-era northern state took steps to end slavery; most extended political rights, including the franchise, to free blacks.[17]

For Jefferson, political equality for blacks was impossible because he thought "the real distinction that nature has made" between the races went beyond color and other physical attributes. Race, more than their status as slaves, doomed blacks to permanent inequality. In *Notes on the State of Virginia,* Jefferson asserted that a harsh bondage did not prevent Roman slaves from achieving distinction in science, art, and literature because "they were of the race of whites"; American slaves could never achieve such distinction because they were not white. Jefferson argued that American Indians had "a germ in their minds which only wants [lacks] cultivation"; they were capable of "the most sublime oratory." But he had never found a black who "had uttered a thought above the level of plain narration; never seen an elementary trait of painting or sculpture." He found "no poetry" among blacks. Jefferson argued that blacks' ability to "reason" was "much inferior" to whites, while "in imagination they are dull, tasteless, and anomalous" and "inferior to the whites in the endowments of body and mind." Jefferson conceded that blacks were brave, but this was due to "a want of fore-thought, which prevents their seeing a danger till it be present."[18]

Jefferson could assert the equality of mankind only by excluding blacks. He admitted some qualms at reaching a "conclusion [that] would degrade a whole race of men from the rank in the scale of beings which their Creator may perhaps have given them." But, qualms or not, he suspected that blacks might be "originally a distinct race, or made distinct by time and circumstances" and that because of this they were "inferior to the whites in . . . body and mind."[19] If they had natural rights, and Jefferson seems uncertain on this point, they could exercise them only outside the United States.

Because Jefferson could not imagine living in a society in which blacks could claim equal rights, he could never comfortably consider emancipation or manumission. He never could overcome the "biases that made it impossible for him to conceive of a color-blind republic devoted to the rights of *all* men."[20] Because Jefferson believed free blacks could never be citizens—despite the fact that they were citizens in the states immediately north and south of Virginia—he assumed they would necessarily become an exploited and ungovernable mob.[21] Jefferson also feared that emancipated slaves would take revenge on their former masters for the "ten thousand . . . injuries they have sustained." He believed "Justice" was "in one scale, self-preservation in the other." He told a fellow slaveholding Virginian that, "if something is not done & soon done, we shall be the murderers of our own children."[22] But he had no idea what that "something" might be. A man who fearlessly pledged his life, fortune, and "sacred Honor" to fight the king of England and his mighty armies trembled at the idea of black slaves acting as free men.

Jefferson's negrophobia was profound. A scientist and naturalist, he nevertheless accepted and repeated absurdly unscientific and illogical arguments about the racial characteristics of blacks, speculating that blackness might come "from the colour of the blood" or that blacks might breed with the "Oran-ootan."[23] His assertion that black men preferred white women was empirically insupportable. However, he had abundant evidence that many white men, including his late father-in-law, maintained sexual liaisons with their female slaves.[24] Indeed, within a few years after he wrote these words, Jefferson would himself begin a sexual relationship with his own slave, Sally Hemings.

Confronted with examples of black achievement, be it Phillis Wheatley's poetry, Benjamin Banneker's mathematics, or the *Literature of Negroes* compiled by Bishop Henri Grégoire, Jefferson found the evidence inconclusive or unpersuasive.[25] Faced with black accomplishment, he reiterated unsubstantiated claims about black biological inferiority.

More than the precursor of the antebellum abolitionists, Jefferson was the intellectual godfather of the racist pseudoscience of the American school of anthropology. William Lloyd Garrison may have learned his political theory from Jefferson, but the antebellum proponents of scientific racism, such as Josiah Nott, Samuel Cartwright, and Samuel G. Morton, apparently learned their science from him.[26] Jefferson's theories about race "became indisputable dogma within a decade after his death."[27]

A Southern Planter in the Age of Enlightenment

Jefferson's attitude toward slavery and his lack of any serious commitment to emancipation reflects his upbringing, class origins, and lifelong status as a wealthy landowner, slave owner, and southern aristocrat. At twenty-one he came into his inheritance: 5,000 acres and 22 slaves. His marriage to Martha Wayles Skelton brought him more slaves and land. By the end of the Revolution, when he was just forty years old, Jefferson commanded a "miniature state," with some 10,000 acres of land and nearly 200 slaves.[28] The only "citizens" in this "state" were Jefferson, his white relatives, and perhaps a few white employees.

As a slave owner, Jefferson was neither sadistic nor vicious. But he bought and sold slaves, punished them, and hunted them down when they escaped.[29] He advised his friends and relatives about purchasing slaves and gave them as gifts. He sold slaves away from their families to punish them and to make examples of them "in terrorem to others." Throughout his life he sold large numbers of slaves to raise cash.[30] In all these respects, Jefferson was an ordinary southern gentleman and master.

The traditional image of Jefferson is that of a slaveholder valiantly trying to come to terms with the inherent contradictions between slavery and the philosophy of the American Revolution. This image collapses under careful scrutiny. It will not do to defend Jefferson on the ground that he was a southerner, a slave owner, and a man of his times. We must compare him to his peers—the intellectual, political, and cultural leaders of his generation— and not to his Virginia neighbors. Jefferson, after all, is not an American icon because he was ordinary and mundane. Who would care if Jefferson had been average? We put him on our coins, currency, and stamps, we build monuments to him and name counties, cities, and state capitals for him, because he was special.

But on issues of slavery, race, and human equality, Jefferson was, as historian Robert McColley concludes "not ahead, but rather far behind, such public advocates of emancipation as John Jay and Alexander Hamilton of New York, Anthony Benezet and Benjamin Franklin of Philadelphia, and Robert Pleasants and Warner Mifflin of Virginia."[31] To this list we might add James Otis of Massachusetts, John and Henry Laurens of South Carolina, Jefferson's lifelong friend Dr. Benjamin Rush of Pennsylvania, Jefferson's mentor at William and Mary, George Wythe, his friend Judge St. George Tucker, and a host of others in Virginia, Maryland, and North Carolina. Reverend Dr. Samuel Stanhope Smith, the president of Princeton University, argued that Jefferson's "remarks upon the genius of the African negro" had "little foundation in true philosophy." Rev. Smith well understood how Jefferson's scientifically baseless conclusions and speculations undermined the concept of human equality in the early republic.[32] After the American Revolution, "European social evolutionists generally assumed that all people had innate abilities that would enable them eventually to ascend to the heights attained by Europeans and Euro-Americans." However, Jefferson, who "harboured doubts as to the abilities of the Negro race," was clearly out of step with this view.[33]

Criticism of Jefferson for his failure to act on slavery must be based on what his own generation expected from him and on his own actions compared with those of others in his generation. There was in fact "much support in the Chesapeake for abolishing slavery by one means or another, not only among leaders . . . but among the generality of people."[34] After the Revolution, many Europeans and Americans turned to Jefferson for answers, encouragement, and moral support in the struggle against human bondage. They were usually disappointed. Jefferson told his correspondents to look to the future, wait for the next generation to take control, or hope that diffusion, population growth, or some other natural process would solve the problem.

Meanwhile, many of his contemporaries set the standard for facing the challenge of slavery. Colonel John Laurens, for example, jeopardized his political career in South Carolina by strenuously urging the legislature to support compensated emancipation of slaves who would be organized in all-black regiments. Laurens believed this would benefit "those who are un-justly deprived of the rights of mankind" while simultaneously helping the patriot cause. Laurens died before he could liberate his own slaves, but his father, Henry, carried out his son's manumission plan.[35] Jefferson never sug-gested enrolling slaves, although as a revolutionary governor he was in a position to do so. Moreover, he never contemplated either enlisting his own slaves in the patriot army or emancipating them.

The dramatic growth of Virginia's free black population after the Revolu-tion suggests that many masters took Jefferson's words about "self-evident truths" at face value. In 1782, when the state adopted a law allowing volun-tary manumissions, about 2,000 free blacks lived in Virginia. By 1790 this figure had risen to 12,766, and it continued to rise to 20,124 in 1800 and 30,570 in 1810. In the three decades after the Revolution, free blacks "were the fastest-growing element in the Southern population." Some of this growth was due to natural increase, but most came from manumissions.[36]

Voluntary manumission attracted leaders of the Revolution with large numbers of slaves as well as relatively unknown individuals with just a few. Virginians with far more slaves than Jefferson freed their bondsmen and bondswomen. In the 1790s Robert "Councillor" Carter manumitted his more than 500 slaves while providing them with land and housing.[37] John and Jonathan Pleasants, who together owned almost as many slaves as Jefferson, attempted to manumit them in their wills by directing their executor, Robert Pleasants, to manumit their slaves if and when Virginia law allowed private manumissions. Through the persistent efforts of Robert Pleasants, these wishes came to fruition. George Washington freed all his slaves in his will and "pro-vided for apprenticeship and tenancy for the able-bodied and lodgings and pensions for the aged." Washington hated slavery and declined to participate in its most seamy aspects, refusing "either to buy or sell slaves, 'as you would do cattle at a market.'" In 1785 Joseph Mayo, an obscure planter from Powhatan, "astonished some of [Jefferson's] acquaintances" by bequeathing freedom to his 150 to 170 slaves. When Jefferson's kinsman John Randolph of Roanoke died in 1833, he manumitted all of his hundreds of slaves and provided money to purchase land for them.[38]

Had Jefferson freed his slaves, he would have given great impetus to this manumission movement. Certainly his well-known condemnations of the institution led some of his contemporaries to believe that he would also act. Yet if Jefferson condemned slavery, it was because he was far more concerned about what slavery did to whites than about what it did to blacks. He feared miscegenation, the moral debasement of whites, and violent conflict between the races. A closer look at his public career and private life illustrates these themes, showing there is little substance to the antislavery Jefferson.[39]

A Young Man with Noble Ideas

Historians have used two events from his prerevolutionary career—his support for a bill in the Virginia legislature to allow voluntary manumission and his failed attempt as a young attorney to win freedom for a man of mixed racial ancestry held in servitude—to argue for Jefferson's early hostility to slavery. However, a careful examination of this history illustrates the weakness of Jefferson's youthful opposition to slavery.

In 1769, as a freshman legislator in the House of Burgesses, Jefferson supported a bill to allow private manumission of slaves. Unfortunately, there are no existing records from 1769 to illuminate the history of this proposed law. The slim documentation of this effort consists of a letter Jefferson wrote in 1814 and an autobiographical note from 1821. The first account came in response to Edward Coles's request that Jefferson endorse Coles's plan to free his slaves. In a long and revealing letter, in which he ultimately urged Coles not to manumit his slaves, Jefferson wrote about his earliest public opposition to slavery:

> I drew to this subject [manumission] the attention of Col. Bland, one of the oldest, ablest, & most respected members, and he undertook to move for certain moderate extensions of the protection of the laws to these people. I seconded his motion, and as a younger member, was more spared in the debate; but he was denounced as an enemy of his country, & treated with the grossest indecorum.

Seven years after he wrote Coles, Jefferson recalled in his autobiography: "I made one effort in that body for the permission of the emancipation of slaves, which was rejected."[40]

The incident shows that Jefferson was troubled by slavery, but not that he wanted to end the institution. Bland's proposal was not radical: it would not have freed a single slave. In simply changing existing Virginia law to allow masters to manumit their slaves, the proposed legislation was fully in accord with revolutionary-era notions of slave owners' property rights. Nor is it clear how, according to Jefferson's claim, it would have extended the "protection of the laws" to slaves. In fact, the law was designed to allow masters to dispose of their slaves as they wished. Only when their masters chose to free them would former slaves have been under the same laws as other free blacks in Virginia. Moreover, in prerevolutionary Virginia, free blacks did not have the same "protection of the laws" as whites.

Still, in a society where manumission was illegal, the Bland proposal would have been a meaningful step toward freedom, one that the Virginia legislature finally did take in 1782. Whether or not Jefferson took the initiative in 1769—and it seems likely that he exaggerated his role in retrospect just as he exaggerated the libertarian nature of the proposal—this would be the last time he stuck out his neck on slavery while holding office. The lesson Jefferson learned in 1769 was to avoid discussions of slavery that might lead to unpleasant confrontations with his colleagues. However troubled he may have been by slavery, Jefferson never again worked for amelioration or reform.

The other "antislavery" incident of his early career was his role in *Howell v. Netherland* (1770), in which he represented Samuel Howell, a man of mixed racial ancestry, who was held in servitude until age thirty-one. His status was based on the fact that he, his mother, and his grandmother were born out of wedlock. A 1705 law required that illegitimate mixed-race children of white women would be bound out by the church wardens until age thirty-one. A 1723 law further provided that if a female held to service under the 1705 law had children before her servitude ended, these children would also be bound out under the same terms.[41]

Howell's grandmother was the bastard child of a white woman and a black or mulatto man and had been bound out according to the 1705 law. When she was no older than eighteen, the grandmother gave birth to a female child, who in turn was bound out until age thirty-one. At nineteen she gave birth to Howell and the court bound him to Netherland. When he was twenty-eight, Howell sued Netherland for his freedom. Using unpersuasive legal arguments and some natural rights theory, Jefferson vainly sought to convince the court that this man should be free.[42]

This case was neither about slavery nor "the surest indication of his attitude [toward slavery] at this time."[43] Samuel Howell, the plaintiff, was not a slave and would soon gain his freedom, no matter what the court decided. In his argument, Jefferson clearly made this point, reminding the court that the plaintiff and his maternal ancestors were all born free, although his mother and grandmother had been subject to an indenture.

More important, Jefferson's arguments focused on race and status, not slavery. We cannot know Howell's color but the evidence suggests he was mostly of white ancestry. His great-grandmother was white and his great-grandfather may have been half-white. We do not know the race of his grandfather and father, but under the 1705 and 1723 laws Howell would have been in servitude until age thirty-one if all of his ancestors except the great-grandfather had been white. The plaintiff's mixed heritage may have affected Jefferson's willingness to take the case. This is a plausible inference from his argument that Netherland's interpretation of the law was dangerous "[b]ecause it would make servants of the children of white servants or apprentices, which nobody will say is right."[44]

It is true that in this case Jefferson articulated the notion that "under law of nature . . . we are all born free."[45] But the key issue in this case—as in so many of Jefferson's writings on slavery, race, and liberty—hinges on what Jefferson meant by the term "we." It is likely that Howell had predominantly white ancestry, appeared white, and was, in Jefferson's view, a white person. Jefferson's argument was that the children of white women should not be made into temporary slaves.

Jefferson's private actions regarding his own slaves' attempts to gain freedom further undermine his antislavery reputation for this early period. Because the proposed 1769 statute failed to pass, no master could, on his own, free a slave within the colony of Virginia. But even without a statute there were ways a master could free his slaves. One was by not interfering with their determined efforts to become free by running away. But Jefferson chased after his slaves, even as he urged the legislature to allow other masters to free theirs. In September 1769, Jefferson advertised that he would pay up to ten pounds for the return of Sandy, a runaway. Sandy was caught and Jefferson later sold him for one hundred pounds.[46] It was also possible to voluntarily manumit slaves in other places, such as Pennsylvania. Between 1775 and 1800, Jefferson lived in or visited a number of free jurisdictions, including Massachusetts, Pennsylvania, and France, but he never voluntarily manumitted a slave in any of them.

The Declaration of Independence

Three years after he sold Sandy, Jefferson pledged his life, fortune, and "sacred honor" to the cause of American independence and liberty. He also lent his brilliant rhetorical skills to the cause. Jefferson considered his paternity of the Declaration of Independence one of his three most important accomplishments, along with drafting Virginia's Statute of Religious Freedom and being the "Father of the University of Virginia." More than anything else, his drafting of the Declaration—and a clause on the slave trade deleted from that draft—has sustained the myth of the antislavery Jefferson.

The most obvious connection between slavery and the Declaration is in the preamble, a clarion call to liberty. Its sentiments undermine the morality of slavery and its legitimacy under natural law. For those who would make Jefferson an antislavery icon, the preamble is crucial. Antebellum opponents of slavery as diverse as William Lloyd Garrison, Frederick Douglass, and Abraham Lincoln relied on this language to bolster their opposition to human bondage. In dedicating the nation to the dismantling of slavery and to a "new birth of freedom," Lincoln hearkened back to the Declaration, which "brought forth . . . a new nation, conceived in Liberty and dedicated to the proposition that all men are created equal."[47]

Before turning to the Declaration itself, it is necessary to examine a clause of Jefferson's left out of the final document. In his original draft, Jefferson complained that King George III had "waged cruel war against human nature itself, violating its most sacred rights of life and liberty" by perpetuating the African slave trade. Calling the African trade "piratical warfare," Jefferson complained that "a CHRISTIAN king of Great Britain" was so "Determined to keep open a market where MEN" were bought and sold that he used his "negative" to suppress "every legislative attempt to prohibit or to restrain this execrable commerce."[48] While condemning the king for supporting the African trade, Jefferson also denounced him for encouraging slaves to enlist in the British army, "exciting those very people to rise in arms among us, and to purchase that liberty of which he has deprived them, by murdering the people on whom he also obtruded them: thus paying off former crimes committed against the LIBERTIES of one people, with crimes which he urges to commit against the LIVES of another."[49]

Although this "vehement philippic against negro slavery," as John Adams called it, never made it into the final version of the Declaration,[50] it has made it into the public mind as proof of Jefferson's opposition to slavery. But Adams's characterization of the clause is misleading. Congress deleted this clause for a variety of reasons, including the complaints of Georgia and South Carolina, still active participants in the transatlantic trade. But, even without the specific complaints of those states, "the charge," as Merrill Peterson suggests, "simply did not ring true. And Jefferson's bloated rhetoric gave it away."[51] In any case, Jefferson was attacking the African slave trade, not slavery. The arguments against the African trade were humanitarian, economic, and prudential. Many Virginians opposed the trade for "selfish considerations, such as protecting the value of their property in slaves and securing their communities from the dangers of an ever-increasing slave population," especially when that population was made up of recent arrivals from Africa, who tended to be more rebellious than other slaves.[52]

Jefferson certainly fit this class of Virginians. Because Jefferson sold slaves throughout his life, the African trade threatened him economically. Similarly, Jefferson always argued for curbs on the growth of America's black population. He almost always tied any discussion of manumission or emancipation to colonization or "expatriation." Ending the African trade would slow the growth of the nation's black population. Thus, the attack on King George III dovetailed with Jefferson's negrophobia and his interests as a Virginia slave owner and did not necessarily indicate opposition to slavery itself.

Jefferson's last charge against the King on the slavery issue—and the only one incorporated into the final document—is one his biographers never discuss. It is his complaint that the King "has excited domestic insurrections against us." The meaning is unmistakable.[53] For southern slave owners, "domestic insurrections" had only one meaning: slave revolts. Jefferson's original draft of the Declaration complains that the king has enslaved people "against human nature itself"; he then proceeds to condemn the king for enabling those people to fight for their freedom. Jefferson failed to consider the irony of Americans rebelling against the king while complaining that slaves were rebelling against them.

For Jefferson, former slaves in uniform were far more threatening than the king's white army. British soldiers killed enemies in battle, but slaves in uniform, fighting for their own liberty, were "murderers." Like so much of Jefferson's writings on slavery, his draft of the Declaration reveals his self-deluding inability to see slaves as human beings. They are mere objects, in this case to be used in the propaganda war against the king. Not a few Englishmen read the Declaration and wondered, as did Samuel Johnson, "How is it that we hear the loudest *yelps* for liberty among the drivers of negroes?"[54] Few of the revolutionaries yelped louder, or with more eloquence, than the master of Monticello; few owned so many Negroes.

Revolutionary Slaveholder

Jefferson might have blunted the biting criticism of Johnson and others if he had taken some actions against slavery during the Revolution. But he did not. Certainly he could have used the Revolution to sever or diminish his personal ties to slavery. During the war, many masters enlisted their male slaves in the revolutionary army. The master got the slave's enlistment bounty and made an important double contribution to the cause of liberty by providing a soldier for the Continental line and giving freedom to a slave. The slave gained his freedom and earned a place in American society.

Thomas Jefferson did not enlist any of his slaves, thus forfeiting a singular opportunity to free some of his slaves, be recompensed for his loss, and, as a revolutionary officeholder, take a lead in recruiting soldiers. At the time, Jefferson had not yet accumulated huge personal debts. This young man with a great future forfeited a chance to make a statement about liberty that went beyond parchment protests.[55]

Jefferson's failure to act is all the more striking in view of his reaction to a wartime event affecting his slaves. In 1781 Lord Cornwallis occupied Jefferson's Elkhill plantation. In addition to taking animals and food, and destroying property, the British troops carried off thirty or so of Jefferson's slaves. Jefferson later wrote to the English intellectual William Gordon, "had this been to give them freedom he would have done right, but it was to consign them to inevitable death from the small pox and putrid fever then raging in his camp." Jefferson's biographer notes that "[t]his, indeed, was the fate of most of the slaves, and Jefferson recovered only five of them."[56]

The important question is not what Cornwallis did with the slaves or what he might have done had he won at Yorktown, but what Jefferson did. He vigorously sought to recover his slaves. Had Jefferson done this to give them freedom, then he "would have done right." But Jefferson chased down his slaves to consign them to lifetime bondage. The fact remains that many slaves—including some owned by Jefferson—gained their freedom by escaping to British lines; none gained it by remaining on the Jefferson plantations.[57]

Revolutionary Lawmaker

Jefferson's failure to take any action to end slavery is underscored by the unique opportunity he had, from 1776 to 1779, to shape the laws of Virginia. Shortly after he signed the Declaration, Jefferson left the national Congress to serve in the Virginia legislature. He remained there until June 1779, when he became governor. A careful examination of Jefferson's role as a revolutionary lawmaker raises further questions about his reputation for opposing slavery. It shows that Jefferson's support for independence and liberty for white America ironically made him less sympathetic to the natural rights claims of blacks.

Jefferson's legislative career was one of the most satisfying and creative periods in his life. Early on he proposed a bill for a complete overhaul of Virginia's laws. As chair of the revision committee, Jefferson was able "to set forth in due course a long-range program emphasizing humane criminal laws, complete religious freedom, and the diffusion of education, and thus to appear on the page of history as a major prophet of intellectual liberty and human enlightenment." During and after Jefferson's service in the legislature, Virginia adopted many of the committee's proposed laws, including bills on religious freedom, the abolition of primogeniture and entail, education, citizenship, and the criminal code. More than two centuries later scholars still praise these legal changes, "and the credit for all of these belongs to [Jefferson]."[58]

The committee provided Jefferson, who was "pre-eminently a political architect, looking to the future,"[59] with a unique opportunity to change the law of slavery in Virginia. Unlike 1769, when he was a freshman legislator, Jefferson was now a respected national leader with an international reputation, chairing a committee to revise the laws of the largest and most important state in the new nation. Here was the moment and the man to strike at slavery. Instead, Jefferson struck at slaves and free blacks.

One of Jefferson's goals was to modernize Virginia's criminal code, incorporating the humane concepts found in the writings of the Italian criminologist, Cesare de Beccari. He reduced the number of capital crimes for white offenders to two and removed various barbaric customs from the criminal code. But, "except for the privilege of knowing that their corpses would not rot on gibbets, the slaves profited little from the enlightened humanitarianism" of Jefferson's draft code. His proposed law tightened the slave code, increased penalties for slave criminals, and "retained most of the inhumane features of the colonial slave law." Indeed, Jefferson's recommendations were so extreme that even the legislature eventually rejected some of the more vicious aspects of Jefferson's proposed criminal code for slaves.[60]

Jefferson was proud of his proposed liberalization of the rules for white immigrants seeking citizenship. But this same law, adopted just before he became governor, prohibited free blacks from becoming citizens. Under another law, Jefferson proposed that any slave manumitted in the state had to leave Virginia within a year or "be out of the protection of the laws." Free blacks coming into the state, except seamen, were to be outlawed. Visiting seamen were given a twenty-four-hour grace period before they were outlawed. Jefferson's proposed laws would have banished any white woman bearing "a child by a negro or mulatto." If she failed to leave the state, the woman would be outlawed and her child would be bound out for an unspecified time before being banished from the state.[61]

The legislature rejected Jefferson's proposed legislation for free blacks, manumitted slaves, and white women who bore mixed-race children. Shortly after Jefferson left the governorship, the legislature passed a liberal manumission law that specifically allowed manumitted slaves to remain in the state.[62] Jefferson's failed proposals nevertheless stand in stark contrast with his earlier support for a manumission law, his arguments against "mak[ing] servants of the children of white servants or apprentices,"[63] and his endorsement of the natural rights of "life, liberty, and the pursuit of happiness." How can we balance Jefferson's support for the 1769 manumission law with the law he proposed a decade later? How do we interpret his arguments against punishing the children of white women in *Howell v. Netherland* in light of his proposal to exile white women and their mulatto children? Had Jefferson soured on black freedom in the preceding decade, or had he never favored manumission in the first place?

The answers to these questions are truly complex but go to the heart of understanding Jefferson's complex views on race and sex. In *Howell v. Netherland,* Jefferson had sought the freedom of the child of a woman who was of mixed ancestry to begin with, but who appeared to be white. She had had a child with someone who was probably white; that child, Howell, also appeared to be white. Thus, in this case Jefferson was attempting to secure the freedom of someone who was white in appearance and whose mother looked white as well. In his proposed laws, Jefferson wanted to stigmatize white women and their offspring if those white women had children with nonwhite men. In other words, in *Howell* Jefferson wanted to privilege whiteness and in his proposed law he wanted to punish those who undermined whiteness.

His advocacy of voluntary manumission in 1769 contrasts with his opposition to the presence of free blacks in the state in the 1780s, and indicates that Jefferson's support for manumission had never been very strong in the first place. The fact that he did not mention this support in any of his letters or writings until 1814 bolsters this theory. The changing circumstances created by the Revolution also may have altered Jefferson's views on black freedom. During the Revolution, Jefferson saw his republican theories about equality and citizenship come into their own. This forced him to confront the problem of race and free blacks in a republican society without any royal government to intervene. During the colonial period, there were considerable barriers to voting. In 1769 blacks could not vote in any of the colonies, and no one was likely to suggest they should.[64] Thus in 1769 Jefferson could favor liberalized manumission laws; he did not have to worry about the free blacks having a political role in his society—under British rule they would have none. But by 1779 free blacks could invoke Jefferson's own stirring words to claim citizenship and the franchise. Jefferson approved of an expanded franchise after the Revolution, but he never envisioned free blacks as voters or citizens. Jefferson's dilemma was that the only alternative to black citizenship was a large nonvoting population of free blacks that he believed would endanger the republic. Blinded by negrophobia and notions of black inferiority, Jefferson could not allow free blacks to remain in republican Virginia.[65]

The free blacks and slaves of Virginia would have been better off if the British had won the war. "From the perspective of the black masses," as the late legal historian A. Leon Higginbotham concluded, "the Revolution merely assured the plantation owners of their right to continue the legal 'tyranny' of slavery."[66] Although he would have been uncomfortable with the word tyranny applied to him, Jefferson could hardly have disagreed with this conclusion.

A Manumission Law That Never Was

As chair of the committee to revise Virginia's laws, Jefferson was in the ideal position to work toward gradual emancipation. But he failed to take the lead. And when legislators approached Jefferson with draft legislation that would have brought gradual emancipation to Virginia, he declined to add it to the proposed revisions. He later explained it was "better that this should be kept back" and only offered as an amendment,[67] although it is unclear why this would have been a better strategy. It seems more likely that Jefferson simply did not want the issue brought to the floor for any debate. Confronted with a chance to work toward public emancipation or private manumission, Jefferson backpedaled.

In his *Notes on the State of Virginia,* Jefferson wrote that a bill "to emancipate all slaves born after passing the act" was not "reported by the revisors," but that "an amendment containing it was prepared, to be offered the legislature whenever the bill should be taken up." Under this proposed amendment, the children of slaves would be educated and then "colonized" out of the state.[68] If Jefferson or anyone else ever prepared such an amendment, no copy of it has survived. The first appearance of the text of this amendment was in the *Notes*.

Jefferson wrote *Notes on Virginia* in 1781, revised it in 1783–1784, and made a final revision in France, "before turning his manuscript over" to his French publisher "late in 1784 or early in 1785." By the time Jefferson left for France, it was clear that no one would introduce the emancipation/colonization scheme. Nevertheless, Jefferson did not revise his account of the emancipation amendment. Jefferson repeated this account in his authorized edition published by John Stockdale in London in 1787.[69] There is no indication why Jefferson persisted in telling his European readers that this law would be introduced, when he knew it had not been, and would not be, proposed.

Curiously, Jefferson never altered the *Notes* to reflect what Virginia *did* do at this time, which was to pass legislation allowing masters to manumit their slaves.[70] Virginia passed this law in 1782, well before Jefferson left for France. Jefferson's silence may reflect the fact that the manumission law was not part of Jefferson's program, but instead resulted from the pleas of citizens seeking to free their own slaves. Jefferson may have ignored the law because he did not like it—this law allowed manumitted blacks to remain in Virginia, whereas Jefferson wanted former slaves to be forced to leave the state. Finally, perhaps, in exaggerating the prospects for a general emancipation, Jefferson may have been telling his European friends what he thought they wanted to hear. His failure to revise the *Notes* created the false impression that Virginia was prepared to act boldly against slavery.

Jefferson later claimed that the revisors of Virginia's laws never proposed the amendment because "the public mind would not yet bear the proposition." This account is diametrically opposed to his assertion in 1774 in *A Summary View of the Rights of British America* that "the abolition of domestic slavery is the great object of desire in those colonies where it was unhappily introduced in their infant state."[71] Yet it is clear that Jefferson was not seriously interested in either allowing for private manumission or ending slavery, whatever the state of the "public mind." He was far more concerned with ridding the state of free blacks and creating a criminal code to keep slaves in line. Jefferson introduced laws, which failed to pass, to make this happen.

When it came to slavery, it seems likely, however, that Jefferson used the term "public mind" to explain what was actually in his own mind. A brief look at Jefferson's role in shaping the public mind in 1776 illustrates this. Before July 1776, most Americans were not prepared to declare their independence; when Jefferson penned the Declaration, public opinion needed to be shaped by argument and debate. Jefferson's brilliant prose in the Declaration helped accomplish that. The manumission movement faced similar obstacles. Many revolutionary Virginians, although surely nothing close to a majority, were ready to consider some form of gradual emancipation. Jefferson might have helped shape the public mind on emancipation, just as he had on independence. Even without Jefferson's lead, the legislature adopted a law allowing private manumission *without* expatriation. The adoption of this law suggests that on this question of manumission the "public mind"—and certainly the collective mind of the Virginia legislature—was far in advance of Jefferson's.

Jefferson's actions on the committee to revise Virginia's laws contrast with those of two prominent Virginia judges, George Wythe and St. George Tucker. During the post-revolutionary period, Wythe, Jefferson's teacher at William and Mary, publicly attacked slavery in *Hudgins* v. *Wrights*, arguing that the Virginia Constitution prohibited bondage.[72] Tucker overturned part of Wythe's ruling on constitutional grounds. But Tucker was on record as favoring a gradual emancipation law. In his *Dissertation on Slavery with a Proposal for the Gradual Abolition of It in the State of Virginia,* Tucker was "much bolder than Jefferson in advocating emancipation."[73] Tucker circulated his pamphlet throughout the state, hoping to attract support for his manumission scheme; Jefferson sought to limit circulation of *Notes on the State of Virginia* in order to avoid "irritation."

Jefferson's legislative service during the Revolution underscores his hostility to free blacks, his growing fear of miscegenation, and his persistent dodging of the problem of slavery. In these crucial respects, there was nothing revolutionary about Jefferson's lawmaking. To the contrary, his proposals concerning slavery and race were reactionary. Fortunately for Virginia's free blacks, masters who wanted to liberate their slaves, white women who chose to have liaisons with black men, and slaves convicted of crimes in Virginia, the legislature rejected most of Jefferson's proposals on slavery and race.

Emancipation Schemes

Despite his hostility to free blacks and his refusal to introduce a gradual emancipation proposal in the Virginia legislature, on two other occasions Jefferson went on record as favoring some sort of emancipation or curb on the spread of slavery. The thrust of both schemes, as well as the emancipation amendment described in the *Notes*, was to eliminate slavery in a jurisdiction (either Virginia or the Northwest) while at the same time preventing the growth of a free black population.

Gradual Emancipation and the Virginia Constitution

In the spring of 1783 it seemed likely that Virginia would call a convention to revise its constitution. In anticipation, Jefferson wrote a draft constitution that he privately shared with James Madison. This document included a provision to gradually end slavery in Virginia:

> The General assembly shall not . . . permit the introduction of any more slaves to reside in this state, or the continuance of slavery beyond the generation which shall be living on the 31st day of December 1800; all persons born after that day being hereby declared free.[74]

The draft constitution is an intriguing document, unfinished and ambiguous. The slavery clause suggests that, in the deepest recesses of his heart and mind, Jefferson *knew* that something had to be done about slavery. Jefferson sent a copy of his draft to Madison, but asked him not to share its contents with his colleagues. The draft might instead "serve as a basis for your amendment, or may suggest amendments to a better groundwork."[75]

Jefferson's proposal is congruent with his other responses to slavery. Characteristically, Jefferson refused to publicly advocate abolition, instead expecting Madison or others to promote his program. Similarly, Jefferson sought to delay any direct or immediate confrontation with the institution—his emancipation program would not go into effect until seventeen years after he wrote it! Finally, the proposal itself was ambivalent. Even if his program succeeded in the convention, the clause, as Jefferson wrote it, was not self-executing. The draft constitution admonished the "General Assembly" to act. If the assembly did not act, the clause would not go into effect.

Jefferson's first provision, banning the importation of slaves, would not have required much new legislation. By the time he wrote this proposal, Virginia had already prohibited the importation of any new slaves, except by bona fide immigrants.[76] The proposal would have changed this law only by preventing immigrants from bringing slaves into Virginia. If there was a departure in this proposal from Jefferson's lifelong views on slavery, it was in the lack of any requirement of expatriation of former slaves. The precedent here was the 1782 act allowing masters to free their slaves *without* requiring expatriation.

For Jefferson, the 1782 law was problematic. He was opposed to the presence of free blacks in Virginia. How, then, could he propose an end to slavery if former slaves could remain in the state? Jefferson's draft gradual emancipation scheme offered at least a partial solution to this problem. The seventeen-year delay in implementing the plan would give Virginia masters years to sell their slaves out of the state. After 1801 masters would have been able to move pregnant women out of the state, so their children would be born as slaves.[77] Jefferson may have hoped to achieve at least a partial expatriation of free blacks because individual masters would make the economic decision to sell their slaves elsewhere.

Slavery in the West

Whatever Jefferson hoped to accomplish in his draft constitution, Virginia did not in the end call a state constitutional convention and thus the emancipation scheme never reached the public. Shortly after he wrote this document, Jefferson was back in politics. In June 1784 Jefferson entered Congress, then operating under the Articles of Confederation. Here he took one more shot at slavery. Even if this salvo had landed on the target—and it did not— it would have been at best a glancing blow. Jefferson's "Plan of Government for the Western Territory" would have banned slavery after 1800.[78] Congress rejected the antislavery proviso. At this time, thousands of slaves were already in the West, and more were arriving daily in what later became Kentucky and Tennessee. Given the large slave population already in the territories south of the Ohio, as well as a fair number in what would become Indiana and Illinois, it seems unlikely that Jefferson's proposal, delaying emancipation for sixteen years, would have been successful. As William M. Wiecek notes, the phrasing of Jefferson's proposed ordinance "was, in effect, a permission to the western territories and states to establish slavery and retain it to the year 1800."[79] Delaying abolition in the West until 1800 would have given slave owners sixteen years to populate the region and to lobby for a change in the law.

Calling for a ban on slavery in the West was nevertheless an attack on the institution, if for no other reason than it would have put the government on record opposing its spread. Had Jefferson's ban passed, and had it worked, he might have continued in the direction of chipping away at slavery at the margins. Whatever his motivations—to reserve the West for free whites, to circumscribe the domestic slave trade, to diminish the demand for slaves in the new nation in order to undermine the African trade, or to strike a blow against an unjust institution—this was certainly a step in the right direction. However, it was a step from which Jefferson would later retreat. During the debates over the Missouri Compromise, Jefferson argued against prohibiting slavery in the West: a "geographical line, coinciding with a marked principle, moral and political," would stir the "angry passions of men." If Jefferson was inconsistent on slavery restriction, he was consistent in promoting what he considered best for white southerners. Always fearful of a concentration of blacks, slave or free, in 1820 he argued that introducing slavery in the West would lead to "diffusion," which would mean fewer blacks in the older slave states.[80]

Emancipation and the Notes on the State of Virginia

The *Notes on the State of Virginia* provide some of Jefferson's most important discussions of slavery, including an elaborate discussion of the emancipation scheme he never in fact proposed in the Virginia legislature. Before examining this scheme, it is worth noting Jefferson's general comments on slavery and race in the *Notes*.

Jefferson began his "Query XIV" of his *Notes on Virginia* with a discussion of the "administration of justice and a description of the laws." Much of this discussion centered on legal questions that had nothing to do with slavery. However, in explaining the laws of Virginia, Jefferson revealed his acceptance of slavery as an economic institution devoid of any moral or ethical concerns. Thus, Jefferson noted that slaves "were entailable under the monarchy," but "the first republican assembly" abolished such restrictions on property. Jefferson then turned to legislation that the assembly had not yet approved. He noted that a "remarkable" proposal pending before the legislature was "to make slaves distributable among the next of kin, as other moveables." That Jefferson thought this was "remarkable" suggests that his commitment to property was far greater than his opposition to slavery. Maintaining restrictions on the transfer of slave property would have made it less valuable, thereby encouraging manumission. Removing those restrictions enhanced the value of the property.[81]

Half a page after his discussion of slaves as "moveables," Jefferson mentioned the proposed bill "to emancipate all slaves born after the passing of the act," discussed above. Neither Jefferson nor anyone else ever introduced into the Virginia legislature the gradual emancipation program that Jefferson described. Nevertheless, he presented it to his European readers as one of the more "remarkable alterations proposed" in the revision of Virginia's laws.[82] Jefferson claimed that the proposal in the *Notes* was the same one that was to be introduced by amendment in the legislature. Since no one ever introduced it in the legislature, we can never know if the bill was ever actually on the agenda. What is clear, however, is that this proposal has all the marks of Jefferson's mature views on slavery, race, and emancipation; moreover, it was presented in the *Notes* in conjunction with Jefferson's most complete elaboration of his theories on slavery and race—an extraordinary discussion in a single paragraph five pages long.

According to Jefferson's proposal, children of slaves would remain with their parents until "a certain age," when they would be trained "to tillage, arts or sciences, according to their geniuses." The males would be fully emancipated at twenty-one, the females at eighteen. Then they would be "colonized to such place as the circumstances of the time should render most proper." Meanwhile, ships would travel "to other parts of the world for an equal number of white inhabitants" to be induced to come to America as paid agricultural laborers.[83]

This program was extremely impractical. The cost of removing Virginia's 200,000 slaves would have been enormous; finding willing white workers to enter Virginia's tobacco fields would have been almost impossible. Had this proposal been brought before the assembly, it probably would have been rejected. Aside from the unlikely chance of making such a program work, Jefferson's other comments in the *Notes* raise doubts about his own support for the proposal. It is in the rest of this rambling five-page paragraph that Jefferson offers his harsh views on the abilities of blacks.

Jefferson describes blacks as lacking "imagination," "reason," "forethought," and talents in poetry, art, oratory, and science. They even lacked basic human emotions: "Their griefs are transient" and their love was more like lust, lacking "a tender delicate mixture of sentiment and sensation." In contrast to white Roman slaves, black American slaves lacked skills in the "arts and sciences" even when they had been "liberally educated" and "lived in countries where the arts and sciences are cultivated to a considerable degree."[84] Jefferson's message is mixed. Under his emancipation scheme, the children of slaves would be educated, trained for freedom, and set free when ready. But they would never be ready for freedom because they were incapable of learning.

The Slave Trade, Louisiana, and the Presidency

As president, Jefferson signed a bill outlawing the African slave trade. Jefferson pushed for this bill. It is likely that the trade would have ended in

1808 if almost any of the early national leaders had been president. The swift passage of the law indicates the strong popular appeal of banning the trade. Opposition to the slave trade did not necessarily signify opposition to slavery.[85] There were significant economic reasons for opposing the trade. A cessation of the trade would preserve the market value of the excess slaves in Virginia and Maryland. Some slave owners opposed the trade on both humanitarian and racist grounds. It was one thing to inherit slaves or buy and sell people who had been raised as slaves, but quite another to enslave free people in Africa. Jefferson sympathized with "the unhappy human beings" who were "brought away from their native country, & whose wives, children & parents are now suffering for want of their aid & comfort."[86] He also opposed the trade because it increased the nation's black population.

As we saw in Chapter 1, in an elaborate bargain—the "dirty compromise" of the Constitutional Convention—the Framers prohibited Congress from banning the African trade before 1808. The Virginia delegation at the Convention, led by Washington and Madison, opposed the slave trade provision. The clause did not *require* Congress to abolish the trade in 1808, and advocates of the trade, mostly from the Carolinas and Georgia, expected to have enough clout in the future to keep the trade open past 1808.

In his annual message to Congress in December 1806, Jefferson recommended legislation to abolish the African trade "to withdraw the citizens of the United States from all further participation in those violations of human rights which have been so long continued on the unoffending inhabitants of Africa, and which the morality, the reputation, and the best interests of our country have long been eager to proscribe."[87] Congress quickly adopted legislation ending the trade on January 1, 1808. Historians have rightly noted that the 1808 law was a significant event in the struggle against slavery. It prevented hundreds of thousands of Africans from being brought to America, even if it probably had little effect on ending slavery in the United States.[88]

Jefferson's successful opposition to the slave trade forces us to ask why he failed to put his prestige, congressional majority, and popularity behind other antislavery reforms. After acquiring Louisiana, he did nothing to ban slavery in that vast territory. He might have used his influence to prohibit slavery throughout the territory, or at least limit it to what became the state of Louisiana. Either approach would have prevented Missouri from becoming a slave state and thus would have preempted the divisive debates of 1819–1821.[89] Jefferson also could have proposed a gradual emancipation bill for the District of Columbia. Similarly, he might have given diplomatic recognition to Haiti, thereby showing his support for ending slavery in the Americas and his commitment to self-determination for free blacks.[90] Haiti would also have provided a place to colonize free blacks, if any state, or the nation, ever implemented the type of emancipation with expulsion that Jefferson advocated. His failure to do any of these things highlights Jefferson's lack of commitment to ending slavery or limiting its growth. It also underscores his racism and his fear and hatred of free blacks. Jefferson might have aided the black revolutionaries in Haiti who emulated his own struggle against Britain. Instead, with "implacable malice" toward the black republic, Jefferson did everything in his power to undermine the Haitian Revolution, including banning trade with the island and offering to aid the French in reconquering the island.[91] In 1806 Congressman John Wayles Eppes, Jefferson's son-in-law, declared he would "pledge the Treasury of the United States that the Negro government should be destroyed." On this issue Eppes was clearly the spokesman for his father-in-law, the president.[92] Jefferson's domestic policy was no different. Instead of working to improve the condition of free blacks, Jefferson signed a law which "excluded blacks from carrying the United States mail," even if these blacks were citizens and voters in the states where they lived.[93]

Manumitting His Slaves

While Jefferson could not, or would not, work emancipation at the state level, or where the federal government had jurisdiction (such as Washington, D.C.), he certainly could have effected personal manumissions. Here was one area where Jefferson had absolute control. Jefferson repeatedly proclaimed his willingness to give up slavery. There was "not a man on earth who would sacrifice more," he claimed, "to relieve us from this heavy reproach, in any *practicable* way." Ending slavery, Jefferson claimed, "would not cost me a second thought, if in that way, a general emancipation and *expatriation* could be effected."[94]

Throughout his life, Jefferson had opportunities to free some or all of his slaves. During the Revolution, Jefferson could have freed his male slaves by enlisting them in the army. From 1782 to 1805, Virginia law allowed masters to manumit slaves without requiring they leave the state. From 1805 until 1815, emancipated slaves could remain in the state with permission of the legislature. After 1815, county courts could grant exemptions for "extraordinary merit." Courts appear to have interpreted this phrase quite loosely.[95] Furthermore, throughout his life Jefferson could have emancipated any or all of his slaves in Pennsylvania or some other free jurisdiction.

With a very few exceptions, Jefferson never took advantage of these opportunities. He believed manumitted slaves could not survive in the United States. "Deep rooted prejudices entertained by whites; ten thousand recollections, by the blacks, of the injuries they have sustained, new provocations; the real distinctions which nature has made; and many other circumstances" made freedom within Virginia impossible. The major "other circumstance" was Jefferson's almost paranoid fear of a "mixture of colour here." "Expatriation" was always part of Jefferson's notion of a proper manumission: "If a slave can have a country in this world, it must be any other in preference to that in which he is born to live and labour for another." Jefferson supported colonization even as he understood that the cost of moving so many people to Africa made it "impossible to look at the enterprise a second time." However, "expatriation to the governments of the W[est] I[ndies] of their own colour" was "entirely practicable and greatly preferable to the mixture of colour here." In 1824 he again urged gradual emancipation combined with colonization in Haiti, forgetting, of course, that as president he had made economic war on Haiti and refused to give diplomatic recognition to that country. This was a reaffirmation of the plan suggested in the *Notes* forty years earlier to ensure that emancipated slaves were "removed beyond the reach of mixture."[96]

Even if colonization was impractical on the grand scale, it was practical on the private scale. But Jefferson never took advantage of this option. Jefferson could have freed any of his slaves by sending them out of the state, or he could have freed the slaves he took to Europe and the North. There were no bars to manumission when he lived in or visited Pennsylvania, Massachusetts, New York, the District of Columbia, Great Britain, and France. Manumission in France would have been the ideal solution for some of his slaves: under French law they were already free and would easily have merged into that country's growing free black community.[97] But Jefferson did not free Sally or James Hemings while they were in France. On the contrary, he carefully avoided any unpleasant encounter with French law that might have led these slaves to claim their liberty. He also advised other Americans there how to retain their slaves in violation of French law. He wrote, no doubt from personal experience, of "an instance where a person bringing in a slave, and saying nothing about it, has not been disturbed in his possession."[98]

Jefferson's biographers tend to avoid saying how many slaves he actually freed. Instead they talk in vague terms about him freeing "particular" slaves who were "faithful" and skilled.[99] This vagueness is not surprising, because the numbers are so embarrassingly small. It would almost be better for Jefferson's reputation if he had freed none—then at least we might plausibly argue that he consistently opposed manumission or that he forgot. But he did not forget to manumit his slaves. He just didn't do it.

During his life and in death Jefferson freed only eight slaves: two in the 1790s, one in 1822, and five by his will in 1826. This small number allows for an instructive, detailed examination of each manumission. These slaves

Only freed members of the
Hemings family (who were his
relatives)

154   *SLAVERY AND THE FOUNDERS*

were indeed "particular" since they represent less than two percent of the total number of slaves Jefferson owned in his lifetime.[100] Despite the claims of his traditional biographers, skills and fidelity were not the tests Jefferson used to free his slaves. What were the characteristics of these emancipated slaves? There seems to have been one major test and one minor test.

The major test was simple: the only slaves Jefferson freed were members of the Hemings family and thus were Jefferson's own relatives by marriage, blood, or both.[101] This relationship has not always been clearly understood. Sally Hemings and her siblings were the children of a slave named Elizabeth Hemings, commonly called Betty, and Betty's master, John Wayles. John Wayles was also the father of Jefferson's wife, Martha. Thus, Sally was Jefferson's half sister-in-law; her siblings were similarly related to Jefferson. Sally's children, as we now know, were also Jefferson's.[102] The second test was gender-based. With only one exception, all the slaves he manumitted were male. Jefferson seems to have had little regard for the liberty of his female relatives in bondage. In the end, Jefferson was never generous with freedom, even for his African-American relatives. Moreover, the three manumissions during his lifetime—including the one woman he freed—were not a result of philanthropic and humane instincts.

In 1794 Robert Hemings, Sally's older brother, purchased his freedom from Jefferson for sixty pounds. His future employer, George Frederick Stras, "advanced the money."[103] Robert was in fact already living with Stras and working for him at the time of the sale. This is a manumission in only the most technical sense. Jefferson did not grant Robert his freedom for his faithful service or out of political conviction; Jefferson sold Robert his freedom. Jefferson apparently agreed to give up Robert only because he was convinced that Stras had already "debauched" Robert, and thus he "complied reluctantly with an agreement by which Stras in essence purchased a number of years of Robert's service and retained the deed of emancipation until Robert had reimbursed him by serving out his time."[104]

Although Jefferson sold him as a slave, Robert was probably entitled to his freedom. Robert had accompanied Jefferson to Boston in 1784 and was therefore legally free under Massachusetts law. It is quite likely that Virginia's courts would have recognized that freedom had Robert pursued it. The most prominent Virginia jurists of this period—such as St. George Tucker and George Wythe—were far more hostile to slavery than Jefferson was.[105]

The case of James Hemings is similar. Like his sister Sally (whom Jefferson never freed), James Hemings had lived with Jefferson in Paris and was clearly free under French law. The great Jefferson biographer Dumas Malone invokes James as another example of Jefferson's judicious manumission policy: while in Philadelphia, Jefferson "signed an agreement to free him after he had returned to Monticello and stayed there long enough to teach somebody else how to cook—presumably in the French manner." Merrill Peterson describes the manumission agreement as a bargain that favored James, "who won his freedom upon fulfilling the pledge to teach his art [of cooking] to a worthy successor."[106] These assessments are implausible and do not comport with the defensive and apologetic language of the agreement.

> Having been at great expence in having James Hemings taught the art of cookery, desiring to befriend him, and to require from him as little in return as possible, I do hereby promise & declare, that if the said James shall go with me to Monticello in the course of the ensuing winter, when I go to reside there myself, and shall continue until he shall have taught such persons as I shall place under him for the purpose to be a good cook, this previous condition being performed, he shall be thereupon made free, and I will thereupon execute all proper instruments to make him free.[107]

This is not the language of a benevolent manumission; it is the language of a contract between Jefferson and a suspicious and hostile party. Indeed, the very existence of the agreement undermines any notion of benevolence. Had he been willing to free James Hemings, Jefferson could have done so without signing an agreement for future manumission. Jefferson could have simply taken James back to Monticello, told him to train another cook, and after he did so freed him. But Jefferson did not do that, because it is clear that "having been at great expence" for Jame's training as cook Jefferson was unwilling to lose James Hemings.

Why, then, did Jefferson sign this agreement? He may have done it to avoid a suit from the Pennsylvania Abolition Society (PAS) in Philadelphia.[108] Under French law, James was free. Once society members or others opposed to slavery found out that James had been in France, they may have threatened a lawsuit to vindicate the right. This is particularly true because almost all of the members of the PAS were Federalists, and by this time some of them might have had few qualms about going after the leader of the emerging opposition party. As Gary Nash has noted, in Philadelphia it was "almost an oddity" to find a Jeffersonian involved with the Pennsylvania Abolition Society.[109] Jefferson surely would have wanted to avoid the embarrassment of a lawsuit over the freedom of a slave who was his wife's half brother. This "voluntary manumission" looks suspiciously like a bargain between Jefferson and whoever was threatening to intervene on behalf of James. James, who remained in bondage an extra three years, was the short-term loser. It is possible he acquiesced in the agreement because it gave him an opportunity to see his family once again before returning to Philadelphia. In 1796 Jefferson finally freed James.[110] Although Virginia law allowed him to remain in the state, James chose to return to Philadelphia, and Jefferson generously gave him thirty dollars for the trip.

The only woman Jefferson freed was Harriet Hemings, the twenty-year-old daughter of Sally. In 1822 she ran away with her brother Beverley. Jefferson freed Harriet while she was on the run, but not her twenty-four-year-old brother.[111] Perhaps he blamed Beverley for the escape. Given the circumstances of Harriet's emancipation, it can hardly be called voluntary. None of Jefferson's biographers discuss this manumission.

This brings us to Jefferson's posthumous manumission of five Hemings family members: Joe Fosset, the son of Sally's sister Mary; Burwell, the son of Sally's sister Bett; Sally's brother, John Hemings; and Sally's sons Madison and Eston Hemings. Jefferson gave money to Burwell and tools to the other two adults. He allowed the adults to live on his lands for free, giving them a log house and an acre of land for their own use. Despite his lifelong opposition to the presence of free blacks in Virginia, he asked his executor to petition the legislature to allow this tiny handful of former slaves to remain in the state.[112]

Yet even in Jefferson's benevolence, much was lacking. He directed his executors to allow the three men to live on land "convenient to them with respect to the residence of their wives."[113] Jefferson owned Joe Fosset's wife, but did not provide for her freedom or the freedom of their children. She would later be sold to pay the debts of Jefferson's estate. Joe Fosset would spend the rest of his life trying to accumulate enough money to purchase his family, who were scattered after they were sold at auction to pay Jefferson's debts. Jefferson's daughter owned the wife of John Hemings. Jefferson made no attempt to acquire her so that she might live in freedom with her husband.[114] John was more fortunate than Joe, since his wife remained at Monticello after most of Jefferson's slaves were auctioned off. While he provided for the freedom of the teenage Madison and Eston Hemings when they turned twenty-one, Jefferson did not manumit their mother, Sally.

Jefferson could have provided for the freedom of more than the five "faithful" slaves manumitted in his will.[115] Jefferson might have asked that his slaves be sent to Liberia: the American Colonization Society probably would have assumed the costs, as it did for less famous masters. In the context of Jefferson's own opposition to slavery, colonization made sense. Providing for the colonization of his slaves would have fit perfectly with Jefferson's lifelong assertions that he would support emancipation with expatriation. Of course, some of his slaves might not have wanted to end their days in a foreign place. Jefferson could have given his slaves the opportunity to choose between slavery in Virginia or freedom in Africa or elsewhere. Only a month before Jefferson died, Herbert Elder, a master in Petersburg, provided just such an opportunity for his slaves. Thirteen of Elder's fourteen slaves chose freedom on the continent of their ancestors.

Like Jefferson, Elder died with many debts. Elder's executor rented the slaves out to pay the debts of the estate; then he made plans to send them to Liberia. In 1833 a Virginia court approved these transactions, including the provision that the slaves make the final choice between being sold for the benefit of the estate or going to Africa.[116] If an obscure master in Petersburg could devise such a solution to the problem of debt and freedom, one could reasonably expect as much from the Sage of Monticello.

While considering the role of property in society, Jefferson once told Madison that the "earth belongs to the living" and that "no man can, by *natural right*, oblige the lands he occupied, or the persons who succeed him in that occupation, to the payment of his debts contracted by him." Otherwise, "the lands would belong to the dead, and not to the living."[117] Late in life he reiterated the theme. "Can one generation bind another . . . ?" He answered, "The Creator has made the earth for the living, not the dead."[118] Jefferson was talking about land. Apparently Jefferson did not see the irony that by his extravagances he would "oblige" living slaves, perhaps for "several generations to come," for "the payment of his debts contracted by him."

In 1817 Jefferson had asserted he was "personally . . . ready and desirous to make any sacrifice which shall ensure their gradual but complete retirement from the State, and effectually, at the same time, establish them elsewhere in freedom and safety."[119] Yet he never made the economies in his lifestyle that would have enabled him to free his slaves in his life or at his death. He even failed to bequeath his slaves to the Colonization Society, missing a chance to accomplish all this *without* any sacrifice. Jefferson was not, in the end, interested in freeing his own slaves, even outside the country. In his will he directed that his tombstone indicate his authorship of the Declaration of Independence. In death, as in life, Jefferson wanted to be remembered for his words, even while failing to act on them with respect to his slaves. We honor him for the words of the Declaration, even as we remember his lifelong failure to implement liberty at the most personal level.

The Time Was Never Right

Delay and avoidance were the hallmarks of Jefferson's proposals to end slavery. He often spoke of the need for abolition, but asserted that the time was not right. "Not here" and "not now" was his philosophy. In the Virginia legislature, he refused to offer an emancipation bill and instead left the task to others, when the time might be right. While in France he refused to manumit his slaves. "No wonder," William Freehling has written, "that posterity scorns this procrastinator" who "mastered dissimulation" and "developed fantastic powers of avoidance" when it came to dealing with slavery.[120]

Always a colonizationist, Jefferson could not conceive of emancipation without expatriation, which he conceded was impossible on any significant scale. He trembled at the thought that God's "justice cannot sleep for ever," but he trembled more at the prospect of free blacks in his community. He thought it was "impossible to be temperate" in discussing solutions to slavery, so he offered none at all: "we must be contented to hope they will force their way into every one's mind." Deluding himself and his reader, Jefferson deferred to the next generation: "I think a change already perceptible, since the origin of the present revolution. The spirit of the master is abating, that of the slave rising from the dust, his condition mollifying, the way I hope preparing, under the auspices of heaven, for a total emancipation, and that this is disposed, in the order of events, to be with the consent of the masters."[121]

This theme of hoping the future would take care of past sins emerged in Jefferson's postrevolutionary correspondence with Richard Price, a "liberal-minded Englishman."[122] Price's letters illustrate how people around the world expected Jefferson to be a leader in a postrevolutionary emancipation. Jefferson's response demonstrates both his hatred of slavery and his persistent belief that others, or the next generation, would have to deal with the problem.

In 1785 Price told Jefferson that "the friends of liberty and humanity in Europe" were disappointed that "the people who have been struggling so earnestly to save *themselves* from slavery are very ready to enslave *others*." Those in Europe who supported the Revolution were now "mortify'd" that "an event which had raised their hopes will prove only an introduction to a new Scene of aristocratic tyranny and human debasement."[123] Price clearly expected Jefferson to lead America in a different direction.

Jefferson responded to Price with a harsh attack on slave owners and "the enormity" of slavery—and an overly optimistic analysis of the prospects for emancipation in Virginia. The struggle over abolishing slavery is "the interesting spectacle of justice, in conflict with avarice and oppression; a conflict wherein the sacred side is gaining daily recruits, from the influx into office of young men grown, and growing up" who had "sucked in the principles of liberty, as it were, with their mother's milk; and it is to them I look with anxiety to turn the fate of this question."[124] Ironically, in condemning slavery and those who would not move against it, Jefferson condemned himself.

A year later, Jefferson wrote that emancipation would happen "at some period of time not very distant" because support for emancipation "is continually recruiting by the addition of nearly the whole of the young men as fast as they come into public life."[125] Yet Jefferson refused to offer leadership or encouragement to the rising generation. A decade later, Jefferson remained fearful of slavery, but still unable to act. He told St. George Tucker, "We shall be the murderers of our own children." Jefferson feared that a conflagration similar to Haiti awaited Virginians, and "only a single spark is wanting."[126] Yet even Jefferson's obsession with slave revolts could not lead him to act. "Soon" would have to be when the next generation came into power.

In *Notes on Virginia,* Jefferson had suggested that slaves be replaced by free workers imported from Europe. But shortly after the Louisiana purchase, Jefferson asserted that the national government was constitutionally precluded from trying to attract European immigrants to take the place of slaves. Reading the Constitution narrowly, he believed that only the states could take such action. Once again, coming to terms with slavery was someone else's responsibility—this time the states'.[127]

But when others did take the initiative, Jefferson refused their requests for aid or moral support. Instead, he counseled delay. In 1814 Edward Coles wrote to Jefferson, asking for support and encouragement in his personal campaign against slavery. Coles had grown up on the "mother's milk" of liberty in the shadow of Monticello. Jeffersonian notions of natural rights, life, liberty, and equality were second nature to Coles. He had gone to Jefferson's alma mater, read *Notes on the State of Virginia*, and been inspired by the antislavery implications of Jefferson's rhetoric. Coles asked Jefferson to endorse his plan to take his slaves to Illinois and free them. Jefferson rebuffed his young neighbor.

Coles represented the future generation that Jefferson had said would bring an end to slavery. He reiterated this belief to Coles: "I had always hoped that the younger generation . . . would have sympathized with oppression wherever found, and proved their love of liberty beyond their own share of it." Jefferson found Coles's letter a "welcome voice" from this generation, making the retired president think "the hour of emancipation is advancing, in the march of time."[128]

But Jefferson favored only a gradual emancipation of the children of slaves and counseled Coles against freeing his adult slaves. People "of this color" were "as incapable as children of taking care of themselves." Free blacks were "pests in society by their idleness, and the depredations to which this leads them." Jefferson feared their "amalgamation with the other color." Refusing to endorse manumission, Jefferson implored Coles to continue to care for his slaves. Merging his lifelong affection for states' rights with his hostility to free blacks, he urged Coles to "reconcile yourself to your country and its unfortunate condition."[129]

Six years later, he told Congressman John Holmes that slavery should be abolished "gradually, and with due sacrifices." It would happen when "*ex-*

patriation could be effected." In his most memorable statement on the subject, Jefferson proclaimed, "We have the wolf by the ear, and we can neither hold him, nor safely let him go. Justice is in one scale, and self-preservation in the other."[130] The image was striking, but misconceived. Jefferson's perception of danger from emancipation resulted from his inability to comprehend free blacks living in his republican society, his fear that manumission would lead to miscegenation, and his extreme dislike of blacks in general.

In old age, Jefferson could not endorse emancipation, even as he repeated the tired litany of his theoretical support for abolition sometime in the future. Confronted with a member of that younger generation doing just what he always claimed he wanted, Jefferson refused to lift a finger or write a word to encourage emancipation. He shrank from the implications of his own rhetoric. Pathetically he declared in the last year of his life, "on the subject of emancipation I have ceased to think because [it is] not to be a work of my day."[131]

"Treason against the Hopes of the World"

The history of Jefferson's relationship to slavery is grim and unpleasant. His words are those of a liberty-loving man of the Enlightenment. His deeds are those of a self-indulgent and negrophobic Virginia planter.

Throughout his life, as he condemned slavery, Jefferson almost always implied that, however bad it was for slaves, the institution was somehow worse for whites. His concerns about the institution had more to do with its effect on whites and white society than on its true victims.

In *Notes on Virginia,* Jefferson emphasized the dangers of slavery by describing how it affected whites. It produced "an unhappy influence on the manners of our people." "[O]ur people" here clearly meant the whites. The "whole commerce between master and slave," he wrote, was "a perpetual exercise of the most boisterous passions, the most unremitting despotism on the one part, and degrading submissions on the other." Jefferson's concern was with the "children [who] see this, and learn to imitate it." Jefferson argued that setting a role model for a child was a reason for "restraining the intemperance of passion toward his slave." Significantly, Jefferson did not suggest manumission as an alternative. Jefferson's concerns were solely with the "morals and manners" of the master class. He was concerned that slavery led to despotism by the masters, but he never expressed regret for the mistreatment of the slave.[132]

Similarly, throughout his life Jefferson expressed his fears of miscegenation and a weakening of white society through contact with blacks. He favored some form of colonization that would put blacks "beyond the reach of mixture."[133] As a key figure in formulating early American foreign policy,

Jefferson was obsessed with the Barbary pirates, who were turning white Americans into slaves. He willingly went to war to protect whites from enslavement, while retaining his own black slaves.

Jefferson also worried about slave revolts and what to do with rebellious slaves. "I tremble for my country when I reflect that God is just," he wrote. Jefferson's point is clear: slavery undermines liberty and republican government and might some day lead to a bloody slave revolt.[134] In the aftermath of the scare surrounding Gabriel's Rebellion, Jefferson endorsed the hanging of the conspirators. However, after nearly a score had been executed and more than thirty blacks were still to be tried, Jefferson suggested to Governor James Monroe that perhaps the executions should end. Since no whites had actually been killed by Gabriel and his cohorts, because in fact the authorities had arrested Gabriel before any rebellion had taken place, Jefferson could afford to be magnanimous. But his reasoning hardly suggests a man concerned about black lives or fundamental justice. Himself a revolutionary a quarter of a century earlier, he had few qualms about executing slaves who wanted their own liberty. But he was concerned about public opinion beyond Virginia. Thus, he urged an end to the executions because "the other states and the world at large will forever condemn us if we indulge a principle of revenge."[135] Significantly, Jefferson did not seem to worry about whether a "just God" might condemn white Virginians for executing slaves who wanted to become free; he was only concerned about the larger political impact of the executions. This of course was always the pattern in his life.

Jefferson despaired at the end of his life. It was not because the slavery question remained unresolved: he had spent his whole life as a slave owner and would die as one; his slaves would live on, working to pay off his debts. Jefferson instead despaired because he feared that his countrymen would throw away what he had worked so hard to achieve—and that they would throw it away over slavery. The rancorous congressional debate caused by the attempt of northern congressmen to prohibit slavery in the new state of Missouri had "like a fire bell in the night, awakened and filled [him] with terror." This was not because he feared a slave rebellion or because he saw the crisis leading to emancipation. Rather, Jefferson feared that the crisis would destroy the nation he had worked so hard to build. "I regret," he wrote Congressman John Holmes, "that I am now to die in the belief, that the useless sacrifice of themselves by the generation of 1776, to acquire self-government and happiness to their country, is to be thrown away by the unwise and unworthy passions of their sons."[136]

How could white people "throw away" the "blessings" of liberty and republicanism for the sake of black people, who were, after all, unsuited for freedom? Why were the children of the Revolution wasting their passions on such an "unwise and unworthy" problem as the fate of slaves and black people in America? Jefferson could not fathom how his fellow whites could "perpetrate this act of suicide on themselves, and of treason against the hopes of the world,"[137] over, of all things, the place in society of a people he believed were inferior.

Truly, Jefferson missed the point. He had proclaimed that the natural rights of all people included life, liberty, equality, and the pursuit of happiness. In half the nation, a growing number of white people were coming to believe that "all" included nonwhites. Since the Revolution, the world had been looking to Jefferson to take the lead on this issue. All his life he had lived in personal and political denial: the problem wasn't there, the problem would go away, the next generation would deal with it, the inferiority of blacks made the problem insoluble. By 1820 some Americans, who had read Jefferson only too well, were beginning to confront the contradiction of slavery in the land of the free.

Yes, there had been "treason against the hopes of the world"—treason by that generation that failed to place the nation on the road to liberty for all. No one bore a greater responsibility for that failure than the author of the Declaration of Independence—the Master of Monticello.

Seven

Thomas Jefferson, Sally Hemings, and Antislavery

Historians and Myths

Thomas Jefferson is certainly the most popular saint of American civil religion. His closest rival is Abraham Lincoln. But Lincoln was merely our greatest president. He burst on the scene like a comet, saved the Union, ended slavery, and then was martyred. Jefferson was ever so much more: coauthor of the Declaration of Independence, president of the United States, father of the University of Virginia, philosopher, cofounder of the nation's oldest political party, patron of the Lewis and Clark expedition, scientist, naturalist, spiritual godfather of religious liberty in Virginia, and the architect and owner of that great house—full of furniture, art, scientific instruments, natural curiosities, gadgets, and other treasures—that continues to fascinate Americans.[1]

The virtual deification of Jefferson is ingrained in the general public, sustained by popular biographers and scholars, supported by the mass media, and bolstered by recent presidents: In 1993 Bill Clinton, a Democrat, began his trek to his first inauguration at Monticello; Ronald Reagan, a Republican, urged Americans to "pluck a flower from Thomas Jefferson's life and wear it in our soul forever." In the 1990s politicians for and against such diverse issues as school prayer and a balanced budget amendment have quoted Jefferson to bolster their position. Both conservatives and liberals look to Jefferson as an icon and a role model.[2]

Jefferson's image in America would be almost perfect,[3] were it not for slavery. But, alas, Jefferson owned slaves throughout his adulthood and freed only a handful during his life and in his will.[4] In the half century from the adoption of the Declaration of Independence, on July 4, 1776, until his death, on July 4, 1826, Jefferson did nothing to help America solve what was clearly its most serious social and political problem. As David Brion Davis has noted, "the most remarkable thing about Jefferson's stand on slavery is his immense silence."[5] He failed to come to terms with the institution on either a personal or political level.

Jefferson and Sally Hemings

The most sensitive aspect of Jefferson's lifelong connection to slavery concerns his sexual relationship with his slave Sally Hemings. On Sunday, November 1, 1998, interest in Jefferson's relations exploded as newspapers throughout the nation reported that Eugene A. Foster, a retired pathologist from Tufts University, asserted that DNA analysis proved that Jefferson was indeed the father of at least one of the mixed-race children of Sally Hemings. Jefferson was once again front-page news, as the *New York Times* declared: "DNA Test Finds Evidence of Jefferson Child by Slave."[6]

In the days that followed, stories of Tom and Sally were everywhere. Public Television's *News Hour* devoted a fifteen-minute segment to the topic, National Public Radio covered it on *All Things Considered*, and even Voice of America interviewed scholars about the news, leading to international discussion of the issue. Network newscasters and papers across the nation discussed the implications of the research, which was fully reported in the November 5, 1998, issue of the prestigious journal *Nature*, in an article by geneticist Eric S. Lander and Jefferson biographer Joseph J. Ellis and in a report by Eugene A. Foster and other scientists.[7]

For a brief moment Jefferson's sex scandal even managed to take the public mind off the sex scandal of that other "Jefferson," William Jefferson Clinton. In the *Nature* article, Ellis and Lander claimed that, "with impeccable timing, Jefferson reappears to remind us of a truth that should be self-evident. Our heroes—and especially Presidents—are not gods or saints, but flesh-and-blood humans, with all the frailties and imperfections that this entails."[8] Some conservative critics of President Clinton, however, suggested that the timing of the reappearance of Jefferson was hardly coincidental and that, on the contrary, Ellis, a supporter of Clinton, published his article when he did to deflect criticism from Clinton.[9]

The DNA evidence about Jefferson and Sally Hemings is surely interesting. It should have settled the issue of Jefferson's relationship with Sally, and for most scholars it has, but at least some of Jefferson's defenders remain unconvinced. They argue that the DNA does not prove conclusively that Jefferson fathered Sally's children, for any male in the Jefferson family—especially Thomas's uncle Fields Jefferson—could have done so. Moreover, the DNA evidence leaves open a minuscule possibility that some other, non-Jefferson male was the father of Sally's children.

Despite the rearguard action of a few, mostly nonscholars and nonscientists, most scholars now accept that Jefferson fathered some or all of Sally's children. Even the Thomas Jefferson Memorial Foundation, which owns Monticello, has now accepted this result. As Lander and Ellis note, there were three pieces of existing evidence to support this conclusion. First, that "several of the children bore a striking physical resemblance to Jefferson. Second, that Sally's fourth child, Madison, testified late in life that Sally had identified Jefferson as the father of her children," and last, that "Jefferson was in residence at his mansion in Monticello in Virginia at the time when each of the children was conceived."[10]

Beyond the reliability of the DNA evidence, what does it mean for our culture that Jefferson fathered children with his slave? What does it tell about ourselves, our past, and the soul of our nation? Why are we so obsessed with this issue? Why, in other words, should we care?

Interest in this issue is certainly not new. The first accusation came in 1802 and debate over its accuracy raged until after Jefferson's death.[11] The debate continued to rage right up until the DNA evidence appeared.[12] For example, before the DNA evidence, Joseph Ellis, who wrote the article in *Nature*, utterly refused to accept the possibility that Jefferson, *his* Jefferson, could have had a sexual relationship with Sally. Ellis even argued that Jefferson could not have had sex with Sally because Jefferson was too "feminine."[13]

To understand the issue, we must first turn back to the original story itself. The allegation dating from 1802 is simple enough. In 1802, the journalist James T. Callender published articles claiming that Jefferson had fathered a number of children with Sally Hemings. The relationship may have begun while Jefferson was in Paris in the late 1780s and continued for much of the rest of Jefferson's life. During this period Sally had at least five children, perhaps seven or more. All the children appear to have had a white father, and more important, all were born nine months after she and Jefferson were in close proximity. As they grew older, some "bore a striking physical resemblance to Jefferson."[14]

Until the advent of the DNA evidence, most modern scholars and many present-day admirers of Jefferson dismissed the possibility that *their* Jefferson could have had a sexual relationship with someone to whom he was not married. Others simply argued that he would not have been involved with a black woman, especially one of his own slaves. Dumas Malone argued against a relationship between Jefferson and Sally Hemings on the ground that it was "virtually unthinkable in a man of Jefferson's moral standards and habitual conduct." Malone did "not claim that" Jefferson "was a plaster saint incapable of moral lapses." But his "weaknesses were not of this sort."[15] This argument, as one historian has noted, "seems to rest heavily upon a rather insistent reading of nineteenth-century Victorian mores into a moral set that must have been formed in the middle of the eighteenth century—an era in which flourished" such people as "Ben Franklin and the fictional Tom Jones."[16]

Most interesting, perhaps, is the argument Joseph Ellis made only a year before the DNA evidence forced him to backtrack. First, Ellis offered a persuasive argument that the story might be true, noting that James Callender, while disreputable, was usually accurate. He even noted the discovery of a "missing" child, born to Sally in 1799 that could also have been fathered by Jefferson.[17] However, Ellis then did an about-face, declaring that "a liaison with Sally Hemings is remote."[18]

Ellis based this conclusion on two quite different arguments. First, he noted that two of Sally's children were born after the scandal broke in 1802, and thus "it is difficult to believe that Jefferson would have persisted in producing progeny with Sally once the secret had been exposed and the Federalist press was poised to report it."[19] The careers of President Bill Clinton and Senator Gary Hart suggest, however, that it is quite possible for a president or a presidential candidate to continue an illicit relationship, even while the press or even a special prosecutor is sniffing around to find evidence of impropriety. With no reporters or prosecutors snooping on Jefferson's mountaintop, he was surely free to act as he wished. That Ellis would not accept this says more about the needs and wishes of a modern historian than we might wish to believe. However, the very fact that Sally had more children after 1802 could be taken to prove Jefferson's innocence, because, as his supporters might have argued, he would not have continued the relationship after Callender reported it, and so, because Sally kept having mulatto children, Jefferson could not be the father.

But the real issue here is not about Ellis and other historians, but about Jefferson. As Ellis so clearly shows in his admirable biography, Jefferson was capable of massive self-deception, so there is no reason to think he could not deceive himself and others on this issue. Just as he condemned the existence of interracial children, he continued to father them.

Ellis's second argument was based on the assertion that "for most of his adult life" Jefferson "lacked the capacity for the direct and physical expression of his sexual energies." Thus, he "consummated his relations with women at a more rarefied level, where the palpable realities of physical intimacy were routinely sublimed to safer and more sentimental regions." Ellis quoted approvingly Henry Adams's comment, made more than half a century after Jefferson's death, that the Virginian was "almost feminine."[20] This is an enormously curious argument about a man who propositioned his neighbor's wife as a young man and then fathered seven children in the first ten years of his marriage[21]—hardly the description of a man incapable of sexual relations. But it was a novel attempt to avoid the overwhelming circumstantial evidence that Jefferson did father children with Sally. Again, however, the question arises, what is it about Jefferson and his secular sainthood that makes it better to suggest he was "feminine" (perhaps gay) than to admit that he was having sexual relations with a slave?

Other scholars who are not necessarily biographers of Jefferson have also gone out of their way to deny even the possibility that he had a relationship with Sally Hemings. For example, Joel Williamson asserted that Jefferson and Sally Hemings were not sexually involved because Jefferson "was a widower" and "by inclination a one-woman man."[22] Williamson also argued against a relationship between Tom and Sally because Jefferson did not treat Sally's children as other masters treated their slave children. Having examined a number of master-slave relationships, Williamson claims to have found certain patterns in them: Jefferson "departed from the role" of master-father "in two important respects: he did not avow paternity, explicitly or implicitly . . . or take very good care of [the children] or their mother; and he did not maintain the relationship with the mistress until death did them part."[23]

These two assertions were unconvincing even before the DNA evidence disproved them. A man of Jefferson's stature and status would have been unlikely to admit to any immoral or questionable behavior. Such an admission could have destroyed his political career and ruined him as a public figure. Moreover, it would cut against his very private nature and persona. Thus, his failure to avow paternity proves nothing. Moreover, the fact that he freed all of Sally's children—or did not go after them when they escaped—may indicate that he was giving them special treatment.[24] Nor can we know whether Jefferson failed to maintain a relationship with Sally Hemings after 1808; we only know that she apparently had no children after 1808, when she was about forty years old and Jefferson was sixty-five. This does not prove that she was no longer in a relationship with Jefferson. She may have suffered miscarriages or simply did not become pregnant.[25]

Most Jeffersonian scholars also argued that the original source of the Sally story, James Callender, was totally untrustworthy and that many of his facts are either wrong or cannot be proved. Malone declared that Callender's "charges are suspect in the first place because they issued from the vengeful pen of an unscrupulous man and were promulgated in a spirit of bitter partisanship."[26] This of course is not much of an argument. We would not expect Jefferson's friends to write about such an embarrassing relationship.

Callender, who had once been allied with Jefferson, attacked the president on a variety of issues. But, as historian Michael Durey demonstrated before the DNA evidence was available, "of the four major accusations he threw at Jefferson, only the Sally Hemings affair is in any doubt." Contemporary journalists or modern historians had long ago corroborated all of

Callender's other charges leveled against Jefferson. Durey also points out that "of all the facts published by Callender on the Sally affair, only one"— involving a suggestion that one of Sally's daughters was working in Richmond—"can be proved to be incorrect." Moreover, when Callender reported this, he offered the caveat "we do not give it as gospel."[27] Despite his vile pen, nasty personality, and vengeful spirit, Callender turns out to have been a fairly good reporter. As Durey concluded:

> Contrary to the opinion of Jefferson's admirers, Callender was not an incorrigible liar. His interpretations of facts frequently were strained and exaggerated, but there is little, if any, evidence of his purposeful invention of stories or falsification of facts. When his published facts, rather than opinions, were found to be false, he usually publicly corrected them. . . . What is surprising is not Callender's penchant for falsification, but his ability to uncover facts that have later been found to be true.[28]

Even before the DNA evidence became available, the general public believed the story, as novelists and moviemakers exploited its sensationalism. My own thoroughly unscientific evidence is that almost every student I have had before the DNA evidence was discovered believed the story on entering college or law school. My colleagues reported a similar acceptance of the story. Scriptwriters and storytellers, free to spin their yarns without regard for historical accuracy, portrayed Jefferson as everything from a brutal rapist who exploited a teen-age Sally Hemings to a man involved in a deeply passionate but forbidden relationship.[29]

By the early 1990s, most scholars—except those obsessed with protecting Jefferson's image—seemed no longer to care much about the issue of Sally Hemings one way or the other. This alteration may be a function of changing attitudes about sex. There is nothing shocking anymore about an American president having a mistress. The shift may also have come because historians working with the existing traditional sources could never resolve the issue, and thus the debate had run out of steam.

In the first edition of this book I argued that if

> it could be shown that Jefferson did father Sally Hemings's children—say through the discovery of new documentary evidence or through DNA testing of the remains of the Hemings offspring and Jefferson—or even the existing locks of his hair—then the debate would take a new turn. Jefferson's character would be questioned on two new grounds. The first question that would arise could never be conclusively answered: Did he take advantage of his position as a master to coerce Sally Hemings into his bed, or was this truly a relationship of love and affection? Second, and perhaps even more

compelling, what does it say about Jefferson to know that he enslaved his own children?[30]

This second question raises a singularly important point. From the perspective of character and morality, the DNA evidence changes little. Partisans on both sides of the issue have been so obsessed with Jefferson's personal relationship with Sally Hemings—with the idea of illicit sex by an American icon—that they have lost sight of the fact that Jefferson was related through marriage, and probably through blood, to the Hemings family, even if he fathered no children with Sally, because Sally Hemings was the half sister of Jefferson's wife, Martha Wayles Skelton.[31] Thus, even without the DNA evidence, the moral question has always been on the table. And, even if better DNA evidence should show that Fields Jefferson, Thomas's uncle, fathered the children, the moral question of enslaving family members would still be there. From a moral perspective, does it matter much whether Jefferson held his nieces and nephews and brothers- and sisters-in-law in slavery or whether he held his own children in slavery?[32]

Virtually all scholars agree with Merrill Peterson that Sally Hemings was the "offspring of John Wayles and Elizabeth Hemings . . . and hence the half-sister of Jefferson's departed wife."[33] That makes Sally Hemings the half sister-in-law of Thomas Jefferson. Furthermore, without the DNA evidence to force them to take a different position, biographers of Jefferson who were most supportive of his image, like Merrill Peterson and Dumas Malone, asserted that Sally's children were fathered by Jefferson's "wayward nephew," Peter Carr, the son of Jefferson's sister.[34] We now know this was not the case, but the historiographical issue remains. To deflect the paternity charge, generations of Jefferson scholars argued that the great man should not be condemned because, after all, he only enslaved his grandnieces and -nephews by blood, who were also his half nieces and nephews by marriage.

Thus, before the DNA evidence changed the debate, the consensus of those who most revere the third president boiled down to this: for most of his adult life, Jefferson enslaved a generation of people—Sally Hemings and her siblings—who were his in-laws. Furthermore, he also enslaved a group of people—the children of Sally Hemings—who were his grandnieces and -nephews through their father and his half grandnieces and -nephews through their mother. They were doubly his relatives. He also held in bondage the children of other Hemings adults, who were also related to him through his deceased wife, Martha. Although all of these people had at least one African ancestor, they were all virtually white—and under Virginia law many were legally white, since they were less than one-quarter black.[35] Indeed, Jefferson privately noted that if he emancipated any male Hemings slave, the ex-slave would become "a free white man, and a citizen of the US to all intents and purposes."[36] Yet Jefferson held many of the Hemings family members as slaves to his dying day, and beyond.

At his death Jefferson provided for the manumission of five male members of the Hemings family, but the rest remained slaves.[37] For the sake of character—Jefferson's or the nation's—does it matter much whether Jefferson held his own children in bondage, or merely his blood relatives and his wife's blood relatives? Merrill Peterson suggested that the "legend" that Jefferson fathered children with Sally Hemings was created by a "wanton man"— James Callender. Peterson argued that "such a mixture of the races, such a ruthless exploitation of the master-slave relationship, revolted [Jefferson's] whole being."[38] Yet, even before the DNA test, the evidence showed that Jefferson tolerated such a relationship and left his own family members in bondage as the relationship continued. Even after he died, Sally Hemings and other members of her extended family—Jefferson's relatives by marriage or birth, or both—remained in bondage.

Jefferson, Critical Historiography, and the Problem of Presentism

Although the debate over Jefferson and Sally Hemings may be currently exciting, because it combines science, sex, and the presidency, the debate over Jefferson's relationship to slavery is in the end even more important. As Peter S. Onuf, who holds the Thomas Jefferson Chair in history at the University of Virginia, has observed, "The most heated current controversy" among scholars "centers on Jefferson's slaveholding."[39]

Because of Jefferson's status as an icon, it is difficult to scrutinize any aspect of his career or personal life without appearing to assault the very core of American society. As Gordon S. Wood has perceptively observed, "Most Americans think of Jefferson much as our first professional biographer James Parton did. 'If Jefferson was wrong,' wrote Parton in 1874, 'America is wrong. If America is right, Jefferson was right.'"[40] The historian who questions Jefferson, it would seem, implicitly questions America.

Wood also notes that "[d]uring the past three decades or so many people, including some historians, have concluded that something was seriously wrong with America. And if something is wrong with America, then something has to be wrong with Jefferson."[41]

Wood's sophisticated analysis illuminates the importance of Jefferson to the way Americans understand their own past. It is a small step, however, to a less subtle conclusion that those historians who criticize Jefferson do so not because he merits the criticism, but rather because such criticisms bolster their modern political agendas. Thus, in a gushing appraisal of Jefferson in the *Atlantic Monthly*, Douglas L. Wilson rails against "presentism" and its application to Jefferson, complaining that people who view Jefferson harshly are unfairly applying modern sensibilities to an eighteenth-century man.[42]

Leonard W. Levy encountered such a response when he published his now classic work, *Jefferson and Civil Liberties: The Darker Side*. Levy showed that Jefferson as a politician was unable to live up to his reputation—largely created by his biographers—as a great civil libertarian. The book was unfairly and inaccurately attacked by Jefferson's biographers, who could not accept any criticism of their hero. Reviewers condemned Levy for testing Jefferson "against the standards of the ACLU" and for complaining that Jefferson did not fit with the "prevailing standards" of the 1960s.[43] Actually, it was Jefferson's biographers who had long proclaimed him to be a civil libertarian along modern lines; Levy merely tested Jefferson against the standards of Jefferson's own era and against Jefferson's own words.

Behind the argument over presentism is the attitude among many Jefferson scholars that if Jefferson was not perfect, then his entire image will be destroyed. Levy encountered this outlook in his discussion of Jefferson's authoritarian inclinations toward the civil liberties of his opponents. Julian P. Boyd, one of the nation's most significant Jefferson scholars, could not even bring himself to read Levy's manuscript before it went to press. Instead, he declared that if Levy's "view was right," then Boyd "had wasted his best years in the wrong profession." Similarly, today some Jefferson scholars and popular biographers cannot come to terms with Jefferson's views on slavery and race. Thus, Gordon Wood has written: "In our present climate the fact that Jefferson was a racist slaveholder seems to defile and discredit all of his great liberal and democratic achievements." Wood, who was not endorsing this position but merely recognizing it, has overstated the point. It is possible to admire Jefferson for many things—such as his advocacy of religious freedom, his brilliant articulation of the patriot position during the revolution, and his lifetime support of public education—while at the same time recognizing his failure to come to terms with slavery and race.[44]

Some scholars deny the validity of any criticism of Jefferson. Douglas Wilson, for example, rhetorically asks, "How should we remember the leading figures of our history? By their greatest achievements and most important contributions or by their personal failures and peccadilloes?"[45] Wilson implies that anyone who critically explores one aspect of Jefferson's life must be seeking to destroy the whole edifice of Jefferson. His argument also suggests that Jefferson's lifelong failure to confront slavery, either as a politician or as a private citizen, was merely a peccadillo.

Although Jefferson's defenders are quick to challenge the style and motivation of historians with a different view, they are nevertheless quite open about their own self-conscious attempts to protect *their* Jefferson and use him to bolster their own political vision of America. Thus, for example, James Parton declared that he was motivated to write a biography of Jefferson "because I think that the best chance for Republican America is an adherence to the general line of politics of which he was the embodiment." He then asserted, as noted above, that "If Jefferson was wrong, America is wrong. If America is right, Jefferson was right."[46] Nearly a century later, Merrill D. Peterson defended the idea that when discussing Jefferson "the historian's obligation to historical truth is compromised, in some degree, by his sense of obligation to the Jefferson symbol." Because Jefferson held "such an important place in the symbolical architecture of this nation," Peterson argued that "objectivity must not be allowed to empty the symbol of meaning for 'Jefferson's children.'"[47] Peterson's point is clear. Jefferson personifies an "image," a "vision" of America. Tamper with Jefferson, and you tamper with that image.

Biographers of Jefferson argue that it is "presentist,"—and therefore illegitimate, to judge historical figures by modern values and goals—yet as Peterson admits, they are willing to distort the historical record to protect Jefferson as a symbol for the modern era. Certainly the craft of history is not served by applying today's standards to Jefferson or any eighteenth-century figures. Such an analysis may tell us a great deal about our own culture but tells us very little about Jefferson and his age. It is important, however, to understand Jefferson's relationship to slavery and race *on his terms* and by the standards of his own era. A frank acknowledgment that understanding Jefferson affects how we understand our own world is not a presentist assessment of Jefferson. It is merely a recognition that history matters—something about which, presumably, scholars in all disciplines can agree.

Jefferson as an Opponent of Slavery

Was Jefferson an opponent of slavery? Did he "hate" the institution, as Gordon Wood has argued?[48] Did he really believe, as Peter Onuf claims, that slavery "was a crime against humanity"?[49] Is it true, as Joseph Ellis has argued, that he "assumed a leadership role in pushing slavery onto the agenda" in the 1760s and 1770s?[50] What did he do, and what might he have done, about slavery? How have Jefferson's biographers dealt with Jefferson and slavery? Was he, as almost all his biographers maintain, a lifelong opponent of slavery who did everything within his power to end his own relationship with the institution and to put it on the road to its ultimate extinction? Or was he, as Ellis also argues, a man "oscillating between outright condemnation of slavery as incompatible with republican values and equally outright pro-crastination when pushed to offer practical remedies to end it"?[51] At best, the evidence shows that Jefferson was theoretically bothered by slavery, but in the end far more concerned about his own welfare, the prosperity of white Virginians, and his fears, bordering on paranoia, about the presence of free blacks in America.

For many Jefferson biographers, any discussion of slavery that challenges the idea of an antislavery Jefferson raises the question of presentism. Thus Alf J. Mapp Jr., in his popular biographies of Jefferson, ignores most of Jefferson's lifelong relationship with slavery but goes out of his way to ar-gue that "judged in the context of his times, Jefferson is relieved of the charge of hypocrisy" and that "[i]t is extremely naive for us to judge him in the context of our time."[52] The implication is that any criticism of Jefferson and slavery is simply taking him out of the context of his times. Such biogra-phers complain that any criticism of Jefferson's relationship to slavery un-fairly applies modern sensibilities to an eighteenth-century man. Joseph Ellis, for example, writes about discussions of slavery and Jefferson as "latter-day revisionism," as though it is an unfair modern approach to Jefferson. Ironi-cally, however, a sentence later he argues that Jefferson was "an outspoken opponent early in his career, but only a tentative and elusive commentator later on."[53] Once again, it seems that one can make Jefferson into a protoabolitionist and *not* be presentist, but to criticize his views on slavery is modern, or "latter-day," revisionism.

Coming to terms with Jefferson and slavery is not easy. To consider that he might not have opposed slavery seems to shake our confidence in this icon of our founding. But as Onuf has correctly observed, "it would be a mistake to emphasize the presentism" of the debate over Jefferson and the peculiar institution.[54] The question is not how Jefferson measures up to mod-ern concepts of race and slavery but, rather, how he compares to three other standards: (1) the portrayal of him offered by most of his biographers; (2) the ideology and goals he set for himself; and (3) the way his contemporaries dealt with slavery in the context of Jefferson's ideals.

Thus, to understand Jefferson's relationship to slavery and race, we must not impose twenty-first century values on a man of the eighteenth century. Rather, we must examine Jefferson on his own terms and on the terms of his own age; as Mapp put it, in "the context of his times." But what is the mea-sure within that context? We consider Jefferson a great man, a leader, an icon. He is praised for his vision; there is nothing ordinary about him. There-fore, it seems reasonable to expect that Jefferson's position on slavery and race should have been at the cutting edge of the late eighteenth century and not somewhere in the middle or at the back of the pack. Furthermore, we must test Jefferson by the standards that Douglas Wilson, Dumas Malone, and a host of others have imposed. In a sense, it is they who have set the agenda by arguing that he believed "slavery was morally wrong and forcefully declare[d] that it ought to be abolished," that he "strongly favored emancipation," that he "regarded [slavery] as fundamentally cruel," that he had an "abhorrence of slavery," an institution he "was resolved to destroy."[55]

Popular biographers follow in the footsteps of Jefferson scholars, often with unrestrained exaggeration or misrepresentation. Willard Sterne Randall, in a popular biography that was thoroughly demolished by serious scholars,[56] assures us that "Jefferson's opposition to slavery was well known." Similarly, Randall distorts beyond all recognition Jefferson's position on slavery while in the Virginia legislature. Randall asserts that Jefferson "favored gradual emancipation" but that his plan was rejected by a legislative committee that he chaired. In fact, Jefferson never proposed such a plan; rather, as chairman of the committee that was charged with revising Virginia's laws, he absolutely refused to allow such a plan, written by others, to be considered by the state's legislature.[57] Following along this same line, apparently, is Clay Jenkinson, a Jefferson impersonator. He tells his audience, according to the account set out by historian Joseph Ellis, that Jefferson "tries his best to persuade his countrymen to end the slave trade and gradually end slavery itself."[58] That Jefferson did neither is apparently irrelevant to the public performance of Jefferson "in person."

Alf J. Mapp Jr. romantically declares, with no supporting evidence, that in the years before the Revolution no one in the House of Burgesses "was more sensitive than Jefferson to the anomaly of their position as slave-owners contending for liberty as a God-given right." Mapp maintains that Jefferson "repeatedly proposed the gradual abolition of slavery," although he provides not a single shred of documentation for this position. Mapp asserts that Jefferson's attitude about slavery was "far too liberal for most of his contemporaries" but ignores those contemporaries who in fact were far more advanced than Jefferson on issues of slavery and race. Indeed, in his first volume on Jefferson, Mapp notes that the early-eighteenth-century planter William Byrd II believed that blacks were "naturally as intelligent as the Caucasian" and that apparent intellectual differences "were the result of culture." In his second volume, however, Mapp argues that "Jefferson's estimate of the abilities of blacks coincided with that of most educated white men of his day." Mapp does not explain why the "liberal" Jefferson was unable to reach a conclusion about equality that was at least as progressive as Byrd's. Nor does he cite those "educated white men of his day," like Benjamin Franklin or Dr. Benjamin Rush, who, unlike Jefferson, believed in racial equality.[59]

Speaking for the defenders of the traditional view of an antislavery

Jefferson, Merrill Peterson asserts, "All of Jefferson's values and goals dictated the extermination of slavery."[60] It is neither presentist nor unreasonable to investigate the extent to which Jefferson lived up to his "values and goals" or if indeed Peterson is correct in asserting that these were his values and goals.

Jefferson was a great leader. It is therefore all the more important to see, and distinguish, where that greatness flourished and where it failed. Understanding Jefferson and finding value in his life and work is not an all-or-nothing proposition. We hold no other figure in American history to such a standard in order to preserve his secular sainthood. Abraham Lincoln, who did more for human freedom than any other sitting president, nevertheless is accepted by scholars and the public as a man with faults and warts. Indeed, Lincoln's greatness is so apparent because he was so human, with limitations, fears, and anxieties. Similarly, those who admire John Adams and correctly see him as perhaps the most intellectually complex Founder nevertheless admit to his many failings and flaws.[61]

Of all our major American leaders, only Jefferson is carved in marble, larger than life, and either perfect or a shattered statue. Jefferson's biographers have set this standard. Because they know that slavery is wrong, they have tried to shape Jefferson into their image of a properly liberal opponent of slavery. They wish to make a lifelong slave owner, a man who sold scores of slaves to support his extravagant lifestyle, into a protoabolitionist so that he will fit into their presentist conceptions of what he believed and felt. Thus, scholars and popular biographers proclaim, as Peterson did, that "all of Jefferson's values and goals dictated the extermination of slavery."[62] They then must either ignore contrary evidence, thereby painting a false picture of Jefferson, or explain away his views and actions in ways that undermine their accounts of his life.

Jefferson and Slavery

It is clear that Jefferson found slavery distasteful, at least on some levels. Gordon Wood asserts that he "hated slavery."[63] Peter Onuf asserts he had a "lifelong opposition to slavery."[64] Yet it is hard to imagine how someone as intelligent, politically powerful, wealthy, and well connected as Jefferson could "hate" an institution, and "oppose" it throughout his life, but be unable to do anything about it. We must wonder why Jefferson, who was willing to risk his life, fortune, and honor[65] to fight for his nation's liberty, was unwilling to take at least some risks to do something about slavery if he truly "hated" it.

Consider the other things Jefferson hated. He hated and opposed the British empire and helped start a revolution to sever his ties with it. He hated religious intolerance and wrote "A Bill for Establishing Religious Freedom," which the Virginia General Assembly eventually passed.[66] He hated primogeniture and entail and proposed legislation to end them. He hated ignorance and proposed a system of public education, even though he (correctly) doubted it would pass. He opposed cruel punishments (at least for whites) and successfully initiated a complete reform of Virginia's criminal code for free people.[67] He hated and opposed the Sedition Act of 1798 and deftly arranged to have the state of Kentucky promulgate his denunciation of the law. He hated and opposed the Federalists and when he came to power turned out of office as many as he could, thereby inventing an early version of the spoils system in America.

Jefferson's "hatred" of slavery—if that's what it was—was a peculiarly cramped "hatred" that took three forms. First, he hated what slavery did to whites. Second, he hated slavery because he feared it would lead to a rebellion that would destroy his society. Third, he hated slavery because it brought Africans to America and kept them there. He cared little for the fate or feelings of these Africans and their African-American descendants, but he could not stand their presence in America. None of these feelings motivated him to do anything about the institution.

The Effect of Slavery on the Whites

Jefferson's most famous outburst against slavery is found in *Notes on the State of Virginia*, in which he argued that slavery had an "unhappy influence on the manners of our people."[68] The designation "our people" here does not include blacks. A careful reading of this famous paragraph shows that Jefferson's concern was for the effects of slavery on the master class. He was afraid that slavery corrupted white Americans.

At first glance, it seems that he had some concern for the slave. Thus he wrote: "[T]he whole commerce between master and slave is a perpetual exercise of the most boisterous passions, the most unremitting despotism on the one part, and degrading submissions on the other." This sentence suggests that Jefferson may have been concerned about the effect of slavery on the slave. He certainly opposed both despotism and "submissions." The rest of this paragraph, however, ignores the slave and concentrates only on how slavery corrupts the master class. Jefferson noted that "our children see this, and learn to imitate it." He was appalled by this prospect:

> If a parent could find no motive either in his philanthropy or his self-love, for restraining the intemperance of passion toward his slave, it should always be a sufficient one that his child is present. But generally it is not

sufficient. The parent storms, the child looks on, catches the lineaments of wrath, puts on the same airs in the circle of smaller slaves, gives a loose to his worst passions, and thus nursed, educated, and daily exercised in tyranny, cannot but be stamped by it with odious peculiarities. The man must be a prodigy who can retain his manners and morals undepraved by such circumstances.[69]

Jefferson's analysis is on target here, as far as it goes. As David Brion Davis suggests, it is impossible to imagine "many planters in any country" writing in this vein.[70] This passage surely illustrates Jefferson's understanding of the inherent danger of slavery to the temperament of the master class. It may even suggest he realized that the presence of slavery might undermine public and private morality in a republican society. Yet his remedy for this danger was curious.

Jefferson did not suggest that citizens of a republican society should work to end slavery. Nor did he even propose that a conscientious parent should free his own slaves or even sell them. No, the parent should only keep his temper when his own children are present. Jefferson "hated" slavery because it undermined the self-control of the white master class. In this diatribe he had nothing to say about the "smaller slaves" who faced the wrath of an immature child, nor did he seem concerned with the physical and emotional dangers adult slaves might face from the passions of an adult owner. Jefferson's only concern here was for his own race and for what slavery might do to its members. Despite his concern, his remedy—restraint in front of the children—was hardly one at all.

Jefferson also hated the institution because it made whites dependent on blacks. Like others of his generation, he was particularly sensitive to the danger of dependency. Jefferson depended on his slaves as much as he believed they depended on him. He could not survive without his bondsmen and bondswomen, and he knew it. Forrest McDonald wryly notes that "by all accounts Jefferson himself agonized a great deal" about slavery, but "agony or no, he retained his slaves and lived in splendor off their labors."[71]

In his most famous statement on the subject, Jefferson wrote, "[W]e have the wolf by the ear, and we can neither hold him, nor safely let him go. Justice is in one scale, and self-preservation in the other."[72] Historians have traditionally read this declaration as an indication of Jefferson's fears of a slave revolt. But Jefferson surely knew that if he emancipated his slaves, the newly freed people would have no need to revolt; if he let the "wolf" of slavery go, he had no reason to fear the emancipated ex-slaves would turn on him. In Haiti freedom had been wrenched from a horribly brutal master class with great violence that continued for nearly a decade; but in the northern

United States a master class had voted itself out of existence without *any* violence after emancipation. Thus, on some level Jefferson must have understood that "self-preservation" was more than merely avoiding a slave rebellion.

Indeed, for Jefferson, "self-preservation" was about a lifestyle and culture based on white supremacy. Jefferson's way of life depended on slavery, and if he let the wolf go, he would lose his servants, his laborers, and those who provided him with wealth and material happiness. Here the image of the wolf is suggestive of the dangers to republican values caused by the peculiar institution. The wolf may also have been the wolf of gluttony and greed. Jefferson was compulsively acquisitive. This behavior violated republican principles, but Jefferson seemed incapable of resisting the temptation to acquire things. As Herbert Sloan has observed, Jefferson was "never able to refuse himself the things he wanted and thought he deserved, even at the cost of running up substantial debts."[73] Slavery and the wealth it produced fostered this behavior. Without his slaves Jefferson could not have purchased his wine, his paintings, and his furniture or built Monticello to house everything. Garry Wills points out that while in France "Jefferson went on a buying spree" that "was staggering in its intensity. At times it must have looked as if he meant to take much of Paris back with him to his mountain 'château.' " When he left France, he shipped eighty-six large crates back to the United States. His treasures included "sixty-three oil paintings, seven busts by Houdon, forty-eight formal chairs, Sèvres table sculptures of biscuit, damask hangings, four full-length mirrors in gilt frames, four marble-topped tables, 120 porcelain plates, and numberless items of personal luxury."[74] While in France and shortly after his return, Jefferson sold at least eighty-five slaves to pay his debts, but he never considered cutting back on his luxurious lifestyle. "Self-preservation" for Jefferson was at least in part economic. He was dependent on slaves and he might not have liked it, but he did not dislike it enough to do anything about it.

Along the same lines, Jefferson may have seen support for slavery as a necessary component of his political self-preservation. As John Chester Miller observes, Jefferson always believed he had to "choose between the preservation of his political 'usefulness' and active opposition to slavery." This conclusion of course assumes that Jefferson wanted to oppose slavery. Other successful Virginia politicians took more public stands against slavery. James Wood managed to serve as governor of Virginia as well as vice president of the Virginia Abolition Society. Judge St. George Tucker proposed a gradual abolition scheme, while Governor Beverley Randolph praised the Pennsylvania Abolition Society. Moreover, Miller's analysis does not explain Jefferson's refusal to take a stand against slavery after he left public office in 1809.[75]

Jefferson often stated he wanted slaves to be free, but he always condi-
tioned his emancipatory goals on the removal from the country of free blacks.
Thus, late in life he wrote that he favored "a general emancipation and *expatriation*" if it "could be effected."[76] If that removal had actually occurred, he
would have lost his slaves' labor and the luxuries it provided, while his be-
loved South would have lost the enormous political leverage the three-fifths
clause gave it in the House of Representatives and the electoral college. Indeed, without the electoral votes provided by the three-fifths clause, Jefferson
would not have defeated John Adams in 1800. These possible consequences
help to explain why Jefferson placed impossible conditions—such as expatriation—on any scheme to end slavery.

Jefferson's Fear of Slaves

The second element of Jefferson's "hatred" of slavery was based on what he
feared the slaves would do to the master class. His writings are filled with his
apprehensions about slave revolts. In 1797, with the image of Haiti fresh in
his mind, he told a fellow Virginian that "if something is not done, & soon
done, we shall be the murderers of our own children." But he was incapable
of recognizing what that "something" might be. During his presidency,
Jefferson did all he could to undermine the black republic in Haiti, including
offering aid to Napoleon in his futile effort to reconquer the island and reim-
pose slavery. The existence of a free black republic just off the American
coast clearly unnerved Jefferson.[77]

In 1814 neighbor Edward Coles urged Jefferson, then in retirement and
above the political fray, "to exert" his "knowledge and influence in devising
and getting into operation some plan for the gradual emancipation of slavery." In response Jefferson suggested that emancipation would come "by
the generous energy of our own minds; or by the bloody process of St.
Domingo." Yet he categorically rejected Coles's plea to take the lead on
proposing some emancipation program: Jefferson's always fertile mind had
no "energy" for emancipation. Instead, he urged Coles not to act on his own
generous impulse to free his slaves.[78]

By 1820, he could only bemoan the danger of holding the wolf by the ear.
Five years later he acknowledged that removing blacks from America would
increase the "happiness and safety" of white Americans, although he refused
to endorse the American Colonization Society because he thought it was
impractical.[79]

"I tremble for my country," he wrote in the *Notes*, "when I reflect that
God is just: that his justice cannot sleep forever: that considering numbers,
nature and natural means only, a revolution of the wheel of fortune, an ex-

change of situation, is among possible events: that it may become probable by supernatural interference!"[80] Slavery surely had a profound effect on Jefferson. Here was the scientist of Monticello, worrying about the "wheel of fortune" and "supernatural interference." Here was Jefferson the deist worried about a wrathful, Calvinist God, punishing the people of America for the sin of slaveholding. Surely Jefferson hated an institution that could make him so fearful and his country so sinful. But he could never act to remove the cause of his fears or take steps to eliminate the sin from his life or that of his nation.

Jefferson's Racism and His Hatred of Slavery

The third element of Jefferson's hatred of slavery resulted from his profound racism. He had little empathy for those who allowed themselves to be reduced to "degrading submissions." He assumed their inferiority, based on their race. He wrote in *Notes on Virginia*:

> In general, their existence appears to participate more of sensation than reflection. To this must be ascribed their disposition to sleep when abstracted from their diversions, and unemployed in labour. An animal whose body is at rest, and who does not reflect, must be disposed to sleep of course. Comparing them by their faculties of memory, reason, and imagination, it appears to me, that in memory they are equal to the whites; in reason much inferior, as I think one could scarcely be found capable of tracing and comprehending the investigations of Euclid; and that in imagination they are dull, tasteless, and anomalous.

Absurdly, he suggested blackness might come "from the colour of the blood."[81] Jefferson collected fossils, kept track of the weather, and carefully observed plants, animals, soil, and people. Surely he was capable of making the casual observation—or serious scientific investigation—necessary to prove or debunk his theory on the color of human blood. His suggestion that blacks might inbreed with the "Oran-ootan" was laughable; his assertion that black men preferred white women was empirically not supportable. The reverse was more likely the case, as he certainly knew. Many white men, including his late father-in-law, maintained sexual liaisons with female slaves.[82] Indeed, as we now know, he would begin his own relationship with a female slave only a few years after he wrote the *Notes*.

He found the very appearance of his black slaves offensive.[83] He could hardly stand the "eternal monotony, which reigns in the countenances, that immoveable veil of black which covers all the emotions of the other race."

He surely "hated" the slave, whom he could not even look at as an individual. In his slaves he saw only a monotony of color and countenance, punctuated by "a very strong and disagreeable odour."[84]

Jefferson hated slavery because he hated the slave and the Negro and because he hated what slavery did to white people. In the end, however, he could do little about it except express his fears about the institution's ill effects on the master class and the problem of self-preservation. What he never understood was that only by striving for justice could he have achieved "self-preservation." Thus, his hatred of slavery was unproductive and limited to complaints about how it affected whites, to frightened letters to close confidants and occasional pious pronouncements about the evils of the institution. With this understanding of Jefferson's "hatred" of slavery, it is possible to scrutinize the way historians and biographers have dealt with the problem of Jefferson and slavery.

Jeffersonian Scholars on Slavery

Three quite separate aspects of Jefferson and slavery reveal the way biographers have often shaped the historical record to protect the "correct" image of Jefferson: Jefferson's public role in opposing slavery, his private relationship with the peculiar institution, and his racial ideas.

The Public Jefferson

The image of Jefferson as a protoabolitionist who did everything in his power to end slavery remains strong in the academy, fueled by some Jeffersonian scholars and biographers writing for the general public. Examples of this assessment include Dumas Malone's multivolume biography of Jefferson, Adrienne Koch and William Peden's Modern Library edition of his works, Merrill Peterson's biography of Jefferson, Douglas Wilson's reverential article in the *Atlantic Monthly*, and the popular biographies by Willard Randall and Alf Mapp.[85]

Scholars such as William Cohen, David Brion Davis, Winthrop D. Jordan, Robert McColley, John Chester Miller, and William W. Freehling have made the case that Jefferson was not in fact antislavery and that he did little to end the institution.[86] Many popular biographers and some Jefferson scholars ignore this literature,[87] clinging to the belief that Jefferson opposed slavery and would have ended it and freed his own slaves if only it had been possible to do so. Speaking to a popular audience in the *Atlantic Monthly*, Douglas Wilson praises Jefferson as a man "who was born into a slaveholding society, whose family and admired friends owned slaves," but who "decide[d] at an early age that slavery was morally wrong and forcefully declare[d] that it ought to be abolished." He maintains that Jefferson "went against his society and own self-interest to denounce slavery and urge its abolition."[88] Wilson neglects, however, to provide any evidence for these conclusions while ignoring the vast amount of documentation that undercuts them.

Moreover, Wilson conveniently fails to tell his readers that Jefferson lived in a society—revolutionary-era Virginia—in which many of his neighbors and friends, including George Washington, publicly and privately acted on their antislavery views. Indeed, even if Jefferson had "forcefully declare[d] that [slavery] ought to be abolished" (which he in fact did not do), he would hardly have been unique in the revolutionary-era South. In South Carolina, Colonel John Laurens, for example, jeopardized his political career by strenuously urging the legislature to support a program whereby slaves would be freed and enlisted in all-black regiments while masters would be recompensed by Congress. Laurens believed this policy would benefit "those who are unjustly deprived of the rights of mankind" while simultaneously helping the patriot cause. At the same time, Laurens had made plans to liberate his own slaves. His tragic death, in one of the last skirmishes of the war, prevented him from acting, but his father, Henry, carried out the plan of manumission.[89] As a war governor and a wartime state legislator, Jefferson was silent on the question of emancipating and enlisting slaves. Moreover, on the personal level, unlike hundreds of Virginia masters, he did not enlist any of his own slaves in the Continental Army, thus denying them the opportunity to fight for their freedom as well as for his.

Dumas Malone argues that Jefferson "strongly favored emancipation" and that his "personal activities against the institution of slavery were greatest in the period of the American Revolution, when he vainly proposed a plan of gradual emancipation for his own commonwealth."[90] In fact, while in the legislature, he never did propose this plan. When others wanted to do so, he stopped them.

Merrill Peterson tells us that Jefferson "set his heart on the eradication of slavery." But as chairman of the committee to revise Virginia's laws, Jefferson refused to propose either a gradual emancipation scheme or a bill to allow individual masters to free their slaves. Peterson says on this issue that Jefferson chose to "let it lie rather than risk the loss of all power of accomplishment by untimely advocacy of so arduous a cause." This analysis assumes that Jefferson wanted to do something about slavery. There is simply no strong evidence for such a conclusion. He not only failed to lead on this point, but he also discouraged others from proposing gradual emancipation. When his colleagues approached him with draft legislation that would have brought gradual emancipation to Virginia, he declined to add it to the proposed revisions because it was "better that this should be kept back" and only offered as an amendment.[91] This statement suggests that Jefferson did not propose any bill on emancipation—even one allowing for voluntary manumission— because he was a hardheaded politician unwilling to lose a vote. A few years later, however, with Jefferson gone from the scene, the Old Dominion easily adopted a law allowing private manumission. On the question of personally separating themselves from the evil of slaveholding, other Virginians, more committed to freedom than Jefferson, readily accomplished something while he refused to attempt anything.

Peterson's overall discussion of Jefferson's legislative record further undercuts his analysis of Jefferson's failure to support any legislation allowing either gradual emancipation or private manumission. Peterson rightly praises Jefferson for attempting, however unsuccessfully, educational reform.[92] This record shows that, on issues that truly mattered to him, Jefferson was willing to risk defeat. On slavery, however, he was not willing to run a risk. Jefferson's sympathetic biographers make excuses and offer explanations for why he could not do what his biographers "know" in their hearts he wanted to do. But the evidence suggests that what is in the hearts of Jefferson's biographers was not very much in Jefferson's heart. Throughout his career, when confronted with a chance to work toward public emancipation or private manumission, Jefferson backpedaled. As Andrew Burstein observes, he was not "tormented enough by racial injustice to risk his political career."[93] Nor for that matter was he willing to take any risks after he left politics. Except for a few private letters arguing for colonization, which he knew was an impossible project, Jefferson was simply not very much concerned about ending slavery as a public policy issue. Nor, as Burstein notes, "did he feel a pressing moral requirement to free his own slaves."[94] In the abstract, Jefferson knew that slavery was wrong, but on this issue, unlike so many others, he was able to completely separate any abstract ideas he had from the reality of his life.

If the test of greatness for a politician is the willingness to lead a nation or state to what is right, even when it is unpopular, then Jefferson fails the test on slavery. His occasional mumblings about the evils of slavery pale in comparison to the eloquent attacks on the institution by Chancellor George Wythe, who, in addition to his role as a leading Virginia jurist, had been Jefferson's mentor at William and Mary. In *Hudgins v. Wrights*, Wythe single-handedly tried to abolish slavery through judicial interpretation.[95]

Douglas Wilson rhetorically asks how a white man born in a slave society could oppose slavery. Wilson's point, I suppose, is that we should admire Jefferson because he theoretically opposed slavery while owning slaves. More to the point, we might ask how Jefferson, who studied under George Wythe, could have been so unable to act on his supposed opposition to slavery.

The best Jefferson could offer was an occasional private thought on the subject. In a letter to James Madison, Jefferson once outlined a program for manumission in Virginia, but he took no steps to make the proposal public, much less implement it. His private suggestions that Virginia somehow, sometime, end slavery are wimpy and trivial compared to his mentor's direct assault in *Hudgins v. Wrights* or the actions of Judge St. George Tucker, a member of Virginia's highest court, who published a detailed plan for gradual emancipation in the commonwealth.[96]

The popular biographers retell the stories of Jefferson's legislative opposition to slavery with even less sophistication. Randall declares that when Jefferson was appointed as chairman of the committee to revise the laws of Virginia, his "opposition to slavery was well known."[97] What Randall has done is to conflate opposition to the importation of slaves with opposition to slaveholding. His confusion on this issue is indeed profound. He somehow believes that because Jefferson had proposed a ban on the importation of slaves, "he did not need to write a separate law banning slavery."[98] Alf Mapp is even more confused. In his first book on Jefferson, he asserts that Jefferson attempted to condemn slavery in the Declaration of Independence, when in fact he only attacked the slave trade. Apparently forgetting what he wrote in his first book, Mapp later asserts that Jefferson "wrote into the Declaration of Independence a pledge to abolish the importation of slaves."[99] This analysis is also inaccurate, because the proposed clause contained no pledge of any kind.

Mapp asserts that "Jefferson repeatedly proposed the gradual abolition of slavery," but offers no examples of these proposals or when they were repeatedly offered.[100] Randall, on the other hand, knows that Jefferson never introduced such a law. Instead, he excuses Jefferson for failing to propose emancipation by declaring that by 1786, "revolutionary fever had cooled to the point that no prominent Virginia politician would risk his friends, his office, or his influence to speak up for the slaves."[101] Assuming for the moment that such "fever" had "cooled" by 1786, this does not explain Jefferson's failure to introduce such legislation from 1776 through 1779, when he was in the legislature, or in 1780 when he was governor. Randall also fails to note the passage of the 1782 law (passed when Jefferson held no public office) that allowed private manumission in Virginia or the thousands of masters who freed their slaves under that law in the next two decades. Furthermore, Randall is blissfully unaware of the opposition to slavery by St. George Tucker and George Wythe during that period. So too will be the popular audience that reads his book.

The Private Jefferson

In addition to explaining why Jefferson never publicly fought slavery, his biographers must explain away his private relationship to it. Jefferson was surely better than many masters, but he was hardly a model. Joseph Ellis, for example, claims that Jefferson was "extremely reluctant to sell slaves against their will."[102] But as a slave owner Jefferson in fact sold scores of slaves—at least eighty-five alone between 1784 to 1794—all the while protesting that he had "scruples about selling negroes but for delinquency or on their own request." In contrast, George Washington refused "either to buy or sell slaves, 'as you would do cattle at a market.'"[103]

Jefferson is noted for advocating a progressive and fair administration of justice. He accomplished a major reform of Virginia's criminal code. For his slaves, however, punishment could be swift, arbitrary, and horrible. For the crime of "delinquency," the notoriously thin-skinned Jefferson permanently banished offenders from friends and family. His determination to sell "delinquent" slaves was calculated to create terror in others. He directed that one slave be sold to "negro purchasers from Georgia" or some "other quarter so distant as never more to be heard of among us." This removal should appear to the other slaves "as if he were put out of the way by death."[104]

Douglas Wilson had the question right: "How could the man who wrote that 'all men are created equal' own slaves?" Wilson in fact never answers his question. Instead, he denies the validity of the inquiry: "Thus the question of why Jefferson didn't free his slaves only serves to illustrate how presentism involves us in mistaken assumptions about historical conditions—in this case that an eighteenth-century slaveholder wanting to get out from under the moral stigma of slavery and improve the lot of his slaves had only to set them free."[105] However, in the late eighteenth century thousands of Americans throughout the South set their slaves free, a number of states abolished the institution, and nearly every major reformer in America and Europe *except* Thomas Jefferson actively opposed slavery. Thus, we may legitimately ask why the Master of Monticello was unable to achieve the same high standards set by the Emancipator of Mount Vernon and thousands of other less famous slave owners.

During his life Jefferson freed only three slaves. The last of these, Harriet Hemings, ran away in 1822, and Jefferson apparently thought it easier to emancipate her than chase after her. This was hardly the act of a benevolent master. Nor were the manumissions of Robert Hemings in 1794 and James Hemings in 1796. A careful examination of these manumissions, which by necessity requires a repetition of some material presented in Chapter 6 of this book, illustrates once again the way historians, both scholarly and popular, have refused to come to terms with Jefferson's dismal record of rarely freeing his slaves.

Jefferson freed Robert Hemings in 1794 only after the slave paid Jefferson sixty pounds, which he borrowed from George Frederick Stras, his white employer. This was a manumission in only the most technical sense. Jefferson did not grant Hemings his freedom for his faithful service or out of political conviction; Jefferson sold Hemings his freedom for sixty pounds, which was his fair market value. Malone, writing about Robert Hemings, asserts that Jefferson only freed a slave when "that individual was prepared for freedom in his opinion."[106] But this was hardly such a case. It was Stras, not Jefferson, who believed Robert Hemings was ready to be free. Jefferson apparently agreed to give up Hemings only because Jefferson was convinced that Stras had already "debauched" the slave by treating him as a free person, and thus he allowed Robert to purchase his own freedom.[107]

In 1796 Jefferson reluctantly emancipated James Hemings. Using this member of the Hemings family as another example of Jefferson's judicious manumission policy, Malone writes that, while in Philadelphia, Jefferson "signed an agreement to free him after he had returned to Monticello and stayed there long enough to teach somebody else how to cook—presumably in the French manner." Merrill Peterson describes the event as a bargain that favored Hemings, who "won his freedom upon fulfilling the pledge to teach his art [of cooking] to a worthy successor"[108]—his brother Peter. Most of the popular biographers repeat this analysis, which, however, hides the reality of this transaction.

James Hemings had lived with Jefferson in France as well as in various parts of the North. Hemings was unquestionably free under French law, as well as the law of some northern states to which he had been taken.[109] While in Philadelphia, Hemings apparently asserted this freedom. Jefferson was clearly reluctant to let James Hemings go, but in a declaration dated September 15, 1793, Jefferson promised to manumit him. The language of the document is defensive and apologetic.

> Having been at great expence in having James Hemings taught the art of cookery, desiring to befriend him, and to require from him as little in return as possible, I do hereby promise & declare, that if the said James shall go with me to Monticello in the course of the ensuing winter, when I go to reside there myself, and shall there continue until he shall have taught such persons as I shall place under him for the purpose to be a good cook, this previous condition being performed, he shall be thereupon made free, and I will thereupon execute all proper instruments to make him free.[110]

This is not the language of a benevolent manumission. Rather, as I have argued in Chapter 6, it is the language of a contract between Jefferson and a suspicious and hostile party. It is likely that opponents of slavery in Philadelphia, perhaps members of the Pennsylvania Abolition Society, were advising Hemings. They might even have offered to help him sue Jefferson. The very existence of the document undermines any notion of benevolence. Had Jefferson been willing voluntarily to free Hemings, he could have done so without signing an agreement for future manumission. Jefferson could have simply taken Hemings back to Monticello, had him train another cook, and then freed him. But Jefferson did not do that, because it is clear that he was unwilling to lose this valuable piece of property named James Hemings. It seems that only in response to outside pressure did Jefferson agree to the manumission. He did so without grace or acknowledgment that Hemings had served him well for many years.

Like Wilson, Dumas Malone argued that freedom was not in the best interest of Jefferson's slaves. "To have emancipated the whole body of his slaves, depriving himself thereby of his entire labor force and a large part of his property while turning them loose in an inhospitable world, would have been neither practicable nor kind," he wrote.[111] Malone never considered whether Jefferson's slaves would have agreed, or whether they would have happily accepted freedom and joined their former master in the "ordeal of liberty." Moreover, Malone and Wilson ignore the examples of thousands of other southerners—led by George Washington, Robert "Councillor" Carter, and John Laurens—who voluntarily freed their slaves during the nation's first few decades.[112] Was Washington impractical? Was Carter unkind? Clearly not.

The popular biographers are, as we might expect, even less adept at dealing with this issue. Alf Mapp declares that Jefferson "would not free his own slaves so long as he lived because the laws of Virginia then exiled freed slaves."[113] This statement is inaccurate, misleading, and begs the question. It is inaccurate because under Virginia's manumission law of 1782, masters could free most of their adult slaves, and those slaves could remain in the state. This act was in force until 1806.[114] Between 1782 and 1806 Jefferson might have freed hundreds of people who could have remained in Virginia. Moreover, after 1806 manumitted slaves could have left the state or petitioned to remain in the state. Surely the county court or the Virginia legislature would have granted such a petition backed by Jefferson. Mapp implies that being "exiled" from Virginia was worse than remaining a slave in the Old Dominion. Surely the thousands of slaves who ran away from the South during and after the Revolution disprove that notion. Moreover, Mapp's argument ignores Jefferson's lifelong assertions that emancipation and expatriation had to be combined.

Mapp's declaration is misleading because it implies, but does not say, that Jefferson freed his slaves *after* "he lived." Conveniently, Mapp fails in his first volume to discuss Jefferson's will and the mere handful of slaves he did free. In his second volume, Mapp notes that Jefferson used his will to manumit "five slaves who had acquired skills that would enable them to support themselves." Mapp fails, however, to discuss the huge number of slaves the former president did not free.[115] His summation begs the question, because had Jefferson wanted to free his slaves, he had numerous opportunities throughout his life to do so. He might have allowed his male slaves to enlist in the revolutionary armies. He took slaves to Paris and Philadelphia but carefully avoided freeing them in either place. He might easily have sent his slaves to a number of other free jurisdictions in his lifetime. Not only did he not do so, but he discouraged others from doing so as well.[116]

If Mapp is misleading, Randall distorts the record beyond all recognition in what appears to be a clumsy effort to protect Jefferson's image. In a paragraph that begins with a discussion of Christmas 1789, Randall writes:

> Over the next few years, Jefferson was to begin to emancipate these devoted slaves, one at a time: Sally Hemings's brother Robert first, then James Hemings. He evidently had decided that the time was not ripe to openly defy the slave system all around him and reopen the debate over emancipation at a time when the new government was so unstable.[117]

It is hard to imagine who or what Randall is writing about. Jefferson manumitted Robert Hemings in 1794 and James in 1796. He freed no other slaves until the 1820s. Thus, the "devoted slaves, one at a time" turn out to be only two. It is even harder to imagine what any of these actions had to do with "defy[ing] the slave system," "reopen[ing] the debate over emancipation," or the "new government." Private manumission had been legal in Virginia since 1782, and, indeed, at this time white opponents of slavery in Virginia were active and openly discussing abolition. Finally, in 1789 the "new government" was the national government, but manumission was strictly a state issue with no federal implications at all, and the Virginia government was certainly stable at this time. Moreover, the state government allowed private manumission.

In his final comments on James Hemings, Randall provides more misinformation, distorting the account, in an attempt to put Jefferson's failure to manumit his slaves in a better light. Following the lead of Malone, Randall writes that Jefferson "considered it irresponsible, indeed cruel, to turn loose his slaves until they were self-sufficient and prepared to remain free." He then misrepresents the tale of James Hemings to support this contention, writing that Jefferson "had freed his favorite chef, James Hemings, who then drifted from job to job, became an alcoholic, begged to be allowed to return to Monticello, and finally committed suicide."[118] The real story is much more complex, although surely tragic.

James Hemings had wanted to remain in Philadelphia in 1793, but Jefferson compelled him to return to Monticello and train his brother Peter to cook; James gained his own freedom only by riveting the chains of bondage more firmly on his brother. When Jefferson finally emancipated James in 1796, he returned to Philadelphia but found it difficult to recreate the life he had built before his forced removal to Monticello. He went to France, came back to America, and wanted to go to Spain, but he could not afford the passage. In 1801 the newly elected president asked James to come to Washington as his cook, but he absolutely refused to work for his former master. James did spend about six weeks at Monticello, where most of his family lived. Depressed and something of an alcoholic, he committed suicide later that year.[119]

This is surely a tragic tale. We can only wonder how the story would have turned out if Jefferson had freed Hemings in France, or in Philadelphia in 1793, when he had a solid community and network of friends. We can also wonder how James would have fared if his family had also gained its freedom in 1796, so that he could have faced the world with the support of his relatives. We can never know what psychological burden Hemings bore by having to teach his brother to be Jefferson's cook, thus ensuring that the Master of Monticello would never free him. We only know that, in the end, the result was devastating.

Contrary to Randall's account, it was Jefferson who had asked Hemings to come to Washington with him; it was Hemings who refused the offer. James Hemings had not "begged" to return to Monticello, and if he had wanted to remain there as Jefferson's servant, he could have. Jefferson had freed Hemings under protest; he was willing to help James and even let him remain near his family, but only if James remained in a subordinate position under Jefferson.

Malone, Wilson, Mapp, and Randall might have compared Jefferson to his young and idealistic neighbor, Edward Coles, who took all of his slaves to Illinois and freed them. Similarly, they might have looked at Robert Carter. In the 1790s—when Jefferson was marketing his slaves to pay for his supply of paintings, books, Bordeaux, and other luxuries—"Councillor" Carter manumitted more than five hundred slaves, providing them with land and housing.[120]

Malone writes that when Jefferson "freed a particular slave, that individual was prepared for freedom in his opinion, and had a good place to go to."[121] This sentence implies that Jefferson granted manumissions with some frequency, and voluntarily, which was not the case. Another biographer wrote that at his death Jefferson emancipated "his ablest and most faithful slaves."[122] These scholars are vague, however, on just how many "able" or "faithful" slaves were actually freed. This fuzziness is not surprising, because the numbers are so embarrassingly small. These authors fail to note that of some 200 slaves, at his death Jefferson found only 5—all male members of the Hemings family—to be "able and faithful" enough to deserve freedom. It would almost be better for Jefferson's reputation if he had freed none of his slaves in his will—then at least we might plausibly argue that he was consistently opposed to manumission, or that he forgot. But Jefferson did not forget to manumit all his slaves. He just did not do it. In the small number of slaves emancipated in his will, Jefferson contrasts with other Virginians, like Washington, Jonathan Pleasants and his two sons John and Robert, Jefferson's kinsman John Randolph of Roanoke, and less well-known people like Joseph Mayo, who bequeathed freedom to some 150 slaves, or Herbert Elder, a master in Petersburg, who emancipated 13 slaves.[123]

Wilson and other scholars maintain that Jefferson could not free his slaves because of "the tangle of legal restrictions and other obstacles faced by the eighteenth-century Virginia slaveholder who might have wished freedom for his slaves." This is utter nonsense. In 1782 Virginia passed a law allowing manumitted slaves to stay in the state. Until the legislature amended it in 1806, this law allowed a master to free healthy adult slaves without any restrictions. The same legislation allowed for the manumission of children, superannuated slaves, and those who lacked a "sound mind and body," provided that they were "supported and maintained by the person so liberating them."[124] This was not a "tangle of legal restrictions" but a straightforward law allowing owners to free slaves and allowing those former slaves to remain in the commonwealth. Over the twenty-three years that this law was in effect, Jefferson could have freed virtually all of his slaves. If he had emancipated only the adult, able-bodied ones, he could have gradually extricated himself from his status as a master. Furthermore, he could have allowed those slaves to remain in Virginia, perhaps working for wages on his lands.

After 1806, masters could still free their slaves, but the former slaves had to leave the state within twelve months.[125] Moreover, for the entire period of Jefferson's adult life, there were no restrictions on freeing slaves in Pennsylvania, New York, and New England. Later in his life Jefferson had the option of sending his manumitted slaves to Liberia. Thousands of Jefferson's fellow Virginians took advantage of the 1782 law, the openness of neighboring jurisdictions, or the American Colonization Society to free their slaves. That Jefferson failed to do so is not a function of the laws of Virginia, but rather of his own hatred of free blacks, his utter inability to understand the humanity of his slaves, and his unrestrained spending habits.

Jefferson and the Problem of Race

Most defenders of the faith simply do not want to face Jefferson's racial views. Some, like Joseph Ellis, simply do not discuss the issue, perhaps because Jefferson's crude and blunt comments on race undermine Ellis's theory that Jefferson is a "sphinx." There is in fact nothing sphinxlike about Jefferson's views on race: they are quite clear and utterly in conflict with the "liberal Jefferson" his biographers have tried to create.

Douglas Wilson, on the other hand, says Jefferson cannot be blamed for "doubting the possibility of integration" because most other Americans could not envision it either.[126] He quotes from *Notes on the State of Virginia* to argue that Jefferson's reasons for opposing an integrated society "are the same reasons often cited by black separatists": "'[D]eep rooted prejudices entertained by the whites; ten thousand recollections, by the blacks, of the injuries they have sustained; new provocations; [and] the real distinctions which nature has made.'" Wilson simply ignores Jefferson's cruder comments that blacks were "inferior to the whites in the endowments of body and mind," that they had a "disagreeable odour," and that black women might mate with the "Oran-ootan." He ignores Jefferson's pseudoscientific observations on the color of the blood of blacks and his absurd assertions that they need "less sleep" than whites, although Jefferson noted a few sentences later "their disposition to sleep when abstracted from their diversions, and unemployed in labour." Jefferson's explanation for this characteristic reveals his true views of blacks: "An animal whose body is at rest, and who does not reflect, must be disposed to sleep of course." For Jefferson, blacks were barely human, an animal-like species that lacked "forethought," that "participate[d] more of sensation than reflection," who were "in reason much inferior" and "in imagination . . . dull, tasteless, and anomalous." Unlike true human beings, they lacked the "tender delicate mixture of sentiment and sensation."[127]

This view of blacks was not merely theoretical. One of the great human tragedies of Jefferson's relationship to slavery occurred when he manumitted five of his male slaves in his will. One of those freed was Joseph Fossett. Revealing his utter inability to see slaves as people with human feelings, Jefferson did not free Fossett's wife and eight children, who were subsequently auctioned off "to at least four different bidders."[128] This might be seen as a perverse kind of cruelty, to free Fossett but not his family. But Jefferson believed that blacks lacked the ability to love the way white people did: "They are more ardent after their female," he wrote in *Notes on Virginia*, "but love seems with them to be more an eager desire, than a tender delicate mixture of sentiment and sensation. Their griefs are transient."[129] If Jefferson thought about his action at all, he doubtless concluded that Fossett would get over the loss of his wife and that the wife and children would get over the loss of Fossett and each other. "Their griefs," after all, were "transient."[130]

In *Notes on Virginia* Jefferson wrote that blacks were not equal to whites in musical ability. Mapp attempts to explain away this absurd statement: "Jefferson had not had the opportunity to hear the composition of W.C. Handy, Scott Joplin, or Duke Ellington." Similarly, Wilson suggests that had Jefferson "lived long enough to meet the ex-slave Frederick Douglass or hear the searing eloquence of his oratory, he would have recognized intellectual gifts in a black man that were superior to those of most whites."[131]

Neither Mapp nor Wilson reveal what kind of Ouija board they used to contact Jefferson to ascertain these facts. We do know, however, that Jefferson privately rejected evidence of black accomplishment, even when others of his generation applauded it. Jefferson found all evidence of black accomplishment inconclusive or unpersuasive. Although slaves provided for his every need at Monticello, he was blind to their talents, skills, or intellectual abilities. A comparison of Jefferson with Benjamin Franklin and George Washington, as well as an examination of Jefferson's private views of the black poet Phillis Wheatley and the black mathematician Benjamin Banneker, illustrate this point.

Jefferson and Franklin were colleagues on the committee that drafted the Declaration of Independence, and both served in the new nation's diplomatic corps. Both were philosophers, inventors, and scientists. Both owned slaves, although Franklin's holdings were negligible compared to Jefferson's, and Franklin manumitted his slaves during his lifetime.

On the significance of race they differed. As early as the 1770s, Franklin asserted that Pennsylvania's free blacks were "improvident and poor," but, unlike Jefferson, he did not attribute their condition to race. Rather, Franklin thought their position was a result of their lack of education. "They are not," he wrote, "deficient in natural understanding." Jefferson, however, believed that in ability to "reason" blacks were "much inferior" to whites and were "inferior to the whites in the endowments of body and mind."[132] As early as 1758, Franklin had proposed a school for free blacks. At the end of his life, this former slave owner was president of the Pennsylvania Abolition Society. Jefferson, on the other hand, opposed both emancipation and black education. He doubted blacks were capable of understanding higher mathematics and asserted they were incapable of producing poetry or music. He believed that even those who had "been liberally educated" were unchanged by the experience.[133]

A comparison with Washington, who freed all his slaves in his will, underscores how much out of step Jefferson was with the leaders of his era on black equality. As early as 1774, Washington argued that "custom and use" made blacks "tame and abject slaves." He understood that slavery, not some innate characteristic of race, made blacks seem less than equal to whites. On his own plantations he proved this conclusion to be so. By 1789, all five of his farms had black overseers.[134]

It would be "presentist" to expect Jefferson to have had the same racial views as enlightened, educated Americans have today. But it is not presentist to think that Jefferson should have been able to join Franklin, Benjamin Rush, Washington, and many of his European friends who attributed the condition of blacks—slave and free—to social factors rather than to race.

An examination of Jefferson's responses to evidence about the abilities of blacks underscores his racism. In his *Notes on Virginia*, Jefferson denied the intellectual abilities of blacks. "Religion, indeed, has produced a Phyllis Whately [*sic*]; but it could not produce a poet." Yet Voltaire praised her poetry, as did George Washington; the *Boston Gazette* applauded her "extraordinary Poetical Genius," and a volume of her poems "went through five editions before 1800."[135]

In 1791 Benjamin Banneker sent Jefferson a draft of his almanac. In a perfunctory, one-paragraph thank-you letter, Jefferson declared that "no body wishes more than I do to see such proofs as you exhibit, that nature has given our black brethren, talents equal to those of other colours of men, and that the appearance of a want of them is owing to the degraded condition of their existence in Africa and America."[136]

Nearly two decades later, Jefferson received from Bishop Henri Grégoire of Paris his volume *Literature of Negroes*. The bishop had written this book to prove the equality of blacks. As in his response to Banneker, Jefferson sent Grégoire a short, one-paragraph letter, thanking the bishop for his book, telling Grégoire what he probably wanted to hear. Jefferson praised the "hopeful advances" blacks were "making toward their re-establishment on an equal footing with the other colors of the human family." Jefferson then declared his hope "to see a complete refutation of the doubts" on black intelligence he had expressed in the *Notes on Virginia*.[137]

These two letters suggest that Jefferson was, at least in private, an egalitarian who believed in racially equality. They are the best available evidence to support the heroic Jefferson on questions of race. Both letters are reprinted in the three most commonly available collections of his writings, *The Life and Selected Writings of Thomas Jefferson*, edited by Adrienne Koch and William Peden, Merrill D. Peterson's *The Portable Jefferson*, and Peterson's more elaborate Library of America edition of Jefferson's *Writings*.

These volumes do not, however, include the text of a letter Jefferson wrote to Joel Barlow, his longtime friend and political ally, nine months after he wrote to Bishop Grégoire. Here Jefferson expressed his true view of the bishop's project to prove the intellectual capacities of blacks and his views of Banneker's abilities. Jefferson told Barlow,

> I believe him [Bishop Grégoire] a very good man, with imagination enough to declaim eloquently, but without judgment to decide. He wrote to me also

on doubts I had expressed five or six and twenty years ago, in the *Notes of Virginia,* as to the grade of understanding of the negroes, and he sent me his book on the literature of the negroes. His credulity has made him gather up every story he could find of men of color (without distinguishing whether black, or of what degree mixture,) however slight the mention or light the authority on which they are quoted. The whole do not amount, in point of evidence, to what we know ourselves of Banneker. We know he had spherical trigonometry enough to make almanacs, but not without suspicion of aid from Ellicot, who was his neighbor and friend, and never missed an opportunity of puffing him. I have a long letter from Banneker, which shows him to have had a mind of very common stature indeed. As to Bishop Gregoire, I wrote him, as you have done, a soft answer.[138]

In sum, Jefferson's views on race are embarrassing, not just by the standards of our age but by the standards of his own age. When corresponding with people of different views, Jefferson purposely misled them as to his true beliefs about race. He gave them "a soft answer."

Tragically, Jefferson's pseudoscientific proclamations fostered the subsequent development of proslavery science, which led to scientific racism. Jefferson helped invent racism as an intellectually credible viewpoint. As Winthrop Jordan notes, Jefferson's positions about race "constituted, for all its qualifications, the most intense, extensive, and extreme formulation of anti-Negro 'thought' offered by any American in the thirty years after the Revolution."[139] The very importance of Jefferson to the founding era—and the power that Peterson calls the "symbol" of Jefferson—helped make racism respectable in antebellum America. Racism might have developed without his support for it in the *Notes,* but it is nevertheless a legacy of Jefferson.

Distorting the Record to Preserve the Image

The protectors of Jefferson's image have usually relied on interpretations of events, letters, and writings to shape Jefferson into a properly enlightened opponent of slavery. Thus, scholars have been quick to reprint Jefferson's letters to Banneker and Bishop Grégoire, but have ignored his letter to Joel Barlow. On at least one significant occasion, editors of his works consciously removed from public view part of a letter because it undermined their concept of who Jefferson was. In 1944 Adrienne Koch and William Peden published the first popularly available edition of Jefferson's papers, *The Life and Selected Writings of Thomas Jefferson.* Most of the correspondence in their book was reprinted in full. One important exception was Jefferson's famous letter to Edward Coles.[140]

Coles, a neighbor of Jefferson and a cousin of Patrick Henry and Dolly Payne, the wife of James Madison, had both physically and politically grown up in the shadow of Monticello. Jeffersonian notions of natural rights, life, liberty, and equality were second nature to him. He had gone to Jefferson's alma mater, read *Notes on the State of Virginia*, and accepted at face value Jefferson's literary attacks on slavery. By the time he left college, Coles was a committed opponent of slavery. When Coles inherited slaves from his father in 1807, he decided that he would free them as soon as possible. Before he could act on his views, Coles became the private secretary to President James Madison, his cousin by marriage. During the War of 1812 he decided to manumit his slaves in the Northwest Territory when the war ended.[141]

In July 1814 the twenty-eight-year-old Coles wrote to the Sage of Monticello, asking for his support and encouragement. Coles praised the former president for his philosophical opposition to slavery and asked Jefferson to help devise a plan to bring about an end to slavery in Virginia. Perhaps because of his longtime close contact with Madison, Coles seemed instinctively to anticipate Jefferson's likely arguments against endorsing an emancipation scheme. Coles pointed out that Jefferson was a "revered father" of the nation who thus had great credibility. Jefferson also had "carried . . . into the shades of old age and retirement" the "confidence and love" of the American people. Thus, no one was better equipped to attack slavery than this aged hero of the Revolution.[142]

Coles seemed to understand that Jefferson had always claimed he could not propose abolition because it might fail. But by 1814 Jefferson was safely in retirement. So Coles told the ex-president that he "hope[d] the fear of failing, at this time, will have no influence in preventing you from employing your pen to eradicate this most degrading feature of British Colonial policy."[143] Appealing to Jefferson's sense of history,[144] Coles told Jefferson that if his attempt failed now, "at some future day your memory will be consecrated by a grateful posterity."[145] Coles also hoped Jefferson would endorse his plan to take his slaves out of Virginia to a place where he could free them.

In the first half of his response, Jefferson praised Coles as a representative of the future generation that Jefferson always said would bring an end to slavery. He reiterated this belief to Coles: "I had always hoped that the younger generation . . . would have sympathized with oppression wherever found, and proved their love of liberty beyond their own share of it." Coles's letter was a "welcome voice" from this group, as "the hour of emancipation is advancing, in the march of time."[146] In their volume, Koch and Peden ended the letter here. This conclusion left the reader with the impression that Jefferson favored and endorsed what Coles was doing.

The deleted material—more than half of the original letter—contains an attack on the Haitian revolution, arguments against miscegenation, racist comments about blacks, and Jefferson's advice to Coles not to emancipate his slaves. Jefferson counseled his neighbor against manumission because slaves "of this color we know" were "as incapable as children of taking care of themselves." Emancipated slaves were "pests in society by their idleness, and the depredations to which this leads them." Jefferson further feared their "amalgamation with the other color." He could not endorse the plan Coles laid out. Instead of proposing an emancipation program, as Coles had urged, Jefferson urged Coles to "softly" advocate change "through the medium of writing and conversation." Finally, he beseeched his idealistic neighbor to continue to care for his slaves. "I hope my dear sir," the author of the Declaration of Independence wrote, "you will reconcile yourself to your country and its unfortunate condition."[147]

It is possible that Koch and Peden self-consciously saw themselves as protecting an image of Jefferson consistent with the wartime goals of America's opposition to fascism.[148] More likely, they deleted the portion of the letter because it did not comport with their understanding of how Jefferson *must* have been. They had a notion of who Jefferson *really* was, and they simply rejected other evidence.

That is the problem for most Jeffersonian scholars. They have created a mythical man—someone who in Peterson's words went up to Mount Olympus.[149] They have further burdened him with an "image" that carries with it our conception of America itself. More than two and a half centuries after his birth, it is time to look at Jefferson for what he was: a person with virtues and faults. His greatest failing lay in his inability to join the best of his generation in fighting slavery and in his working instead to prevent any significant change in America's racial status quo. When we understand that about him, we can better understand something about ourselves and our country's past. We can then have a greater appreciation of Jefferson's many virtues and the power of his ideas because we will see them in the context of his own humanity.

Notes

Chapter One. Making a Covenant with Death: Slavery and the Constitutional Convention

1. William Lloyd Garrison to Rev. Samuel J. May, July 17, 1845, in Walter M. Merrill, ed., *The Letters of William Lloyd Garrison* (Cambridge: Harvard University Press, 1973) 3:303. *The Liberator*, May 6, 1842. See also William M. Wiecek, *The Sources of Antislavery Constitutionalism in America, 1760–1848* (Ithaca, N.Y.: Cornell University Press, 1977), chap. 10; and James Brewer Stewart, *Holy Warriors: The Abolitionists and American Slavery*, rev. ed., (New York: Hill and Wang, 1996), 98–99, 113, 162; William E. Cain, ed., *William Lloyd Garrison and the Fight Against Slavery: Selections from the Liberator* (Boston: Bedford Books, 1995), 36.

2. Wendell Phillips, *Can Abolitionists Vote or Take Office Under the United States Constitution* (New York: American Anti-Slavery Society, 1845), 3.

3. Justice Joseph Story, a native of Massachusetts, in fact took this position in *Prigg v. Pennsylvania*, 16 Pet. (U.S.) 539 (1842). See also Paul Finkelman, "Story Telling on the Supreme Court: *Prigg v. Pennsylvania* and Justice Joseph Story's "Judicial Nationalism," *Supreme Court Review* 1994 (1995): 247–294.

4. James Henry Hammond, "Speech on the Admission of Kansas," March 4, 1858, in Eric McKitrick, ed., *Slavery Defended: The Views of the Old South* (Englewood Cliffs, N.J.: Prentice Hall, 1963), 121.

5. Samuel J. May, *Some Recollections of Our Antislavery Conflict* (Boston: Fields, Osgood, 1869), 143–144. May offered this confession after the Civil War was over, when he could "rejoice, therefore, with joy unspeakable that the question is at length practically settled."

6. [Wendell Phillips], *The Constitution: A Pro-Slavery Compact; or, Selections from the Madison Papers*, 2d ed. (New York: American Anti-Slavery Society, 1845), v-vi.

7. Eric Foner, *Free Soil, Free Labor, Free Men: The Ideology of the Republican Party before the Civil War* (New York: Oxford University Press, 1970), chap. 3; Salmon P. Chase, *Reclamation of Fugitives from Service* (Cincinnati: R.P. Donough, 1847). This was Chase's written brief in *Jones v. Van Zandt*, 5 How. (U.S.) 215 (1847). Here Chase was unsuccessful in his attempt to persuade the Supreme Court to overturn the verdict against Van Zandt for helping a group of fugitive slaves claimed by Jones. William M. Wiecek, "Slavery and Abolition before the United States Supreme Court, 1820–1860," *Journal of American History*, 65 (1978–1979): 34–59. Chase's only success before the Supreme Court was in *Norris v. Cocker*, 13 How. (U.S.) 429 (1851),

which turned on a technical aspect of a statute. For a discussion of that case, see Paul Finkelman, "Fugitive Slaves, Midwestern Racial Tolerance, and the Value of Justice Delayed," *Iowa Law Review* 78 (1992): 89, 105–107. The only other antislavery success before the Supreme Court was in *United States v. The Amistad*, 15 Pet. (U.S.) 518 (1841), which involved the illegal African slave trade and issues of international law. George Bradburn to Gerrit Smith, December 15, 1846, Gerrit Smith Papers, box 4, Syracuse University, Syracuse, New York. The Garrisonian analysis was not, of course, designed to give aid and comfort to defenders of slavery. The Garrisonians merely read the Constitution and the debates of the Convention and analyzed what they found. Similarly, an acceptance of the Garrisonian view of the Constitution—that it was a document that explicitly protected the institution of slavery—is not an endorsement of the Garrisonian cure: a rejection of political activity and disunion.

8. Max Farrand, ed., *The Records of the Federal Convention of 1787*, rev. ed., 4 vols. (New Haven: Yale University Press, 1966), 1:561; 2:415; Jonathan Elliot, *The Debates in the Several State Conventions on the Adoption of the Federal Constitution*, 5 vols. (New York: Burt Franklin, 1987, reprint of 1888 edition), 4:176. See also Staughton Lynd, "The Abolitionist Critique of the Constitution," in *Class Conflict, Slavery, and the United States Constitution: Ten Essays* (Indianapolis: Bobbs-Merrill, 1967), 159–160.

9. Curiously, Don Fehrenbacher found that "only three [clauses of the Constitution] were directly and primarily concerned with the institution of slavery." Fehrenbacher acknowledged only that other clauses "impinged upon slavery." Fehrenbacher also asserted that "the Constitution had some bias toward freedom but was essentially open-ended with respect to slavery." Fehrenbacher failed, however, to explain what part of the Constitution was profreedom, while at the same time ignoring many proslavery aspects of the Constitution. Don E. Fehrenbacher, *The Federal Government and Slavery* (Claremont, Calif.: Claremont Institute, 1984), 3, 6. For an analysis of the Constitution similar to the one presented here, see Wiecek, *Sources of Antislavery Constitutionalism*. Wiecek lists eleven separate clauses in the Constitution that "directly or indirectly accommodated the peculiar institution," but makes no distinction between direct and indirect protections of slavery (62–63).

10. Wendell Phillips considered this clause, and the one of Article IV, Section 4, among the five key proslavery provisions of the Constitution (*The Constitution: A Pro-Slavery Compact*, vi).

11. Although no slave state would have levied such a tax, a free state like New York, Massachusetts, or Pennsylvania might conceivably have taxed products produced in other states but exported through the harbors of New York, Boston, or Philadelphia.

12. If the fifteen slave states that existed in 1860 all remained in the Union, and all still retained slavery, they would to this day be able to prevent an amendment on any subject. In a fifty-state union, it takes only thirteen states to block any amendment.

13. William W. Freehling, "The Founding Fathers and Slavery," *American Historical Review* 77 (1972): 81, quote at 82.

14. The proslavery implications of this clause did not become fully apparent until the Supreme Court issued its opinion in *Dred Scott v. Sandford*, 19 How. (U.S.) 393 (1857). There the Court held that even free blacks could not sue in diversity in federal courts.

15. *Dred Scott v. Sandford*, 19 How. (U.S.) 393 (1857). Throughout the antebellum period the slave states refused to grant privileges and immunities to free blacks from

other states or countries. Most of the slave states prohibited free blacks from even entering their jurisdictions. In *Elkison v. Deliesseline*, 8 F. Cas. 493 (1823) Supreme Court Justice William Johnson refused to strike down such a law in South Carolina, although he believed it to be unconstitutional. For more on this problem, see my books *An Imperfect Union: Slavery, Federalism, and Comity* (Chapel Hill: University of North Carolina Press, 1981), 109n and *Slavery in the Courtroom* (Washington, D.C.: Library of Congress, 1985) 256–263, and my articles "States Rights North and South in Antebellum America," in Kermit L. Hall and James W. Ely Jr., eds., *An Uncertain Tradition: Constitutionalism and the History of the South* (Athens: University of Georgia Press, 1989), 125–158, and "The Protection of Black Rights in Seward's New York," *Civil War History* 34 (1988): 211–234.

16. In *Dred Scott*, Chief Justice Taney held unconstitutional the Missouri Compromise, which banned slavery in most of the western territories.

17. Under various clauses of the Constitution, the Congress might have protected, limited, or prohibited the interstate slave trade (Article I, Section 8, Paragraph 3), slavery in the District of Columbia or on military bases (Article I, Section 8, Paragraph 17), or slavery in the territories (Article IV, Section 3, Paragraph 2). None of these clauses permitted Congress to touch slavery in the states. Some radical abolitionists argued that under the guarantee clause, Article IV, Section 4, Congress had the right to end slavery in the states. See Wiecek, *Sources of Antislavery Constitutionalism*, 269–271. The delegates in Philadelphia did not debate these clauses with slavery in mind, although, as will be shown later in this chapter, the commerce clause was accepted as part of a bargain over the African slave trade.

18. Pinckney quoted in Elliot, ed., *Debates*, 4:286. Patrick Henry, using any argument he could find to oppose the Constitution, feared that, "among ten thousand implied powers which they may assume, they may, if we be engaged in war, liberate every one of your slaves if they please." Elliot, ed., *Debates*, 3:589. Ironically, the implied war powers of the president would be used to end slavery, but only after the South had renounced the Union.

19. Fehrenbacher, *Federal Government and Slavery*, 6, n. 2; Earl Maltz, "Slavery, Federalism, and the Structure of the Constitution," *The American Journal of Legal History* 36 (1992): 468. Maltz argues that because of its respect for federalism the Constitution did not affect slavery as it existed in the states. However, the Constitution interfered with the power of the states in other areas, such as denying them the right to abridge contracts, coin money, set up their own foreign policy, or tax exports of imports. Surely it would not have been beyond the scope of the Constitution to allow Congress to regulate slavery in the states in a number of ways.

20. Elliot, ed., *Debates*, 3:598–599 (Randolph) (emphasis in the original), 4:286 (Pinckney).

21. It is perhaps an exaggeration to assert, as Staughton Lynd has, that the "sectional conflict between North and South was the major tension in the Convention," simply because there were so many other "major" tensions; it is clear, however, that sectional conflicts and the role of slavery in the new nation caused as much tension as any other individual issue ("Abolitionist Critique," in Lynd, *Class Conflict*, 160).

22. Farrand, ed., *Records*, 1:18.

23. In the first Congress, the North had thirty-five representatives and the South had thirty. However, after the first federal census, the original northern states had fifty-five members of Congress, and the southern states had only forty-four. Had slaves not been counted for congressional representation, the South's members of the House

after 1790 would have been only about thirty-four. In this book I consider the North to be those states that ended slavery before the beginning of the Civil War and the South to include those states that retained slavery until the War. Thus, I consider Delaware to be a southern state, but not New Jersey or New York, although neither had taken steps to end slavery before the Convention. New York passed its gradual emancipation act in 1799, New Jersey in 1804.

24. Farrand, ed., *Records*, 1:20. In 1790 Virginia had a free population of 454,983. The next largest free populations were Pennsylvania, 430,630; Massachusetts, 378,693; and New York, 318,824. Virginia also had 292,627 slaves, whereas the entire North had only 40,089 slaves.

25. Farrand, ed., *Records*, 1:36–38. It seems likely that the Delaware delegation exaggerated the constraints on their commission in a shrewd attempt to avoid a potentially catastrophic debate over slavery and representation. When the Convention did in fact adopt representation based on population, the Delaware delegates remained and did not threaten to leave.

26. Approval by the Convention did not mean permanent adoption, for until June 20 the Convention debated the proposed Constitution as a Committee of the Whole, which allowed for full discussion without binding the delegates to any final resolution of an issue. Anything approved by the Convention as a Committee of the Whole would have to be voted on again when the Convention was in regular session. Furthermore, under the standing rules of the Convention, delegates were free to ask for a reconsideration of decisions on one day's notice. Finally, all clauses of the new Constitution were eventually sent to two drafting committees, the Committee of Detail and the Committee of Style. The reports of these committees were also subject to full debate and amendment by the entire Convention.

27. Historians presenting the traditional view include Francis Newton Thorpe, *The Story of the Constitution of the United States* (New York: Chautauqua Press, 1891), 131; Max Farrand, *The Framing of the Constitution of the United States* (New Haven: Yale University Press, 1913), 108; Charles Warren, *The Making of the Constitution* (Boston: Little, Brown, 1928), 290–291, 584–586; and Clinton Rossiter, *1787: The Grand Convention* (New York: Macmillan, 1966), 173, 188–189.

28. Farrand, ed., *Records*, 1:196. This motion by Sherman somewhat undermines the traditional notion of a split between the "small" and "large" states over representation. Sherman, from the small state of Connecticut, was willing to accept population as a basis for representation in the lower house of the legislature, as long as slaves were not counted, and provided that there was equality in the upper house. A week earlier, George Mason of Virginia had suggested the importance of sectionalism in a long speech arguing for an executive "vested in three persons, one chosen from the Northern, one from the Middle, and one from the Southern States." Farrand, ed., *Records*, 1:112–113.

29. For a more complete discussion of Wilson's position on slavery, see Paul Finkelman, "Slavery, The Pennsylvania Delegation, and the Constitutional Convention: The Two Faces of the Keystone State," *Pennsylvania Magazine of History and Biography* 112 (1988): 49–72.

30. Gerry's arguments must be pieced together from the various notes taken by Madison, Yates, Paterson, Butler and Lansing found in *Records*, 201, 205–206, 208, and James H. Hutson, ed., *Supplement to Max Farrand's The Records of the Federal Convention of 1787* (New Haven: Yale University Press, 1987), 69–70.

31. The debate over the three-fifths ratio in the Congress is in Worthington Chauncey

Ford et al., eds., *Journals of the Continental Congress, 1774–1789,* 34 vols. (Washington, D.C.: Government Printing Office, 1904–1937), 25:948–952 (debates of March 28 to April 1, 1783); 24:214–216, 223–224.

32. Rossiter, *Grand Convention,* 173; Donald L. Robinson, *Slavery in the Structure of American Politics, 1765–1820* (New York: Harcourt Brace Jovanovich, 1971), 156–158. Max Farrand adopts a similar analysis in *Framing of the Constitution,* arguing that "one finds references in contemporary writings to the 'Federal ratio,' as if it were well understood what was meant by that term" (108). It is probably true that many of the delegates at the Convention accepted the ratio of three to five as a proper one for determining the value of slaves in society, but this does not mean that they agreed that the ratio ought to be applied to representation.

33. Farrand, ed., *Records,* 1:227. The final draft of the Constitution would omit the word "white," thus leading the antislavery radical Lysander Spooner to argue that the "other persons" referred to resident aliens. Spooner's argument seems more polemical than serious. Lysander Spooner, *The Unconstitutionality of Slavery* (Boston: B. Marsh, 1845), 94. Whatever strength it had lay in the ambiguity of the wording of the Constitution, which avoided such terms as "slave," "white," and "black."

34. Staughton Lynd makes this argument in "The Compromise of 1787," in *Class Conflict.* Gunning Bedford of Delaware observed in the debates of June 30 that Georgia, "though a small State at present," was "actuated by present interest and future prospects" and that North Carolina had "the same motives of present and future interest." Farrand, ed., *Records,* 1:491.

35. Farrand, ed., *Records,* 1:486–487. The day before, June 29, Alexander Hamilton had made a similar observation. Hamilton, not surprisingly perhaps, saw the issue solely in economic terms: "The only considerable distinction of interests, lay between the carrying and non-carrying States, which divide instead of uniting the largest States" (466).

36. As if to directly refute Madison's sectional arguments, Delaware's Gunning Bedford argued that his state had little in common with "South Carolina, puffed up with the possession of her wealth and negroes," or Georgia and North Carolina. All three states had "an eye" on "future wealth and greatness," which was predicated on slavery, and thus they were "united with the great states" against the smaller states like Delaware (ibid., 500 [Yates's notes]). Nevertheless, Delaware would remain a slave state until the adoption of the Thirteenth Amendment. New Jersey, which also opposed representation based on population, might also be considered a slave state, since at this time it had taken no steps to end slavery. New Jersey would be the last northern state to pass a gradual emancipation statute, not doing so until 1804. See, generally, Arthur Zilversmit, *The First Emancipation: The Abolition of Slavery in the North* (Chicago: University of Chicago Press, 1967). In the Virginia ratifying convention, James Madison asserted that New York and New Jersey would "probably oppose any attempts to annihilate this species of property" (Elliot, ed., *Debates,* 3: 459). However, as William Paterson's subsequent antislavery statements suggest, the New Jersey delegates were even more offended by counting slaves for purposes of representation than they were fearful of population-based representation.

37. Farrand, ed., *Records,* 1: 516 (from Yates's notes), 510 (from Madison's notes).

38. Ibid., 526.

39. Ibid., 542.

40. Ibid., 560–561. Paterson's animosity toward counting slaves is indicated in an analysis of state population reprinted in Farrand 572. Paterson tried to estimate the

population of each state and the numbers of slaves that would augment representation. For the Deep South, he noted, "In the lower States the acc[oun]ts are not to be depended on." Paterson was of course correct about the allocation of representation in the slave states. No slave state at this time based representation solely on population. In Virginia, for example, each county had two representatives in the lower house of the state legislature. In South Carolina, the representatives per parish varied, but the allocations were not based on slave population. In 1808, when South Carolina did go to a population-based system, the representatives were allocated according to "the whole number of white inhabitants in the State."

41. Ibid., 562.

42. Ibid., 563; U.S. Constitution, Article I, Section 2, Paragraph 3.

43. Farrand, ed., *Records*, 1:566.

44. Ibid., 566–567.

45. Ibid., 567.

46. Ibid., 568–570.

47. Ibid., 580–581.

48. Ibid., 586–588. South Carolina apparently opposed the three-fifths clause because the state was holding out for full representation for slaves. Maryland opposed the clause because of its current wording. Thus, even though the three-fifths clause had been defeated, it seemed that a majority in favor of it could be found. Delaware, also a slave state, voted no, but this was because that state consistently opposed any representation scheme based on population.

49. Ibid., 594.

50. Ibid., 593.

51. Ibid., 593.

52. Ibid., 597. The two divided delegations were Massachusetts and South Carolina. In the former delegation some members apparently opposed this concession to the South. In the latter, some members apparently were holding out for full representation for slaves. In this debate Pierce Butler had argued for full representation for blacks (ibid., 592). The two negative votes came from Delaware and New Jersey, states that had consistently opposed population-based representation.

53. Ibid., 592.

54. Ibid., 601–602. Gouverneur Morris would later argue that the application of the three-fifths clause to direct taxes was inserted "as a bridge to assist" the Convention "over a certain gulph" caused by slavery. Once the Convention had passed this point, Morris was ready to abandon direct taxation based on the three-fifths clause (ibid., 2:106).

55. Ibid., 1:602–603.

56. Ibid., 603–604.

57. Ibid., 605.

58. Ibid., 2:9–10.

59. Ibid., 13, 15. The negative votes were from Virginia, South Carolina, Georgia, and Pennsylvania.

60. Ibid., 17. The recommittal vote ended in a tie (and thus lost). The only northern state to vote for it was Connecticut, which almost always voted with the Deep South on issues concerning slavery. The only Deep South state to oppose the recommittal was North Carolina.

61. Ibid., 1:500; 2:27.

62. Ibid., 2:30–32. Roger Sherman, who virtually always voted with the South on

important matters, also opposed direct election of the president.

63. Ralph Louis Ketcham, *James Madison: A Biography* (New York: Macmillan, 1971), 181, 186–89. Madison did not have unlimited faith in the people, as his essay "Vices of the Political System of the United States" indicates, and, indeed, he had some sympathies for the indirect election of officials because such a system limited the power of the people. However, this is not the position he took in the Convention, where he argued for the theoretical value of direct election, but in the end opposed it, at least in part because of slavery.

64. Farrand, ed., *Records*, 2:56–57. The acceptance of the electoral college based on the House of Representatives took place on July 20, the day after Madison's speech (64). On July 25 the Convention reconsidered this vote. Once again Madison argued that the North would have an advantage in a popular election, although here Madison did not specifically mention slavery (111).

65. Ironically, this antidemocratic system that Madison ultimately supported subsequently had a major impact on his career: Thomas Jefferson's victory in the election of 1800, and Madison's elevation to the position of secretary of state and heir apparent, would be possible only because of the electoral votes that the southern states gained on account of their slaves. This point is made by Lynd in "The Abolitionist Critique," in *Class Conflict,* 178; and Robinson, *Slavery in the Structure of American Politics*, 405. Many northerners believed that the outcome of the 1812 election also would have been different if it were not for the three-fifths clause, although this is probably not the case. However, without the three-fifths clause, John Quincy Adams might have had more electoral votes than Andrew Jackson and might have been elected outright in 1824.

66. Farrand, ed., *Records*, 2:95.

67. Ibid., 177–189. All references to numbered sections are to those of the printed report, as reproduced in Farrand. That report goes up to Article XXII because there are two articles numbered VI.

68. Ibid., 220.

69. Ibid., 220–222.

70. Ibid., 222–223.

71. Ibid., 223.

72. For example, North Carolina's Richard Spaight expressed fear that the capital would always remain in New York City, "especially if the President should be a Northern Man" (ibid., 261). In debates over qualifications for officeholding, clear sectional differences emerged. Southerners usually favored property qualifications and strict residency or even nativity qualifications. Northerners did not. Ellsworth of Connecticut argued that a meaningful property qualification in the South would preclude almost all northerners from holding office, and a fair qualification in the North would be meaningless in the South, where the delegates presumed there was more wealth (ibid., 248–249, 267–272).

73. Ibid., 305–308.

74. Ibid., 306.

75. Ibid., 360, 363–364.

76. Ibid., 363–365.

77. Ibid., 369–370. During the ratification process, proponents of the Constitution would similarly confuse the power to end "the slave trade" after 1808, which Congress had, with congressional power to end slavery itself, which Congress clearly did not have. James Wilson, for example, told the Pennsylvania ratifying convention that

after "the lapse of a few years . . . Congress will have power to exterminate slavery from within our borders" (Elliot, ed., *Debates*, 2:484). Since Wilson attended all the debates over this clause, it is impossible to accept this statement as his understanding of the slave trade clause. More likely, he simply made this argument to win support for the Constitution. In New Hampshire, a supporter of the Constitution also argued that the slave trade clause gave Congress the power to end slavery. He was quickly disabused of this notion by Joshua Atherton, Elliot, ed., *Debates*, 2:207.

78. Farrand, ed., *Records,* 2:369–370. On scholarly and popular misunderstandings of Mason's views on slavery, see Peter Wallenstein, "Flawed Keepers of the Flame: The Interpreters of George Mason," *Virginia Magazine of History and Biography* 102 (1994): 229–260.

79. Farrand, ed., *Records*, 2:378 (McHenry's notes).

80. Ibid., 370–371.

81. Ibid., 371–375.

82. Ibid.

83. Ibid.

84. Ibid., 372–373. Wilson's position here must be contrasted with the position he took in the state ratifying convention (see above, n. 76). Nathaniel Gorham of Massachusetts also registered his opposition to the slave trade, but only after the issue was recommitted.

85. Ibid., 374. McHenry's notes on this debate are quite revealing. Although not attributing remarks to any particular delegate, McHenry's notes make clear that part of the conflict between Virginia and the Deep South on the issue was economic. Virginia had surplus slaves to sell south, and the value of those slaves would be undermined by the African trade.

86. Ibid., 414–415.

87. Ibid., 415–416. The Convention then changed the wording of the tax provision of the clause, limiting the tax on slaves to ten dollars. Walter Berns, in "The Constitution and the Migration of Slaves," *Yale Law Journal*, 78 (1968): 198, argues that the term "migration" in the slave trade clause referred to the interstate slave trade and that the term "importation" referred to the African slave trade. If this analysis were correct, then it would appear that the delegates from the Deep South were willing to allow Congress to prohibit the domestic slave trade as well as the African slave trade after 1808. This analysis defies all understanding of the Convention. Berns, moreover, provides no evidence that anyone at the Constitutional Convention or in any of the state ratifying conventions believed this. As William Wiecek more accurately argues in *Sources of Antislavery Constitutionalism*, 75, the term "migration" was "potentially a weapon in the hands of moderate abolitionists" of the mid-nineteenth century. But certainly no one in the Convention saw it that way. More important, in the nineteenth century only a few radical opponents of slavery thought the clause could be used this way. At no time before 1861 did any president, leader of Congress, or majority in either house of Congress accept this analysis.

88. Farrand, ed., *Records*, 2:443. This problem is examined in Finkelman, *An Imperfect Union*.

89. Farrand, ed., *Records*, 2:443. James Hutson has found a draft of the fugitive slave clause in the Pierce Butler papers that is not in Butler's handwriting and concludes that this unknown "author would seem to challenge Butler for the dubious honor of being the father of the fugitive slave clause" ("Pierce Butler's Records of the Federal Constitutional Convention," *Quarterly Journal of the Library of Congress,*

37 (1980): 64, quote at 68). The draft of the bill is reprinted in Hutson, *Supplement*, 246. Butler was not one of the great minds of the Convention, and it is certainly likely that he collaborated in drafting the provision with someone else, especially Charles Pinckney. It seems clear, however, that Butler was the delegate who actually introduced, and pushed for, the fugitive slave provision at the Convention. In any event, the idea for the fugitive slave clause probably came from the Northwest Ordinance, which the Congress, sitting in New York, had passed in July. The Ordinance contained the first national fugitive slave provision.

90. Farrand, ed., *Records*, 2:449.

91. Ibid., 449–452. Luther Martin, *The Genuine Information Delivered to the Legislature of the State of Maryland Relative to the Proceedings of the General Convention Lately Held at Philadelphia*, in Herbert J. Storing, ed., *The Complete Anti-Federalist,* 7 vols. (Chicago: University of Chicago Press, 1981), 2:60–61. Martin, who later opposed the Constitution, made this point in his letter to the Maryland ratifying convention. He had been on the committee that drafted the compromise over commerce and the slave trade.

92. Farrand, ed., *Records*, 2:451–453. Other scholars have noted this compromise as well, but most have done so approvingly. Charles Warren believed that slavery was relatively insignificant in the making of the Constitution. Arguing that the morality of the slave trade was unimportant, he wrote that "historians have underestimated the importance of the concession made on commerce by the South." He approvingly quoted George T. Curtis: "The just and candid voice of History has also to thank the Southern statesmen who consented to this arrangement for having clothed a majority of the two Houses with a full commercial power." Warren, *Making of the Constitution*, 585, 585n, quoting Curtis, *History of the Origin, Formation, and Adoption of the Constitution of the United States* (New York: Harper & Brothers, 1854–1858), 2:306–307. Curtis was a northern ally of the South—a "doughface" in the language of antebellum America—and his history clearly reflected his political biases. Warren's analysis follows Max Farrand, "Compromises of the Constitution," in *Annual Report of the American Historical Association for the Year 1903* (1904), 1:73–84. The historiography of this issue is discussed in Lynd, " Abolitionist Critique," in Lynd, *Class Conflict*.

93. Farrand, ed., *Records*, 2:453–454.

94. Freehling, "Founding Fathers and Slavery," 81, quote at 84.

95. Freehling has recently reiterated his position, calling mine "cynical." Freehling writes that "I believe Carolinians meant their ultimatum—and that a majority of the delegates so believed." William W. Freehling, *The Road to Disunion: Secessionists at Bay, 1776–1854* (New York: Oxford University Press, 1990), 584, n. 30. However, Freehling hedges a little by also noting that Jefferson was "not present to cave in when South Carolina threatened not to join the Union if the Constitutional Convention of 1787 empowered Congress to end the African slave trade immediately." Ibid., 135. It strikes me that "cave in" is much more on the mark, implying that there might have been greater room for tough negotiation or actual opposition to this position.

96. Maltz, "Slavery, Federalism, and the Structure of the Constitution," 469.

97. Ibid., 469.

98. Many South Carolinians expected to be able to maintain the trade after 1808. They expected that the new western states would favor the trade, at least in part because the states of the Southwest — what became Kentucky, Tennessee, Mississippi, and Alabama — would want imports because that would lower the price of slaves for them. Some leaders in the Deep South also expected New Englanders to support the

trade. During the ratification struggle, David Ramsey, one of the leading intellectuals and politicians in South Carolina, argued that this same sort of economic self-interest would prevail after 1808. He argued in favor of ratification, noting: "Though Congress may forbid the importation of negroes after 21 years, it does not follow that they will. On the other hand, it is probable that they will not. The more rice we make, the more business will be for their shipping: their interest will therefore coincide with our's." Civis [David Ramsey], "To the Citizens of South Carolina," *Charleston Columbian Herald*, February 4, 1788, reprinted in Merrill Jensen, ed., *Documentary History of the Ratification of the Constitution*, 16:25 (Madison: Wisconsin Historical Society, 1986).

99. Farrand, ed., *Records*, 2:371, 373; Freehling; "Founding Fathers," 84.

100. Farrand, ed., *Records*, 2:466–467. The vote on the Dickinson motion was three to eight. The three yes votes came from the middle states, New Jersey, Pennsylvania, and Delaware. Delaware was also a slave state and would remain one until the adoption of the Thirteenth Amendment in 1865. But, by this time in the Convention, it was clear that Delaware did not think of itself as a slave state.

101. For example, in a vote to limit the president's treaty power, Maryland, South Carolina, and Georgia voted yes, and the other states present voted no (ibid., 2:541).

102. Ibid., 537–538, 541–542, 543. On August 31 he had declared "that he would sooner chop off his right hand than put it to the Constitution" (ibid., 479). Ultimately, he refused to sign the Constitution. On September 12, Mason would use sectional arguments in an attempt to create a stronger prohibition on states levying an export tax (ibid., 588–589, 631).

103. Ibid., 559–561.

104. Ibid., 623–627.

105. Ibid., 601–602, 628 (square brackets in Farrand); there is no indication who requested this change. A similar change of wording was made in the three-fifths clause at the suggestion of Edmund Randolph, changing the word "servitude" to "service" for describing indentured whites. Randolph argued that the original term "being thought to express the condition of slaves" would be inappropriate, while the new term described "the obligations of free persons" (ibid., 607). There was also a little more discussion about the amendment clause as it affected the slave trade, but nothing resulted from this (ibid., 629).

106. Ibid., 443.

107. Elliot, ed., *Debates*, 4:286.

108. Farrand, ed., *Records*, 2:633, 640.

109. Letters from a Countryman from Dutchess County (letter of Jan. 22, 1788), in Storing, ed., *Complete Anti-Federalist*, 6:62; Elliot, ed., *Debates*, 2:203. Essays by Republicus (essay of March 12, 1788), in Storing, ed., *Complete Anti-Federalist*, 5:169.

110. Consider Arms, Malichi Maynard, and Samuel Field, "Reasons for Dissent," in Storing, ed., *Complete Anti-Federalist*, 4:262–263.

Chapter Two. Slavery and the Northwest Ordinance 1787: A Study in Ambiguity

1. Northwest Ordinance, Art. VI.

2. Salmon P. Chase, ed., *The Statutes of Ohio and of the Northwestern Territory*, 3 vols. (Cincinnati: Corey and Fairbanks, 1833–1835), 1:18; Edward Coles, *History*

of the Ordinance of 1787 (Philadelphia: Historical Society of Pennsylvania, 1856), 32–33. Peter S. Onuf, "From Constitution to Higher Law: The Reinterpretation of the Northwest Ordinance," *Ohio History* 94 (1985): 5–7, 31–33, discusses nineteenth-century views of the Ordinance. For one politician's views of the Ordinance, see Abraham Lincoln's various speeches between 1854 and 1860 in Roy P. Basler, ed., *The Collected Works of Abraham Lincoln,* 9 vols. (New Brunswick, N.J.: Rutgers University Press, 1953–1955), especially Lincoln's speech at Cincinnati, Ohio, in September 1859, at 3:454–457. Post–Civil War historians also interpreted the ordinance in this way. See B.A. Hinsdale, *The Old Northwest* (New York: Townsend MacCoun, 1888), 263, 273; Wager Swayne, *The Ordinance of 1787 and the War of 1861* (New York, [1892?]); and William Frederick Poole, *The Ordinance of 1787, and Dr. Manasseh Cutler as an Agent in its Formation* (Cambridge, Mass.: Welch, Bigelow, 1876). During the Missouri Compromise debates, southerners denied that the Ordinance could in fact prevent any state from adopting slavery once that state was admitted into the union. Glover Moore, *The Missouri Controversy, 1819–1821* (Lexington: University of Kentucky Press, 1953), 121–122.

Whether the Ordinance actually prevented slavery in the Northwest from ultimately surviving is open to question. Robert McColley, *Slavery and Jeffersonian Virginia* 2d. ed. (Urbana: University of Illinois Press, 1973), 181, argues that "What prevented the slaveholding planters from dominating Illinois, and possibly even Indiana, was, of all things, cotton." McColley suggests that cotton pulled slavery south, because that was where slavery was most profitable. This variation on the "natural limits" theory of slavery is persuasive as a partial explanation of why slavery did not expand into Illinois. Had it not been for political factors, however, it is likely that Illinois would have become a slave state in the 1820s.

3. Ulrich B. Phillips, *American Negro Slavery* (New York: D. Appleton, 1918), 128. For nineteenth-century analyses, see George Bancroft, *History of the United States of America, From the Discovery of the American Continent*, 10 vols. (Boston: Little, Brown) 6:290; Jacob Piatt Dunn, Jr., *Indiana: A Redemption from Slavery* (Boston and New York: Houghton Mifflin, 1888), 177–218; and Poole, *Ordinance of 1787*. See also Hinsdale, *Old Northwest*, 276–277, for his statement that "no act of American legislation has called out more eloquent applause than the Ordinance of 1787. In one respect it has a proud preeminence over all other acts on the American statute-books. It alone is known by the date of its enactment, and not by its subject matter."

Recent historiography is striking for the lack of interest in the Ordinance in general and the slavery provision in particular. From World War II until 1986, no article in either the *Journal of American History* (originally the *Mississippi Valley Historical Review*) or the *William and Mary Quarterly* focused on the Ordinance. The indexes of these two journals reveal that the Ordinance is mentioned in only seven *Journal of American History* articles and only three *William and Mary Quarterly* articles during this period. The slavery provision is discussed in passing in only one article: William Cohen, "Thomas Jefferson and the Problem of Slavery," *Journal of American History*, 56 (1969): 511. In his glowing account of the image of the Founding Fathers, William W. Freehling mentions Article VI of the Ordinance but does not analyze it in "The Founding Fathers and Slavery," *American Historical Review*, 77 (1972): 87–89; and Robert F. Berkhofer Jr., in "Jefferson, the Ordinance of 1784, and the Origins of the American Territorial System," *William and Mary Quarterly*, 29 3d. ser. (1972): 231–262, briefly mentions Jefferson's attempt to prohibit slavery in the national territories in 1784 but does not discuss the Ordinance of 1787. Similarly, Jack Ericson

Eblen, *The First and Second United States Empires: Governors and Territorial Government, 1784–1912* (Pittsburgh: University of Pittsburgh Press, 1968), says little about the slavery provision, and the same is true of Peter S. Onuf's excellent book, *The Origins of the Federal Republic: Jurisdictional Controversies in the United States, 1775–1787* (Philadelphia: University of Pennsylvania Press, 1983). Donald L. Robinson, *Slavery in the Structure of American Politics, 1765–1820* (New York: Harcourt Brace Jovanovich, 1971) deals at some length with Article VI of the Ordinance. In his magisterial *The Problem of Slavery in the Age of Revolution, 1770–1823* (Ithaca: Cornell University Press, 1975), David Brion Davis discusses the Ordinance and places it in the larger context of the era. The only important article of the two decades before 1986 devoted to the slavery provision is Staughton Lynd's "The Compromise of 1787," reprinted in his book *Class Conflict, Slavery, and the United States Constitution: Ten Essays* (Indianapolis: Bobbs-Merrill, 1967), 185–213.

State historical society journals have shown more interest in the Ordinance. See Onuf, "From Constitution to Higher Law"; Ray A. Billington, "The Historians of the Northwest Ordinance," *Journal of the Illinois State Historical Society*, 40 (1947): 397–413; and J. David Griffin, "Historians and the Sixth Article of the Ordinance of 1787," *Ohio History*, 78 (1969): 252–260. See also Phillip R. Shriver, "America's Other Bicentennial," *The Old Northwest* 9 (1983): 219–235. During the bicentennial of the Ordinance, a number of journals and books appeared that dealt with the Ordinance. See, for example, Frederick D. Williams, ed., *The Northwest Ordinance: Essays on Its Formulation, Provisions, and Legacy* (East Lansing, Mich.: Michigan State University, 1989); Lloyd Hunter, ed., *Pathways to the Old Northwest* (Indianapolis: Indiana Historical Society, 1988); Andrew R.L. Cayton and Peter S. Onuf, *The Midwest and the Nation: Rethinking the History of an American Region* (Bloomington: Indiana University Press, 1990); and the articles in Volume 84, No. 1 (1988) of *Indiana Magazine of History*.

4. Staughton Lynd first suggested this analysis in "The Compromise of 1787," *Class Conflict* 189–200, to explain why southerners supported the slavery prohibition. The clause may also have strengthened slavery in the South by preventing competition between the Ohio Valley and Virginia or Kentucky. This point is discussed in more detail below.

5. The fugitive slave clause of the Ordinance was the first important protection given to slavery by the national government. The Constitutional Convention did not consider a fugitive slave provision until August 28, a month and a half after the Ordinance provided such protection for slave owners. It is likely that the South Carolinians at the convention who demanded this clause got the idea for such a clause from the Ordinance. Max Farrand, ed., *The Records of the Federal Convention of 1787*, rev. ed., 4 vols. (New Haven: Yale University Press, 1966), 2:443, 453–454. The vigorous defense of slavery by the Deep South delegates at the Constitutional Convention stands in contrast to the adoption of Article VI of the Ordinance, if that article is seen as "antislavery." It is likely, however, that the Deep South delegates in Congress thought Article VI would protect slavery where it was and allow it to spread to the Southwest. Thus, they may have seen the article as proslavery, or at least as protective of slavery.

6. David Brion Davis, "The Significance of Excluding Slavery from the Old Northwest in 1787," *Indiana Magazine of History*, 84, (1988): 75–89. I discuss the continuation of slavery in the territory in Chapter 3 of this volume. See also Onuf, "From Constitution to Higher Law," 23–29. In *Statehood and Union: A History of the Northwest Ordinance* (Bloomington and Indianapolis: Indiana University Press, 1987),

123, Peter S. Onuf demonstrates, as earlier scholars have failed to do, that the vote against the convention was "decisive": 6,640 to 4,972. While a margin of under 1,700 votes might seem slim by today's standards, as a percentage of votes cast (and voters in the state), this was a landslide victory of 43 percent for the convention and 57 percent opposed to it. These figures come from Theodore C. Pease, ed., *Illinois Election Returns, 1818–1848* (Springfield, Ill.: Trustees of the Illinois State Historical Library, 1923), 27.

7. Cases throughout the antebellum period raised the problem that persons might be held as slaves in an area where slavery itself was prohibited. See Paul Finkelman, *An Imperfect Union: Slavery, Federalism, and Comity* (Chapel Hill: University of North Carolina Press, 1981). The problem of enslavement without the sanction of law persists to this day. In *United States v. Mussry*, 726 F. 2d 1448 (1984), a federal court in California ruled that the coercion necessary to produce slavery need not be physical, but could be a result of threats, especially if those enslaved were aliens unfamiliar with the laws of the United States. In *Mussry*, the court allowed the prosecution for enslavement of persons who had enticed Indonesian aliens to the United States, then seized their passports and return airline tickets, and told the Indonesians that they would suffer terrible penalties if they tried to escape. Such a case illustrates the power of a "master" over illiterate minorities, be they Indonesians in late twentieth-century California or "indentured servants" in late eighteenth-century Indiana and Illinois.

8. *Marchand v. Negro Peggy*, 2 Sergeant & Rawle (Pa.) 18 (1815). Holding Peggy to be a slave, Tilghman declared: "The only just mode of extirpating the small remains of slavery in the state, would be by purchasing the slaves at a reasonable price, and paying their owners out of the public treasury." Ibid., 19. In *Jarrot (colored Man) v. Jarrot*, 2 Gilman (Ill.) 1 (1845), the Illinois Supreme Court held that the descendants of slaves owned by the original settlers, born after Illinois statehood, were free. It is significant that the Illinois court used the year of statehood, 1818, and not the year of the Ordinance, to determine freedom.

9. *Somerset v. Stewart*, Loft (G.B.) 1 (1772); 20 Howell State Trials 1 (1772). See also William M. Wiecek, *The Sources of Antislavery Constitutionalism in America, 1760–1848* (Ithaca: Cornell University Press, 1977), 20–39. On the problems of slavery and the conflict of laws, see Finkelman, *An Imperfect Union*. For discussions on slavery in the North, see arguments of counsel in *Commonwealth v. Aves*, 18 Pick. (Mass.) 193 (1836), and *Lemmon v. The People*, 20 NY 562 (1860).

10. Northwest Ordinance, Art. VI.

11. Ibid., Sec. 14.

12. Worthington Chauncey Ford, *Journals of the Continental Congress, 1774–1789*, 34 vols. (Washington, D.C.: Government Printing Office, 1904–1937), 32:281–283, 292, 313–320, 333–334. The only dissenting vote in Congress came from Abraham Yates of New York.

13. The nineteenth-century historians cited above sought to determine who deserved the credit for the Ordinance in general and Article VI in particular. Ducking the issue altogether, George Bancroft wrote: "Thomas Jefferson first summoned Congress to prohibit slavery in all the territory of the United States; Rufus King lifted up the measure when it lay almost lifeless on the ground . . . a congress . . . headed by William Grayson, supported by Richard Henry Lee, and using Nathan Dane as scribe, carried the measure to the goal." *History of the United States*, 6:290.

14. Lynd, "Compromise of 1787," in *Class Conflict*, 99; Onuf, *Origins of the Federal Republic*, 169–171. Lynd also argues that the South was anxious to pass the

Ordinance so that the American side of the Mississippi River would be quickly settled. Such a settlement would strengthen America's hand in negotiations with the Spanish for access to New Orleans. This would explain why southerners were anxious to have some bill for organizing the territory, but does not explain why southerners should have been willing to give up slavery in the area.

15. William Grayson to James Monroe, Aug. 8, 1787, in Paul H. Smith, ed., *Letters of Members of Delegates to Congress, 1774-1789,* 26 vols. (Washington, D.C.: Library of Congress, 1996), 24:393-396. Grayson's argument suggests that Deep South congressmen may have supported Article VI because prohibiting slavery in the Northwest would lower the price of slaves in the Southeast and Southwest while Upper South congressmen supported the ordinance to avoid economic competition from north of the Ohio River. See also Peter Force, "The Ordinance of 1787, and Its History," in William Henry Smith, ed., *The St. Clair Papers: The Life and Public Services of Arthur St. Clair,* 2 vols. (Cincinnati: R. Clarke, 1882), 2:611–612.

16. Richard Henry Lee to Francis Lightfoot Lee, July 14, 1787, in Smith, ed., *Letters of Members of Delegates to Congress,* 24:353-355; Richard Henry Lee to George Washington, July 15, 1787, ibid., 356-357. Poole, *Ordinance of 1787,* 27, 26.

17. Poole, *Ordinance of 1787,* 29; Ford, *Journals of the Continental Congress,* 32:343. Eblen, *First and Second United States Empires,* 43n, denies that Cutler could have had any effect on the Ordinance because "it is clear that by the time Cutler arrived in New York in 1787, there was nothing really new to be offered." However, Article VI, containing the slavery prohibition and the quite new fugitive slave provision, was in fact added to the Ordinance *after* Cutler left New York. Eblen is also confused about when Cutler appeared in New York. He states that Cutler arrived in New York on May 9 (page 37) and predicates his analysis accordingly. Cutler, however, did not come to New York until July 6.

18. Cutler's son Ephraim recalled, in a statement written after Cutler's death, that Cutler had personally claimed to be the author of the slavery prohibition. William Parker Cutler and Julia Perkins Cutler, *Life, Journals and Correspondence of Rev. Manasseh Cutler* 2 vols. (Cincinnati: R. Clarke, 1888), 1:343–344. This claim, or the memory of it by his descendants, may be an example of the filiopietism common in the nineteenth century among the descendants of the revolutionary-era patriots. Cutler himself left no written documentation to support his claim of authorship. Cutler's presence at the Congress is ambiguous. He arrived on July 6, wrote down some suggestions for amendments to the pending bill, and left on the tenth. On the eleventh, after Cutler had left New York, the bill, as read to the Congress, did not include the antislavery amendments. Not until the thirteenth, when the bill had its third and final reading, did Nathan Dane introduce the slavery prohibition in Congress. See also Edmund Cody Burnett, *The Continental Congress* (New York: Macmillan, 1941), 685. On July 19, when Cutler saw the final bill, as passed, he noted in his diary that all but one of his suggestions had been accepted. At no time, however, did Cutler indicate in his diary, or a letter, what those suggestions were. Cutler and Cutler, *Life, Manasseh Cutler, LL.D.,* 1:230, 242, 293. The reliability of the printed version of Cutler's journals has also been questioned, although not on this point. Lee Nathaniel Newcomer, "Manasseh Cutler's Writings: A Note on Editorial Practice," *Mississippi Valley Historical Review* 47 (June 1960): 88–101. Jay A. Barrett, *Evolution of the Ordinance of 1787* (New York: G.P. Putnam's Sons, 1891), 74–77, argues against Cutler's antislavery credentials on the basis of subsequent votes in the United States Congress.

19. Poole, *Ordinance of 1787*, 31; Berkhofer, "Jefferson"; Onuf, *Origins of the Federal Republic*, ch. 7.

20. Berkhofer, "Jefferson," discusses the defeat of Jefferson's prohibition on slavery. See also Cohen, "Thomas Jefferson and the Problem of Slavery," 511, and Merrill D. Peterson, *Thomas Jefferson and the New Nation* (New York: Oxford University Press, 1970), 283. No one, as far as I know, discusses the potential enforcement problems of Jefferson's proposal in any detail.

21. Nathan Dane to Rufus King, July 16, 1787, in Smith, ed., *Letters of Members of Delegates to Congress,* 24:353-355. Except for the letters cited above, there are no existing letters in which anyone in Congress even mentioned the slavery prohibition. This in part may undermine Lynd's theory of concerted effort between the convention and Congress. Manasseh Cutler could not have brought news of the slavery prohibition to the Convention because he did not find out the exact wording of the Ordinance until July 19.

22. For example, for Missouri, see *Merry v. Tiffin and Menard*, 1 Mo. 725 (1827); *Theoteste v. Chouteau*, 2 Mo. 144 (1829); *Nancy v. Trammel*, 3 Mo. 306 (1836); *Chouteau and Keizer v. Hope*, 7 Mo. 428 (1842); *Chouteau v. Pierre (of Color)*, 9 Mo. 3 (1845); and *Charlotte (of Color) v. Chouteau*, 11 Mo. 193 (1847), reargued at 21 Mo. 590 (1855), 25 Mo. 465 (1857), and 33 Mo. 194 (1862). In Illinois the leading case is *Jarrot v. Jarrot*, 2 Gilman 1 (1845). A number of other Illinois cases involved slaves brought into the Illinois territory after 1787 by the French settlers: *Boon v. Juliet*, 1 Scammon 258 (1836); *Choisser v. Hargrave*, 1 Scammon 317 (1836); and *Borders v. Borders*, 4 Scammon 341 (1843). Apparently a number of cases involving the "French" slaves went unreported. Roger D. Bridges, ed., "John Mason Peck on Illinois Slavery," *Journal of the Illinois State Historical Society*, 75 (1982): 201. Slaves brought to Illinois before 1787 were referred to as "French" slaves even if they were owned by Anglo-Americans.

23. In *Dred Scott v. Sandford*, 19 How. (U.S.) 393 (1857), Chief Justice Taney would ultimately make a similar argument, claiming that Congress could not emancipate slaves brought into federal territories. Taney's argument may have been inapplicable for the introduction of slavery into a totally unsettled territory. However, it seems somewhat more reasonable to apply the concept to slaves already present in a territory at the time the federal government extended its jurisdiction over the area.

24. In *State v. Hoppess*, 2 *Western Law Journal* (Ohio) 279 (1845), Judge Nathaniel Read of the Ohio Supreme Court refused to free a slave whose master voluntarily allowed him to leave a boat that was temporarily docked in Cincinnati. Read believed that the Ohio River and its wharves were open to unrestricted transit for all Americans, including masters traveling with their slaves. Finkelman, *Imperfect Union*, 167–72.

25. It is unlikely that the congressmen were making a distinction between indentured servants and others when they used the term "free inhabitants." For one thing, indentured servants, like apprentices, were usually considered "free," even though they might be under some sort of long-term contract. This is clearly the understanding of the Constitution's three-fifths clause (Article I, Section 2). The Articles of Confederation are less clear on this issue. Article IV talks about "the free inhabitants of each of these states" and excludes "paupers, vagabonds, and fugitives from justice." It seems likely that this clause included indentured persons as "free inhabitants." Article IX of the Articles of Confederation allocates quotas for military enlistments based on "the number of white inhabitants." This certainly included white indentured

servants. In a strictly legal sense, indentured servants were free persons who voluntarily contracted to serve someone for a term of years. As such, they were not in "involuntary servitude."

26. "An Ordinance for ascertaining the mode of disposing of Lands in the Western Territory," Act of May 20, 1785, in Ford, *Journals of the Continental Congress*, 28:375–381, 378.

27. Onuf, "From Constitution to Higher Law," 19.

28. Davis, "Significance of Excluding Slavery from the Old Northwest," 86.

29. "An Act for the Gradual Abolition of Slavery," *Pennsylvania Acts, 1780*; "An Act authorizing the manumission of negroes, mulattoes, and others, and for the gradual abolition of slavery," *Rhode Island Laws, 1784*; "An Act concerning Indian, mulatto, and negro servants and slaves," *Connecticut Laws, 1784*. Massachusetts had abolished slavery through its constitution and judicial decisions. Emancipation had been a political issue in Massachusetts only to the extent that the 1778 Massachusetts constitution did not have a free and equal clause and because it discriminated against blacks. Willi Paul Adams, *The First American Constitutions: Republican Ideology and the Making of State Constitutions in the Revolutionary Era* (Chapel Hill: University of North Carolina Press, 1980), 184.

30. Lynd, "The Compromise of 1787," 186. The only other obvious victories for "liberty" were the constitutional and statutory abolition of slavery in the North (see Arthur Zilversmit, *The First Emancipation: The Abolition of Slavery in the North* [Chicago, 1967]) and the Virginia manumission statute of 1782, "An act to authorize manumission of slaves," 11 Hening *Statutes of Virginia* 39, act of May 1782. For a different view, see Freehling, "The Founding Fathers and Slavery."

31. Quoted in Robinson, *Slavery in the Structure of American Politics*, 80.

32. While population figures for this period are unreliable, all evidence indicates that nearly all the slaves in the Northwest lived in what would become Indiana and Illinois. N. Dwight Harris, *The History of Negro Servitude in Illinois* (Chicago: A.C. McClurg, 1904); Emma Lou Thornbrough, *The Negro in Indiana: A Study of a Minority* (Indianapolis: Indiana Historical Bureau, 1957).

33. See Onuf, *Origins of the Federal Republic*, 75–77; William M. Malloy, ed., *Treaties, Conventions, International Acts, Protocols, and Agreements Between the United States of America and Other Powers, 1776–1937*, 4 vols. (Washington, D.C.: Government Printing Office, 1910–1938), 1:586; and "An act to authorize the delegates of this state in congress, to convey to the United States, in congress assembled, all the rights of this commonwealth to the territory north westward of the river Ohio," 11; Hening, *Statutes of Virginia* 326.

34. An ex post facto law makes conduct criminal (or changes the punishment or penalty for such conduct, or the rules of evidence to prove such conduct) subsequent to the conduct.

35. "Memorial of Barthelemi Tardiveau, July 8, 1788," in Clarence W. Alvord, ed., *Kaskaskia Records, 1778–1790* (Springfield: Illinois State Library, 1909), 485–488. See also Arthur C. Boggess, *The Settlement of Illinois 1778–1830* (1908; reprint, Freeport, N.Y.: Books of the Libraries Press, 1970), 50–53.

36. "Memorial of Barthelemi Tardiveau, September 17, 1788," in Alvord, ed., *Kaskaskia Records*, 491–493.

37. Technically an ex post facto law only applies to criminal conduct. Since the holding of slaves was not made criminal under the Ordinance, Article VI could not be considered an ex post facto law. The taking of property by the state, or altering the

nature of property by the state, has never been considered ex post facto legislation.

38. Major John Hamtramck to General Josiah Harmar, July 29, Aug. 14, 1789, in Alvord, ed., *Kaskaskia Records*, 506–508, 508–509.

39. Tardiveau to St. Clair, June 30, 1789, in William Henry Smith, ed., *St. Clair Papers: The Life and Public Services of Arthur St. Clair,* 2 vols. (Cincinnati: R. Clarke, 1882), 2:117–118.

40. Ibid; Hamtramck to Harmar, Aug. 14, 1789, in Alvord, ed., *Kaskaskia Records*, 508–509.

41. Ford, *Journals of the Continental Congress*, 34:540–543, quotation, 541.

42. Drew McCoy, *The Last of the Fathers: James Madison and the Republican Legacy* (Cambridge: Cambridge University Press, 1989) 260–261, 268.

43. Governor Arthur St. Clair to President George Washington, May 1, 1790, in Carter, ed., *The Territorial Papers of the United States*, 28 vols. (Washington, D.C.: Government Printing Office, 1934-1975), 2:244–248.

44. "Report of Governor St. Clair to the Secretary of State [Thomas Jefferson]," Feb. 10, 1791, in Carter, ed., *Territorial Papers*, 2:332–337, quotation, 333.

45. St. Clair to Luke Decker, Oct. 11, 1793, ibid; 3:415–416. In *Groves v. Slaughter*, 15 Peters (U.S.) 449 (1841), the U.S. Supreme Court would make a similar analysis of a provision of the Mississippi Constitution of 1832, which prohibited the importation of slaves as merchandise. The court would assert that this provision could not become enforceable without legislative action.

46. Judge George Turner to Governor St. Clair, June 14, 1794, in Smith, ed., *St. Clair Papers*, 2:325–326; St. Clair to Turner, Dec. 14, 1794, ibid, 2:330–332.

47. St. Clair to Winthrop Sargent, Apr. 28, 1795, ibid, 2:340–343; "Inquiry into the Official Conduct of a Judge of the Supreme Court of the Northwestern Territory," *American State Papers, Class X, Miscellaneous,* 2 vols. (Washington, D.C.: Gales and Seton, 1834), 1:151–152, 157; Governor St. Clair to William St. Clair, June 3, 1795, in Smith, ed., *St. Clair Papers*, 2:372–373.

48. For a discussion of these petitions see Chapter 3, "Evading the Ordinance: The Persistence of Bondage in Indiana and Illinois," in this volume. The petitions are collected in Jacob Piatt Dunn, "Slavery Petitions and Papers," *Indiana Historical Society Publications* (Indianapolis: Bowen-Merrill Company, 1894), 2:443–529. See esp. "Memorial of Randolph and St. Clair Counties, Jan. 17, 1806," 498; "Legislative Resolutions of 1807 [1806]," 507; "Petition of Randolph and St. Clair Counties, February 20, 1807," 510; "Legislative Petition of 1807," 515; and, against slavery, "Petition of Randolph County, February 20, 1807, Counter to the Preceding Petition," 512; "Counter Petition of Clark County," 518; and "Report on the Preceding," 521. "The Report of General W. Johnston, Chairman of the Committee to which the Petitions on the Slavery Question had been Referred," reprinted from the *Vincennes Sun*, Dec. 17, 1808, is on 522. See also "Slavery in the Indiana Territory," No. 222, 9th Cong., 2d sess., House of Representatives, *American State Papers, Miscellaneous*, 1:477–478; and "Slavery in the Indiana Territory," No. 222, 10th Cong., 1st sess., Senate, *American State Papers, Miscellaneous*, 1:484–486.

49. "A Law concerning Servants. Adopted from the Virginia code, and published at Vincennes, the twenty-second day of September one thousand eight hundred and three . . . ," in Francis S. Philbrick, ed., *Laws of Indiana Territory, 1801–1809* (Springfield: Illinois State Library, 1930), 42; Illinois Constitution, 1848, Art. XIII, Sec. 16.

50. Poole, *Ordinance of 1787*, 8–9.

51. Davis, "Significance of Excluding Slavery," 78.

52. *State v. Lasselle*, 1 Black. (Ind.) 60 (1820). In 1820, the United States Census reported 190 slaves living in Indiana. As late as 1840, the census found three slaves in the state.

53. Harris, *Negro Servitude in Illinois*, 18; Moore, *Missouri Controversy*, 34, 54. See also Chapter 3 in this volume.

54. Illinois Constitution, 1818, Art. VI, declared that slavery shall not "hereafter be introduced into this State," which implied that slaves already in the state could be retained. This article also upheld certain forms of indentured servitude and allowed slaves to be brought from other states for limited amounts of time to work in the salt-making industry. See also Moore, *Missouri Controversy*, 258–287. For a handy list of Illinois laws supporting slavery passed before 1840, see *Slave Code of The State of Illinois* (Julilet [*sic*]: Will County Anti-Slavery Society, 1840), reprinted in Paul Finkelman, ed., *Statutes on Slavery: The Pamphlet Literature* (New York: Garland, 1988) 2:81.

55. For example, see *Hays v. Borders*, 1 Gilman (Ill.) 46 (1844), upholding indentures made before statehood that amounted to lifetime slavery. Illinois Constitution, 1848, Art. XIII, Sec. 16, finally abolished all slavery in the state.

56. Davis argues that better drafting would have undermined its passage in 1787: its "very ambiguity was probably essential for the initial congressional consensus." Davis, "Significance of Excluding Slavery," 88. Yet, this is not at all clear. If Congress intended to exclude slavery from the Northwest, then it seems that more direct language would been more likely to accomplish this goal.

57. The exact number of slaves living in Indiana and Illinois is impossible to determine. The 1810 census listed 237 slaves and 393 free blacks in Indiana, "although many of the latter group were undoubtedly held under indentures." Thornbrough, *Negro in Indiana*, 22. The 1820 census found 917 slaves in Illinois and 190 slaves in Indiana. Undoubtedly many of the 1,677 free blacks in those two states were also held in some form of servitude. As late as 1840, Illinois had 331 slaves. It is likely that more than 2,000 persons were held in slavery in Indiana and Illinois between 1787 and 1848.

Chapter Three. Evading the Ordinance: The Persistence of Bondage in Indiana and Illinois

1. See, generally, Chapter 2 of this volume.

2. See, for example, James Willard Hurst, *Law and the Conditions of Freedom in the Nineteenth-Century United States* (Madison: University of Wisconsin Press, 1956); Morton J. Horwitz, *The Transformation of American Law, 1780–1860* (Cambridge: Harvard University Press, 1977).

3. On the South Carolinian defense of slavery at the Constitutional Convention, see Chapter 1 of this volume.

4. "Petition of October 1, 1800," in Jacob Piatt Dunn, "Slavery Petitions and Papers," *Indiana Historical Society Publications*, vol. 2 (Indianapolis: Indianapolis Historical Society, 1894), 2:456.

5. "Legislative Petition of Dec. 18, 1805," ibid., 478.

6. "Memorial of Barthelemi Tardiveau, July 8, 1788," in Clarence W. Alvord, ed., *Kaskaskia Records, 1778–1709* (Springfield: Illinois State Library, 1909), 485–488; Worthington Chauncey Ford, et al., eds. *Journals of the Continental Congress, 1774–1789,* 34 vols. (Washington, D.C.: Government Printing Office, 1904–1937), 34:540–542.

7. See Chapter 2 of this volume. Governor Arthur St. Clair to President George Washington, May 1, 1790, in Clarence Edwin Carter, ed., *The Territorial Papers of the United States,* 28 vols. (Washington, D.C.: Government Printing Office, 1934–1975), 2:244–248.

8. Chapter 2 of this volume; St. Clair to Luke Decker, Oct. 11, 1793, in Carter, ed., *Territorial Papers,* 3:415–416.

9. Dunn, "Slavery Petitions," 2:447, 451.

10. Ibid., 448–449; Chapter 1 of this volume.

11. Dunn, "Slavery Petitions," 2:448. The suggestion that settlers might move across the Mississippi to the "Spanish dominions" also implied a threat to the security of the nation. Eric Foner, *Free Soil, Free Labor, Free Men: The Ideology of the Republican Party before the Civil War* (New York: Oxford University Press, 1970), chs. 1, 2.

12. Dunn, "Slavery Petitions," 2:449.

13. Robert McColley, *Slavery and Jeffersonian Virginia,* 2d ed. (Urbana: University of Illinois Press, 1973), 173–75.

14. Dunn, "Slavery Petitions," 2:447–449.

15. The petitioners came close to articulating, at the political level, Thomas Jefferson's radical notions of inheritance, "'that the earth belongs in usufruct to the living': that the dead have neither powers nor rights over it." Jefferson believed that this theory of inheritance should apply to all laws, because the "earth belongs always to the living generation." Thus, Jefferson felt that "no society can make a perpetual constitution or even a perpetual law." Jefferson would have limited all laws to a life span of nineteen years. Thomas Jefferson to James Madison, Paris, Sept. 6, 1789, in Julian P. Boyd et al., eds., *The Papers of Thomas Jefferson* (Princeton: Princeton University Press, 1950–), 15:392–397. The Illinois petitioners seem to have adopted this concept from the Ordinance of 1787. On Jefferson and inheritance, see also Stanley N. Katz, "Republicanism and the Law of Inheritance in the American Revolutionary Era," *Michigan Law Review,* 76 (1977): 1–29; Adrienne Koch, *Jefferson and Madison: The Great Collaboration* (New York: Knopf, 1950), ch. 4.

16. Dunn, "Slavery Petitions," 2:452–453.

17. William Henry Smith, ed., *The St. Clair Papers: The Life and Public Services of Arthur St. Clair,* 2 vols. (Cincinnati: R. Clarke, 1882), 2:447–448n, 451n.

18. Ibid.

19. "An Act to divide the territory of the United States northwest of the Ohio, into two separate governments," Act of May 7, 1800, *U.S. Statutes at Large,* 2:58–59.

20. Dunn, "Slavery Petitions," 2:455–461.

21. Ibid., 456–457.

22. Ibid., 462.

23. Ibid., 471; *Illinois Constitution,* 1818, Art. VI, Sec. 2.

24. Dunn, "Slavery Petitions," 2:471. On the military insecurity of the Northwest, see Gordon T. Stewart, "The Northwest and the Balance of Power in North America," in Frederick D. Williams, ed., *The Northwest Ordinance: Essays on Its Formulation, Provisions, and Legacy* (East Lansing: Michigan State University, 1989), 21–38.

25. Dunn, "Slavery Petitions," 2:473–475.

26. Ibid. 2:476–77.

27. The committee, chaired by Jeremiah Morrow of Ohio, included James M. Garnett (Virginia), Matthew Walton (Kentucky), O'Brien Smith (South Carolina), Benjamin Parke (Indiana Territory), Philip Van Cortlandt (New York), and John

Hamilton (Pennsylvania). Van Cortlandt and Hamilton were Jeffersonian Democrats, who may have sympathized with their proslavery colleagues. In addition, Hamilton was from Washington County, an area in southwest Pennsylvania that had been claimed by Virginia until the 1780s. This county had a high percentage of southern-born inhabitants, and as late as 1799 residents of the county were attempting to claim as slaves blacks who had gained their freedom under the state's gradual emancipation act of 1780. See Paul Finkelman, *An Imperfect Union: Slavery, Federalism, and Comity* (Chapel Hill: University of North Carolina Press, 1981), 60–62.

28. Dunn, "Slavery Petitions," 2: 494–95. The proslavery bias of the committee is suggested by the fact that the report ignored a petition from settlers opposed to slavery in Dearborn County, Indiana. Dunn, "Slavery Petitions," 492.

29. "Slavery in the Indiana Territory," No. 222, 9th Cong., 2d sess., House of Representatives, *American State Papers, Class X, Miscellaneous*, 1:477–78; "Slavery in the Indiana Territory," No. 229, 10th Cong., 1st sess., Senate, ibid., 484–86; Dunn, "Slavery Petitions," 2:498, 507, 521; 515.

30. "Slavery in the Indiana Territory," No. 222; "Slavery in the Indiana Territory," No. 229; Dunn, "Slavery Petitions," 512; 518; 521; 522.

31. Homer J. Webster, "William Henry Harrison's Administration of Indiana Territory," *Indiana Historical Society Publications*, vol. 4 (Indianapolis: Indiana Historical Society, 1907); Dorothy Burne Goebel, *William Henry Harrison: A Political Biography* (Indianapolis: Historical Bureau of the Indiana Library and Historical Department, 1926), 76-77; Logan Esarey, ed., *Messages and Letters of William Henry Harrison,* 2 vols. (Indianapolis: Indiana Historical Commission, 1922), 1:60–67; Jacob Piatt Dunn, *Indiana: A Redemption from Slavery* (Boston and New York: Houghton Mifflin, 1888), 312–13.

32. Peter S. Onuf, *Statehood and Union: A History of the Northwest Ordinance* (Bloomington and Indianapolis: Indiana University Press, 1987), 118.

33. "A Law concerning Servants. Adopted from the Virginia code, and published at Vincennes, the twenty-second day of September one thousand eight hundred and three," in Francis S. Philbrick, ed., *Laws of Indiana Territory, 1801–1809* (Springfield: Illinois State Library, 1930), 42.

34. Ibid., 42–45. On the seventeenth century, see generally, Edmund Morgan, *American Slavery, American Freedom: The Ordeal of Virginia* (New York: W.W. Norton, 1975).

35. Philbrick, ed., *Laws of Indiana Territory*, 42–43.

36. "A Law in addition to a law intitled a law to regulate the practice of the General Court upon Appeals and Writs of Error, and other purposes. Adopted from the Virginia and Kentucky codes," Sept. 20, 1803, ibid., 33, 40.

37. "An Act concerning the introduction of Negroes and Mulattoes into this Territory," Aug. 26, 1805, ibid., 136–139. New Jersey remained a slave state until 1804, and thus Parke might well have been raised in a slaveholding community. It was the last northern state to adopt a gradual emancipation statute. See Arthur Zilversmit, "Liberty and Property: New Jersey and the Abolition of Slavery," *New Jersey History* 88 (1970): 215–226, and Simeon F. Moss, "The Persistence of Slavery and Involuntary Servitude in a Free State (1685–1866)," *Journal of Negro History* 35 (1950): 289–314.

38. See N. Dwight Harris, *The History of Negro Servitude in Illinois* (Chicago: A.C. McClurg, 1904), 258–262, for examples of indentures; Emma Lou Thornbrough, *The Negro in Indiana: A Study of a Minority* (Indianapolis: Indiana Historical Bureau, 1957), 9.

39. Philbrick, ed., *Laws of Indiana Territory*, 203–204; 463–467; 523–526; 657–558; 399–425; 481–495; and 284–288.

40. Onuf, *Statehood and Union*, 118; "An Act to repeal the act entitled 'An act for the introduction of negroes and mulattoes into this territory,'" in Louis Ewbank and Dorothy Riker, eds., *The Laws of Indiana Territory, 1809–1816* (Indianapolis: Indiana Historical Bureau, 1934), 138–139.

41. Indiana Constitution, 1816, Art. XI, Sec. 7.

42. Ibid., Art. VIII, Sec. 1.

43. *Harry v. Decker and Hopkins*, 1 Walker (Miss.) 36 (1818), involves Indiana slave owners who attempted to take their slave Harry out of the state and sell him in Mississippi. In *State v. Lasselle*, 1 Blackf. (Ind.) 60 (1820), the Indiana Supreme Court ruled that all slaves living in the state were free under the Constitution of 1816. In *In re Mary Clark, a Woman of Color*, 1 Blackf. (Ind.) 122 (1821), the Indiana court ruled that adult blacks could not be held as indentured servants against their will. U.S. Bureau of the Census, *Negro Population in the United States, 1790–1915* (Washington, D.C.: Government Printing Office, 1918), 57. The census probably undercounted the number of people actually held in servitude. An 1830 town census in Vincennes found thirty-two slaves. Thornbrough, *Negro in Indiana*, 30.

44. The exact number of slaves and black servants is unclear. An 1818 census taken shortly before statehood found 847 "slaves" and 326 "free blacks" in Illinois. There are, however, no existing returns for Randolph and Edwards counties and only partial returns for St. Clair County. Randolph and St. Clair, in fact, had large slave populations at the time. The 1820 state census found only 668 "slaves" and 469 "free blacks," but this does not include 375 "blacks" of unknown status in Randolph and Washington counties. The federal census in 1820 found 917 "slaves" and 457 "free blacks" in the state. It is quite likely that many of the "free blacks" listed in all three censuses were actually indentured for long periods of time. There are discrepancies between all of the censuses. For example, the 1820 state census found more slaves than the federal census did in four counties, and fewer slaves than the federal census in six counties. The state census recorded 342 "blacks" in Randolph, while the federal census found only 317, of which 233 were slaves. All of these numbers are inexact. It seems likely that slaves were undercounted in all three censuses. Masters might have tried to hide slaves to avoid taxation. For political reasons masters might have passed slaves off as free workers, and also for political reasons census takers might have chosen to count indentured blacks (even those with lifetime indentures) as free. If we take the largest number of slaves found by the various censuses for each county, the total is 1,165. It is probably safe to assume that this number is closest to the true number of slaves in the state between 1818 and 1820. These data are from Margaret Cross Norton, *Illinois Census Returns. 1810, 1818* (Springfield: Illinois State Library, 1935), xxx–xxxii.

45. Webster, "William Henry Harrison's Administration," 177, 198, 218.

46. Francis S. Philbrick, ed., *Laws of the Illinois Territory 1809–1818* (Springfield: Illinois State Historical Library, 1950), 91–92; "Act of Jan. 25, 1807," *Laws of Ohio*, 1807, 1–5. Northern laws on this subject are discussed in Paul Finkelman, "Prelude to the Fourteenth Amendment: Black Legal Rights in the Antebellum North," *Rutgers Law Journal* 17 (1986): 430–443.

47. Philbrick, ed., *Laws of the Illinois Territory*, 157–158.

48. Ibid.

49. Harris, *Negro Servitude in Illinois*, 15.

50. Philbrick, ed., *Laws of the Illinois Territory*, 154–155. Eugene H. Berwanger, *The Frontier Against Slavery: Western Anti-Negro Prejudice and the Slavery Extension Controversy* (Urbana: University of Illinois Press, 1967), 12; Thomas Forsyth to Governor Edwards, Dec. 8, 1815, in Carter, ed., *Territorial Papers*, 17:259–260.

51. Census figures for this period are very unreliable. A census in 1818 found 1,173 blacks in the state, including 847 slaves. There are no records, however, of this census for a few counties, including Randolph, which had the largest slave and black population in Illinois. This census probably undercounted the number of slaves, indentured servants, and free blacks. Masters who feared they might lose their slaves under the Ordinance or state constitution, or those who simply wanted to avoid taxes, had great incentives for not reporting their slaves and for reporting slaves and servants as "free persons." Free blacks who may have entered Illinois in violation of restrictive legislation, or who were fugitives, were also inclined to avoid the census takers whenever possible. Norton, *Illinois Census Returns*, xxx-xxxii. *Western Intelligencer* quoted in Onuf, *Statehood and Union*, 123.

52. Harris, *Negro Servitude in Illinois*, 19.

53. McColley, *Slavery and Jeffersonian Virginia*, 175. The ability of slave owners to settle lands more quickly than non–slave owners remained a constant factor of western expansion. Between 1787 and 1821, only three western free states (Ohio, Indiana, and Illinois) entered the union, while six western slave states (Kentucky, Tennessee, Louisiana, Mississippi, Alabama, and Missouri) were admitted. Four slave states west of the Mississippi (Louisiana, Missouri, Arkansas, and Texas) entered the union before the first free state (Iowa) was admitted from that region. In 1850, before the admission of California to the union, the fifteen free states had only 463,361 square miles of land, while the same number of slave states contained 816,204 square miles.

54. On ideology, see James Oakes, *The Ruling Race: A History of American Slaveholders* (New York: Knopf, 1982), 90; see also 77–78, 90–91. Whether slave owners would have moved to Illinois is uncertain. Robert McColley persuasively argues that, by 1818, if not earlier, the direction of slave migration had been permanently pushed south and west by the profitability of cotton. "What prevented the slaveholding planters from dominating Illinois, and possibly even Indiana, was, of all things, cotton. . . . [B]y 1800 cotton was rapidly becoming known as a plantation crop without parallel, and the migration of slavery took a distinct turn toward those latitudes where the growing season would sustain the fibrous plant. The very success of cotton on the lower Mississippi created new opportunities for planters growing grain in the more temperate climates, and slavery was handsomely maintained, for this reason, in Kentucky and Missouri. But planters on the move had little reason to grow grain and hogs in competition with free labor when an obliging government, abetted by eager vigilantes, was continually clearing the Indians from choice cotton lands in the Southwest." *Slavery and Jeffersonian Virginia*, 181.

55. Harris, *Negro Servitude in Illinois*, 18, 24–25; Donald L. Robinson, *Slavery in the Structure of American Politics, 1765–1820* (New York: Harcourt Brace Jovanovich, 1971), 378–423, esp. 408, 412–413; Glover Moore, *The Missouri Controversy, 1819–1821* (Lexington: University of Kentucky Press, 1953).

56. Illinois Constitution, 1818, Art. VI, Sec. 1.

57. Ibid., Sec. 2.

58. Ibid., Sec. 3.

59. Ibid., Sec. 3.

60. On gradual emancipation, see, generally, Zilversmit, *First Emancipation*, and Finkelman, *Imperfect Union*, 3–101.

61. Berwanger, *Frontier Against Slavery*, 14.

62. Unfortunately there are no remaining records of the 1818 convention, so it is impossible to know what kind of debate, if any, there was over this section of the constitution.

63. "An Act respecting Free Negroes, Mulattoes, Servants, and Slaves," approved Mar. 30, 1819, Illinois Session Laws, 1819, 354, reenacted and reprinted in *The Revised Laws of Illinois* (Vandalia: Printed by Greiner & Sherman, 1833), 457.

64. *Jarrot (colored Man) v. Jarrot*, 2 Gilman (III.) 1 (1845).

65. Onuf, *Statehood and Union*, 123.

66. Ibid., 123–130. See also note 6 of Chapter 2.

67. *Strader v. Graham*, 10 How. (U.S.) 82 (1850), discussed in Finkelman, *Imperfect Union*, 222–227, 271–278, and passim. It is possible that Congress could bind a territory in the law admitting the territory as a state. Congress did this in 1812 when it required that Louisiana adopt jury trials and the English language. However, once a territory becomes a state, it cannot be bound by previous congressional actions.

68. Quoted in Onuf, *Statehood and Union*, 124.

69. Ibid., 133–152.

Chapter Four. Implementing the Proslavery Constitution: The Adoption of the Fugitive Slave Law of 1793

1. Jonathan Elliot, ed., *The Debates in the Several State Conventions on the Adoption of the Federal Constitution*, 5 vols. (New York: Burt Franklin, 1987, reprint of 1888 ed.), 4:286.

2. U.S. Constitution, Art. IV, Sec. 2, Par. 3.

3. The only other response to Pinckney and Butler's proposal was Roger Sherman's sarcastic observation that he "saw no more propriety in the public seizing and surrendering a slave or servant, than a horse." Max Farrand. ed., *The Records of the Federal Convention of 1787*, rev. ed. 4 vols. (New Haven: Yale University Press, 1966), 2:443 (quotations in text and note), 453–454. The history of this clause is discussed in Chapter 1 in this volume. See also, William M. Wiecek, "The Witch at the Christening: Slavery and the Constitution's Origins," in Leonard W. Levy and Dennis J. Mahoney, eds., *The Framing and Ratification of the Constitution* (New York: Macmillan, 1987), 167–184.

4. On the debates in the convention, see Chapter 1; "An Act for the Gradual Abolition of Slavery," Act of March 1, 1780, *Laws of the Commonwealth of Pennsylvania*, 4 vols. (Philadelphia: 1810), 1:492–93. Section 9 of this law provided for the return of fugitive slaves. The gradual abolition acts of Rhode Island and Connecticut, both passed in 1784, had similar provisions.

5. "An Act respecting fugitives from justice, and persons escaping from the service of their masters," Act of February 12, 1793, in *U.S. Statutes at Large*, 1:302 (hereinafter cited as Act of 1793). William R. Leslie, "A Study in the Origins of Interstate Rendition: The Big Beaver Creek Murders," *American Historical Review*

57 (1951): 63–76, argues that the 1793 law resulted from a conflict between Pennsylvania and Virginia over the rendition of four men charged with killing peaceful Delaware Indians. Coincidentally, some of those wanted for killing the Indians were also involved in the kidnapping of the free black John Davis. However, as this chapter demonstrates, the 1793 law regulating both the extradition of fugitives from justice and the rendition of fugitive slaves was a result of Governor Thomas Mifflin's seeking the return of the three Virginians for kidnapping John Davis, who the Virginians claimed was a fugitive slave. Critical to this analysis is the fact that on August 24, 1791, Governor Mifflin praised Governor Beverley Randolph for his cooperation in seeking the arrest of the men charged with killing the Delaware Indians. Yet this was over a month after Governor Mifflin had written to President George Washington complaining about Virginia's noncompliance in the extradition of the men who kidnapped John Davis. This chronology shows that the connection of this case, and the 1793 law, to the Big Beaver Creek murders is coincidental. Thomas Mifflin, "To the Assembly Concerning the State of the Commonwealth," August 24, 1791, in George Edward Read, ed., *Pennsylvania Archives: Fourth Series*, (Harrisburg: State Printer, 1900), 4:178–81.

6. There were numerous well-known antebellum conflicts over the return of both fugitives from justice and fugitive slaves. On fugitive slave rendition, see Thomas D. Morris, *Free Men All: The Personal Liberty Laws of the North, 1780–1861* (Baltimore: Johns Hopkins University Press, 1974); Robert M. Cover, *Justice Accused: Antislavery and the Judicial Process* (New Haven: Yale University Press, 1975); and my own articles, "The Treason Trial of Castner Hanway," in Michal Belknap, ed., *American Political Trials* (rev. ed., Westport, Conn.: Greenwood, 1994), 77–96; "Sorting Out Prigg v. Pennsylvania," *Rutgers Law Journal* 24 (1993): 605–665; "Fugitive Slaves, Midwestern Racial Tolerance, and the Value of Justice Delayed," *Iowa Law Review*, 78 (1992): 89–141; "State Constitutional Protections of Liberty and the Antebellum New Jersey Supreme Court: Chief Justice Hornblower and the Fugitive Slave Law," *Rutgers Law Journal*, 23 (1992): 753–787; "International Extradition and Fugitive Slaves: The John Anderson Case," *Brooklyn Journal of International Law* 18 (1992): 765–810. On conflicts over the interstate rendition of fugitives from justice, see my articles, "States' Rights, North and South in Antebellum America," in Kermit L. Hall and James W. Ely Jr., eds., *An Uncertain Tradition: Constitutionalism and the History of the South* (Athens: University of Georgia Press, 1989), 125–58; and "The Protection of Black Rights in Seward's New York," *Civil War History* 34 (1988), 211–234.

7. For a discussion of this problem in the first Congress, see Joseph C. Burke, "The Proslavery Argument in the First Congress," *Duquesne Review* 14 (1969): 3–15, and Howard A. Ohline, "Slavery, Economics, and Congressional Politics, 1790," *Journal of Southern History* 46 (1980): 335–360. See generally Donald L. Robinson, *Slavery in the Structure of American Politics, 1765–1820* (New York: Harcourt Brace Jovanovich, 1971).

8. On the controversy over the boundary between Virginia and Pennsylvania, see Peter S. Onuf, *The Origins of the Federal Republic: Jurisdictional Controversies in the United States, 1775-1787* (Philadelphia: University of Pennsylvania Press, 1983), 49–66. On the general support for slavery in Virginia in the early national period, see Robert McColley, *Slavery and Jeffersonian Virginia*, 2d ed. (Urbana: University of Illinois Press, 1973), 182–189.

9. The indenture period was intended to allow masters time to educate the chil-

dren of their slaves and to teach them a trade. It also enabled the master to recoup most or all of the cost of raising the children of their slaves. Robert William Fogel and Stanley L. Engerman, "Philanthropy at Bargain Prices: Notes on the Economics of Gradual Emancipation," *Journal of Legal Studies* 3 (1974): 377–401.

10. "Act for the Gradual Abolition of Slavery," *Laws of the Commonwealth of Pennsylvania*, 1:492–93. The drafting and adoption of this act are discussed in Arthur Zilversmit, *The First Emancipation: The Abolition of Slavery in the North* (Chicago: University of Chicago Press, 1967), 124–137. The law is put in a larger context in William M. Wiecek, *The Sources of Antislavery Constitutionalism in America, 1760–1848* (Ithaca, N. Y.: Cornell University Press, 1977); David Brion Davis, *The Problem of Slavery in the Age of Revolution, 1770-1823* (Ithaca, N.Y.: Cornell University Press, 1975); and A. Leon Higginbotham, *In the Matter of Color: Race and the American Legal Process: The Colonial Period* (New York: Oxford University Press, 1978), 299–310.

11. Onuf, *Origins of the Federal Republic*, 49–60 (quotations on p. 60).

12. Acceptance of Pennsylvania's jurisdiction, which registration implied, threatened many land titles in the area, which were based on Virginia claims. Thus in 1780 some slave owners in the area faced the dilemma that they could only protect their slave property by jeopardizing their land claims.

13. "Virginia Claims to Land in Western Pennsylvania," in William Henry Egle, ed., *Pennsylvania Archives: Third Series*, (Harrisburg: Wm. Stanley Ray, 1894), 3:485–504. See Onuf, *Origins of the Federal Republic*, 57–59.

14. "An act to Redress Certain Grievances, Within the Counties of Westmoreland and Washington," Act of April 13, 1782. *Laws of the Commonwealth of Pennsylvania*, 1:496. For a discussion of the judicial construction of this law, see Paul Finkelman, *An Imperfect Union: Slavery, Federalism, and Comity* (Chapel Hill: University of North Carolina Press, 1981), 60–62, 230 n.70.

15. June 23, 1780, *Journal of the House of Delegates*, 1780 session, 60–61, quoted and cited in Onuf, *Origins of the Federal Republic*, 60–61 and n.70.

16. Its formal name was the Pennsylvania Society for Promoting the Abolition of Slavery, the Relief of Free Negroes Unlawfully Held in Bondage, and for Improving the Condition of the African Race.

17. Wm. Mimachan and Benj. Biggs to the Governor [Beverley Randolph], November 20, 1791, in William R. Palmer and Sherwin McRae, eds., *Calendar of Virginia State Papers . . .* Vol. 5 (Richmond: Virginia State Library, 1885), 396–398; Mifflin, "To the Assembly Concerning the State of the Commonwealth." A court of "oyer and terminer" (to hear and determine) is a minor trial court.

18. Alex. Addison to [the Committee of Correspondence of] the Pennsylvania Society for promoting the Abolition of Slavery, the Relief of Free Negroes Unlawfully Held in Bondage, and for Improving the Condition of the African Race [hereinafter to be called the Pennsylvania Abolition Society], December 6, 1790, Committee of Correspondence, Letterbook, Vol. 1, page 72, Papers of the Pennsylvania Abolition Society (Historical Society of Pennsylvania, Philadelphia; hereinafter cited as PAS Papers), microfilm reel 11.

19. Ibid.; Pennsylvania Abolition Society, General Meeting Minutebook, Vol. 1, page 154, minutes of May 30, 1791, PAS Papers, microfilm reel 11; "To Thomas Mifflin, Governor of Pennsylvania: The Memorial of the Pennsylvania Society for Promoting the abolition of slavery . . . ," in *American State Papers: Class X. Miscellaneous*, 2 vols. (Washington, D.C.: Gales and Seton, 1834), 1:39.

20. Governor Thomas Mifflin to Governor Beverley Randolph, June 4, 1791, in *American State Papers: Class X. Miscellaneous*, 1:40.

21. Beverley Randolph to Innes, June 14, 1791, and Innes to Beverley Randolph, undated, in Palmer and McRae, eds., *Calendar of Virginia State Papers*, 5:326–328 (first and second quotations on p. 326; third through sixth quotations on p. 327). Randolph's refusal to cooperate contrasts with his willingness, a month earlier, to issue a proclamation for the arrest of two Virginians for the murder of four Indians in Pennsylvania. Randolph later rescinded the proclamation, and this became the second instance in which Virginia refused to comply with a Pennsylvania extradition requisition. "Proclamation of Governor Beverley Randolph," May 3, 1791, and "In Council," January 3, 1792, both ibid., 298–299, 421–422. The relationship between these two incidents is discussed in Leslie, "Study in the Origins of Interstate Rendition," *American Historical Review* 57 (1951): 63–76.

22. Innes to Randolph, undated, in Palmer and McRae, eds., *Calendar of Virginia State Papers,* 5:327.

23. Governor Randolph to Mifflin, June 20, 1791, and July 8, 1791, ibid., 329, 340–341; Mifflin to President Washington, July 18, 1791; Attorney General Edmund Randolph to Washington, July 20, 1791, both in Alford, *American State Papers: Class X. Miscellaneous*, 1:38–39, 41–43 (quotations on p. 39).

24. Edmund Randolph to Washington, July 20, 1791, in Alford, *American State Papers: Class X. Miscellaneous*, 1:41–42. A few weeks later, on August 2, Governor Mifflin informed President Washington that Wells was in fact in custody but that the other two men remained at large. Mifflin to President Washington, August 2, 1791, and certification of Edward Burd [Prothonotary of the Pennsylvania Supreme Court], November 10, 1788, ibid., 43.

25. Ibid., 42.

26. Ibid.

27. Ibid., 42–43.

28. Mifflin to Washington, August 2, 1791, ibid., 43; Mifflin, "To the Assembly concerning the State of the Commonwealth," ibid., 180. Randolph's biographer states that Washington fully followed the attorney general's advice and that Mifflin, in turn, accepted Randolph's suggestions. John J. Reardon, *Edmund Randolph: A Biography* (New York: Macmillan, 1974), 202. This is true only to the extent that Washington passed Randolph's suggestions on to the two governors and to the extent that Mifflin continued to negotiate with Governor Randolph. However, Washington clearly ignored Attorney General Randolph's advice about not asking Congress to become involved in the controversy. Washington turned the entire matter over to Congress shortly after the new session opened in October 1791. President Washington to "Gentlemen of the Senate and of the House of Representatives," October 27, 1791, in Alford, *American State Papers: Class X. Miscellaneous*, 1:38.

29. Wm. Mimachan and Benj. Biggs to the Governor, November 20, 1791, in Palmer and McRae, eds., *Calendar of Virginia State Papers*, 5:397 (quotations); see also John Waller and Horatio Hall to the Governor, November 20, 1791, ibid., 402–403.

30. Thomas Mifflin, "To the Assembly concerning . . . the surrender of fugitives . . . ," January 25, 1792, in Reed, ed. *Pennsylvania Archives: Fourth Series*, 4:218–221 (quotation on p. 221).

31. President Washington to "Gentlemen of the Senate and of the House of Representatives," October 27, 1791, in *American State Papers: Class X. Miscellaneous*, 1:38; *Journal of the House of Representatives* 4, 2d Cong., 1st sess., 15, 17 (first and

second quotations), 30 (third quotation) (House debates of October 28, October 31, and November 15, 1791); *Annals of Congress*, 2d Cong., 1st sess., 18 (Senate debate of October 27, 1791), and 147, 148 (House debate of October 28, 1791).

32. U.S. House of Representatives, 2d Cong., 1st sess., *A Bill Respecting Fugitives from Justice and from the Service of Masters*, printed broadside (New York: New-York Historical Society; hereinafter cited as House Bill of 1791). This appears to be the only extant copy of the bill. None is known to exist in the National Archives.

33. Farrand, ed., *Records of the Federal Convention*, 2:11, 443, 453. For a discussion of this see Chapter 1 of this book.

34. House Bill of 1791, paragraph one.

35. Ibid., paragraph two (quotation). Paragraph one of the 1791 bill, which deals with the extradition of fugitives from justice, is explicit about such matters as requiring an extradition requisition "in writing, authenticated by the signature of the Governor" and "by the seal of such state." Similarly, the bill required that the governor arresting the fugitive issue a warrant "under his hand and the seal of the same state . . ." In the description of the "deposition" necessary to arrest a fugitive slave, such details are omitted. Thus it is not clear if the drafters of this bill intended to require a sworn deposition, taken before a judge. It seems that, if they had meant this, they would have spelled out these requirements. The drafters of the bill probably did not intend a deposition in chancery, which is the precursor of the modern interrogatory, in which the witness is questioned under oath by attorneys for either or both sides of the case. It obviously would have been impossible for an alleged fugitive to send an attorney to a southern state to depose a person who might offer evidence against him. Thus the meaning of "deposition" in this bill is unclear. An early treatise on American law (although one written many years after this law was debated) noted that depositions were "not favored by the law." Francis Hilliard, *The Elements of Law: Being a Comprehensive Summary of American Jurisprudence* (Boston: Hilliarad Gray; New York: Halstead and Voorhies, 1835), 308.

36. Even in the late antebellum period, when tensions were much greater and opposition to slavery much stronger, many, perhaps even a majority, of northerners complied with the Fugitive Slave Law of 1850 when confronted with the actual enforcement of the law. Although I think his thesis of northern support for the 1850 law is overstated, Stanley W. Campbell, *The Slave Catchers: Enforcement of the Fugitive Slave Law, 1850–1860* (Chapel Hill: University of North Carolina Press, 1968), vii-viii, does demonstrate that many northerners willingly enforced the law. However, this apparent support for the law may also have been a result of selective enforcement attempts. For example, Frederick Douglass argued that violent opposition to the law at Christiana, Pennsylvania, and Syracuse, New York, both in 1851, made it "almost a dead letter." Frederick Douglass, *The Life and Times of Frederick Douglass* (1892; reprint, New York: Macmillan, 1962), 282.

37. House Bill of 1791; *Prigg v. Pennsylvania*, 16 Pet. (4. U.S.) 539 (1842). For a fuller discussion of this case, see Finkelman, "Sorting Out *Prigg v. Pennsylvania*," and Finkelman, "Story Telling on the Supreme Court: *Prigg v. Pennsylvania* and Justice Joseph Story's Judicial Nationalism," *Supreme Court Review*, 1994:(1995), 247–294.

38. *Journal of the House of Representatives*, 4, 2d Cong., 1st sess., 30, 32–34 (debates of November 15, 18, 1791). Leslie, "A Study in the Origins of Interstate Rendition," n. 73.

39. *Journal of the Senate*, IV, 2 Cong., 1 Sess., 170 (debate of March 30, 1792), *Annals of Congress*, 2d Cong., 1st sess., 115 (quotation).

40. U.S. Senate, 2d Cong., 2 sess., "Bill respecting fugitives from Justice and persons escaping from the service of their masters, Dec. 20, 1792," handwritten draft in file Sen. 2A-DI, Bills and Resolutions, 1789–1968, Records of the United States Senate, Record Group 46 (National Archives and Records Service, Washington; hereinafter cited as RG 46). The same file also contains a three-page version of the bill, which was printed by John Fenno, and is hereinafter cited as Senate Bill 1. The Senate journal does not indicate when this printing was ordered. U.S. Senate, 2d Cong., 2d sess., "Amendments Reported by the Committee on the Bill respecting fugitives from justice and persons escaping from the service of their masters," ibid. There is no known printed version of this bill, which is hereinafter cited as Senate Bill 2. U.S. Senate, 2d Cong., 2d sess., "Amendments reported on the report of the Committee respecting fugitives from Justice and Persons escaping from the service of their masters January 14, 1793," ibid. (hereinafter cited as Senate Bill 3). These amendments, along with the text of Senate Bill 2, were printed by John Fenno as *The Report of the Committee on the Bill Respecting Fugitives from Justice and Persons Escaping from the Service of their Masters, as Proposed and Amended* ([Philadelphia, 1793]). The only printed version of this I have found is marked up with the amendments that were added between January 15 and 17. A handwritten notation on this heavily marked-up printed bill reads "The Bill passed the Senate, January 18th 1793." This version is found in file Sen. 2A-DI, RG 46, and is hereinafter cited as Printed and Amended Senate Bill 3.

41. Senate Bill 1.

42. *Journal of the Senate*, 5, 2d Cong., 2d sess., 16, 24–26 (debates of November 22, 1792; and December 20, 21, 24, 26, 27, 28, 1792). All members of the committee were chosen by ballot. In the vote to choose the original committee members and the vote to expand the committee, southern senators appear to have been more unified than their northern colleagues about whom they wanted on the committee. Both Johnston of North Carolina and Taylor of Virginia received the most votes in the balloting for the committee spots. This suggests that the southerners in the Senate understood that the issue here was vital to their section's needs. U.S. Senate, 2d Cong., 2d sess., "Lists of the Yeas and Nays," 2d Cong., Sen. 2A-J1, RG46.

43. *Journal of the Senate*, 5, 2d Cong., 2d sess., 28 (debate of January 3, 1793); Senate Bill 2.

44. Senate Bill 2. Robinson, *Slavery in the Structure of American Politics*, 286. In general, American law, at least until the decision in the 1857 *Dred Scott v. Sandford*, 19 How. (U.S.) 393 (1857), gave the states complete autonomy over the status of their residents. Thus this provision would have been consistent with most American law. However, the entire purpose of the fugitive slave provision was to nullify the common law and prevent localities from altering the status of slaves who escaped to their jurisdiction. This provision would have, in effect, nullified at least part of the Constitution's fugitive slave clause.

45. Senate Bill 2.

46. Printed and Amended Senate Bill 3; U.S. Senate, 2d Cong., 2d sess., "Mr. Butlers motion fugitives from Justice &c.," Sen. 2A-BI, RG 46.

47. Printed and Amended Senate Bill 3. *Journal of the Senate*, 5, 2d Cong., 2d sess., 33–34 (debates of January 14–16, 1793).

48. Ibid. (debates of January 14–17, 1793).

49. The Court held this in *Prigg v. Pennsylvania.*

50. Printed and Amended Senate Bill 3. An alternative would have been to create more federal courts and judgeships, but this was not a realistic possibility at the time, and no one in the Senate contemplated this solution. Ultimately, slave owners found northern courts inhospitable to their claims, and they were forced to rely on the federal courts. This is just one of many reasons that southerners eventually found the 1793 law unsatisfactory. Paul Finkelman, *"Prigg v. Pennsylvania* and Northern State Courts: Anti-Slavery Use of a Pro-Slavery Decision," *Civil War History* 25 (1979), 5–35.

51. *Journal of the Senate,* 5, 2d Cong., 2d sess., 35 (February 22, 1793).

52. *Journal of the House of Representatives,* 5, 2d Cong., 2d sess., 87–88, 104, 105, 106, 113, 116, 121 (debates of January 21, February 4, 5, 8, 9, 14, 1793); *Annals of Congress,* 2d Cong., 2d sess., 862 (House debate of January 21, 1793); *Philadelphia Gazette,* January 30 and February 13, 1793; *Philadelphia Pennsylvania Journal and Weekly Advertiser,* January 30 and February 13, 1793 (quotation); *Philadelphia Gazette of the United States,* February 6, 1793.

53. Boudinot and Dayton do not appear to have traded their support for the bill for economic gain or other special interests. Ohline, "Slavery, Economics, and Congressional Politics," 350, argues that in 1790 some northerners, although significantly *not* Elias Boudinot, failed to support an aggressively antislavery position because it would undermine their desire for southern support for economic legislation, such as assumption of the state war debts: "some New Englanders did admit privately that the assumption of state debts took precedence over antislavery." Ibid., 350. This was consistent with the position that New Englanders took at the Constitutional Convention, trading their support for the slave trade for South Carolinian support for the commerce clause. See Chapter 1 of this volume.

54. *Journal of the Senate,* 5, 2d Cong., 2d sess., 47, 48, 51, 53, 57 (February 5, 6, 8, 11, 14, 1793).

55. Act of 1793.

56. Ibid.; *Kentucky v. Dennison,* 24 How. (U.S.) 66 (1861).

57. See copy of the bill with handwritten notations in Manumissions Box 4B, PAS Papers, microfilm reel 24, p. 184; J[ames] P[emberton] [Chairman of the Committee of Correspondence] to Alex. Addison, February 12, 1793, Committee of Correspondence, Letterbook, 1789–1794, Vol. 1, 103–104 (quotation on p. 104), PAS Papers, microfilm reel 11.

58. See, for example, Finkelman, "State Constitutional Protections of Liberty." See also the opinion of Chancellor Reuben Walworth of New York in *Jack v. Martin,* 14 Wendell (N.Y.) 512 (1835). Walworth declared that the 1793 law was unconstitutional, but still upheld the return of the fugitive slave Jack on the grounds that the states should enforce the constitutional clause on their own.

59. Gary B. Nash and Jean Soderlund, *Freedom by Degrees: Emancipation in Pennsylvania and Its Aftermath* (New York: Oxford University Press, 1991), 136. Philip Foner claims four men who were members of both the Democratic Society of Pennsylvania and the PAS: George Logan, Peter S. Du Ponceau, Dr. James Hutchinson, and Absalom Baird. Philip S. Foner, *The Democratic-Republican Societies, 1790– 1800* (Westport, Conn.: Greenwood Press, 1976), 12. While twice as many as Nash and Soderlund found, the small number Foner found simply underscores the point that Federalists, not Republicans, supported abolition in Pennsylvania. Gary B. Nash, *Forging Freedom: The Formation of Philadelphia's Black Community* (Cambridge: Harvard University Press, 1988), 181–82.

60. Pinckney quoted in Elliot, ed., *Debates*, 4:286.

61. "An Act for the Gradual Abolition of Slavery," reprinted in *Laws of the Commonwealth of Pennsylvania* (Philadelphia, 1810), 1:492–496, Section 9. Gradual Emancipation Act of 1784, reprinted in *Public Laws of Rhode Island* (Providence, 1822), 441–444; Gradual Emancipation Act of 1784, reprinted in *Laws of Connecticut* (Hartford, 1821), tit. 22, 23. Act of Mar. 26, 1788, *Massachusetts General Laws* 680–682, repealed *sub silentio* by Act of Mar. 29, 1834, *Massachusetts Statutes, 1834*. Zilversmit, *First Emancipation*. These laws and this analysis are discussed at greater length in Finkelman, "Sorting Out *Prigg v. Pennsylvania*."

62. Wiecek, *Sources of Antislavery Constitutionalism*, 16.

63. Ohline, "Slavery, Economics, and Congressional Politics."

64. Marion G. McDougall, *Fugitive Slaves: 1619–1865* (Boston: Ginn, 1891), lists most of the southern attempts to amend the 1793 law prior to the passage of the Fugitive Slave Law of 1850, which was technically an amendment of the 1793 law. Finkelman, "*Prigg v. Pennsylvania* and Northern State Courts."

Chapter Five. The Problem of Slavery in the Age of Federalism

1. William M. Wiecek, "The Witch at the Christening: Slavery and the Constitution's Origins," in Leonard W. Levy and Dennis J. Mahoney, eds., *The Framing and Ratification of the Constitution* (New York: Macmillan, 1987), 167–184. Scholars of slavery, on the other hand, have written extensively on slavery in this period. Among others, see James Oliver Horton and Lois E. Horton, *In Hope of Liberty: Culture, Community, and Protest Among Northern Free Blacks, 1700–1860* (New York: Oxford University Press, 1997); Ira Berlin and Ronald Hoffman, eds., *Slavery and Freedom in the Age of the American Revolution* (Charlottesville: University Press of Virginia, 1983); Gary B. Nash and Jean Soderlund, *Freedom by Degrees: Emancipation in Pennsylvania and Its Aftermath* (New York: Oxford University Press, 1991); Shane White, *Somewhat More Independent: The End of Slavery in New York City, 1770–1810* (Athens: University of Georgia Press, 1991); Graham Russell Hodges, *Slavery, Freedom and Culture Among Early American Workers* (Armonk, N.Y.: M.E. Sharpe, 1998); Douglas R. Egerton, *Gabriel's Rebellion: The Virginia Slave Conspiracies of 1800 and 1802* (Chapel Hill: University of North Carolina Press, 1993); Donald L. Robinson, *Slavery in the Structure of American Politics, 1765–1820* (New York: Harcourt Brace Jovanovich, 1971); David Brion Davis, *The Problem of Slavery in the Age of Revolution, 1780–1823* (Ithaca, N.Y.: Cornell University Press, 1975); William M. Wiecek, *The Sources of Antislavery Constitutionalism in America, 1760–1848* (Ithaca, N.Y.: Cornell University Press, 1977); Robert McColley, *Slavery and Jeffersonian Virginia*, 2d ed. (Urbana: University of Illinois Press, 1973); Arthur Zilversmit, *The First Emancipation: The Abolition of Slavery in the North* (Chicago: University of Chicago Press, 1967).

2. Stanley Elkins and Eric McKitrick, *The Age of Federalism* (New York: Oxford University Press, 1993), 163. For a recent book that seems to better understand the importance of slavery to the politics of this period, see James Roger Sharp, *American Politics in the Early Republic: The New Nation in Crisis* (New Haven: Yale University Press, 1993).

3. For a discussion of scholarship on Thomas Jefferson and slavery, see Chapter

7 of this book. Historians of foreign affairs are equally uninterested in the troublesome question of Haiti. Lawrence S. Kaplan, *Entangling Alliances with None: American Foreign Policy in the Age of Jefferson* (Kent, Ohio: Kent State University, 1987), for example, has no references at all to Haiti, St. Domingue, slavery, the African slave trade, or blacks, even though all these topics were integral parts of American foreign policy at this time.

4. Slavery comes up nine times in the index, but all of the references are to passing mentions of slavery as part of some larger discussion. Thus, the authors note that treaty negotiations with the British included "the issue of slaves carried off" and that it is possible to gain insight into Thomas Jefferson's mind by knowing that he "could seriously persuade himself that the difference of one vote by a New Jersey delegate in the Confederation Congress on the Ordinance of 1784 would have kept slavery out of the territories forever." Elkins and McKitrick, *Age of Federalism*, 199, 401. Curiously, there are a few other passing references to slavery and a significant discussion of the Haitian Revolution, but they are not indexed under "slavery." This lack of any discussion of race is all the more peculiar given the previous work of both authors, which recognized the central importance of slavery to the development of America in the eighteenth and nineteenth centuries. See Stanley Elkins, *Slavery* (Chicago: University of Chicago Press, 1959 and various revised editions); Eric McKitrick, *Slavery Defended: The Views of the Old South* (Englewood Cliffs, N.J.: Prentice-Hall, 1963); Eric McKitrick, *Andrew Johnson and Reconstruction* (Chicago: University of Chicago, 1960).

5. See generally, Zilversmit, *First Emancipation.* The northern states passed gradual emancipation statutes as follows: Pennsylvania (1780), Connecticut (1784), Rhode Island (1784), New York (1799), New Jersey (1804). Massachusetts (1780), New Hampshire (1784), and Vermont (1791) ended slavery by their state constitutions. On the implementation of these laws, see Nash and Soderlund, *Freedom by Degrees,* and Paul Finkelman, *An Imperfect Union: Slavery, Federalism, and Comity* (Chapel Hill: University of North Carolina Press, 1981).

6. Elkins and McKitrick, *Age of Federalism*, 4.

7. See Chapter 1 of this book; Wiecek, "Witch at the Christening" and *Sources of Antislavery Constitutionalism.*

8. Joseph E. Ellis argues that Adams did not leave Washington in anger. *Passionate Sage: The Character and Legacy of John Adams* (New York: W.W. Norton, 1993) 19–25.

9. In 1812 the Federalists came very close to defeating James Madison by running DeWitt Clinton, a disgruntled Republican. Had Clinton won, the Federalists would surely have gained a new lease on life. As late as 1820, the Federalists remained a political force in much of the North, even if they were already dead as a national party. Moreover, even while out of power at the national level, Federalists retained influence and power in a number of states through at least 1821.

10. Alvin Kass, *Politics in New York State, 1800–1830* (Syracuse: Syracuse University Press, 1965), 4. In New York, fifty leading Federalists declared an end to their party in January 1820; however, as late as 1821 Federalists still operated as a recognizable faction in the state. Ibid., 80–81. It is hard to know when the "age of federalism" began. I would start it with the Constitutional Convention, although the Federalist Party does not emerge until the 1790s.

11. Michael F. Holt, *The Rise and Fall of the American Whig Party: Jacksonian Politics and the Onset of the Civil War* (New York: Oxford University Press, 1999),

persuasively argues that "the Whig party evolved not from the Federalists but from divisions within the Jeffersonian Republican Party" (p. 2). This is certainly true, but it seems quite clear that many early Whigs, like John Quincy Adams, began their political life as Federalists. Holt describes Adams as a member of the "Madisonian nationalist wing" of the Jeffersonian Republicans (p. 5). This seems true enough, but a good deal of Madison's later nationalism, like his support of a national bank and federally sponsored internal improvements, looked a lot like the program of the Federalist Party.

12. 1 Cranch (U.S.) 137 (1803).

13. Sharp, *American Politics in the Early Republic*, 34.

14. Hornblower characterized himself as an "Old Federalist." See Paul Finkelman, "State Constitutional Protections of Liberty and the Antebellum New Jersey Supreme Court: Chief Justice Hornblower and the Fugitive Slave Law," *Rutgers Law Journal* 23 (1992): 753–787. Fessenden had been a Federalist member of the Massachusetts and Maine legislatures, as well as being the most prominent lawyer in Maine. William Jay "was a self-described Federalist 'of the old Washington school.'" Wiecek, *Sources of Antislavery Constitutionalism*, 154.

15. James Brewer Stewart, *William Lloyd Garrison and the Challenge of Emancipation* (Arlington Heights, Ill: Harlan Davidson, 1992), 13, 14–15; Linda Kerber, *Federalists in Dissent: Imagery and Ideology in Jeffersonian America* (Ithaca: Cornell University Press, 1970), 59, 62–63.

16. Kerber, *Federalists in Dissent*, 63–64, suggests this.

17. James M. Banner, *To the Hartford Convention: The Federalists and the Origins of Party Politics in Massachusetts, 1789–1815* (New York: A.A. Knopf, 1970), 101–109. Banner argues that the abolitionists represented "New England sectionalism" as well as opposition to slavery.

18. [Wendell Phillips], *The Constitution A Pro-Slavery Compact; or, Selections from the Madison Papers*, 2d ed. (New York: American Anti-Slavery Society, 1845), v-vi.

19. Kerber, *Federalists in Dissent*, 23–66.

20. Ulrich B. Phillips, *American Negro Slavery* (New York: D. Appleton, 1918), 128. See Chapters 2 and 3 of this book.

21. See Chapters 2 and 3 of this book.

22. David Hackett Fischer, *The Revolution of American Conservatism: The Federalist Party in the Era of Jeffersonian Democracy* (New York: Harper & Row, 1986), 245–247.

23. Max Farrand, ed., *The Records of the Federal Convention of 1787*, rev. ed., 4 vols. (New Haven: Yale University Press, 1966), 1:486, 603–604. Hamilton argued that "the only considerable distinction of interests, lay between the carrying and non-carrying States, which divide instead of uniting the largest States," Farrand, ed., *Records* 1:466. For a detailed discussion of this debate, see Chapter 1 of this book and Wiecek, "Witch at the Christening."

24. Farrand, *Records*, 2:220–223.

25. "Letters from a Countryman from Dutchess County" (letter of Jan. 22, 1788), in Herbert J. Storing, ed., *The Complete Anti-Federalist,* 7 vols. (Chicago: University of Chicago Press, 1981), 6:62; "A Friend to the Rights of the People," in Storing, ed., *Complete Anti-Federalist*, 4:238–239. A few southern Anti-Federalists also complained about the clause allowing for the continuation of the African slave trade until at least 1808. For example, in Kentucky, "Republicus" thought that the slave trade provision to be "an excellent clause . . . in an Algerian Constitution." Essays by Republicus (essay of Mar. 1, 1788), in Storing, ed., *Complete Anti-Federalist*, 5:169.

26. Jonathan Elliot, ed., *The Debates in the Several State Conventions on the Adoption of the Federal Constitution,* 5 vols. (New York: Burt Franklin, 1987, reprint of 1888 edition), 2:484.

27. Robinson, *Slavery in the Structure of American Politics,* 299, 300. It is almost impossible to tie the slave trade to party politics. Republicans and Federalists both supported and opposed taxes on importing slaves. Illustrative of this may be the man who proposed the first tax on imported slaves, Josiah Parker of Virginia, who was associated with the Republicans in the early 1790s but was a "half-Federalist" by the fifth Congress and voted against Jefferson's election in 1800. Fischer, *Revolution of American Conservatism,* 376. On one vote in 1806, on taxing imported slaves, the vote does not seem to split along coherent party lines. Gales and Seton, *History of Congress,* 9th Congress, 519.

28. Robinson, *Slavery in the Structure of American Politics,* 299–305.

29. See Chapter 4 of this book.

30. This conflict of course would culminate with the debate over the territories in the 1850s. Then Stephen Douglas, a true Jeffersonian, would declare that he did not care if slavery was voted up or down. Similarly, Chief Justice Roger B. Taney's decision in *Dred Scott v. Sandford,* 19 How. (U.S.) 393 (1857), constitutionalized Jeffersonian notions of expansion. Taney's appointment to the Court, as the replacement for John Marshall, symbolized the final nail in the coffin of federalism.

31. Although he supported Madison while in Congress, Story, before going on the Court, often worked closely with Federalists. Jefferson always distrusted Story's commitment to Republican policies and believed that Madison had erred in appointing him.

32. Jefferson to John Holmes, April 22, 1820, Paul Ford, *Writings of Thomas Jefferson,* 10:157–58.

33. Garry Wills, *Cincinnatus: George Washington and the Enlightenment* (Garden City, NY: Doubleday, 1984), 234.

34. Samuel Flagg Bemis, *Jay's Treaty: A Study in Commerce and Diplomacy* (New Haven: Yale University Press, 1962), 131, 284, 290; Jerald A. Combs, *The Jay Treaty: Political Battleground of the Founding Fathers* (Berkeley: University of California Press, 1970) 127.

35. Wills, *Cincinnatus,* 234; "Resolutions Adopted on Jay's Treaty, September 28, 1795," in Philip S. Foner, *The Democratic-Republican Societies, 1790–1800* (Westport, Conn.: Greenwood Press, 1976), 404; Combs, *Jay Treaty,* 161.

36. Charles R. Ritcheson, *Aftermath of Revolution: British Policy Toward the United States, 1783–1795* (Dallas: Southern Methodist University Press, 1969), 337.

37. Donald H. Stewart, *The Opposition Press of the Federalist Period* (Albany: State University of New York Press, 1969), 180, 206–207, 320. Stewart, a fan of the Jeffersonians, adopts their proslavery language here, talking about the "kidnapping" of slaves. The slaves themselves might have used such terms as "liberating" or "emancipating" to describe what the British had done for them, rather than to them.

38. See generally, Davis, *Problem of Slavery.*

39. Robinson, *Slavery in the Structure of American Politics.*

40. Banner, *To the Hartford Convention,* 104.

41. Work on Washington and slavery is still in its formative stage, but see Fritz Hirschfeld, *George Washington and Slavery: A Documentary Portrayal* (Columbia: University of Missouri Press, 1997).

42. James H. Broussard, *The Southern Federalists, 1800–1816* (Baton Rouge: Louisiana State University Press, 1978), 314.

43. Banner, *To the Hartford Convention*, 104. While I accept Banner's argument on where antislavery went, I believe that antislavery was far stronger in the North than he suggests. Part of his argument is based on what I believe is a misreading of some of the legislation passed in Massachusetts and elsewhere in the North during this period. See Paul Finkelman, "Prelude to the Fourteenth Amendment: Black Legal Rights in the Antebellum North," *Rutgers Law Journal* 17 (1986): 415–482. Banner's argument fails to take into account the strong support for black voting rights among Federalists throughout the North.

44. I realize that John Quincy Adams was not elected as a "Federalist," and, indeed, the Federalist Party was effectively dead when he took office. Nevertheless, his pre-presidential career was as a Federalist and an opponent of Jeffersonianism. He was, arguably, the last "Federalist" president.

45. Van Buren was a doughface for most of his career, although late in life he abandoned the South and embraced free soil.

46. To some extent so was Madison. Both men, for example, voted to give Congress the power to regulate trade with a simple majority—something generally opposed by slaveholders.

47. Wills, *Cincinnatus*, 234. See Chapters 6 and 7 of this book.

48. Zilversmit, *First Emancipation*, 205. Bloomfield was a Washington-Adams elector in 1792. Glover Moore, *The Missouri Controversy, 1819–1821* (Lexington: University of Kentucky Press, 1953), 67–69.

49. Fischer, *Revolution of American Conservatism*, 165. Merrill D. Peterson, for example, wants to blame Jefferson's nephew Peter Carr for fathering Sally's children. *Thomas Jefferson and the New Nation* (New York: Oxford University Press, 1970), 707. For a fascinating history of the defense of Jefferson, see Scot A. French and Edward L. Ayers, "The Strange Career of Thomas Jefferson: Race and Slavery in the American Memory, 1943–1993," in Peter S. Onuf, ed., *Jeffersonian Legacies* (Charlottesville: University Press of Virginia, 1993), 418–456.

50. Sally Hemings was less than half Jefferson's age when their relationship began, and as a slave she had little if any opportunity to refuse a sexual relationship with her master.

51. Kerber, *Federalists in Dissent*, 27.

52. Ibid., 52.

53. Ibid., 23, 25–26.

54. Banner, *To the Hartford Convention*, 276 n.

55. As I argue below, the embargo hurt free blacks disproportionately more than whites.

56. Nash and Soderlund, *Freedom by Degrees*, 136. Philip Foner claims four men who were members of both the Democratic Society of Pennsylvania and the PAS: George Logan, Peter S. Du Ponceay, Dr. James Hutchinson, and Absalom Baird. Foner, *The Democratic-Republican Societies*, 12. While twice as many as Nash and Soderlund found, the small number Foner found simply underscores the point that Federalists, not Republicans, supported abolition in Pennsylvania. Logan appears to be one of the few Republican leaders from the North who challenged southerners on issues of slavery.

57. Nash and Soderlund, *Freedom by Degrees*, 136; Gary B. Nash, *Forging Freedom: The Formation of Philadelphia's Black Community* (Cambridge: Harvard University Press, 1988), 181–182.

58. Edmund Morgan, *American Slavery, American Freedom: The Ordeal of Virginia* (New York: W.W. Norton, 1975), 327.

59. Nash and Soderlund, *Freedom by Degrees*, 136. There is some evidence of Federalists alleging that the Jeffersonians were courting the black vote. According to Fischer, *Revolution of American Conservatism*, 165, "Before 1800, even in northern states, Federalist polemicists were openly contemptuous of Negroes."

60. Leon Litwack, *North of Slavery* (Chicago: University of Chicago Press, 1961), 81–82. Zilversmit, *First Emancipation*, 183. See also Edgar McManus, *A History of Negro Slavery in New York* (Syracuse: Syracuse University Press, 1966) 175 n, and Dixon Ryan Fox, "The Negro Vote in Old New York," *Political Science Quarterly* 32 (1917): 252, 254. Fox argues that the vote was entirely partisan, but Zilversmit argues that Fox incorrectly identifies some supporters of the bill as Federalists when in fact they were Republicans.

61. A few Republicans in New York joined the Manumission Society in that state. They included James Nicholson, Tunis Wortman, Samuel L. Mitchill, Melancton Smith, and Philip Freneau. Philip Foner, *The Democratic-Republican Societies*, 12. Aaron Burr voted for gradual emancipation in the New York legislature, but does not otherwise appear to have taken a stand on the issue.

62. Zilversmit, 184; Kass, *Politics in New York State*, 82, 88–89. King quoted in ibid., 88. Sharp, *American Politics in the Early Republic*.

63. Dixon Ryan Fox, *The Decline of the Aristocracy in the Politics of New York, 1801–1840* (1919; reprint, New York: Harper and Row, 1965), 269 n.

64. Kerber, *Federalists in Dissent*, 41–50, contains an excellent discussion of Federalist support for the Haitian revolution.

65. McManus, *History of Negro Slavery in New York*, 187.

66. Philip Foner, *The Democratic-Republican Societies*, 12–13.

67. See generally, W. Jeffrey Bolster, *Black Jacks: African American Seamen in the Age of Sail* (Cambridge: Harvard University Press, 1977); McManus, *History of Negro Slavery in New York*, 187; Fischer, *Revolution of American Conservatism*, 166. I am indebted to Rob Forbes of Yale University for pointing out the important connection between free blacks and maritime industry in the North.

68. Horton and Horton, *In Hope of Liberty*, 168; Phyllis E. Field, *The Politics of Race in New York* (Ithaca, N.Y.: Cornell University Press, 1982); Litwack, *North of Slavery*, 81–82.

69. Litwack, *North of Slavery*, 82–83; Kent quoted at 83. See also Fox, "The Negro Vote," 257–263.

70. Thomas Jefferson to St. George Tucker, August 28, 1797, Paul Ford, ed., *Writings of Thomas Jefferson*, 7:168.

71. Philip Foner, *The Democratic-Republican Societies*, 13.

72. Michael Zuckerman, *Almost Chosen People: Oblique Biographies in the American Grain* (Berkeley: University of California Press, 1993), 188.

73. Elkins and McKitrick, 654.

74. Ibid., 658.

75. Ibid., 659.

76. Rayford Logan, *Diplomatic Relations of the United States with Haiti, 1776–1891* (Chapel Hill: The University of North Carolina Press, 1941), 177–178 shows that the vote in both houses of Congress was almost entirely along party lines. Elkins and McKitrick, 662.

77. Charles C. Tansill, *The United States and Santo Domingo, 1798–1873: A Chapter in Caribbean Diplomacy* (Baltimore: The Johns Hopkins Press, 1938), 82–83.

78. Zuckerman, *Almost Chosen People*, 180, 185.

79. Tansill, *United States and Santo Domingo*, 104-105.

80. Zuckerman, *Almost Chosen People*.

81. Gales and Seton, *History of Congress,* 9th Congress, 117, 125.

82. Gales and Seton, *History of Congress*, 513, 515, 516; Tansill, *United States and Santo Domingo*, 105. One New York Democrat voted no as did the mercurial Matthew Lyon, who at the time represented Kentucky.

83. Zuckerman, *Almost Chosen People*, 186.

84. Broussard, *Southern Federalists*, 314.

85. Fischer, *Revolution of American Conservatism*, 384.

86. Broussard, *Southern Federalists*, 315–316.

87. Paul Finkelman, "'Hooted Down the Page of History': Reconsidering the Greatness of Chief Justice Taney," *Journal of Supreme Court History*, 1994 (1994): 83–102.

88. John Hope Franklin, *The Free Negro in North Carolina, 1790–1860* (Chapel Hill: University of North Carolina Press, 1943), 106, 181, 246. Blacks could also vote in Tennessee, but little is known about how they voted.

89. Davis, *Problem of Slavery in the Age of Revolution*, 178; Winthrop Jordan, *White Over Black: American Attitudes Toward the Negro, 1550-1812* (Chapel Hill: University of North Carolina Press, 1968), 481; and Chapters 6 and 7 of this book.

90. David R. Roediger, *The Wages of Whiteness: Race and the Making of the American Working Class* (London and New York: Verso, 1991).

91. Morgan, *American Slavery, American Freedom*.

92. See Broussard, *Southern Federalists*, 316–320; on Jefferson's great fear of free blacks, see Chapters. 6 and 7 of this book.

93. Bolster, *Black Jacks*, especially Chapter 5.

94. Thomas Jefferson to John W. Eppes, June 30, 1820, in Edwin Morris Betts, ed., *Thomas Jefferson's Farm Book.* (Princeton: American Philosophical Society, 1953), 45. Hirschfeld, *George Washington and Slavery*, 4–5, 51. John Chester Miller, *The Wolf by the Ears: Thomas Jefferson and Slavery* (New York: Free Press, 1977), 107.

95. Sharp, *American Politics*, 22.

Chapter Six. "Treason Against the Hopes of the World": Thomas Jefferson and Slavery

1. Edmund Morgan, *American Slavery, American Freedom: The Ordeal of Virginia* (New York: W.W. Norton, 1975), 376.

2. Leonard W. Levy, *Jefferson and Civil Liberties: The Darker Side*, rev. ed. (Chicago: Ivan Dee, 1989) 1.

3. Jefferson to Edward Coles, August 25, 1814, reprinted in Merrill Peterson, ed., *The Portable Jefferson* (New York: Penguin Books, 1975), 544.

4. "Revisal of the Laws," in Julian Boyd et al., eds., Vol. 18, *The Papers of Thomas Jefferson* (Princeton: Princeton University Press, 1950) 2:470–478, 503–504; David Brion Davis, *The Problem of Slavery in the Age of Revolution, 1770–1823* (Ithaca: Cornell University Press, 1975), 174–175. Jefferson also would have expelled white women bearing interracial children.

5. Certainly "after his return to America" in late 1789, "the most remarkable thing about Jefferson's stand on slavery is his immense silence." Davis, *Problem of Slavery in the Age of Revolution*, 179. Two other aspects of his discussions on slavery are striking. First, he sometimes referred to "God" in his discussion of slavery—

especially a vengeful Calvinist God, which was contrary to his personal religious beliefs. Second, after his retirement from the presidency, he claimed to be ignorant of public affairs when writing about slavery. Neither claim rings true. "I had little opportunity of knowing the progress of public sentiment here on this subject." Jefferson to Edward Coles, August 25, 1814; "I had for a long time ceased to read newspapers, or pay any attention to public affairs." Jefferson to John Holmes, April 22, 1820, in Peterson, *Portable Jefferson*, 544.

6. "Both in power, when the responsibilities of office might have affected his judgement, and in retirement, when he presumably had a free range of options, Jefferson was a loyal member of the planter class to which he belonged." Duncan MacLeod, *Slavery, Race, and the American Revolution* (Cambridge: Cambridge University Press, 1974), 128.

7. Dumas Malone, *Jefferson and His Times*. 6 vols. (Boston: Little, Brown, 1948–1981): 2:xxiii.

8. Joseph J. Ellis, *American Sphinx: The Character of Thomas Jefferson* (New York: Alfred A. Knopf, 1997), 89.

9. Jefferson to Marquis de Chastellux, June 7, 1785, Boyd, ed., Papers of Jefferson, 8:174, 184; Jefferson to James Monroe, June 17, 1785, 8:229; and Jefferson to Charles Thomson, June 21, 1785, 8:245.

10. Davis, *Problem of Slavery in the Age of Revolution*, 177; William W. Freehling, *The Road to Disunion: Secessionists at Bay* (New York: Oxford University Press, 1990), 142.

11. Andrew Burstein, *The Inner Jefferson: Portrait of Grieving Optimist* (Charlottesville: University Press of Virginia, 1995), 22.

12. Examples of this communication in his correspondence include the following: James Madison to Jefferson, Oct. 17, 1784, Boyd, *Papers of Jefferson*, 7:446 (the "hobbyhorse" of the Marquis de Lafayette is "the *manumission* of the *slaves*" which "*does him real honor*, as it is *proof of his humanity*"); G.K. van Hogendorp to Jefferson, May 22, 1784, 7:284 ("I should wish to know whether Your Negroes marry, or what proportion do"); John Adams to Jefferson, May 22, 1785, 8:160 ("The passages upon Slavery [in *Notes on the State of Virginia*], are worth Diamonds. They will have more effect than Volumes written by mere Philosophers"). See also 8:174, 184, 229, 245, and 667.

13. Davis, *Problem of Slavery in the Age of Revolution*, 178.

14. Jefferson to John W. Eppes, June 30, 1820, in Edwin Morris Betts, ed., *Thomas Jefferson's Farm Book*, 35 (Princeton: American Philosophical Society, 1953), 45; Lucia Stanton, "'Those Who Labor for My Happiness': Thomas Jefferson and His Slaves," in Peter S. Onuf, ed., *Jeffersonian Legacies* (Charlottesville: University Press of Virginia, 1993), 172 n. 6; Drew McCoy, *The Last of the Fathers: James Madison and the Republican Legacy* (Cambridge: Cambridge University Press, 1989) 258–259.

15. Morgan, *American Slavery, American Freedom*, 380. See also David R. Roediger, *The Wages of Whiteness: Race and the Making of the American Working Class* (London and New York: Verso, 1991).

16. John Hope Franklin, *Racial Equality in America* (Chicago: University of Chicago Press, 1976), 19; William M. Wiecek, *The Sources of Antislavery Constitutionalism in America, 1760–1848* (Ithaca: Cornell University Press, 1977), 51; J.R. Pole, *The Pursuit of Equality in American History* (Berkeley, University of California Press, 1978), 26–27; see also Donald L. Robinson, *Slavery in the Structure of American Politics, 1765–1820* (New York: Harcourt Brace Jovanovich, 1971).

234 NOTES TO CHAPTER SIX

17. *Commonwealth v. Jennison* (unreported, Mass., 1783), reprinted in Paul Finkelman, *The Law of Freedom and Bondage: A Casebook* (New York: Oceana Press and NYU School of Law, 1986), 36–37. See generally, Arthur Zilversmit, *The First Emancipation: The Abolition of Slavery in the North* (Chicago: University of Chicago Press, 1967); Paul Finkelman, *An Imperfect Union: Slavery, Federalism, and Comity* (Chapel Hill: University of North Carolina Press, 1981); and Paul Finkelman, "Prelude to the Fourteenth Amendment: Black Legal Rights in the Antebellum North," *Rutgers Law Journal* 17 (1986): 415–482. By the end of the Revolution, only Rhode Island and Connecticut among the northern states prohibited free blacks from voting.

18. Thomas Jefferson, *Notes on the State of Virginia*, ed. William Peden (Chapel Hill: University of North Carolina Press, 1954), 138–143.

19. Ibid., 142–143.

20. Ralph L. Ketcham, *From Colony to Country: The Revolution in American Thought, 1750–1820* (New York: Macmillan, 1974), 238.

21. Free blacks could vote and own property in both Pennsylvania and North Carolina from the Revolution until after Jefferson's death. Theoretically, they could have held office in both states, although none did.

22. Jefferson, *Notes*, 138; Jefferson to John Holmes, April 22, 1820; Paul Leicester Ford, ed., *The Writings of Thomas Jefferson,* 12 vols. (New York: G.P. Putnam's Sons, 1904–1905) 10:157; Jefferson to St. George Tucker, August 28, 1797, Ford, ed. *Writings,* 7:168.

23. Jefferson, *Notes*, 138, 139.

24. On the issue of relationships between masters and slaves, see Joel Williamson, *New People: Miscegenation and Mulattoes in the United States* (New York: New York University Press, 1984). For more on Jefferson and Sally Hemings, see Chapter 7 of this volume.

25. John Chester Miller, *Wolf by the Ears: Thomas Jefferson and Slavery* (New York: Free Press, 1977), 74–78.

26. William Stanton, *The Leopard's Spots: Scientific Attitudes Toward Race in America, 1815–59* (Chicago: University of Chicago Press, 1960). Larry E. Tise, *Proslavery: A History of the Defense of Slavery in America, 1701–1840* (Athens: University of Georgia Press, 1987), 231, writes that Jefferson's *Notes* "cast doubt on the equality of men and thereby on the common origin of the human species. Such notions pandered easily to growing beliefs that Negroes were of an inferior race."

27. John Hope Franklin, *Race and History: Selected Essays, 1938–1988* (Baton Rouge: Louisiana State University Press, 1989), 326.

28. Merrill Peterson, *Thomas Jefferson and the New Nation* (New York: Oxford University Press, 1970), 9, 27, quoted at 28; Noble E. Cunningham Jr., *In Pursuit of Reason: The Life of Thomas Jefferson* (Baton Rouge: Louisiana State University Press, 1987), 9; William Cohen, "Thomas Jefferson and the Problem of Slavery," *Journal of American History* 56 (1969): 506.

29. See Betts, *Farm Book*, 13–40, for numerous examples of Jefferson buying and selling slaves and hunting down runaways.

30. "Advertisement for a Runaway Slave," [Sept. 7, 1769] in Boyd, *Papers of Jefferson*, 1:33; Jefferson to Thomas Mann Randolph, Apr. 7, 1791, 20:160 (advice on buying slaves); Jefferson to Thomas Mann Randolph Sr., Feb. 4, 1790, 16:154 ("I propose to give to my daughter . . . 25. negroes little and big"); "Marriage Settlement for Martha Jefferson," Feb. 21, 1790, 16:189 (giving as a wedding present six slave families totaling twenty-seven slaves); "Jefferson's Deed of Gift of Certain Slaves,"

Nov. 6, 1790, 16:12; William Cohen, "Thomas Jefferson and the Problem of Slavery," 506. For examples of Jefferson selling slaves, see Jefferson to Francis Eppes, Oct. 31, 1790, 17:657 ("I shall sell 1000£ worth of negroes this time twelvemonth"); Jefferson to Robert Lewis, Oct. 5, 1791, 22:186 ("My attornies found it necessary in 1785 to sell negroes to answer these demands"); Jefferson to John Bolling, Oct. 7, 1791, 22:198–199 ("I find myself obliged this winter to make a very considerable sale of negroes"). Mary Beth Norton, Herbert G. Gutman, and Ira Berlin, "The Afro-American Family in the Age of Revolution," in Ira Berlin and Ronald Hoffman, eds., *Slavery and Freedom in the Age of the American Revolution* (Charlottesville: University Press of Virginia, 1983), 185; Ronald Takaki, *Iron Cages: Race and Culture in Nineteenth-Century America* (New York: Alfred A. Knopf, 1979), 44; Jefferson to Thomas Mann Randolph, June 8, 1803, in Betts, *Farm Book*, 19 (in order to "make an example of him in terrorem to others, in order to maintain the police so rigorously necessary among the nail boys," Jefferson directs that the slave Cary be sold to "negro purchasers from Georgia" or to "any other quarter so distant as never more to be heard of among us, it would to the others be as if he were put out of the way by death"); Daniel Bradley to Jefferson, Oct. 6, 1805, and Jefferson to Bradley, Jan. 19, 1806, Betts, *Farm Book*, 21, 22 (correspondence about one of Jefferson's runaway slaves Bradley had captured); Jefferson to Joseph Daugherty, July 31, 1806, and Daugherty to Jefferson, Aug. 3, 1806, Betts, *Farm Book*, 22–23 (correspondence about recapturing a fugitive blacksmith).

31. Robert McColley, *Slavery and Jeffersonian Virginia*, 2d ed. (Urbana: University of Illinois Press, 1973), 131.

32. Gary B. Nash, *Race and Revolution* (Madison, Wisc.: Madison House, 1990), 12, 16; MacLeod, *Slavery, Race and the American Revolution*, 15. Smith quoted in Stanton, *The Leopard's Spots*, 12; Patricia Bradley, *Slavery, Propaganda, and the American Revolution* (Jackson: University of Mississippi Press, 1998), xiii.

33. Pole, *Pursuit of Equality in American History*, 119.

34. Nash, *Race and Revolution*, 12.

35. Robinson, *Slavery in the Structure of American Politics*, 118–122.

36. St. George Tucker estimated there were 2,000 free blacks in Virginia in 1782, when the state legalized private manumission. Virginia's 200 percent increase in free blacks from 1790 until 1810 far outstripped the growth rate of slaves or whites. Similar growth rates occurred in other states. In Maryland free blacks grew to one quarter of the entire black population in this period. By 1810 free blacks outnumbered slaves in Delaware. Manumissions continued in Virginia in large numbers until at least 1805. This percentage growth in free blacks nationally occurred despite the fact that South Carolina imported more than 80,000 new African slaves between 1803 and 1808. Ira Berlin, *Slaves Without Masters: The Free Negro in the Antebellum South* (New York: Patheon, 1974), 46–50.

37. Gerald W. Mullin, *Flight and Rebellion: Slave Resistance in Eighteenth Century Virginia* (New York: Oxford University Press, 1972), 70. Berlin, *Slaves Without Masters*, 59; Norton et al., "The Afro-American Family," 176.

38. *Pleasants v. Pleasants*, 2 Call 319 (1799); Finkelman, *Law of Freedom and Bondage*, 116–123; James Currie to Jefferson, August 5, 1785, Boyd, *Papers of Jefferson*, 8:342–343; Miller, *Wolf by the Ears*, 107. Russell Kirk, *John Randolph of Roanoke: A Study in American Politics* (Chicago: Regnery, 1964), 189; Berlin, *Slaves Without Masters*, 59. Under his will, Washington's slaves gained their freedom at the death of his wife. See Fritz Hirschfeld, *George Washington and Slavery: A Documen-*

tary Portrayal (Columbia: University of Missouri Press, 1977); see also "An act concerning the emancipation of certain slaves of Joseph Mayo, late of Henrico County," act of December 13, 1787, *The Statutes at Large: Being a Collection of the Law of Virginia from the First Session of the Legislature in the Year 1619,* edited by William Waller Hening, (Richmond: Printed by and for Samuel Pleasants, Junior, printer to the Commonwealth; United States, 1823), 12:611.

39. The persistence of this image is remarkable. Writing in 1968, Winthrop Jordan noted, "Many school books still say that Jefferson freed his slaves." Winthrop Jordan, *White Over Black: American Attitudes Toward the Negro, 1550–1812* (Chapel Hill: University of North Carolina Press, 1968), n. 431. For a further examination of this theme, see Chapter 7 in this volume.

40. Jefferson to Edward Coles, August 25, 1814, reprinted in Peterson, *Portable Jefferson*, 544. *Autobiography of Thomas Jefferson* (1821), reprinted in Adrienne Koch and William Peden, *The Life and Selected Writings of Thomas Jefferson* (New York: Modern Library, 1944), 4.

41. *Acts of Virginia, 1705,* c. 49, sec. 18. "If any woman servant shall have a bastard child, by a negro or mulatto, or if a free Christian white woman shall have such bastard child by a negro or mulatto; in both the said cases the churchwardens shall bind the said child to be a servant until it shall be of thirty-one years of age," *Acts of Virginia, 1723,* c. 4, sec. 22.

42. *Howell v. Netherland,* Jefferson (Va.) 90 (1770); "Argument in the Case of Howell *vs.* Netherland," [April, 1770], in Ford, *Works of Jefferson,* 1:373–81. Malone, *Jefferson and His Times,* 1:121.

43. Ibid., 1:141n; Cunningham, *In Pursuit of Reason,* 13.

44. "Argument in the Case of Howell *vs.* Netherland," Ford, *Works of Jefferson,* 1:378, 380. Throughout his life, Jefferson's views of race were complex, but it is worth noting that the only slaves he liberated at his death were those of mixed ancestry.

45. Ibid., 1:380.

46. Boyd, *Papers of Jefferson,* 1:33.

47. "Final Version, Gettysburg Address," in Roy P. Basler, ed., *The Collected Works of Abraham Lincoln,* 9 vols. (New Brunswick, N.J.: Rutgers University Press, 1953–1955), 7:23.

48. *Autobiography of Jefferson,* in Koch and Peden, *Life and Writings,* 25–26. Jefferson similarly attacked the king in *A Summary View of the Rights of British America* (1774), in Boyd, *Papers of Jefferson,* 1:130: "The abolition of domestic slavery is the great object of desire in those colonies where it was unhappily introduced in their infant state. But previous to the infranchisement of the slave we have, it is necessary to exclude all further importations from Africa. Yet our repeated attempts to effect this by imposing duties which might amount to a prohibition, have been hitherto defeated by his majesty's negative."

49. *Autobiography of Jefferson,* in Koch and Peden, *Life and Writings,* 25–26.

50. Adams quoted in Robinson, *Slavery in the Structure of American Politics,* 82.

51. Peterson, *Jefferson and the New Nation,* 92.

52. Peterson, *Jefferson and the New Nation,* 91; Peter Wood, *Black Majority: Negroes in Colonial South Carolina from 1670 Through the Stono Rebellion* (New York: W.W. Norton, 1974); Mullin, *Flight and Rebellion.* Peter Wallenstein, "Flawed Keepers of the Flame: The Interpreters of George Mason," *Virginia Magazine of History and Biography* 102 (April 1994): 247–250, discusses the ways historians have confused opposition to the African slave trade with opposition to slavery.

53. One of the few scholars to discuss this is Benjamin Quarles, *The Negro in the American Revolution* (Chapel Hill: University of North Carolina Press, 1961) 42–43.

54. Quoted in Robinson, *Slavery in the Structure of American Politics*, 80.

55. During the Revolution a number of states, including New York, Pennsylvania, and Maryland, allowed masters to gain some financial compensation by manumitting and enlisting their slaves in the army. Although Virginia did not authorize this, Jefferson could easily have enlisted his slaves in the militia of another state or in the Continental Army. Even without the sanction of state law, many Virginia masters did enlist their slaves. In fact, this apparently happened so frequently that, as the war wound down, the commonwealth declared that slaves who served "a full term" in any "continental or state [military] establishment" or had been legally discharged from service "shall be held and deemed free." This law, adopted at a time when Jefferson held no state office, "required" Virginia's attorney general to sue "in behalf" of any black soldiers who were subsequently reenslaved. "An Act Directing the Emancipation of Certain Slaves who Have Served as Soldiers in this State," *Laws of Virginia, 1782–1783*, Chap. 190.

56. Jefferson to William Gordon, July 16, 1788, in Boyd, *Papers of Jefferson*, 13:363–364. Peterson, *Jefferson and the New Nation*, 236, places the number of slaves taken at twenty-seven. In 1786 Jefferson told his Scottish creditor Alexander McCaul that "Ld. Cornwallis's army took off 30 of my slaves, burnt one year's crop of tobacco in my houses" and destroyed other property "to the amount of three or four thousand pounds." Jefferson to Alexander McCaul, Apr. 19, 1786, Boyd, *Papers of Jefferson*, 9:389.

57. Even Jefferson admitted that some of the slaves that the British carried off eventually became free in Canada. Jefferson to William Gordon, July 16, 1788, in Boyd, *Papers of Jefferson*, 13:363–364. On the escape of Virginia slaves to British lines during the war, see Sylvia R. Frey, *Water from the Rock: Black Resistance in a Revolutionary Age* (Princeton, N.J.: Princeton University Press, 1991), 141–242.

58. Malone, *Jefferson and His Times*, 1:247–263, quoted at 247, 251, 263.

59. Ibid., 1:247.

60. Miller, *Wolf by the Ears*, 20; Davis, *Slavery in the Age of Revolution*, 174.

61. "A Bill concerning Slaves," Boyd, *Papers of Jefferson*, 2:470–473. "An act declaring who shall be deemed citizens of this commonwealth," 10 Hening's Statutes at Large 129 (May 1779).

62. "An act to authorize the manumission of slaves," 11 Hening 39 (May 1782).

63. "Argument in the Case of *Howell vs. Netherland*," Ford, *Works of Jefferson*, 1:378, 380.

64. Jack P. Greene, *All Men Are Created Equal: Some Reflections on the Character of the American Revolution* (Oxford: Clarendon Press, 1976), 16.

65. "A Bill Declaring Who Shall be Deemed Citizens of This Commonwealth," Boyd, *Papers of Jefferson*, 2:476. This stands in marked contrast with the changes in the states to the north and the south of Virginia, which gave free blacks political rights. Finkelman, "Prelude to the Fourteenth Amendment"; on free blacks in North Carolina, see John Hope Franklin, *The Free Negro in North Carolina* (Chapel Hill: University of North Carolina Press, 1943).

66. A. Leon Higginbotham, *In the Matter of Color: Race and the American Legal Process: The Colonial Period* (New York: Oxford University Press, 1978), 371. At least one Virginia patriot understood this. When some of his slaves joined the British army, Robert Pleasants wrote General William Phillips, urging him to guarantee their

freedom, if they served in his army. Robert Pleasants to General William Phillips, May 14, 1781, reprinted in Roger Bruns, ed., *Am I Not a Man and a Brother: The Antislavery Crusade of Revolutionary America, 1688–1788* (New York: Chelsea House, 1977), 465.

67. Jefferson quoted in Peterson, *Jefferson and the New Nation*, 153.

68. Jefferson, *Notes*, 137–138.

69. Peden's introduction to Jefferson, *Notes*, xi, quoted at xiv–xvi.

70. "An Act to Authorize the Manumission of Slaves," *Laws of Virginia, 1782*, Chap. 61.

71. *Autobiography of Jefferson*, in Koch and Peden, *Life and Writings*, 51; Boyd, *Papers of Jefferson*, 1:130.

72. *Hudgins v. Wrights*, 11 Hen. & M. (Va.) 133 (1806). Wythe also provided for the manumission of his slaves at his death.

73. McColley, *Slavery in Jeffersonian Virginia*, 132. Tucker's pamphlet on gradual emancipation was also published in St. George Tucker, *Tucker's Blackstone* (1803; reprint Union, N.J.: Lawbook Exchange, 1997), 2: Appendix H.

74. "Jefferson's Draft for a Constitution for Virginia," [May-June, 1783], Boyd, *Papers of Jefferson*, 6:298.

75. Jefferson to James Madison, June 17, 1783, Boyd, *Papers of Jefferson*, 6:277.

76. "An Act for Preventing the farther importation of slaves," *Laws of Virginia, 1778*, 471–472.

77. Jefferson's draft constitution can be compared with the Pennsylvania Gradual Emancipation Act of 1780. The Pennsylvania law went into effect the day it passed. "An Act for the gradual abolition of slavery," Act of March 1, 1780, 1 *Laws of the Commonwealth of Pennsylvania*, 492–496, reprinted in Finkelman, *Law of Freedom and Bondage*, 42–45. The gradual emancipation laws of Connecticut (1784) and Rhode Island (1784), and later New York (1799) and New Jersey (1804), also went into effect immediately. Massachusetts, New Hampshire, and the fourteenth state, Vermont, abolished slavery outright, rather than gradually.

78. "Revised Report of the Committee," March 22, 1784, Boyd, *Papers of Jefferson*, 6:608.

79. Wiecek, *Sources of Antislavery Constitutionalism*, 60. On slavery north of the Ohio river, see Chapters 2 and 3 in this volume.

80. Jefferson to John Holmes, April 22, 1820, Ford, *Writings of Jefferson*, 10:157; McCoy, *Last of the Fathers*, 268–274, discusses Jefferson's defense of this position.

81. Jefferson, *Notes*, at 134, 137.

82. Ibid.,137.

83. Ibid., 137–138.

84. Ibid., 138–142.

85. In 1740, following the Stono Rebellion, South Carolina restricted the trade, not out of any antislavery conviction, but because of the fear that freshly imported Africans were dangerous. Wood, *Black Majority*, 325. See also Wallenstein, "Flawed Keepers of the Flame," 247–250.

86. Jefferson to Christopher Ellery, May 19, 1803, Ford, *Writings of Jefferson*, 8:231.

87. Thomas Jefferson, "Sixth Annual Message," December 2, 1806, in James D. Richardson, ed., *Messages and Papers of the Presidents*, 20 vols. (New York: Bureau of National Literature, 1897), 2:306.

88. One might even construct a counterfactual argument that slavery would have

ended faster if the nation had been flooded with slaves from Africa, thus driving down the value of slaves and undermining slavery in the border states, while at the same time leading to more slave revolts in the deep South.

89. Some slavery existed in Missouri in 1803 and would have probably lingered there as it did in Illinois. See Chapter 3 of this volume; Freehling, *Road to Disunion*, 142.

90. "The Moral Legacy of the Founding Fathers," in Franklin, *Race and History*, 161.

91. See Michael Zuckerman, "The Power of Blackness: Thomas Jefferson and the Revolution in St. Domingue," in *Almost Chosen People: Oblique Biographies in the American Grain* (Berkeley: University of California Press, 1993), 175–218, quoted at 188. See also Douglas Egerton, *Gabriel's Rebellion: The Virginia Slave Conspiracies of 1800 and 1802* (Chapel Hill: University of North Carolina Press, 1993), 168–172.

92. Charles C. Tansill, *The United States and Santo Domingo, 1798–1873: A Chapter in Caribbean Diplomacy* (Baltimore: The Johns Hopkins Press, 1938), 104–105.

93. Franklin, *Racial Equality in America*, 25.

94. Jefferson to John Holmes, April 22, 1820; for similar expressions see also Jefferson to Doctor Thomas Humphreys, Feb. 8, 1817, Ford, *Works of Jefferson*, 10:157, 77.

95. The relevant statutes are found in Finkelman, *Law of Freedom and Bondage*, 109–114.

96. Jefferson, *Notes*, Queries XIV, XVIII, 138, 163. Jefferson to John Holmes, April 22, 1820; Jefferson to Jared Sparks, Feb. 4, 1824; Jefferson to William Short, January 18, 1826; Jefferson to Albert Gallatin, Dec. 26, 1820; Ford, *Works of Jefferson*, 10:157, 291, 362, 178, and Jefferson to James Monroe, Nov. 24, 1801, and June 2, 1802, 8:105, 153. See also David Brion Davis, "American Slavery and the American Revolution," in Ira Berlin and Ronald Hoffman, eds., *Slavery and Freedom in the Age of the American Revolution* (Charlottesville: University Press of Virginia, 1983), 279.

97. Sue Peabody, *There Are No Slaves in France* (New York: Oxford University Press, 1996).

98. Jefferson to Paul Bentalou, Aug. 25, 1786, Boyd, *Papers of Jefferson*, 10:296.

99. Malone, *Jefferson and His Times*, 3:208; Peterson, *Jefferson and the New Nation*, 1007.

100. No one has ever made an exact count of all the individual slaves Jefferson owned. At his death he had about 200. During the Revolution he lost over 30, and after the Revolution he sold at least 85. This means he held, over his lifetime, at least 315 different people in bondage. Given births and deaths over the period from 1764, when he came into possession of his slaves, until 1826, it is likely that the total number exceeds 400.

101. Malone, *Jefferson and His Times*, 6:513; Miller, *Wolf by the Ears*, 162. Sally Hemings and her siblings were the children of Jefferson's father-in-law, John Wayles, and thus the half sisters and half brothers of Jefferson's late wife. Peterson, *Jefferson and the New Nation*, 707; Freehling, *Road to Disunion*, 128. Who fathered Sally's children no longer remains a mystery. It was Jefferson, as James Callender, Fawn Brodie, Page Smith, and the oral traditions of the Hemings family have argued. Sally's children were Jefferson's children. But before the DNA evidence confirmed this, the other likely candidates for the paternity were Jefferson's nephews Peter and Samuel Carr. If they had fathered Sally's children, then the children would still have been doubly related to Jefferson — through marriage and blood.

102. See Chapter 7 of this book.

103. Malone, *Jefferson and His Times*, 3:208.

104. James A. Bear Jr., "The Hemings Family of Monticello," *Virginia Cavalcade* 29 (1979): 80–81.

105. Under *Somerset v. Stewart*, 1 Loft 1, 98 Eng. Rep. 499 (K.B. 1772), slaves became free the moment they entered a free jurisdiction. *Somerset* was part of American common law in all of the new states at the time of the Revolution. When cases hinging on this issue arose in the 1830s, Chief Justice Lemuel Shaw, of the Massachusetts Supreme Judicial Court, expressed surprise that there was any doubt on the subject, because the law of Massachusetts had always been that slaves became free the moment they entered the state. Leonard W. Levy, *The Law of the Commonwealth and Chief Justice Shaw* (Cambridge: Harvard University Press, 1957); Finkelman, *Imperfect Union*, 20–25, 100–145. *Commonwealth v. Aves*, 18 Pick. (Mass.) 193 (1836).

106. Malone, *Jefferson and His Times*, 3:209; Peterson, *Jefferson and the New Nation*, 535.

107. Agreement dated September 15, 1793, in Betts, *Farm Book*, 15–16.

108. For examples of the activities of the Pennsylvania Abolition Society, see Finkelman, *Imperfect Union*, 46–69, and Chapter 6 of this book. In the 1790s the Pennsylvania court freed a number of slaves based on residence in Pennsylvania, including one owned by Senator Pierce Butler, a former delegate to the Constitutional Convention.

109. Gary B. Nash and Jean Soderlund, *Freedom by Degrees: Emancipation in Pennsylvania and Its Aftermath* (New York: Oxford University Press, 1991), 136. For more discussion of the politics of members of the PAS, see Chapter 4 in this volume.

110. Betts, *Farm Book*, 15–16.

111. James A. Bear, *Jefferson at Monticello* (Charlottesville: University of Virginia Press, 1967), Hemings family genealogical tables, after page 24. Jefferson did not chase after Beverley, and that might,be seen as a de facto emancipation. But under Virginia law, Jefferson's heirs, or perhaps his creditors, might have seized Beverley after Jefferson's death. A fugitive slave *always* lived in fear of being seized; an emancipated slave, while concerned about kidnapping, was far more secure. The first fugitive slave case to reach the U.S. Supreme Court, *Prigg v. Pennsylvania*, 16 Pet. (U.S.) 539 (1842), involved a slave whose owner allowed her to live free, but who was later seized by an heir.

112. Jefferson's will, Ford, *Writings of Jefferson*, 10:395–396. The Hemings family tree is found in Bear, *Jefferson at Monticello*, 25–26. By 1826 Virginia no longer allowed manumitted slaves to remain in the state without the permission of the legislature.

113. Jefferson's will, Ford, *Writings of Jefferson*, 10:395–396.

114. This could easily have been accomplished by making his daughter's legacy contingent on freeing this one slave. Benjamin Franklin, for example, made a legacy to his grandson Richard Bache contingent on Bache's manumitting "his Negro man Bob." Carl Van Doren, *Benjamin Franklin* (New York: Viking, 1941), 761.

115. According to Peterson, "neither the state of his property nor the state of the laws, he felt permitted him to do more." Peterson, *Jefferson and the New Nation*, 1007. The law was but a minor impediment. Jefferson asked his heirs to petition the legislature to allow five of his manumitted slaves to remain in the state; he could have asked his heirs to petition the legislature to allow all of them to remain. It is inconceivable that the commonwealth would have denied this final request of one of its greatest citizens.

116. *Elder v. Elder's Ex'or*, 4 Leigh (Va.) 252 (1833). Under Virginia law, a creditor had a claim against any emancipated slave if the estate lacked sufficient assets to settle the debts of the deceased. "An Act reducing to one, the several acts concerning slaves, free negroes and mulattoes," Act of March 2, 1819, Sec. 54, 1 *Revised Code of Virginia* 421, at 434 (Richmond, 1819).

117. Jefferson to James Madison, Sept. 6, 1789, Boyd, *Papers of Jefferson*, 15:395.

118. Jefferson to Major John Cartwright, June 5, 1824, in Peterson, *Portable Jefferson*, 580.

119. Jefferson to Doctor Thomas Humphreys, February 8, 1817, in Ford, *Writings of Jefferson*, 1:77.

120. Freehling, *Road to Disunion*, 127, 128.

121. Jefferson, *Notes*, Query XVIII.

122. Malone, *Jefferson and His Times*, 2:95.

123. Richard Price to Jefferson, July 2, 1785, Boyd, *Papers of Jefferson*, 8:258–259.

124. Jefferson to Price, August 7, 1785, Boyd, *Papers of Jefferson*, 8:356–357. In 1786 Jefferson presented a similarly overly optimistic analysis of the possibility of manumission to the French scholar Demeunier. "The disposition to emancipate them is strongest in Virginia. . . . I flatter myself it will take place there at some period of time not very distant." Here, as in his letter to Price and in much subsequent correspondence, Jefferson asserted that the next generation would do the job, because support for emancipation "is continually recruiting by the addition of nearly the whole of the young men as fast as they come into public life." Answers to Demeunier's First Queries, January 24, 1786, Boyd, *Papers of Jefferson*, 10:18.

125. Ibid.

126. Jefferson to St. George Tucker, August 28, 1797, Ford, *Writings of Jefferson*, 7:168.

127. Jefferson to J.P. Reibelt, December 21, 1805, ibid., 8:402.

128. Jefferson to Edward Coles, August 25, 1814, Peterson, *Portable Jefferson*, 544. This correspondence is brilliantly analyzed in Davis, *Slavery in the Age of Revolution*, 180–183. Curiously, Jefferson's letter to Coles was not fully reprinted in the most popular and easily available edition of Jefferson's letters, *The Life and Writings of Thomas Jefferson*, edited by Adrienne Koch and William Peden in 1944, P. 641–642. The editors ended the letter with this quotation about the "hour of emancipation." This would leave the reader with the impression that Jefferson favored what Coles was doing and endorsed it. This was not the case. The deleted material—more than half of the original letter—contains an attack on the Haitian Revolution, arguments against miscegenation, and Jefferson's advice to Coles not to emancipate his slaves. This is just one of many examples of historians trying to cover for Jefferson, trying to turn him into something he was not—an abolitionist.

129. Jefferson to Edward Coles, August 25, 1814, in Peterson, *Portable Jefferson*, 546.

130. Jefferson to John Holmes, April 22, 1820, Ford, *Writings of Jefferson*, 10:157. Researchers at the Jefferson papers have discovered that the original letter used the word "ear," not "ears." I am grateful to Lucinda Stanton for pointing this out.

131. Jefferson to William Short, January 18, 1826, Ford, *Writings of Jefferson*, 1:362. In contrast to Jefferson, Benjamin Franklin, who had once owned slaves, spent the last years of his life fighting slavery as the president of the Pennsylvania Abolition Society. His last public act was to petition Congress to end slavery and to write a brilliant satire demolishing the arguments of southern politicians who had denounced

Franklin in Congress. Robinson, *Slavery in the Structure of American Politics*, 303; Zilversmit, *First Emancipation*, 164–165.

132. Jefferson, *Notes*, 162–163.

133. Ibid., 143.

134. Jefferson even admitted that such revolts might be "just" and that "[t]he Almighty has no attribute which can take side with us in such a contest." Ibid., Query XVIII.

135. Jefferson to James Monroe, Sept. 20, 1800, quoted in Egerton, *Gabriel's Rebellion*, 93.

136. Jefferson to John Holmes, April 22, 1820, Ford, *Writings of Jefferson*, 10:157–158.

137. Ibid., 158.

Chapter Seven. Thomas Jefferson, Sally Hemings and Antislavery: Historians and Myths

1. For a discussion of Monticello and its original furnishings, art, and eclectic, fantastic collection of the thousands of things that Jefferson put together, see Garry Wills, "The Aesthete," *New York Review of Books* 40 (12 Aug. 1993): 6–10. As Wills notes, "When all the goods from a lifetime of buying were stuffed into it, the house must have resembled the most crowded parts of John Sloane's famous museum-house in London. It is hard . . . to imagine what it would have been like to pick one's way through the jumble of Jefferson's collected prizes," including French paintings and sculpture, twenty-eight Windsor chairs, an Indian headdress, mastodon bones, a "mounted moose, and elk antlers," 7.

2. Ronald Reagan, quoted in Joyce Appleby, "Introduction: Jefferson and His Complex Legacy," in Peter S. Onuf, ed., *Jeffersonian Legacies* (Charlottesville, 1993), 1. On March 24, 1995, the television commentator Rush Limbaugh cited Jefferson in support of tougher sanctions on criminals.

3. In 1963 Leonard W. Levy single-handedly demolished Jefferson's reputation as a great civil libertarian in *Jefferson and Civil Liberties: The Darker Side* (1963; revised edition. Chicago: Ivan Dee, 1989). Despite the overwhelming evidence that Levy marshaled, biographers of Jefferson have by and large ignored his work. The third president remains, in the public image and much of the scholarly world, an icon of liberty, despite evidence to the contrary. Thus, in the face of Levy's persuasive evidence that Jefferson's civil libertarian reputation was overblown, Alpheus T. Mason concludes, "as a libertarian theorist, Jefferson is without peer" (ibid., xviii).

4. He freed three members of the Hemings family during his life and five members of the family at his death.

5. David Brion Davis, *The Problem of Slavery in the Age of Revolution, 1770–1823* (Ithaca, N.Y.: Cornell University Press, 1975), 179.

6. Dinitia Smith and Nicholas Wade, "DNA Test Finds Evidence of Jefferson Child by Slave," *New York Times*, Nov. 1, 1998, 1.

7. Eric S. Lander and Joseph J. Ellis, "Founding Father," November 5, 1998, 13–14; E.A. Foster et al., "Jefferson Fathered Slave's Last Child," *Nature*, "Founding Father," November 5, 1998, 27–28.

8. Lander and Ellis, "Founding Father," 14.

9. *New York Times*, Nov. 2, 1998 (editorial and op-ed pages); *Wall Street Journal*,

Feb. 26, 1999, W-15; Joseph J. Ellis, "Jefferson: Post-DNA," *William and Mary Quarterly* 57 (January 2000): 137–138.

10. Lander and Ellis, "Founding Father," 13.

11. In "The Strange Career of Thomas Jefferson: Race and Slavery in American Memory, 1943–1993," in Peter S. Onuf, ed., *Jeffersonian Legacies*, (Charlottesville: University Press of Virginia, 1993), 418–456, Scot A. French and Edward L. Ayers have provided an important discussion of how historians—especially what Fawn Brodie called the "Jefferson Establishment"—have dealt with Jefferson's relationship to Sally Hemings. In 1836 two English ministers noted that "the slave who was the Mother of Jefferson's children, and who was left in bondage, or if liberated, was unprovided for, had her humble abode" only a short distance from Jefferson's home. Commenting on the late president's grave, they wrote: "The granite column may stand for ages; but on the brass tablet to be inserted, it might be engraven that he was literally the *Father* of some of his own slaves." F.A. Cox and J. Hoby, *The Baptists in America; A Narrative of the Deputation from the Baptist Union in England, to the United States and Canada* (New York, Boston: Leavitt, Lord, 1836), 41–42.

12. Most recently, see Annette Gordon-Reed, *Thomas Jefferson and Sally Hemings: An American Controversy* (Charlottesville: University Press of Virginia, 1997).

13. Joseph J. Ellis, *American Sphinx: The Character of Thomas Jefferson* (New York: Alfred A. Knopf, 1997), 305–306.

14. See generally Fawn Brodie, *Thomas Jefferson: An Intimate History* (New York: W.W. Norton, 1974), for the earliest account sympathetic to Jefferson that accepted the Callender charges. Brodie counts seven children, including the mysterious "Tom." Lander and Ellis, "Founding Father," 13.

15. Dumas Malone, *Jefferson and His Time*, (Boston: Little, Brown, 1948–1981), 4:214. Before the DNA evidence, it was possible to argue that Jefferson would not have been involved with Sally Hemings because of his lifelong hatred of miscegenation and his own prejudices against blacks. In *Notes on the State of Virginia*, he argued that blacks were less attractive than whites—"are not the fine mixtures of red and white . . . preferable to that eternal monotony, which reigns in the countenances, that immovable veil of black which covers the emotions of the other race." Similarly, he disliked getting too close to blacks: "they secrete less by the kidneys, and more by the glands of the skin, which gives them a very strong and disagreeable odor." Although he thought that black women were "more ardent," he doubted that blacks were capable of a serious relationship: "love seems with them to be more an eager desire, than a tender delicate mixture of sentiment and sensation." Thomas Jefferson, *Notes on the State of Virginia*, ed. William Peden (Chapel Hill: University of North Carolina Press, 1954), 138–139. Neither of these arguments is conclusive. Jefferson's words on slavery often conflicted with his deeds. Therefore, his hatred of race-mixing did not stop him from doing it, just as his hatred of slavery never prevented him from exercising all the privileges and duties of a master. Similarly, there is ample evidence that throughout the history of the South white men who professed to be disgusted with blacks nevertheless maintained sexual relationships with black women. Furthermore, Sally Hemings was of mostly white ancestry and probably appeared more white than black to Jefferson. Jefferson privately admitted that many of the members of the Hemings family were legally white. Lucia Stanton, "'Those Who Labor For My Happiness': Thomas Jefferson and His Slaves," in Onuf, *Jeffersonian Legacies* (Charlottesville: University Press of Virginia), 152.

16. Joel Williamson, *New People: Miscegenation and Mulattoes in the United States* (New York: New York University Press, 1984), 45.

17. Ellis, *American Sphinx,* 303–304.

18. Ibid., 305.

19. Ibid., 305.

20. Ibid., 305–306.

21. Ibid., 66. Only three of the children survived childbirth.

22. Williamson, *New People,* 47.

23. Ibid., 45. Williamson of course fails to consider that many masters may have had long-term relationships with slaves that they kept hidden from the public, never admitted to anyone, and that many masters did not take care of their slave children.

24. Williamson writes that Jefferson "was wantonly careless about the children. Two were allowed to run away, disappear, and were left like orphans to find their way in the world." Ibid., 45. However, an alternative interpretation of these facts would be that while Jefferson often tracked down runaway slaves and forced them to return to their bondage, when the children of Sally Hemings—who were also his children—ran away, he allowed them to keep the freedom they acquired. They were not then "orphans" in the world, but rather free people liberated from slavery.

25. Ibid., 47. Williamson also argues, although without any evidence, that Sally fails to fit the pattern of a woman who was involved with her master; instead "Sally fits the pattern of the mulatto maid who had a number of lovers in sequence "and" that she herself could not be absolutely certain who was the father of a particular child." However, if this were so, then by Williamson's own analysis she probably would have had more children after 1808.

26. Malone, *Jefferson and His Time,* 3:214.

27. Michael Durey, *"With the Hammer of Truth": James Thomson Callender and Early America's National Heroes* (Charlottesville: University Press of Virginia, 1990), 159–160, Callender quoted at 159.

28. Durey, *"With the Hammer of Truth,"* 160.

29. Gordon-Reed, *Thomas Jefferson and Sally Hemings,* argues for the relationship as loving and caring.

30. Paul Finkelman, *Slavery and the Founders: Race and Liberty in the Age of Jefferson,* 1st ed. (Armonk, N.Y.: M.E. Sharpe, 1996), 142.

31. Some discussion of this connection is found in Jan Ellen Lewis and Peter Onuf, *Sally Hemings and Thomas Jefferson: History, Memory, and Civic Culture* (Charlottesville: University Press of Virginia, 1999), 52–84.

32. A good example of the refusal to consider the moral implications of Jefferson's owning, and selling, his relatives (and his children) is Ellis, "Jefferson: Post-DNA," 125-138.

33. Merrill D. Peterson, *Thomas Jefferson and the New Nation* (New York: Oxford University Press, 1970), 707. At a conference on Jefferson held at the University of Virginia in October 1992, one researcher from Monticello noted that, despite the consensus among Jeffersonian scholars like Malone and Peterson on the paternity of John Wayles, there is no better evidence for John Wayles fathering Sally Hemings than there is for Jefferson fathering her children. When I asked if this meant that Jefferson did father Hemings's children, the researcher replied, "No," because "we must give Mr. Jefferson the benefit of the doubt."

34. Peterson, *Thomas Jefferson and the New Nation,* 707. John Chester Miller also suggests that Peter Carr's brother, Samuel, may have been the father of Sally Hemings's

children. John Chester Miller, *The Wolf by the Ears: Thomas Jefferson and Slavery* (New York: Free Press, 1977), 171.

35. Under a 1785 law, which remained in force until emancipation, blacks or mulattoes were defined as people with at least one-quarter black ancestry. Act of 1785, 12 Hening 184. Sally Hemings was at most one-quarter black. According to her son, Madison Hemings, Sally's grandmother (Madison's great-grandmother) was "a fullblooded African, and possibly a native of that country." Sally's grandfather (Madison's great-grandfather) was an English sea captain named Hemings. Sally's mother, Elizabeth, the offspring of that union, was thus half white. Sally's father was John Wayles. "Reminiscences of Madison Hemings," reprinted in Brodie, *Thomas Jefferson: An Intimate History,* 471. Thus Sally was one-quarter black, and her children, fathered by some white man, were only one-eighth black and thus, under Virginia law, were "white." Similarly, so were virtually all of the children born to other Hemings women, who almost all "formed relationships with white men." Stanton, "'Those Who Labor For My Happiness,'" 152.

36. Jefferson quoted in Stanton, "'Those Who Labor For My Happiness,'" 152.

37. Under Virginia law, slave status was inherited through the mother; thus, even while freeing these slaves, Jefferson did not contribute to the long-term growth of the free African-American population in the country.

38. Peterson, *Thomas Jefferson and the New Nation,* 707.

39. Peter S. Onuf, "The Scholars' Jefferson," *William and Mary Quarterly* 50, 3d ser. (1993): 675.

40. Gordon S. Wood, "The Trials and Tribulations of Thomas Jefferson," in Peter S. Onuf, ed., *Jeffersonian Legacies* (Charlottesville: University Press of Virginia, 1993), 395.

41. Ibid., 395.

42. Douglas L. Wilson, "Thomas Jefferson and the Character Issue," *Atlantic Monthly,* Nov. 1992, 62. Curiously, Wilson goes out of his way to show how "modern" Jefferson was, noting he believed in exercise, ate little red meat, and was "something of a health-food prophet" (p. 65).

43. Levy details this criticism in the preface to the 1989 paperback edition of *Jefferson and Civil Liberties*, pp. xi-xxxvi (quotations on pp. xxiii-xxiv).

44. Ibid., xii; Gordon S. Wood, "Jefferson at Home," *New York Review of Books,* May 13, 1993, 6.

45. Wilson, "Jefferson and the Character Issue," 62.

46. James Parton, *The Life of Thomas Jefferson, Third President of the United States* (Boston: Houghton Mifflin, 1874), iii.

47. Merrill D. Peterson, *The Jefferson Image in the American Mind* (New York: Oxford University Press, 1960), 447.

48. Wood, "Jefferson at Home," 6.

49. Peter Onuf, *Jefferson's Empire: The Language of American Nationhood* (Charlottesville: University Press of Virginia, 2000), p. 147.

50. Ellis, *American Sphinx*, 145.

51. Ibid.

52. Alf J. Mapp Jr., *Thomas Jefferson: A Strange Case of Mistaken Identity* (Lanham, Md.: Madison Books, 1987), 406–407; Alf J. Mapp Jr., *Thomas Jefferson, Passionate Pilgrim: The Presidency, the Founding of the University and the Private Battle* (Lanham, Md.: Madison Books, 1991), 367.

53. Ellis, *American Sphinx,* 263.

54. Onuf, "Scholars' Jefferson," 675.

55.Wilson, "Jefferson and the Character Issue," 66; Malone, *Jefferson and His Time*, 3:264, 266; Miller, *Wolf by the Ears*, xi, 1.

56. See, for example, Peter S. Onuf, "Peerless Tom," *New York Times Book Review* Sept. 26, 1993, 26. In her intelligent and extremely witty review, Jan Lewis writes that Randall's book "bears a superficial resemblance to a serious work of scholarship" but that "this slapdash book is not so much the 'authoritative biography' that its publisher proclaims as a student term paper that has metastasized to grotesque proportions" Jan Lewis, "Pieces of a President," *Washington Post Book World,* Aug. 22, 1993, 10).

57. Willard Sterne Randall, *Thomas Jefferson: A Life* (New York: Henry Holt, 1993), 301. See also Chapter 6 of this volume.

58. Ellis, *American Sphinx,* 6. In his PBS program on Jefferson, Ken Burns persistently turned to Jenkinson to explain Jefferson, never for a moment revealing that Jenkinson was not a scholar, but an actor. Burns always identified him as a "historian."

59. Mapp, *A Strange Case of Mistaken Identity*, 53, 407, 167; Mapp, *Passionate Pilgrim*, 367.

60. Peterson, *Thomas Jefferson and the New Nation*, 998.

61. In his prepresidential career, Ulysses S. Grant was critical in bringing freedom to millions of Americans. On Lincoln and his faults and virtues, see Paul Finkelman, "Civil Liberties and the Civil War: The Great Emancipator as Civil Libertarian," *Michigan Law Review* 91 (1993): 1353–81. Unfortunately, no biographer of Jefferson has treated him as honestly as Joseph J. Ellis has recently treated John Adams in his brilliant *Passionate Sage: The Character and Legacy of John Adams* (New York: W.W. Norton, 1993).

62. Peterson, *Jefferson and the New Nation*, 998.

63. Wood, "Jefferson at Home," 6.

64. Onuf, *Jefferson's Empire*, 185.

65. I paraphrase the closing sentence of the Declaration of Independence: "And for the support of this Declaration with a firm Reliance on the Protection of divine Providence, we mutually pledge to each other our Lives, our Fortunes, and our Sacred Honor."

66. Merrill D. Peterson, ed., *The Portable Thomas Jefferson* (New York: Penguin Books, 1975), 251.

67. This code did not apply to blacks, for whom Jefferson proposed harsher laws. Thus, "except for the privilege of knowing that their corpses would not rot on gibbets, the slaves profited little from the enlightened humanitarianism" in Jefferson's draft code. His revision tightened the slave code, increased penalties for slave criminals, and "retained most of the inhumane features of the colonial slave law" (Miller, *Wolf by the Ears*, 20; Davis, *Slavery in the Age of Revolution*, 174). The legislature eventually rejected some of the more vicious aspects of Jefferson's proposed criminal code for slaves and free blacks.

68. Jefferson, *Notes on the State of Virginia,* 162.

69. Ibid. It is worth noting that this paragraph probably reflects Jefferson's own fears of what slavery might be doing to him, a subject beyond the scope of this essay. Slavery must have constantly challenged Jefferson's self-control.

70. Davis, *Slavery in the Age of Revolution*, 171.

71. On dependency in the revolutionary era, see Gordon S. Wood, *The Radicalism of the American Revolution* (New York: Knopf, 1992), 43–77. On white southern

men's fear of dependency in the nineteenth century, see Joan E. Cashin, *A Family Venture: Men and Women on the Southern Frontier* (New York: Oxford University Press, 1991), chap 2. Forrest McDonald, *Presidency of Jefferson* (Lawrence: University of Kansas Press, 1976), 22.

72. Thomas Jefferson to John Holmes, Apr. 22, 1820, in Paul Leicester Ford, ed., *The Writings of Thomas Jefferson,* 10 vols. (New York: G.P. Putnam's Sons, 1892–1899), 10:157–58. Researchers at the Jefferson papers project have discovered that the original letter used the word "ear," not "ears." I am grateful to Lucia C. Stanton, director of research at the Thomas Jefferson Memorial Foundation, for pointing this out.

73. Herbert Sloan, "'The Earth Belongs in Usufruct to the Living," in Onuf, *Jeffersonian Legacies,* 290.

74. Wills, "Aesthete," 6.

75. Miller, *Wolf by the Ears,* 279; Davis, *Slavery in the Age of Revolution,* 170.

76. Thomas Jefferson to John Holmes, Apr. 22, 1820, in Ford, ed., *Writings of Jefferson,* 10:157–158.

77. Jefferson to St. George Tucker, Aug. 28, 1797, in ibid., 7:168. On Haiti and Jefferson, see Michael Zuckerman, "The Power of Blackness: Thomas Jefferson and the Revolution in St. Domingue," in Zuckerman, *Almost Chosen People: Oblique Biographies in the American Grain* (Berkeley: University of California Press, 1993), 175–218. Douglas R. Egerton, *Gabriel's Rebellion: The Virginia Slave Conspiracies of 1800 and 1802* (Chapel Hill: University of North Carolina Press, 1993), 151–172.

78. Thomas Jefferson to Edward Coles, Aug. 25, 1814, in Peterson, ed., *Portable Jefferson,* 545; Edward Coles to Jefferson, July 31, 1814, reprinted in Clarence Walwroth Alvord, ed., *Governor Edward Coles,* Collections of the Illinois State Historical Library, Vol. 15 (Springfield: Illinois State Library, 1920), 23.

79. Thomas Jefferson to Jared Sparks, Feb. 4, 1824, in Andrew A. Lipscomb and Albert Ellery Bergh, *The Writings of Thomas Jefferson,* 20 vols. (Washington, D.C.: The Thomas Jefferson Memorial Foundation, 1903–1905), 16:9.

80. Thomas Jefferson to Edward Coles, Aug. 25, 1814, in Peterson, ed., *Portable Jefferson,* 545; Jefferson, *Notes on the State of Virginia,* 163.

81. Ibid., 162, 138. On Jefferson as a scientist, see Silvio A. Bedini, *Thomas Jefferson: Statesman of Science* (New York: Macmillan, 1990), esp. 89–124.

82. Jefferson, *Notes on the State of Virginia,* 138–139. On the intersection of sex, psychology, and southern masters, see Nell Irvin Painter, "Of *Lily,* Linda Brent, and Freud: A Non-Exceptionalist Approach to Race, Class, and Gender in the Slave South," *Georgia Historical Quarterly* 76 (1992): 241–59. Painter's analysis may go a long way in explaining Jefferson's writing on this subject. See also Cashin, *Family Venture*; and Catherine Clinton, "'Southern Dishonor': Flesh, Blood, Race, and Bondage," in Carol Bleser, ed., *In Joy and Sorrow: Women, Family, and Marriage in the Victorian South, 1830–1900* (New York: Oxford University Press, 1991), 52–68.

83. It is important to remember that his slave mistress, Sally Hemings, was mostly white.

84. Jefferson, *Notes on the State of Virginia,* 138–139.

85. Malone, *Jefferson and His Time*; Adrienne Koch and William Peden, eds., *The Life and Selected Writings of Thomas Jefferson* (New York: Modern Library, 1944); Peterson, *Jefferson and the New Nation*; Wilson, "Jefferson and the Character Issue"; Randall, *Thomas Jefferson: A Life*; Mapp, *A Strange Case of Mistaken Identity*; Mapp, *Passionate Pilgrim.*

86. William Cohen, "Thomas Jefferson and the Problem of Slavery," *Journal of American History* 56 (1969): 503–526; David Brion Davis, *Was Thomas Jefferson an Authentic Enemy of Slavery?* (Oxford: Oxford University Press, 1970); Davis, *Slavery in the Age of Revolution*, esp. 166–184; Winthrop Jordan, *White Over Black: American Attitudes Toward the Negro, 1550–1812* (Chapel Hill: University of North Carolina Press, 1968); Robert McColley, *Slavery and Jeffersonian Virginia*, 2d ed. (Urbana: University of Illinois Press, 1973); William W. Freehling, *The Road to Disunion: Secessionists at Bay, 1776–1854* (New York: Oxford University Press, 1990). In his book Freehling completely reverses his earlier apologetic view of Jefferson in "The Founding Fathers and Slavery," *American Historical Review* 77 (1972): 81–93. Miller, for all his attacks on Jefferson, refused to accept that Jefferson was not somehow, in some way, a secret abolitionist. Thus, he asserts at the beginning of his important book on the subject that Jefferson "was resolved to destroy" slavery (Miller, *Wolf by the Ears*, xi, 1).

87. Randall's book, *Thomas Jefferson: A Life,* which has extensive notes and bibliography and appears to be a serious work of scholarship, does not list Cohen's article or Davis's book as a source. Although Randall does have Miller, Jordan, and McColley in the bibliography, he does not cite them in his notes, and his few discussions of slavery do not indicate that he is aware of the arguments these scholars have made. Mapp lists only Jordan and Miller in his bibliography and cites neither of them in his two discussions of slavery in his first book, *A Strange Case of Mistaken Identity.* He similarly ignores this literature in his second volume, *Passionate Pilgrim.* Elizabeth C. Langhorne, *Monticello: A Family Story* (Chapel Hill: Algonquin Books, 1987), ignores all secondary work on this subject and explains, incorrectly, that Jefferson could not free his slaves because of his debts and because it was against the law (253). Although Langhorne's book includes extensive discussions of some of Jefferson's bondspeople, the terms "slave" and "slavery" do not appear in her index. Noble E. Cunningham Jr., *In Pursuit of Reason: The Life of Thomas Jefferson* (Baton Rouge: Louisiana State University, 1987) cites Davis, Miller, and Jordan in his few discussions of Jefferson and slavery. Cunningham accepts Jefferson's racism, in a way that earlier biographers did not, although he writes it off to Jefferson's being a "product of his age in his views on race" (62). Yet Cunningham persists in painting Jefferson as an opponent of slavery. He does not confront the persuasive critique of Jefferson by Cohen and Davis. McDonald, *Presidency of Thomas Jefferson. . .*, dismisses any discussion of Jefferson's private life, which presumably includes his role as a slaveholder, as "irrelevant to his qualities as a public man" (179). McDonald, however, acknowledges the importance of slavery to the founding of the republic, makes no attempt to paint Jefferson as an antislavery icon, and points out, as other biographers do not, that even while he was in the White House Jefferson purchased slaves. McDonald notes that the meaning of "liberty" to Jefferson "can scarcely have been a conventional one, since Jefferson owned several hundred human beings during his lifetime" (30).

88. Wilson, "Jefferson and the Character Issue," 66–67.

89. Donald L. Robinson, *Slavery in the Structure of American Politics, 1765–1820* (New York: Harcourt Brace Jovanovich, 1971), 118–122; James Thomas Flexner, *George Washington*, vol. 4, *Anguish and Farewell (1793–1799)* (Boston: Little, Brown, 1972), 116; McColley, *Slavery and Jeffersonian Virginia*. For further discussion of Laurens, see Chapter 6 in this volume.

90. Malone, *Jefferson and His Time*, vol. 3:264, 3:207.

91. Peterson, *Jefferson and the New Nation*, 152–153.

92. Ibid., 145–149.

93. Andrew Burstein, *The Inner Jefferson: Portrait of a Grieving Optimist* (Charlottesville: University Press of Virginia, 1995).

94. Burstein, *Inner Jefferson*, 289.

95. *Hudgins v. Wrights*, 1 Hen. & Munf., (Va.) 134 (1806). For a discussion of the case, see Robert M. Cover, *Justice Accused: Antislavery and the Judicial Process* (New Haven: Yale University Press, 1975), 51–55.

96. St. George Tucker, *A Dissertation on Slavery: With A Proposal for the Gradual Abolition of It, in the State of Virginia* (Philadelphia: Mathew Carey, 1796). For a discussion of Jefferson's proposal to Madison, see Chapter 6 in this volume.

97. Randall, *Thomas Jefferson: A Life*, 301.

98. Ibid. Peter Wallenstein, "Flawed Keepers of the Flame: The Interpreters of George Mason," *Virginia Magazine of History and Biography* 102 (April 1994): 247–250, discusses the ways historians have confused opposition to the African slave trade with opposition to slavery.

99. Mapp, *Strange Case of Mistaken Identity*, 406; Mapp, *Passionate Pilgrim*, 366. I do not doubt the sincerity of Jefferson's distaste for the slave trade, but his attack on the trade—or rather his attempt to blame the king for the trade— was hardly a "pledge" to end it. Many slave owners thought the trade was immoral, cruel, dangerous, and generally a bad policy but still had no objections to slavery itself. Many Virginians, including Jefferson, would benefit financially from an end to the trade, which would increase the price of their slaves.

100. Mapp, *Strange Case of Mistaken Identity*, 407. In spring 1783, Jefferson privately suggested a gradual emancipation program for Virginia. Anticipating a state constitutional convention, Jefferson wrote a draft constitution that provided: "The General assembly shall not . . . permit the introduction of any more slaves to reside in this state, or the continuance of slavery beyond the generation which shall be living on the 31st day of December 1800; all persons born after that day being hereby declared free." "Jefferson's Draft for a Constitution for Virginia," [May-June, 1783], Julian P. Boyd, et al., eds. *The Papers of Jefferson* (Princeton: Princeton University Press, 1950), 6:298. However, the convention never took place and Jefferson never revealed his proposal to the public. Curiously, few Jefferson scholars mention the antislavery provision of the draft constitution. Neither Malone, Peterson, Boyd, nor Cunningham discusses the clause in their biographies. Malone, *Jefferson and His Times*, 3:400; Peterson, *Jefferson and the New Nation*, 132, 267, 381; "Editorial Note," Boyd, *Papers of Jefferson*, 6:278–284; Cunningham, *In Pursuit of Reason*, 84–85. Adrienne Koch, *Jefferson and Madison: The Great Collaboration* (New York: Knopf, 1950), 13, notes that the slavery provision should be considered "by all who remember him as a 'slave holding Virginia planter,'" but she refuses further "speculation" on the clause.

101. Randall, *Thomas Jefferson: A Life*, 302. Mapp notes that Jefferson "had to defer his efforts for gradual emancipation of the slaves." Mapp, *Strange Case of Mistaken Identity*, 123. Mapp fails to note that Jefferson had in fact never made such an effort.

102. Ellis, *American Sphinx*, 149.

103. Stanton, "'Those Who Labor For My Happiness,'" 172, n.6. Thomas Jefferson to John W. Eppes, June 30, 1820, in Edwin Morris Betts, ed., *Thomas Jefferson's*

Farm Book, (Princeton: American Philosophical Society, 1953), 45. He also gave away at least seventy-one slaves to his sisters and his daughters. While not gaining money for slaves he gave away, Jefferson nevertheless destroyed families by doing so. Miller, *Wolf by the Ears*, 107. See also Fritz Hirschfeld, *George Washington and Slavery: A Documentary Portrayal* (Columbia: University of Missouri Press, 1997).

104. Thomas Jefferson to Thomas Mann Randolph, June 8, 1803, in Betts, ed., *Jefferson's Farm Book*, 19.

105. Wilson, "Jefferson and the Character Issue," 66, 69.

106. Malone, *Jefferson and His Time*, 3:208.

107. Ibid.; James A. Bear Jr., "The Hemings Family of Monticello," *Virginia Cavalcade* 29 (1979–1980): 80–81.

108. Malone, *Jefferson and His Time*, 3:209; Peterson, *Jefferson and the New Nation*, 535.

109. Paul Finkelman, *An Imperfect Union: Slavery, Federalism, and Comity* (Chapel Hill: University of North Carolina Press, 1981), 37–38, 41–45.

110. Declaration, Sept. 15, 1793, in Betts, ed., *Jefferson's Farm Book*, 15–16.

111. Malone, *Jefferson and His Time*, 3:208.

112. For a discussion of Washington, see Flexner, *George Washington: Anguish and Farewell*, 122–125. For other examples of Virginians who opposed slavery in the late eighteenth century, see Davis, *Slavery in the Age of Revolution*, 169–171.

113. Mapp, *Strange Case of Mistaken Identity*, 407.

114. "An Act to Authorize the Manumission of Slaves," *Laws of Virginia, 1782*, chap. 61, reprinted in Paul Finkelman, *The Law of Freedom and Bondage: A Casebook* (New York: Oceana Press and NYU School of Law, 1986), 109.

115. Mapp, *Passionate Pilgrim*, 350–351. Mapp also fails to note that the only slaves Jefferson ever freed were members of the Hemings family. It appears that family ties—and a substantial amount of white ancestry—had far more to do with Jefferson's decision to manumit slaves than any skills they might have had.

116. See, for example, Thomas Jefferson to Edward Coles, Aug. 25, 1814, in Peterson, ed., *Portable Jefferson*, p. 544.

117. Randall, *Thomas Jefferson: A Life*, 494.

118. Ibid., 591.

119. The best account of James Hemings is found in Langhorne, *Monticello: A Family Story*, 104–108. Some of the information presented here is also based on files at Monticello.

120. Gerald W. Mullin, *Flight and Rebellion: Slave Resistance in Eighteenth-Century Virginia* (New York: Oxford University Press, 1972), 70; Ira Berlin, *Slaves Without Masters: The Free Negro in the Antebellum South* (New York: Pantheon, 1974), 59; Mary Beth Norton, Herbert G. Gutman, and Ira Berlin, "The Afro-American Family in the Age of Revolution," in Ira Berlin and Ronald Hoffman, eds., *Slavery and Freedom in the Age of the American Revolution* (Charlottesville: University Press of Virginia, 1983), 176.

121. Malone, *Jefferson and His Time,* 3:208.

122. Peterson, *Jefferson and the New Nation*, 1007.

123. For further discussion of these people and documentation of their manumissions, see Chapter 6 of this volume. Some scholars have argued that Jefferson could not free his slaves because of his debts. This assertion begs the question. Throughout his life, Jefferson was profligate. He bought and bought and bought. Had freeing slaves been even a mildly important goal, he might easily have cut back on his consumption and

lavish lifestyle. That he did not suggests where his priorities lay. Even with his debts, Jefferson might have arranged to have his slaves hired out to pay what he owed, with the understanding that once the debts were cleared, the slaves would be freed. Only a month before Jefferson died, Herbert Elder, a master in Petersburg, provided in his will that his slaves be allowed to work to meet the debts of the estate, after which they could choose freedom in Liberia or remain slaves in Virginia. Thirteen of Elder's fourteen slaves chose freedom on the continent of their ancestors (see *Elder v. Elder's Ex'or*, 4 Leigh, (Va.) 252 [1833]). Under Virginia law, a creditor had a claim against any emancipated slave if the estate lacked sufficient assets to settle the debts of the deceased ("An Act reducing into one, the several acts concerning Slaves, Free Negroes and Mulattoes," enacted Mar. 2, 1819, sec. 54, 1 *Revised Code of Virginia* 421 [Richmond, 1819], 434).

124. Wilson, "Jefferson and the Character Issue," 69. "An Act to Authorize the Manumission of Slaves," *Laws of Virginia, 1782*, chap. 61, reprinted in Finkelman, *Law of Freedom and Bondage*, 109.

125. "An Act to Amend the Several Laws Concerning Slaves," *Laws of Virginia, 1805*, chap. 63, reprinted in Finkelman, *Law of Freedom and Bondage*, 111.

126. Wilson, "Jefferson and the Character Issue," 69, 72. I assume Wilson here construed "other Americans" as white citizens. In fact, there is a great deal of evidence that black Americans were quite willing to risk freedom and strive for integration.

127. Wilson, "Jefferson and the Character Issue," 72; Jefferson, *Notes on the State of Virginia*, 138–143.

128. Stanton, "'Those Who Labor for My Happiness,'" 147, 169.

129. Jefferson, *Notes on the State of Virginia*, 139.

130. Fossett spent the next decade heroically trying to put his family back together. In 1837 he manumitted his wife, five children (including two born after Jefferson's death), and four grandchildren.

131. Mapp, *Strange Case of Mistaken Identity*, 171; Wilson, "Jefferson and the Character Issue," 72.

132. Albert Henry Smyth, ed., *The Writings of Benjamin Franklin,* 10 vols. (New York: Macmillan, 1905–1907), 6:222, quoted in Carl Van Doren, *Benjamin Franklin* (New York: Viking, 1938), 479. Jefferson, *Notes on the State of Virginia*, 138, 142–143.

133. Van Doren, *Benjamin Franklin*, 774; Jefferson, *Notes on the State of Virginia*, 139–140. Generally, see Miller, *Wolf by the Ears*, 255–257.

134. Flexner, *George Washington: Anguish and Farewell*, 113–125 (quotation on 114); Garry Wills, *Cincinnatus: George Washington and the Enlightenment* (Garden City, N.Y.: Doubleday, 1984), 234–235.

135. Miller, *Wolf by the Ears*, 75–76.

136. Banneker to Jefferson, August 19, 1791, and Jefferson to Banneker, August 30, 1791, in Boyd, *Papers of Jefferson*, 22:49, 97.

137. Jefferson to Henri Grégoire, in Peterson, *Portable Jefferson*, 517.

138. Jefferson to Joel Barlow, October 8, 1809, in Lipscomb and Bergh, *Writings of Thomas Jefferson*, 12:321–322.

139. Jordan, *White Over Black*, 481.

140. Thomas Jefferson to Edward Coles, Aug. 25, 1814, in Peterson, ed., *Portable Jefferson*, 544; partially reprinted in Koch and Peden, eds., *Life and Selected Writings of Jefferson*, 641–642.

141. Ralph L. Ketcham, "The Dictates of Conscience: Edward Coles and Slavery," *Virginia Quarterly Review* 36 (1960): 47–49.

142. Edward Coles to Jefferson, July 31, 1814, in Alvord, *Governor Edward Coles,* 22–24.

143. Ibid., 23.

144. As Fawn Brodie notes: "Jefferson had a superb sense of history and an exact understanding of his own role in it. He preserved a legacy of over 25,000 letters from his friends and acquaintances, as well as copies of his own letters . . . that numbered 18,000." Brodie, *Thomas Jefferson: An Intimate History,* 22.

145. Coles to Jefferson, in Alvord, *Governor Edward Coles,* 23.

146. Thomas Jefferson to Edward Coles, Aug. 25, 1814, in Peterson, ed., *Portable Jefferson,* 544. This correspondence in brilliantly analyzed in Davis, *Slavery in the Age of Revolution,* 180–183.

147. Thomas Jefferson to Edward Coles, Aug. 25, 1814, in Peterson, *Portable Jefferson,* 546.

148. For a discussion of the reinvention of Jefferson as part of the war effort, see French and Ayers, "Strange Career of Thomas Jefferson," 419–421.

149. Peterson, *Jefferson Image,* 447. The two most important exceptions to this are Onuf, *Jefferson's Empire,* and Burstein, *Inner Jefferson,* although neither is a full-scale biography.

Bibliography

Secondary Sources

Adams, Willi Paul. *The First American Constitutions: Republican Ideology and the Making of State Constitutions in the Revolutionary Era.* Chapel Hill: University of North Carolina Press, 1980.

Appleby, Joyce. "Introduction: Jefferson and His Complex Legacy," in Peter S. Onuf, ed. *Jeffersonian Legacies.* Charlottesville: University Press of Virginia, 1993.

Bancroft, George. *History of the United States of America, From the Discovery of the American Continent.* 6 vols. Boston: Little, Brown, 1883–1885.

Banner, James M. *To the Hartford Convention: The Federalists and the Origins of Party Politics in Massachusetts, 1789–1815.* New York: Alfred A. Knopf, 1970.

Barrett, Jay A. *Evolution of the Ordinance of 1787.* New York: G.P. Putnam's Sons, 1891.

Bear, James A. Jr., "The Hemings Family of Monticello." *Virginia Cavalcade* 29 (1979–80): 78–87.

———. *Jefferson at Monticello.* Charlottesville: University Press of Virginia, 1967.

Bedini, Silvio A. *Thomas Jefferson: Statesman of Science.* New York: Macmillan, 1990.

Bemis, Samuel Flagg. *Jay's Treaty: A Study in Commerce and Diplomacy.* New Haven: Yale University Press, 1962.

Berkhofer, Robert F. Jr. "Jefferson, the Ordinance of 1784, and the Origins of the American Territorial System." *William and Mary Quarterly* 29, 3d. ser. (1972): 231–262.

Berlin, Ira. *Slaves Without Masters: The Free Negro in the Antebellum South.* New York: Pantheon, 1974.

Berlin, Ira, and Ronald Hoffman, eds. *Slavery and Freedom in the Age of the American Revolution.* Charlottesville: University Press of Virginia, 1983.

Berns, Walter. "The Constitution and the Migration of Slaves." *Yale Law Journal* 78 (1968): 198–228.

Berwanger, Eugene H. *The Frontier Against Slavery: Western Anti-Negro Prejudice and the Slavery Extension Controversy.* Urbana: University of Illinois Press, 1967.

Billington, Ray A. "The Historians of the Northwest Ordinance." *Journal of the Illinois State Historical Society* 40 (1947): 397–413.

Bleser, Carol, ed. *In Joy and in Sorrow: Women, Family, and Marriage in the Victorian South, 1830–1900.* New York: Oxford University Press, 1991.

Boggess, Arthur C. *The Settlement of Illinois, 1778–1830.* 1908 Reprint, Freeport, N.Y.: Books for Libraries Press, 1970.

Bolster, W. Jeffrey. *Black Jacks: African American Seamen in the Age of Sail.* Cambridge: Harvard University Press, 1977.

Bradley, Patricia. *Slavery, Propaganda, and the American Revolution.* Jackson: University of Mississippi Press, 1998.

Bridges, Roger D., ed. "John Mason Peck on Illinois Slavery." *Journal of the Illinois State Historical Society* 75 (1982): 201.

Brodie, Fawn. *Thomas Jefferson: An Intimate History.* New York: W.W. Norton, 1974.

Broussard, James H. *The Southern Federalists, 1800–1816.* Baton Rouge: Louisiana State University Press, 1978.

Burke, Joseph C. "The Proslavery Argument in the First Congress." *Duquesne Review* 14 (1969): 3–15.

Burnett, Edmund Cody. *The Continental Congress.* New York: Macmillan, 1941.

Burstein, Andrew. *The Inner Jefferson: Portrait of a Grieving Optimist.* Charlottesville: University Press of Virginia, 1995.

Cain, William E., ed. *William Lloyd Garrison and the Fight Against Slavery: Selections from the Liberator.* Boston: Bedford Books, 1995.

Campbell, Stanley W. *The Slave Catchers: Enforcement of the Fugitive Slave Law, 1850–1860.* Chapel Hill: University of North Carolina Press, 1968.

Cashin, Joan E. *A Family Venture: Men and Women on the Southern Frontier.* New York: Oxford University Press, 1991.

Cayton, Andrew R.L., and Peter S. Onuf, *The Midwest and the Nation: Rethinking the History of an American Region.* Bloomington: Indiana University Press, 1990.

Clinton, Catherine. "'Southern Dishonor': Flesh, Blood, Race, and Bondage." In Carol Bleser, ed., *In Joy and in Sorrow: Women, Family, and Marriage in the Victorian South,* 1830–1900. New York: Oxford University Press, 1991.

Cohen, William. "Thomas Jefferson and the Problem of Slavery." *Journal of American History* 56 (1969): 503–526.

Coles, Edward. *History of the Ordinance of 1787.* Philadelphia: Historical Society of Pennsylvania, 1856.

Combs, Jerald A. *The Jay Treaty: Political Battleground of the Founding Fathers.* Berkeley: University of California Press, 1970.

Cover, Robert M. *Justice Accused: Antislavery and the Judicial Process.* New Haven: Yale University Press, 1975.

Cunningham, Noble E. Jr. *In Pursuit of Reason: The Life of Thomas Jefferson.* Baton Rouge: Louisiana State University Press, 1987.

Curtis, George Ticknor. *History of the Origin, Formation, and Adoption of the Constitution of the United States.* New York: Harper & Brothers, 1854–1858.

Davis, David Brion. "American Slavery and the American Revolution." In Ira Berlin and Ronald Hofftnan, eds., *Slavery and Freedom in the Age of the American Revolution,* 262–280. Charlottesville: University Press of Virginia, 1983.

———. *The Problem of Slavery in the Age of Revolution, 1770–1823.* Ithaca: Cornell University Press, 1975.

———. *The Problem of Slavery in Western Culture.* Ithaca: Cornell University Press, 1966.

———. "The Significance of Excluding Slavery from the Old Northwest in 1787." *Indiana Magazine of History* 84 (1988): 75–89.

———. *Was Thomas Jefferson an Authentic Enemy of Slavery?* Oxford, U.K.: Oxford University Press, 1970.

Douglass, Frederick. *The Life and Times of Frederick Douglass.* 1892. Reprint, New York: Macmillan, 1962.

Du Bois, W. E. B. *The Suppression of the African Slave Trade to the United States of America, 1638–1870.* Cambridge: Harvard University Press, 1896.

Dunn, Jacob Piatt Jr. *Indiana: A Redemption from Slavery.* Boston and New York: Houghton Mifflin, 1888.

Durey, Michael. *"With the Hammer of Truth": James Thomson Callender and Early America's National Heroes.* Charlottesville: University Press of Virginia, 1990.

Eblen, Jack Ericson. *The First and Second United States Empires: Governors and Territorial Government, 1784–1912.* Pittsburgh: University of Pittsburgh Press, 1968.

Egerton, Douglas R. *Gabriel's Rebellion: The Virginia Slave Conspiracies of 1800 and 1802.* Chapel Hill: University of North Carolina Press, 1993.

Egle, William Henry, ed. "Virginia Claims to Land in Western Pennsylvania." *Pennsylvania Archives: Third Series* 3 (Harrisburg, 1894): 485–504.

Elkins, Stanley. *Slavery: A Problem in American Institutional and Intellectual Life.* Chicago: University of Chicago Press, 1959 and various revised editions.

Elkins, Stanley, and Eric McKitrick. *The Age of Federalism.* New York: Oxford University Press, 1993.

Ellis, Joseph J. *American Sphinx: The Character of Thomas Jefferson.* New York: Alfred A. Knopf, 1997.

———. "Jefferson: Post-DNA." *William and Mary Quarterly* 57, 3d ser. (2000): 125–138.

———. *Passionate Sage: The Character and Legacy of John Adams.* New York: W.W. Norton, 1993.

Farrand, Max. "Compromises of the Constitution." *Annual Report of the American Historical Association for the Year 1903* 1 (1904): 73–84.

———. *The Framing of the Constitution of the United States.* New Haven: Yale University Press, 1913.

Fehrenbacher, Don E. *The Dred Scott Case: Its Significance in American Law and Politics.* New York: Oxford University Press, 1978.

———. *The Federal Government and Slavery.* Claremont, Calif: Claremont Institute, 1984.

Field, Phyllis E. *The Politics of Race in New York.* Ithaca: Cornell University Press, 1982.

Finkelman, Paul. "Civil Liberties and the Civil War: The Great Emancipator as Civil Libertarian." *Michigan Law Review* 91 (1993): 1353–1381.

———. "Fugitive Slaves, Midwestern Racial Tolerance, and the Value of Justice Delayed." *Iowa Law Review* 78 (1992): 89–141.

———. "'Hooted Down the Page of History': Reconsidering the Greatness of Chief Justice Taney." *Journal of Supreme Court History, 1994.* (1994): 83–102.

———. *An Imperfect Union: Slavery, Federalism, and Comity.* Chapel Hill: University of North Carolina Press, 1981.

———. "International Extradition and Fugitive Slaves: The John Anderson Case." *Brooklyn Journal of International Law* 18 (1992): 765–810.

———. "The Kidnapping of John Davis and the Adoption of the Fugitive Slave Law of 1793." *Journal of Southern History* 56 (1990): 397–422.

———. *The Law of Freedom and Bondage: A Casebook.* New York: Oceana Press and NYU School of Law, 1986.

————. "Prelude to the Fourteenth Amendment: Black Legal Rights in the Antebellum North." *Rutgers Law Journal* 17 (1986): 415–482.

————. *"Prigg v. Pennsylvania* and Northern State Courts: Anti-Slavery Use of a Pro-Slavery Decision." *Civil War History* 25 (1979): 5–35.

————. "The Protection of Black Rights in Seward's New York." *Civil War History* 34 (1988): 211–234.

————. *Slavery and the Founders: Race and Liberty in the Age of Jefferson,* 1st ed., Armonk, N.Y.: M.E. Sharpe, 1996.

————. *Slavery in the Courtroom.* Washington, D.C.: Library of Congress, 1985.

————. "Slavery, the Pennsylvania Delegation, and the Constitutional Convention: The Two Faces of the Keystone State." *Pennsylvania Magazine of History and Biography* 112 (1988): 49–72.

————. "Sorting out *Prigg v. Pennsylvania." Rutgers Law Journal* 24 (1993): 605–665.

————. "State Constitutional Protections of Liberty and the Antebellum New Jersey Supreme Court: Chief Justice Hornblower and the Fugitive Slave Law." *Rutgers Law Journal* 23 (1992): 753–787.

————. "States Rights, North and South, in Antebellum America." In Kermit L. Hall and James W. Ely, Jr., eds. *An Uncertain Tradition: Constitutionalism and the History of the South.* Athens, Ga.: University of Georgia Press, 1989, 125–58.

————."Story Telling on the Supreme Court: *Prigg v. Pennsylvania* and Justice Joseph Story's Judicial Nationalism." *Supreme Court Review* 1994 (1995): 247–294.

————. "The Treason Trial of Castner Hanway." In Michal Belknap, ed., *American Political Trials.* Rev. ed. Westport, Conn.: Greenwood, 1994, 77–96.

Fischer, David Hackett. *The Revolution of American Conservatism: The Federalist Party in the Era of Jeffersonian Democracy.* New York: Harper & Row, 1986.

Flexner, James Thomas. *George Washington.* Vol. 4, *Anguish and Farewell (1793–1799).* Boston: Little, Brown, 1972.

Fogel, Robert William, and Stanley L. Engerman. "Philanthropy at Bargain Prices: Notes on the Economics of Gradual Emancipation." *Journal of Legal Studies* 3 (1974): 377–401.

Foner, Eric. *Free Soil, Free Labor, Free Men: The Ideology of the Republican Party before the Civil War.* New York: Oxford University Press, 1970.

Foner, Philip S. *The Democratic-Republican Societies, 1790–1800.* Westport, Conn.: Greenwood Press, 1976.

Force, Peter. "The Ordinance of 1787, and Its History." In William Henry Smith, ed., *The St. Clair Papers: The Life and Public Services of Arthur St. Clair.* 2 vols. Cincinnati: R. Clarke, 1882.

Foster, E.A. et al. "Jefferson Fathered Slave's Last Child." *Nature,* November 5, 1998, 27–28.

Fox, Dixon Ryan. "The Negro Vote in Old New York." *Political Science Quarterly* 32 (1917): 252, 254.

————. *The Decline of the Aristocracy in the Politics of New York, 1801–1840.* 1919. Reprint, New York: Harper and Row, 1965.

Franklin, John Hope. *The Free Negro in North Carolina, 1790–1860.* Chapel Hill: University of North Carolina Press, 1943.

————. *Race and History: Selected Essays, 1938–1988.* Baton Rouge: Louisiana State University Press, 1989.

————. *Racial Equality in America.* Chicago: University of Chicago Press, 1976.

Frederickson, George. *The Black Image in the White Mind: The Debate on Afro-American Character and Destiny, 1817–1914.* New York: Harper and Row, 1971.

Freehling, William W. "The Founding Fathers and Slavery." *American Historical Review* 77 (1972): 81–93.

———. *The Reintegration of American History: Slavery and the Civil War.* New York: Oxford University Press, 1994.

———. *The Road to Disunion: Secessionists at Bay, 1776–1854.* New York: Oxford University Press, 1990.

French, Scott A. and Edward L. Ayers, "The Strange Career of Thomas Jefferson: Race and Slavery in the American Memory, 1943–1993." In Peter S. Onuf, ed., *Jeffersonian Legacies.* Charlottesville: University of Virginia Press, 1993, 418–456.

Frey, Sylvia R. *Water from the Rock: Black Resistance in a Revolutionary Age.* Princeton: Princeton University Press, 1991.

Goebel, Dorothy Burne. *William Henry Harrison: A Political Biography.* Indianapolis: Historical Bureau of the Indiana Library and Historical Department, 1926.

Gordon-Reed, Annette. *Thomas Jefferson and Sally Hemings: An American Controversy.* Charlottesville, Va.: University Press of Virginia, 1997.

Greene, Jack P. *All Men Are Created Equal: Some Reflections on the Character of the American Revolution.* Oxford: Clarendon Press, 1976.

Grégoire, Henri. *An Inquiry Concerning the Intellectual and Moral Faculties, and Literature of Negroes* (Graham Russell Hodges, ed.) Armonk, N.Y.: M. E. Sharpe, 1997.

Griffin, J. David. "Historians and the Sixth Article of the Ordinance of 1787." *Ohio History* 78 (1969): 252–260.

Hall, Kermit L., and James W. Ely Jr., eds. *An Uncertain Tradition: Constitutionalism and the History of the South.* Athens: University of Georgia Press, 1989.

Harris, N. Dwight. *The History of Negro Servitude in Illinois.* Chicago: A.C. McClurg, 1904.

Higginbotham, A. Leon. *In the Matter of Color: Race and the American Legal Process: The Colonial Period.* New York: Oxford University Press, 1978.

Hinsdale, B.A. *The Old Northwest.* New York: Townsend MacCoun, 1888.

Hirschfeld, Fritz. *George Washington and Slavery: A Documentary Portrayal.* Columbia, Mo.: University of Missouri Press, 1997.

Hodges, Graham Russell. *Slavery, Freedom and Culture Among Early American Workers.* Armonk, N.Y.: M.E. Sharpe, 1998.

Holt, Michael F. *The Rise and Fall of the American Whig Party: Jacksonian Politics and the Onset of the Civil War.* New York: Oxford University Press, 1999.

Horton, James Oliver, and Lois E. Horton. *In Hope of Liberty: Culture, Community, and Protest Among Northern Free Blacks, 1700–1860.* New York: Oxford University Press, 1997.

Horwitz, Morton J. *The Transformation of American Law, 1780–1860.* Cambridge: Harvard University Press, 1977.

Hunter, Lloyd, ed., *Pathways to the Old Northwest.* Indianapolis: Indiana Historical Society, 1988.

Hurst, James Willard. *Law and the Conditions of Freedom in the Nineteenth-Century United States.* Madison: University of Wisconsin Press, 1956.

Hutson, James. "Pierce Butler's Records of the Federal Constitutional Convention." *Quarterly Journal of the Library of Congress* 37 (1980): 64–73.

Jensen, Merrill. *The Articles of Confederation.* Madison: University of Wisconsin Press, 1940.

Jordan, Winthrop. *White Over Black: American Attitudes Toward the Negro, 1550–1812*. Chapel Hill: University of North Carolina Press, 1968.

Kaplan, Lawrence S. *Entangling Alliances with None: American Foreign Policy in the Age of Jefferson*. Kent, Ohio: Kent State University, 1987.

Kass, Alvin. *Politics in New York State, 1800–1830*. Syracuse: Syracuse University Press, 1965.

Katz, Stanley N. "Republicanism and the Law of Inheritance in the American Revolutionary Era" *Michigan Law Review* 76 (1977): 1–29.

Kerber, Linda. *Federalists in Dissent: Imagery and Ideology in Jeffersonian America*. Ithaca: Cornell University Press, 1970.

Ketcham, Ralph Louis. "The Dictates of Conscience: Edward Coles and Slavery." *Virginia Quarterly Review* 36 (1960): 47–49.

————. *From Colony to Country: The Revolution in American Thought, 1750–1820*. New York: Macmillan, 1974.

————. *James Madison: A Biography*. New York: Macmillan, 1971.

Kirk, Russell. *John Randolph of Roanoke: A Study in American Politics*. Chicago: Regnery, 1964.

Koch, Adrienne. *Jefferson and Madison: The Great Collaboration*. New York: Alfred A. Knopf, 1950.

Lander, Eric S., and Joseph J. Ellis. "Founding Father." *Nature,* November 5, 1998, 13–14.

Langhorne, Elizabeth C. *Monticello: A Family Story*. Chapel Hill, N.C.: Algonquin Books, 1987.

Leslie, William R. "A Study in the Origins of Interstate Rendition: The Big Beaver Creek Murders." *American Historical Review* 57 (1951): 63–76.

Levy, Leonard W. *Jefferson and Civil Liberties: The Darker Side*. Rev. ed., Chicago: Ivan Dee, 1989.

————. *The Law of the Commonwealth and Chief Justice Shaw*. Cambridge: Harvard University Press, 1957.

Lewis, Jan Ellen. "Pieces of a President." *Washington Post Book World,* August 22, 1993, 10.

Lewis, Jan Ellen, and Peter S. Onuf, eds. *Sally Hemings and Thomas Jefferson: History, Memory, and Civic Culture*. Charlottesville: University Press of Virginia, 1999.

Litwack, Leon F. *North of Slavery: The Negro in the Free States, 1790–1860*. Chicago: University of Chicago Press, 1961.

Locke, Mary Stoughton. *Anti-Slavery in America from the Introduction of African Slaves to the Prohibition of the Slave Trade, 1619-1808*. Boston: Ginn, 1901.

Logan, Rayford. *The Diplomatic Relations of the United States with Haiti, 1776–1891*. Chapel Hill: The University of North Carolina Press, 1941.

Lynd, Staughton. *Class Conflict, Slavery, and the United States Constitution: Ten Essays*. Indianapolis: Bobbs-Merrill, 1967.

McColley, Robert. *Slavery and Jeffersonian Virginia*. 2d ed. Urbana: University of Illinois Press, 1973.

McCoy, Drew. *The Last of the Fathers: James Madison and the Republican Legacy*. Cambridge, U.K.: Cambridge University Press, 1989.

McDonald, Forrest. *The Presidency of Thomas Jefferson*. Lawrence: University of Kansas Press, 1976.

McDougall, Marion G. *Fugitive Slaves: 1619–1865*. Boston: Ginn, 1891.

McKitrick, Eric. *Andrew Johnson and Reconstruction.* Chicago: University of Chicago, 1960.

MacLeod, Duncan. *Slavery, Race, and the American Revolution.* Cambridge, U.K.: Cambridge University Press, 1974.

McManus, Edgar. *Black Bondage in the North.* Syracuse: Syracuse University Press, 1973.

————. *A History of Negro Slavery in New York.* Syracuse: Syracuse University Press, 1966.

Malone, Dumas. *Jefferson and His Time.* 6 vols. Boston: Little, Brown, 1948–1981.

Maltz, Earl. "Slavery, Federalism, and the Structure of the Constitution." *The American Journal of Legal History* 36 (1992): 466–498.

Mapp, Alf J. Jr. *Thomas Jefferson, Passionate Pilgrim: the Presidency, the Founding of the University and the Private Battle.* Lanham, Md.: Madison Books, 1991.

————. *Thomas Jefferson: A Strange Case of Mistaken Identity.* Lanham, Md.: Madison Books, 1987.

Matthewson, Tim. "Jefferson and Haiti." *Journal of Southern History* 61 (1995): 209–248.

Miller, John Chester. *The Wolf by the Ears: Thomas Jefferson and Slavery.* New York: Free Press, 1977.

Moore, Glover. *The Missouri Controversy, 1819–1821.* Lexington: University of Kentucky Press, 1953.

Morgan, Edmund. *American Slavery, American Freedom: The Ordeal of Virginia.* New York: W.W. Norton, 1975.

Morris, Thomas D. *Free Men All: The Personal Liberty Laws of the North, 1780–1861.* Baltimore: Johns Hopkins University Press, 1974.

Moss, Simeon F. "The Persistence of Slavery and Involuntary Servitude in a Free State (1685–1866)." *Journal of Negro History* 35 (1950): 289–314.

Mullin, Gerald W. *Flight and Rebellion: Slave Resistance in Eighteenth-Century Virginia.* New York: Oxford University Press, 1972.

Nash, Gary B. *Forging Freedom: The Formation of Philadelphia's Black Community.* Cambridge: Harvard University Press, 1988.

————. *Race and Revolution.* Madison, Wisc.: Madison House, 1990.

Nash, Gary B., and Jean Soderlund. *Freedom by Degrees: Emancipation in Pennsylvania and Its Aftermath.* New York: Oxford University Press, 1991.

Newcomer, Lee Nathaniel. "Manasseh Cutler's Writings: A Note on Editorial Practice." *Mississippi Valley Historical Review* 47 (1960): 88–101.

Norton, Mary Beth, Herbert G. Gutman, and Ira Berlin. "The Afro-American Family in the Age of Revolution." In Ira Berlin and Ronald Hoffman, eds., *Slavery and Freedom in the Age of the American Revolution,* 173–191. Charlottesville: University Press of Virginia, 1983.

Oakes, James. *The Ruling Race: A History of American Slaveholders.* New York: Knopf, 1982.

Ohline, Howard A. "Slavery, Economics, and Congressional Politics, 1790." *Journal of Southern History* 46 (1980): 335–360.

Onuf, Peter S. "From Constitution to Higher Law: The Reinterpretation of the Northwest Ordinance." *Ohio History* 94 (1985): 5–33.

————. *Jefferson's Empire: The Language of American Nationhood.* Charlottesville: University Press of Virginia, 2000.

———. *The Origins of the Federal Republic: Jurisdictional Controversies in the United States, 1775–1787.* Philadelphia: University of Pennsylvania Press, 1983.

———. "Peerless Tom." *New York Times Book Review,* September 26, 1993, 26.

———. "The Scholars' Jefferson." *William and Mary Quarterly* 50, 3d ser. (1993): 671–699.

———. *Statehood and Union: A History of the Northwest Ordinance.* Bloomington and Indianapolis: Indiana University Press, 1987.

———, ed. *Jeffersonian Legacies.* Charlottesville: University Press of Virginia, 1993.

Painter, Nell Irvin. "Of *Lily,* Linda Brent, and Freud: A Non-Exceptionalist Approach to Race, Class, and Gender in the Slave South." *Georgia Historical Quarterly* 76 (1992): 241–259.

Parton, James. *The Life of Thomas Jefferson, Third President of the United States.* Boston: Houghton Mifflin, 1874.

Peabody, Sue. *There Are No Slaves in France.* New York: Oxford University Press, 1996.

Peterson, Merrill D. *The Jefferson Image in the American Mind.* New York: Oxford University Press, 1960.

———. *Thomas Jefferson and the New Nation.* New York: Oxford University Press, 1970.

———. ed. *The Portable Thomas Jefferson.* New York: Penguin Books, 1975.

Phillips, Ulrich B. *American Negro Slavery.* New York: D. Appleton, 1918.

Pole, J.R. *The Pursuit of Equality in American History.* Berkeley: University of California Press, 1978.

Poole, William Frederick. *The Ordinance of 1787, and Dr. Manasseh Cutler as an Agent in its Formation.* Cambridge, Mass.: Welch, Bigelow, 1876.

Quarles, Benjamin. *The Negro in the American Revolution.* Chapel Hill: University of North Carolina Press, 1961.

Randall, Willard Sterne. *Thomas Jefferson: A Life.* New York: Henry Holt, 1993.

Reardon, John J. *Edmund Randolph: A Biography.* New York: Macmillan, 1974.

Ritcheson, Charles R. *Aftermath of Revolution: British Policy Toward the United States, 1783–1795.* Dallas: Southern Methodist University Press, 1969.

Robinson, Donald L. *Slavery in the Structure of American Politics, 1765–1820.* New York: Harcourt Brace Jovanovich, 1971.

Roediger, David R. *The Wages of Whiteness: Race and the Making of the American Working Class.* London and New York: Verso, 1991.

Rossiter, Clinton. *1787: The Grand Convention.* New York: Macmillan, 1966.

Sharp, James Roger. *American Politics in the Early Republic: The New Nation in Crisis.* New Haven: Yale University Press, 1993.

Sloan, Herbert. "The Earth Belongs in Usufruct to the Living," in Onuf, *Jeffersonian Legacies,* 290.

Shriver, Phillip R. "America's Other Bicentennial." *The Old Northwest* 9 (1983): 219–235.

Simpson, Albert F. "The Political Significance of Slave Representation, 1787–1821." *Journal of Southern History* 7 (1941): 315–342.

Stampp, Kenneth. *The Peculiar Institution: Slavery in the Ante-Bellum South.* New York: Random House, 1956.

Stanton, Lucia. "'Those Who Labor For My Happiness': Thomas Jefferson and His Slaves," in Onuf, *Jeffersonian Legacies.* Charlottesville: University Press of Virginia, 1993.

Stanton, William. *The Leopard's Spots: Scientific Attitudes Toward Race in America, 1815–1859.* Chicago: University of Chicago Press, 1960.

Stewart, Donald H. *The Opposition Press of the Federalist Period*. Albany: State University of New York Press, 1969.

Stewart, Gordon. "The Northwest and the Balance of Power in North America," in Frederick D. Williams, ed., *The Northwest Ordinance: Essays on Its Formulation, Provisions, and Legacy*. East Lansing: Michigan State University, 1989.

Stewart, James Brewer. *Holy Warriors: The Abolitionists and American Slavery*. Rev. ed. New York: Hill and Wang, 1996.

————. *William Lloyd Garrison and the Challenge of Emancipation*. Arlington Heights, Ill: Hatlan Davidson, 1992.

Swayne, Wager. *The Ordinance of 1787 and the War of 1861*. New York: C.G. Burgoyne, 1892?.

Takaki, Ronald. *Iron Cages: Race and Culture in Nineteenth-Century America*. New York: Knopf, 1979.

Tansill, Charles C. *The United States and Santo Domingo, 1798–1873: A Chapter in Caribbean Diplomacy*. Baltimore: The Johns Hopkins Press, 1938.

Thornbrough, Emma Lou. *The Negro in Indiana: A Study of a Minority*. Indianapolis: Indiana Historical Bureau, 1957.

Thorpe, Francis Newton. *The Story of the Constitution of the United States*. New York: Chautauqua Press, 1891.

Tise, Larry E. *Proslavery: A History of the Defense of Slavery in America, 1701–1840*. Athens: University of Georgia Press, 1987.

Van Doren, Carl. *Benjamin Franklin*. New York: Viking, 1938.

Wallenstein, Peter. "Flawed Keepers of the Flame: The Interpreters of George Mason." *Virginia Magazine of History and Biography* 102 (1994): 229–260.

Warren, Charles. *The Making of the Constitution*. Boston: Little, Brown, 1928.

Webster, Homer J. "William Henry Harrison's Administration of Indiana Territory." *Indiana Historical Society Publications*. Vol. 4. Indianapolis: Indiana Historical Society, 1907.

White, Shane. *Somewhat More Independent: The End of Slavery in New York City, 1770–1810*. Athens: University of Georgia Press, 1991.

Wiecek, William M. "Slavery and Abolition before the United States Supreme Court, 1820–1860." *Journal of American History* 65 (1978–1979): 34–59.

————. *The Sources of Antislavery Constitutionalism in America, 1760–1848*. Ithaca, N.Y.: Cornell University Press, 1977.

————. "The Witch at the Christening: Slavery and the Constitution's Origins." In Leonard W. Levy and Dennis J. Mahoney, eds., *The Framing and Ratification of the Constitution*. New York: Macmillan, 1987.

Williams, Frederick D., ed. *The Northwest Ordinance: Essays on Its Formulation, Provisions, and Legacy*. East Lansing: Michigan State University Press, 1988.

Williamson, Joel. *New People: Miscegenation and Mulattoes in the United States*. New York: New York University Press, 1984.

Wills, Garry. "The Aesthete." *New York Review of Books,* August 12, 1993, 6–10.

————. *Cincinnatus: George Washington and the Enlightenment*. Garden City, N.Y.: Doubleday, 1984.

Wilson, Douglas L. "Thomas Jefferson and the Character Issue." *Atlantic Monthly,* November 1992.

Wood, Gordon S. "Jefferson at Home." *New York Review of Books,* May 13, 1993, 6–9.

————. *The Radicalism of the American Revolution*. New York: Alfred A. Knopf, 1992.

————. "The Trials and Tribulations and Thomas Jefferson," in Onuf, ed., *Jeffersonian Legacies,* Charlottesville: University Press of Virginia, 1993.

Wood, Peter. *Black Majority: Negroes in Colonial South Carolina from 1670 Through the Stono Rebellion.* New York: W.W. Norton, 1974.

Zilversmit, Arthur. *The First Emancipation: The Abolition of Slavery in the North.* Chicago: University of Chicago Press, 1967.

————. "Liberty and Property: New Jersey and the Abolition of Slavery." *New Jersey History* 88 (1970): 215–226.

Zuckerman, Michael. *Almost Chosen People: Oblique Biographies in the American Grain.* Berkeley: University of California Press, 1993.

Printed Primary Sources

Alvord, Clarence Walworth, ed. *Governor Edward Coles.* Collections of the Illinois State Historical Library. Vol. 15. Springfield: Illinois State Library, 1920.

————. *Kaskaskia Records, 1778–1790.* Springfield: Illinois State Library, 1909.

American State Papers: Class X. Miscellaneous. 2 vols. Washington, D.C.: Gales and Seton, 1834.

Basler, Roy P., ed. *The Collected Works of Abraham Lincoln.* 9 vols. New Brunswick, N.J.: Rutgers University Press, 1953–1955.

Betts, Edwin Morris, ed. *Thomas Jefferson's Farm Book.* Princeton: American Philosophical Society, 1953.

Boyd, Julian P. et al., eds. *The Papers of Thomas Jefferson.* Princeton: Princeton University Press, 1950.

Bruns, Roger, *ed. Am I Not a Man and a Brother: The Antislavery Crusade of Revolutionary America, 1688–1788.* New York: Chelsea House, 1977.

Burnett, Edmund C., ed. *Letters of Members of the Continental Congress.* 8 vols. Washington, D.C.: Carnegie Institute of Washington, 1921–1936.

Carter, Clarence Edwin, ed. *The Territorial Papers of the United States,* 28 vols. Washington, D.C.: Government Printing Office, 1934–1975, 2: 244–248.

Chase, Salmon P. *Reclamation of Fugitives from Service.* Cincinnati: R.P. Donough, 1847.

————, ed. *The Statutes of Ohio and of the Northwestern Territory.* 3 vols. Cincinnati: Corey and Fairbanks, 1833–1835.

Cobb, Thomas R.R. *An Inquiry into the Law of Negro Slavery in the United States of America to Which Is Prefaced, An Historical Sketch of Slavery.* Philadelphia and Savannah: T. & J.W. Johnson, 1858.

Cox, F.A., and J. Hoby. *The Baptists in America; A Narrative of the Deputation From the Baptist Union in England, to the United States and Canada.* New York, Boston: Leavitt, Lord, 1836.

Cutler, William Parker, and Julia Perkins Cutler. *Life, Journal and Correspondence of Rev. Manasseh Cutler, LL.D.* 2 vols. Cincinnati: R. Clarke, 1888.

Dunn, Jacob Piatt. "Slavery Petitions and Papers." *Indiana Historical Society Publications* 2: 443-529. Indianapolis: Bowen-Merrill Company, 1894.

Elliot, Jonathan, ed. *The Debates in the Several State Conventions on the Adoption of the Federal Constitution.* 5 vols. New York: Burt Franklin, 1987, reprint of 1888 edition.

Esarey, Logan, ed. *Messages and Letters of William Henry Harrison.* 2 vols. Indianapolis: Indiana Historical Commission, 1922.

Ewbank, Louis, and Dorothy Riker, eds. *The Laws of Indiana Territory, 1809–1816* Indianapolis: Indiana Historical Bureau, 1934.

Farrand, Max, ed. *The Records of the Federal Convention of 1787.* Rev. ed., 4 vols. New Haven: Yale University Press, 1966.

Ford, Paul Leicester, ed. *The Writings of Thomas Jefferson.* 12 vols. New York: G.P. Putnam's Sons, 1892–1899.

Ford, Worthington Chauncey et. al., eds. *Journals of the Continental Congress, 1774–1789.* 34 vols. Washington, D.C.: Government Printing Office, 1904–1937.

Hening, William Waller, ed. *The Statutes at Large: Being a Collection of the Law of Virginia from the First Session of the Legislature in Year 1619* (Richmond: Printed by and for Samuel Pleasants, Junior, printer to the Commonwealth; United States, 1823), 12:611.

Hilliard, Francis. *The Elements of Law: Being a Comprehensive Summary of American Jurisprudence.* Boston: Hilliard Gray; New York: Halsted and Voorhies, 1835.

Hutson, James H., ed. *Supplement to Max Farrand's The Records of the Federal Convention of 1787.* New Haven: Yale University Press, 1987.

Jefferson, Thomas. *Notes on the State of Virginia.* Edited by William Peden. Chapel Hill: University of North Carolina Press, 1954.

Jensen, Merrill, ed. *Documentary History of the Ratification of the Constitution.* 18 vols. Madison: Wisconsin Historical Society, 1976.

Koch, Adrienne, and William Peden, eds. *The Life and Selected Writings of Thomas Jefferson.* New York: Modern Library, 1944.

Lipscomb, Andrew A., and Albert Ellery Berg, eds. *The Writings of Thomas Jefferson.* 20 vols. Washington, D.C.: The Thomas Jefferson Memorial Association, 1903–1905.

McKitrick, Eric, ed. *Slavery Defended: The Views of the Old South.* Englewood Cliffs, N.J.: Prentice-Hall, 1963.

Malloy, William M., ed. *Treaties, Conventions, International Acts, Protocols, and Agreements Between the United States of America and Other Powers, 1776–1937.* 4 vols. Washington, D.C.: Government Printing Office, 1910–1938.

May, Samuel J. *Some Recollections of Our Antislavery Conflict.* Boston: Fields, Osgood, 1869.

Merrill, Walter M., ed. *The Letters of William Lloyd Garrison.* 6 vols. Cambridge: Harvard University Press, 1973.

Norton. Margaret Cross. *Illinois Census Returns. 1810, 1818.* Springfield: Illinois State Library, 1935.

Palmer, William R., and Sherwin McRae, eds. *Calendar of Virginia State Papers. . . .*Vol. 5. Richmond: Virginia State Library, 1885.

Pease, Theodore C., ed. *Illinois Election Returns, 1818–1848.* Springfield Ill.: Trustees of the Illinois State Historical Library, 1923.

Peterson, Merrill, ed. *The Portable Jefferson.* New York: Penguin Books, 1975.

————, *Thomas Jefferson: Writings.* New York: Viking Press, 1984.

Philbrick, Francis S. *Laws of the Illinois Territory 1809–1818.* Springfield: Illinois State Library, 1950.

————, ed., *Laws of Indiana Territory, 1801–1809.* Springfield: Illinois State Library, 1930.

————, ed., *Laws of Ohio, 1807.*

Phillips, Wendell. *Can Abolitionists Vote or Take Office Under the United States Constitution.* New York: American Anti-Slavery Society, 1845.

[————.] *The Constitution A Pro-Slavery Compact; or, Selections from the Madison Papers.* 2d ed. New York: American Anti-Slavery Society, 1845.

Richardson, James D., ed. *Messages and Papers of the Presidents.* 20 vols. New York: Bureau of National Literature, 1897.

Smith, Paul H., ed. *Letters of Members of Delegates to Congress, 1774–1789,* 26 vols., Washington, D.C.: Library of Congress, 1996.

Smith, William Henry, ed. *The St. Clair Papers: The Life and Public Services of Arthur St. Clair.* 2 vols. Cincinnati: R. Clarke, 1882.

Smyth, Albert Henry, ed. The *Writings of Benjamin Franklin.* 10 vols. New York: Macmillan, 1905–1907.

Spooner, Lysander. *The Unconstitutionality of Slavery.* Boston: B. Marsh, 1845.

Storing. Herbert J., ed. *The Complete Anti-Federalist.* 7 vols. Chicago: University of Chicago Press, 1981.

Tucker, St. George. A *Dissertation on Slavery: With a Proposal for the Gradual Abolition of It, in the State of Virginia.* Philadelphia: Mathew Carey, 1796.

———. *Tucker's Blackstone.* 1803; reprint Union, N.J.: Lawbook Exchange, 1977, 2: Appendix H.

U.S. Bureau of the Census. *Negro Population in the United States, 1790–1915.* Washington, D.C.: Government Printing Office, 1918.

Will County Anti-Slavery Society. *Slave Code of The State of Illinois.* Julilet [sic], Il.: Will County Anti-Slavery Society, 1840. Reprinted in Paul Finkelman, ed., *Statutes on Slavery: The Pamphlet Literature.* 2:81. New York: Garland, 1988.

Cases

Boon v. Juliet, 1 Scammon (Ill.) 258 (1836).

Borders v. Borders, 4 Scammon (Ill.) 341 (1843).

Charlotte (of Color) v. Chouteau, 11 Mo. 193 (1847); reargued at 21 Mo. 590 (1855), 25 Mo. 465 (1857), and 33 Mo. 194 (1862).

Choisser v. Hargrave, 1 Scammon (Ill.) 317 (1836).

Chouteau and Keizer v. Hope, 7 Mo. 428 (1842).

Chouteau v. Pierre (of Color), 9 Mo, 3 (1845).

Commonwealth v. Aves, 18 Pick. (Mass.) 193 (1836).

Commonwealth v. Jennison (unreported, Mass., 1783). Reprinted in Paul Finkelman, *The Law of Freedom and Bondage: A Casebook.* New York: Oceana, 1986, 36–37.

Dred Scott v. Sandford, 19 How. (U.S.) 393 (1857).

Elder v. Elder's Ex'or, 4 Leigh (Va.) 252 (1833).

Elkison v. Deliesseline, 8 F. Cas. 493 (1823).

Groves v. Slaughter, 15 Pet. (U.S.) 449 (1841).

Harry v. Decker and Hopkins, 1 Walker (Miss.) 36, (1818).

Hays v. Borders, 1 Gilman (Ill.) 46 (1844).

Howell v. Netherland, Jefferson (Va.) 90 (1770).

Hudgins v. Wrights, 1 Hen. & M. (Va.) 133 (1806).

In re Mary Clark, a Woman of Color, 1 Blackf. (Ind.) 122 (1821).

Jack v. Martin, 14 Wendell (N.Y.) 512 (1835).

Jarrot (colored Man) v. Jarrot, 2 Gilman (Ill.) 1 (1845).

Jones v. Van Zandt, 5 How. (U.S.) 215 (1847).

Kentucky v. Dennison, 24 How. (U.S.) 66 (1861).

Lemmon v. The People, 20 NY 562 (1860).

Marbury v. Madison, Ranch. (U.S.) 137 (1803).

Marchand v. Negro Peggy, 2 Sergeant & Rawle (Pa.) 18 (1815).

Merry v. Tiffin and Menard, 1Mo. 725 (1827).

Nancy v. Trammel, 3 Mo. 306 (1836).
Norris v. Cocker, 13 How. (U.S.) 429 (1851).
Pleasants v. Pleasants, 2 Call (Va.) 319 (1799).
Prigg v. Pennsylvania, 16 Pet. (U.S.) 539 (1842).
Scale v. Lasselle, 1 Blackf. (Ind.) 60 (1820).
Somerset v. Stewart, Loft (G. B) 1 (1772); 98 Eng. Rep. 499; 20 Howell State Trials 1 (K.B. 1772).
State v. Hoppess, 2 Western Law Journal (Ohio) 279 (1845).
State v. Lasselle, 1 Blackf. (Ind.) 60 (1820).
Strader v. Graham, 10 How. (U.S.) 82 (1850).
Theoteste v. Chouteau, 2 Mo. 144 (1829).
United States v. The Amistad, 15 Pet. (U.S.) 518 (1841).
United States v. Mussry, 726 F. 2d 1448 (1984).

Index

Import taxation *(continued)*
  Constitutional Convention (1787), 23,
    24, 26–29, 204n.86
Indenture system
  Illinois, 60, 65, 74, 76, 77
  Indiana, 60, 69–70, 71
Indiana
  abolition and, 56, 80
    Constitution (1816), 72–73
    statehood (1816), 72
    Supreme Court, 73, 217n.43
  African slave trade, 62
  Age of Federalism, 112
  black diffusion, 60, 62–63
  Connecticut and, 64
  Free Soilers, 62
  generational slavery, 71
  gradual emancipation, 59–60, 61
  indenture system, 60, 69–70, 71
  involuntary servitude, 59, 69–70, 71
  Northwest Ordinance (1787)
    resistance to, 49–50, 55, 212n.32
    state law conflict, 40
  private property, 63
  proslavery legislation and, 68–72
    Congressional response, 70–71
    1803 law, 69–70, 216n.33
    1804 law, 70–71, 216n.37
    1806 law, 71
    1807 law, 71
    1808 law, 71
    full faith and credit clause, 69
    generational slavery, 71
    indenture system, 69–70, 71
    involuntary servitude, 69–70, 71
    leadership, 68–69, 70
    servant rights, 70
    "servant" terminology, 68–69, 70,
      71
    servant testimony, 70, 216n.36
    slave code, 69, 70, 71
    Virginia, 68, 69
    voluntary servitude, 69

Import taxation *(continued)*
  proslavery petitions and
    African slave trade, 62
    arguments for, 61–63
    Article VI repeal, 61, 63, 68
    black diffusion, 62–63
    Congressional rejection, 64
    Connecticut, 64
    leadership, 61
    private property, 63
    Republicanism, 63, 64
    South Carolina, 62
    sovereignty, 63, 64, 215n.15
    Virginia, 63, 64
  Republicanism, 59, 62, 63, 64
  slave code, 69, 70, 71
  slave population, 214n.57, 217n.44
  South Carolina and, 62
  statehood (1816), 72, 112
  Supreme Court, 73, 217n.43
  Virginia and
    proslavery legislation, 68, 69
    proslavery petitions, 63, 64
Ingersoll, Jared, 116
Innes, James, 86–87, 88, 222n.21
In re Mary Clark, a Woman of Color
  (1821), 217n.43
Involuntary servitude
  Illinois, 59, 66, 76–77
  Indiana, 59, 69–70, 71
Iredell, James, 6
Izard, Ralph, 92

J

Jackson, Andrew, 107, 120, 125
Jackson, James, 111, 123
Jarrot (colored Man) v. *Jarrot* (1845),
  209n.8, 211n.22
Jay, John
  Age of Federalism, 113–14, 116,
    118–19
  Fugitive Slave Law (1793), 100, 101

Pinckney, Charles Cotesworth *(continued)*
  Congressional representation, 10,
    15, 16, 17–18, 19, 21,
    199n.18
  export taxation, 22
  import taxation, 28, 29
  privileges and immunities clause,
    29–30
  slave trade, 22, 30, 32, 34, 82, 101
  state authority, 9
Platt, Jonas, 120
Pleasants, John, 136, 190
Pleasants, Jonathan, 136, 190
Pleasants, Robert, 135, 190
Pole, Jack, 132
Poole, William F., 42, 43
Population
  census 1810, 214n.57
  census 1818, 217n.44, 218n.51
  census 1820, 214n.57, 217n.44
  census 1790, 11
  Congressional representation and
    census, 11, 17, 19
    state population, 11, 12–15, 20–21,
      23–25, 201n.34
  Illinois, 73, 214n.57, 218n.51
  Indiana, 214n.57, 217n.44
  Virginia, 136, 235n.36
Portable Jefferson, The (Peterson), 193
Presentism, 170–72, 173
Presidential election. *See* Executive
  branch
Price, Richard, 158, 241n.124
Prigg v. *Pennsylvania* (1842), 91,
  197n.3, 240n.111
Private property ideology
  Fugitive Slave Law (1793), 83, 84
  Indiana, 63
  Northwest Ordinance (1787), 39–40,
    45, 48–50, 52, 212n.33
Privileges and immunities clause, 9,
  29–30, 198n.15
Public Television, 164

Q

Quakers, 100, 118
Quincy, Edmund, 108
Quincy, Josiah, 107, 108, 116, 117

R

Racism, 180–81, 190–94
Ramsey, David, 205n.97
Randall, Willard Sterne, 174, 184, 188,
  189, 246n.56
Randolph, Beverley, 81, 86, 87–89,
  219n.5, 222n.21
Randolph, Edmund
  Committee of Detail, 23
  Constitutional proslavery, 10
  Fugitive Slave Law (1793), 88, 89,
    222n.28
  terminology debate, 206n.104
  three-fifths clause, 18, 20,
    206n.104
  Virginia Plan, 10–12
Randolph, John
  manumission, 136, 190
  proslavery petitions, 65–66
Read, George, 19, 93
Read, Nathaniel, 211n.24
Reagan, Ronald, 163
Religious freedom, 139, 175–76
Republicanism
  Illinois, 59, 62
  Indiana, 59, 62, 63, 64
  Jefferson analysis, 132–34
Republican Party
  emergence of (1854), 126
  Northwest Ordinance (1787), 38
Republicans, Age of Federalism
  economic ideology, 127
  Federalist slavery opposition, 115,
    124–25
  free blacks, 118, 119–20, 231n.59
  Haiti, 119–24

About the Author

Paul Finkelman is the Chapman Distinguished Professor of Law at the University of Tulsa College of Law. He earned his doctorate in American history from the University of Chicago and was a Fellow in Law and History at Harvard Law School. Professor Finkelman has taught at a number of universities and law schools. His book *Slavery in the Courtroom* won the Joseph L. Andrews award from the American Association of Law Libraries. He has also won awards and prizes for his books *Impeachable Offenses* (1998), *Religion and the American Law: An Encyclopedia* (2000), and the two-volume Macmillan *Encyclopedia of World Slavery* (1998).